D1472673

ABOUT THE AUTHOR

~~~~~~

Nicolás Kanellos is founding publisher of the noted Hispanic literary journal *The Americas Review* (formerly *Revista Chicano-Riqueña*) and of the nation's oldest and most esteemed Hispanic publishing house, Arte Público Press. He has been professor of Hispanic literature at the University of Houston since 1980. In 1994 Dr. Kanellos was appointed by President Clinton to the council for the National Endowment for the Humanities (NEH).

Kanellos's four-volume reference book *Handbook of Hispanic Cultures in the United States* has received two awards: the American Library Association Denali Press Award for best reference work, and outstanding reference work of 1994 by Choice. His work *The Hispanic American Almanac* won a Reference and Adult Services Division (RASD) Award for Outstanding Reference Source of the Year from the American Library Association in 1993. Dr. Kanellos is also the director of a major national research project, Recovering the Hispanic Literary Heritage of the United States, a ten-year program to identify, preserve, study, and make accessible tens of thousands of literary documents from the colonial period to 1960.

Dr. Kanellos has been honored with numerous awards for his publishing achievements, including the 1996 Annual Hispanic Publication Award, the 1995 Annual PREMIO Award, and the 1995 Annual Achievement in Publishing Award from the National Hispanic Academy of Media Arts and Sciences.

ALSO AVAILABLE FROM VISIBLE INK PRESS

THE HISPANIC LITERARY COMPANION

Unique in its expansive scope, this collection provides a balanced selection from the wide spectrum of Latino writing today. The accomplishments of 35 Hispanic playwrights, poets, and novelists are represented through biographical profiles, quotes, complete bibliographies and selections from their works. Coverage includes Cristina Garcia, author of the award-winning novel *Dreaming in Cuban,* and Rudolfo Anaya, winner of the American Book Award for *Tortuga* and author of the highly acclaimed *Rain of Gold.*

Nicolás Kanellos 7¼ X 9¼ paperback 416 pages 35 photos ISBN 0-7876-1014-3

LATINAS! WOMEN OF ACHIEVEMENT

"A collection rich with the diverse accomplishments of 70 *hermanas.*"— *Latina* magazine

Celebrating the accomplishments of 70 prominent Hispanic women in the United States, this collection of biographical profiles represents all fields of endeavor—from astronaut Ellen Ochoa to zoologist Maxine Baca Zinn. Foreword by award-winning writer and illustrator Nicholasa Mohr.

Edited by Diane Telgen and Jim Kamp 7¼ X 9¼ paperback 408 pages 70 photos ISBN 0-7876-0883-1

HISPANIC ALMANAC: FROM COLUMBUS TO CORPORATE AMERICA

"Documents Hispanic achievements over the ages, from politics to business to art."—*Evansville Courier*

Take an intriguing look at the people, places, and events that shape American life. Includes hundreds of profiles of entertainers, artists, athletes and other major figures, from Ponce de León to Henry Cisneros, plus thoughtful discussion of current issues and topics. Foreword by writer/director Luis Valdez, founder of the revolutionary theater company El Teatro Campesino.

Nicolás Kanellos 7¼ X 9¼ paperback 644 pages 200 photos and line drawings ISBN 0-7876-0030-X

THESE BOOKS ARE AVAILABLE AT YOUR LOCAL BOOKSTORE, OR BY CALLING 1-800-776-6265.

GCLS/GLASSBORO BRANCH
2 CENTER STREET
GLASSBORO, NJ 08028

WITHDRAWN

HISPANIC
FIRSTS

**500 YEARS OF
EXTRAORDINARY
ACHIEVEMENT**

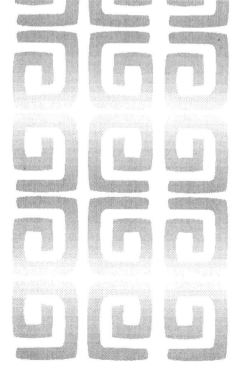

HISPANIC
FIRSTS

**500 YEARS OF
EXTRAORDINARY
ACHIEVEMENT**

NICOLÁS
KANELLOS

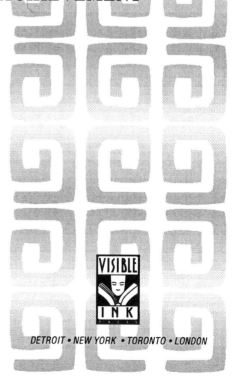

VISIBLE INK PRESS

DETROIT • NEW YORK • TORONTO • LONDON

HISPANIC FIRSTS

Copyright © 1997 by Visible Ink Press™

This publication is a creative work fully protected by all applicable copyright laws, as well as by misappropriation, trade secret, unfair competition, and other applicable laws. The authors and editors of this work have added value to the underlying factual material herein through one or more of the following: unique and original selection, coordination, expression, arrangement, and classification of the information.

No part of this book may be reproduced in any form without permission in writing from the publisher, except by a reviewer who wishes to quote brief passages in connection with a review written for inclusion in a magazine or newspaper.

All rights to this publication will be vigorously defended.

Published by **Visible Ink Press™**
a division of Gale Research
835 Penobscot Building
Detroit, MI 48226-4094

Visible Ink Press™ is a trademark of Gale Research

Most Visible Ink Press™ books are available at special quantity discounts when purchased in bulk by corporations, organizations, or groups. Customized printings, special imprints, messages, and excerpts can be produced to meet your needs. For more information, contact the Special Markets Manager at the above address. Or call 1-800-877-4253.

Senior Art Director: Pamela A. E. Galbreath

ISBN 0-7876-0519-0

Library of Congress Cataloging-in-Publication Data

Kanellos, Nicolás.
    Hispanic Firsts : 500 years of extraordinary achievement / by Nicolás Kanellos.
        p. cm.
    Includes bibliographical references.
    ISBN 0-7876-0519-0
        1. Hispanic Americans—History—Miscellanea. 2. World records—United States.
    I. Title
    E1840S75K36 1997
    973' . 0468073—dc21   97–10499
                                                                                        CIP

Printed in the United States of America
All rights reserved

10 9 8 7 6 5 4 3 2 1

This volume of firsts is dedicated to the next two generations, who will create their own firsts: John Michael, Laura, Miguel and Sonja. And as always, I thank my wife Cristelia and my parents Inés and Charlie for all their support and faith.

Dedico este libro de primeros logros a las dos generaciones que siguen. Lograrán mucho por primera vez en la historia: John Michael, Laura, Miguel y Sonja. Y, como siempre, les agradezco a mi esposa Cristelia y a mis padres Inés y Charlie por su apoyo y fe en mi.

CONTENTS

INTRODUCTION

〰〰〰〰〰〰〰〰〰〰〰〰〰〰〰〰〰〰〰〰

Hispanic Firsts is the first effort to organize the contributions and achievements of Hispanics as pioneers of American culture. In an easily readable and digestible form, these pages document and detail the accomplishments of Hispanics chronologically according to the various fields of their endeavors, from the arts to the sciences. Whereas what has reigned in popular culture and even the teaching of history for more than a century is a stereotypical vision of Hispanics as less than desirable neighbors and citizens, the record clearly shows that Hispanic peoples are responsible for laying the foundation for much of American industry and civilization. Although Hispanics are growing into the largest minority group in the United States, and are forecast to become one-third of the population by 2050, little is generally known of their contributions to U.S. culture and civilization, and far too little is known about their current participation in every field and at every level of the American enterprise.

The writing of *Hispanic Firsts* is governed by two concepts: (1) the development of U.S. civilization owes much to pioneering Hispanics; and (2) Hispanics are also pioneers for breaking barriers to success in American society. Therefore, most of the entries for the early years in this book represent the coming of the Spanish and their Afro- and Indo-Hispanic progeny to areas that would become the United States. These Hispanic peoples introduced European concepts of agriculture, architecture, city planning, education, law, literature, religion, science, writing, and almost every other social organization and intellectual endeavor that was imported to the New World or was developed here as the product of the wedding of European and Amerindian cultures. Once the thirteen colonies that became the United States began to expand southward and westward, Hispanic civilization in North America and the Caribbean was the object of conquest, subjugation, and, to some extent, assimilation. Despite Hispanic peoples having been conquered and incorporated as citizens of the United States, and despite their having been imported for a century and a half to toil in factories and fields, they too often remained outsiders, seen as foreigners and even enemies. Their accomplishments as a people in North America have often been maligned, ignored, or forgotten, even while the United States benefitted from their pioneering work and genius. Thus, the second organizing principle of this book is to recognize those Hispanics and their organizations that succeeded in breaking barriers: the first Hispanics to establish labor unions, publish newspapers, run publishing houses, gain entrance to major sports and even be named to the Halls of Fame; the first Hispanics to discover scientific processes and to fly in outer space; and most important, the first Hispanics to make important gains in civil rights and government and to fight for the dignity of people everywhere.

Most entries are brief mentions of important historical achievements; however, events of greatest resonance are highlighted in the text and are often accompanied by an illustration or photograph. To enable easier scanning and identification of the various achievements of Hispanics, four indexes are included: a timeline, a calendar, an index of entries, and a complete subject index. Also, each entry is accompanied by a reference to sources of information or books and articles for further reading. A complete bibliography is also included for those readers who desire to continue learning about the history of Hispanic peoples in the United States.

In conducting the research for *Hispanic Firsts,* it became obvious that many of the great accomplishments by Hispanics in the United States could not be included simply because they were not the first in history but had built on an already existing tradition. Therefore, some very important names of extraordinary people are absent from this text. Also, there are many deeds that have gone unrecorded, many accomplishments for which we do not have a precise date or the name of the individual or individuals involved. For instance, which Hispanic pioneer established the first mine in the Southwest? Who was the first to grow wheat, or cotton, or rice? At this time in history, many of the documentary sources are lost—perhaps forever. Hundreds of newspapers and books were written and published in Hispanic communities of the United States but were never collected or preserved by libraries and institutions of learning in this society. How much more information could they have added to our storehouse of historical data? How much will we never know about the life and culture of Hispanic peoples in this land?

As a pioneering effort unto itself, *Hispanic Firsts* relies on a wide variety of sources, some of which may have erred in precision. If any errors are detected, I beg the reader's indulgence and forgiveness, and invite the reader to forward corrections to Visible Ink Press in order that the following editions of the work may be corrected. But in all, both Visible Ink Press and I believe that we have broadened the scope of American history and helped to provide more detail and accuracy as to its actual development by acknowledging and documenting the Hispanic contribution that has been absent for so long!

Nicolás Kanellos; Houston, Texas

PHOTO CREDITS

The photographs and illustrations appearing in *Hispanic Firsts* were received from the following sources:

Cover: César Chavéz, courtesy of the Bettmann Archive/Newsphotos Inc.

Art and Design: *p. 2: La Piedad,* by José Campeche (courtesy of Institute of Puerto Rican Culture); *p. 4: Our Lady of Sorrows,* by the Laguna Santero (courtesy of Spanish Colonial Arts Society); *p. 5: Self-Portrait,* by Francisco Oller (courtesy of Museum of the University of Puerto Rico); *p. 10: Casa Singer,* installation by Antonio Martorell (courtesy of *The Américas Review); p. 14: Vaquero,* by Luis Jiménez (courtesy of Arte Público Press); *p. 16:* Carolina Herrera (courtesy of Carolina Herrera); *p. 18: Homenaje a Frida Kahlo,* by Irene Cervántez (courtesy of Arte Público Press).

Business and Commerce: *p. 22:* Illustration by Theodore De Bry of Indians at a sugar plantation and mill in 1590 (courtesy of Library of Congress, Prints and Photographs Division); *p. 25:* A cattle round-up at the San Gabriel Mission in early California (courtesy of California State Library); *p. 27:* A *vaquero* in early California (courtesy of Bancroft Library, University of California); *p. 29:* A sugar refinery in mid-nineteenth century Cuba (courtesy of Library of Congress, Prints and Photographs Division); *p. 31:* Mule trains in the freighting business in Arizona in 1888 (courtesy of Arizona Historical Society); *p. 30:* Leopoldo Carrillo (courtesy of Arizona Historical Society); *p. 32:* Downtown Ybor City in the 1890s (courtesy of Arte Público Press); *p. 34:* Roberto C. Goizueta (courtesy of Coca-Cola Inc); *p. 35:* Luis Nogales (courtesy of Luis Nogales); *p. 33:* Katherine D. Ortega (courtesy of Library of Congress, Prints and Photographs Division); *p. 36:* Lionel Sosa (courtesy of Sosa and Associates); *p. 37:* Linda Alvarado (courtesy of Linda Alvarado).

Education: *p. 44:* Antonio Coronel (courtesy of Southwest Museum); *p. 45:* Esteban Ochoa (courtesy of Arizona Historical Society); *p. 46:* Rita Ricardo-Campbell (courtesy of Rita Ricardo-Campbell); *p. 51:* Tomás Rivera (courtesy of Arte Público Press); *p. 52:* Modesto Maidique (courtesy of Arte Público Press); *p. 53:* Jaime Escalante (courtesy of Arte Público Press); *p. 54:*

Américo Paredes (courtesy of Arte Público Press); *p. 54:* Elsa Gómez (courtesy of Arte Público Press); *p. 55:* Joseph A. Fernández (courtesy of Arte Público Press).

Film: *p. 59:* Dolores del Río (courtesy of AP/Wide World); *p. 61:* Rita Hayworth (courtesy of AP/Wide World); *p. 60:* José Ferrer (courtesy of Arte Público Press); *p. 63:* Anthony Quinn in *The Children of Sánchez* (courtesy of Arte Público Press); *p. 64:* Rita Moreno (courtesy of AP/Wide World); *p. 65:* Ricardo Montalbán (courtesy of Arte Público Press); *p. 66:* Nestor Almendros (courtesy of Arte Público Press); *p. 67:* Elizabeth Peña (courtesy of AP/Wide World); *p. 68:* A scene from Gregory Nava's *El Norte* (courtesy of Arte Público Press); *p. 69:* Edward James Olmos (courtesy of Arte Público Press).

Government: *p. 76:* Pedro Menéndez de Avilés (courtesy of Library of Congress, Prints and Photographs Division); *p. 78:* Palace of the Governors, Santa Fe (courtesy of Library of Congress, Prints and Photographs Division); *p. 79:* The Spanish Governor's Palace (courtesy of Library of Congress, Prints and Photographs Division); *p. 80:* Junípero Serra (courtesy of Library of Congress, Prints and Photographs Division); *p. 83:* Governor Pío Pico (courtesy of California Historical Society); *p. 84:* Governor Romualdo Pacheco (courtesy of Library of Congress, Prints and Photographs Division); *p. 87:* Ladislao Lázaro (courtesy of Library of Congress, Prints and Photographs Division); *p. 88:* Octaviano Larrazolo (courtesy of Library of Congress, Prints and Photographs Division); *p. 90:* Dennis Chávez (courtesy of Library of Congress, Prints and Photographs Division); *p. 91:* Governor Luis Muñoz Marín (courtesy of Library of Congress, Prints and Photographs Division); *p. 92:* Henry B. González (courtesy of Library of Congress, Prints and Photographs Division); *p. 93:* Edward R. Roybal (courtesy of Library of Congress, Prints and Photographs Division); *p. 94:* Herman Badillo (courtesy of Library of Congress, Prints and Photographs Division); *p. 97:* Mari-Luci Jaramillo (courtesy of Library of Congress, Prints and Photographs Division); *p. 104:* Linda Chávez (courtesy of Library of Congress, Prints and Photographs Division); *p. 103:* Governor Bob Martínez (courtesy of Library of Congress, Prints and Photographs Division); *p. 105:* Ileana Ros-Lehtinen (courtesy of Library of Congress, Prints and Photographs Division); *p. 106:* Raymond Orozco (courtesy of Chicago Fire Department); *p. 106:* Antonia C. Novello (courtesy of AP/Wide World); *p. 107:* Ed Pastor (courtesy of Library of Congress, Prints and Photographs Division); *p. 108:* Henry Bonilla (courtesy of Library of Congress, Prints and Photographs Division); *p. 108:* Nydia Velásquez (courtesy of Library of Congress, Prints and Photographs Division); *p. 108:* Lucille Roybal-Allard (courtesy of Library of Congress, Prints and Photographs Division); *p. 112:* Fort Mose, 1760 (courtesy of National Library, Madrid, Spain); *p. 114:* Lola Rodríguez de Tió (courtesy of Arte Público Press); *p. 118:* Order of the Sons of America, Council No. 4, Corpus Christi, 1927 (courtesy of Arte Público Press); *p. 119:* Ninth Annual LULAC Convention, Houston, Texas, 1937 (courtesy of Arte Público Press); *p. 124:* Rodolfo "Corky" Gonzales (courtesy of Denver Public Library, Denver, Colorado); *p. 125:* Swearing in of Vicente Treviño Ximenes, with President Lyndon B. Johnson, photo by Yoichi Okamoto (courtesy of L.B.J. Library, University of Texas, Austin); *p. 128:* Vilma Martínez (courtesy of Arte Público Press); *p. 132:* Willie Velásquez (courtesy of Arte Público Press).

Labor: *p. 135:* Mexican miners in Arizona in the early 1900s (courtesy of Arizona Historical Society); *p. 136:* Mexican workers bailing hay in the San Gabriel Valley, 1890s (courtesy of Natural History Museum of Los Angeles County, California); *p. 143:* Pecan shellers in San Antonio during the 1930s (courtesy of Library of Congress, Prints and Photographs Division); *p. 146:* César Chávez on the picket line during the national grape boycott (courtesy of Archives of Labor and Urban Affairs, Wayne State University, Detroit, Michigan).

Literature: *p. 152:* Title page of Villagrá's epic of the colonization of New Mexico (courtesy of Arte Público Press); *p. 154:* Félix Varela (courtesy of Arte Público Press); *p. 155:* Juan Nepomuceno Seguín (courtesy of Library of Congress, Prints and Photographs Division); *p. 156:* George Santayana (courtesy of Library of Congress, Prints and Photographs Division); *p. 159:* Gabriela Mistral (courtesy of Library of Congress, Prints and Photographs Division); *p. 159:* Floyd Salas (courtesy of Arte Público Press); *p. 160:* Jose Yglesias (courtesy of Arte Público Press); *p. 162:* Cover of *Yo soy Joaquín,* by Rodolfo "Corky" Gonzales (courtesy of Arte Público Press); *p. 165:* Nicholasa Mohr, photo by Phil Cantor (courtesy of Arte Público Press); *p. 168:* Rolando Hinojosa (courtesy of Arte Público Press); *p. 171:* Sandra María Esteves (courtesy of Arte Público Press); *p. 175:* Carolina Hospital, photo by Phil Roche (courtesy of Arte Público Press); *p. 178:* Sandra Cisneros (courtesy of AP/Wide World); *p. 177:* Lucha Corpi (courtesy of Arte Público Press); *p. 179:* Lorna Dee Cervantes (courtesy of Arte Público Press); *p. 183:* Alba Ambert (courtesy of Arte Público Press).

Media: *p. 188:* Harry Caicedo (courtesy of Arte Público Press); *p. 190:* Roberto Suárez (courtesy of Arte Público Press); *p. 192:* Pedro J. González's singing group for his radio show, *Los Madrugadores* (courtesy of Arte Público Press); *p. 194:* María Hinojosa (courtesy of María Hinojosa); *p. 197:* Luis Santeiro (courtesy of Luis Santeiro); *p. 200:* Giselle Fernández (courtesy of CBS Inc); *p. 202:* Nelly Galán (courtesy of AP/Wide World).

The Military: *p. 205:* A drawing of free black soldiers in Havana, 1795 (courtesy of Library of Congress, Prints and Photographs Division); *p. 206:* Francisco de Miranda (courtesy of U.S. Department of Defense); *p. 208:* Bernardo de Gálvez (courtesy of Arte Público Press); *p. 210:* General Juan Nepomuceno Cortina (courtesy of Arte Público Press); *p. 213:* Admiral Horacio Rivero (courtesy of U.S. Department of Defense); *p. 214:* Richard E. Cavazos (courtesy of U.S. Department of Defense).

The Performing Arts: *p. 217:* José Limón (courtesy of Library of Congress, Prints and Photographs Division); *p. 222:* Carlos Chávez (courtesy of Library of Congress, Prints and Photographs Division); *p. 225:* Tania J. León (courtesy of Tania J. León); *p. 229:* Celia Cruz (courtesy of Hollywood Palladium).

Religion: *p. 233: Virgin of Guadalupe* (courtesy of Arte Público Press); *p. 236:* Concelebration of mass near site of Mission San Francisco de los Tejos (courtesy of *Texas Catholic Herald*); *p. 238:* Father Antonio José Martínez (courtesy of Arte Público Press); *p. 241:* Patrick F. Flores (courtesy of Arte Público Press); *p. 243:* Pablo Sedillo (courtesy of *Texas Catholic Herald*).

Science and Technology: *p. 248:* Christopher Columbus (courtesy of Library of Congress, Prints and Photographs Division); *p. 249:* Hernando de Soto (courtesy of Library of Congress, Prints and Photographs Division); *p. 252:* Ellen Ochoa (courtesy of AP/Wide World); *p. 255:* Frederic Remington's depiction of Coronado's trek across the Southwest (courtesy of Library of Congress, Prints and Photographs Division); *p. 261:* Alvar Núñez Cabeza de Vaca (courtesy of Arte Público Press); *p. 264:* Luis Walter Alvarez (courtesy of Library of Congress, Prints and Photographs Division); *p. 266:* George Castro (courtesy of George Castro); *p. 267:* Franklin Chang-Díaz (courtesy of NASA); *p. 268:* Adriana Ocampo (courtesy of Adriana Ocampo); *p. 269:* Eloy Rodríguez, photo by Frank DiMeo (courtesy of Cornell University Photography); *p. 271:* Mario Molina, photo by Donna Coveney (courtesy of Mario Molina).

Sports: *p. 278:* Roberto Clemente (courtesy of Arte Público Press); *p. 282:* Rachel Elizondo McLish (courtesy of AP/Wide World); *p. 284:* "Kid Chocolate" (courtesy of Library of Congress, Prints and Photographs Division); *p. 285:* José "Chegüi" Torres (courtesy of José "Chegüi" Torres); *p. 290:* Thomas Flores (courtesy of Los Angeles Raiders); *p. 291:* "Chi Chi" Rodríguez (courtesy of NBC); *p. 293:* Lee Treviño (courtesy of The National Archives); *p. 299:* Rosemary Casals (courtesy of Archive Photos).

Theater: *p. 305:* A touring theatrical company in Arizona in the 1890s (courtesy of Arte Público Press); *p. 309:* La Chata Noloesca (courtesy of Arte Público Press); *p. 310:* Manuel Aparicio in a Federal Theater Project play (courtesy of Dorothea Lang Collection, Federal Theater Project Archives, George Mason University); *p. 312:* Chita Rivera (courtesy of AP/Wide World); *p. 317:* Scene from Luis Valdez's play *Zoot Suit* (courtesy of Universal City Studios); *p. 319:* Miriam Colón (courtesy of Arte Público Press); *p. 321:* Josefina López (courtesy of Arte Público Press).

CALENDAR OF FIRSTS

JANUARY

FEBRUARY

MARCH

JUNE

JULY

AUGUST

SEPTEMBER

ART AND DESIGN

∼∼

1503 • European-style architecture and design were introduced to the New World with the construction of the church of San Nicolás de Bari, from 1503 to 1508, in the city of Santo Domingo. Other religious, civil, and military architecture, design, and decoration, including all types of pictorial and plastic arts, followed as the Spaniards colonized the Caribbean islands and North, Central, and South America.

Kanellos, *Chronology of Hispanic American History,* p. 14.

1751 • On December 23, 1751, one of the first colonial artists to gain international fame, José Campeche (1751–1809), was born in San Juan, Puerto Rico. Campeche was the fifth of seven children of María Josefa Jordán Marqués, a Canary Islander, and Tomás de Rivafrecha Campeche, a freed slave who became a painter and musician employed by his local church. As a child, José worked in his father's studio, learning both painting and music while receiving his education at the Dominican convent of Saint Thomas Aquinas.

In 1772, Campeche began painting religious figures; his two earliest known paintings are portraits of Brother Sebastián Lorenzo Pizarro and Saint Joseph with the Christ Child. In 1776, Campeche became an associate of the exiled Spanish painter Luis Paret y Alcázar, who had recently arrived in Puerto Rico. Under Paret's influence and instruction, Campeche was transformed from a competent local painter into a colonial master.

In the course of his career, Campeche would eventually outgrow the rigid academic training of Paret as he developed his own more fluid and humanistic style. In 1785, Campeche painted *La dama a caballo* (The Lady on a Horse), which marked his maturity as a draftsman and colorist. During this period, Campeche became one of the leading portrait artists of the nobility and of the government. At the same time, he also developed his career as a musician and teacher of instrumental music at the Cathedral of San Juan. In San Juan in 1789, he painted portraits of the new king of Spain and the royal family when Charles IV inherited the throne; and from 1790 on, he became the principal portrait artist of the most prominent members of San Juan society. In 1797, Campeche began to receive commissions from

other Spanish colonies. He painted *La Piedad* (Piety) for the Caracas Cathedral in Venezuela, among other works. In 1801, Campeche began to receive a number of distinguished commissions to paint religious scenes and portraits of saints; that same year he painted *La visión de San Francisco* (Saint Frances's Vision) for the Church of Saint Frances.

On November 7, 1809, José Campeche died of an infectious disease in the same house in which he had lived his whole life. He was buried at the Dominican convent.

Kanellos, *Chronology of Hispanic American History,* pp. 55, 62.

1760 • The earliest easel painting by a professional artist rendering an event in Texas history was *The Destruction of the Mission of San Sabá* (near present-day Menard). The painting, commissioned by Pedro Romero de Terreros, depicts events that transpired in 1758.

Chipman, *Spanish Texas, 1519–1821,* p. 255.

1783 • The first Academies of Fine Arts were founded in Mexico and Guatemala—these were the first in the Western Hemisphere, and Mexico's was the first in North America.

Kanellos, *Chronology of Hispanic American History,* p. 60.

1796 • A unique style of religious painting and sculpture was started in New Mexico by an unknown wood-carver, subsequently called the Laguna Santero by art historians. This sculptor and painter of religious works, including wooden saints, was active in New Mexico from 1796 to 1808, long enough for him to inspire a school of artists who copied his style. The design of his altar screens and paintings indicates that he may have been from the provinces of Mexico. The expression of religious piety in the works by the Laguna Santero are closer to the images of medieval Europe than they are to the baroque style prevalent in Mexico during his life.

Santeros (carvers of religious statuary) had been carving statues in New Mexico from about 1700, most of them anonymously and copying styles popular in Mexico.

Kanellos, *The Hispanic American Almanac,* p. 471; Quirarte, *Mexican American Artists,* pp. 26–33.

1858 • Puerto Rican painter Francisco Oller (1833–1917) traveled to Paris for a stay of seven years and became the only Latin American artist to participate in the development of impressionism. After studying and inter-acting with the French founders of impressionism, Oller returned to Puerto Rico, introducing much of what he had learned. During the rest of his life, he continued to visit France and Spain in the development of his career.

Born Francisco Manuel Oller y Cestero on July 17, 1833, in San Juan, Oller is also noted as being one of the first artists to really inspire his work with the landscape of Puerto Rico and the customs of its everyday people. As a young student in elementary and secondary school, Oller was consid-

OPPOSITE PAGE:
LA PIEDAD,
BY JOSÉ CAMPECHE.

ered an art prodigy by his teachers. On June 1, 1849, Oller was hired as an art teacher at the College of Saint Thomas, a secondary school; from that date on, he began accepting commissions from churches to paint religious scenes and portraits of saints. In 1851, Oller traveled to Spain and studied at the Academy of San Fernando with Federico Madrazo y Kunts, director of the Prado Museum. In 1853, Oller returned to Puerto Rico, and in 1854 he received the silver medal in the first Puerto Rican Exposition.

OUR LADY OF
SORROWS, BY THE
LAGUNA SANTERO.

In 1858, Oller moved to Paris, where he studied with Thomas Couture and became an official copyist at the Louvre. While living in Paris, Oller took on a number of jobs, including singing as a baritone with an Italian opera company. In 1859, he became a member of the Atelier de Gleyre with Pierre Renoir, Claude Monet, and Alfred Sisley, among others. In the following years, he became associated with many of the pioneers of impressionism, including Camille Pissarro and Paul Cézanne, with whom he lived for a while. In 1865, Oller returned to Puerto Rico but continued to correspond with Cézanne, Pissarro, and other painters in Paris and to send his works there for exhibit and sale. In 1868, Oller exhibited forty-five paintings at the San Juan Fair and was immediately proclaimed the best painter on the island. On September 1 of the same year, Oller opened and directed a Free Academy of Drawing and Painting, with an immediate enrollment of two hundred students.

On November 10, 1869, Oller was knighted by order of the king of Spain. On January 22, 1872, Oller was named painter to the royal court in Spain. From 1873 to 1884, Oller worked in Europe. Upon his return to Puerto Rico in 1884, he learned that his school had been closed. In 1889, he founded the School of Painting and Drawing for Young Ladies. In 1892, Oller finished his monumental painting *El Velorio* (The Wake), based on Puerto Rican rural customs. In 1893, Oller won the gold medal in the Puerto Rico Exposition for his forty-six works exhibited.

In 1895, he settled once again in Paris, where his *El Velorio* also became a sensation. Oller returned to Puerto Rico in 1896 with various paintings exhibiting the impressionist style. In 1901, he opened another academy of drawing in San Juan. In 1902, Oller was named drawing professor in the Normal School, which would later become the University of Puerto Rico. Upon being fired from that post in 1904, he opened yet another school of art for young ladies. He later worked as a teacher in Bayamón and received a stipend while suffering a long illness that eventually resulted in his death on May 17, 1917.

Tardiff and Mabunda, *Dictionary of Hispanic Biography,* pp. 623–24.

1872 • Francisco Oller became the first Puerto Rican painter to be named painter to the royal court of Spain. In 1869, he had been knighted by the king of Spain. Oller was born in San Juan, where he received his early education, but later traveled to Spain to study at the Academy of San Fernando. He went on to an outstanding career, exhibiting works and winning awards in both Europe and the Americas. Oller is noted as the first artist to really inspire his works with the Puerto Rican landscape and customs of its everyday folk. He is also noted as having introduced impressionism to Puerto Rico.

Kanellos, *Chronology of Hispanic American History,* pp. 87–88.

SELF-PORTRAIT, BY
FRANCISCO OLLER.

1876 · The first Hispanic to win a major art award in the United States was the famed Mexican landscape artist José María Velasco at the Centennial International Exposition in Philadelphia. This was just one of the many international awards Velasco received during his career.

Kanellos, *Chronology of Hispanic American History,* pp. 92–119.

1893 · Mexican landscape painter José María Velasco won first prize at the World's Fair in Chicago. Velasco was born in 1840 into a bourgeois family that moved to Mexico City when he was nine. He was educated in Catholic schools until age fifteen and then he began to study at the San Carlos Academy. He began full-time instruction there in landscape painting in 1858 under Italian artist Eugenio Landesio. In 1868, Velasco was appointed professor of perspective at the academy.

During the 1860s, Velasco executed various large-scale landscapes. In the 1870s, he began to develop his interest in photography and eventually made a transition to lithography. In 1875, Velasco was appointed professor of landscape painting at the San Carlos Academy. In 1876, he received a prize at the Centennial International Exposition in Philadelphia. In 1889, he went to Europe and exhibited seventy-eight paintings at the Universal Exposition in Paris and was made a Chevalier de la Légion d'Honneur. In 1890, Velasco received the highest Austrian award, the Franz Joseph Cross, and in 1893 was awarded first prize at the Chicago World's Fair. Velasco died in Mexico City in 1912.

Kanellos, *Chronology of Hispanic American History,* p. 119.

1921 · *Mexican Painters and Photographers of California,* one of the first exhibitions of contemporary Mexican art in the United States, opened in Los Angeles.

Griswold et al., *Chicano Art,* p. 207.

1930 · The three greatest muralists of the twentieth century, Diego Rivera, David Alfaro Siqueiros, and José Clemente Orozco, were all receiving commissions and were very active in art circles in California from 1930 to 1931, inspiring U.S. artists to follow their example. All three had started a revolution in wall painting in Mexico, recovering colors, materials, and techniques from the pre-Columbian Indians as well as from Renaissance European painters, showing how wall painting could be a democratic and national art.

Quirarte, *Mexican American Artists,* p. 32.

1930 · Painter Antonio García graduated from the Art Institute of Chicago and became the first, or one of the first, Mexican American painters of note. He was one of a generation of Mexican-origin artists born between 1901 and

1912 who were raised and educated in the United states and developed an intercultural sensibility. Others were Octavio Medellín, Chelo González Amezcua, Pedro Salinas, and Margaret Herrera Chávez. García was born in Monterrey, Mexico, in 1901, and moved to San Diego, Texas, with his family when he was twelve. In addition to exhibiting his paintings internationally, García also painted murals, illustrated books, and taught art at Del Mar College in Corpus Christi.

Chelo González Amezcua was the first female painter to be considered a Mexican American artist. Born in Mexico in 1903, González was a completely self-taught artist raised in Del Rio, Texas. She was offered a scholarship from the San Carlos Academy, Mexico City, during the 1930s but she had to refuse because of the need to support her family when her father died. In her early work and techniques, González used ballpoint pen on paper, revealing no influence of other artists in her work. Only in the late 1960s was her work recognized and did she begin to exhibit at museums and galleries outside of Del Rio.

Quirarte, *Mexican American Artists,* pp. 41–42, 44–49.

1930 ⋅ One of the first Hispanic folk artists to gain national attention was New Mexican *santero* (carver of religious statuary) Patrocinio Barela, whose work was exhibited and studied throughout the 1930s. Since his time, santeros have continued to command attention in the art world.

Griswold et al., *Chicano Art,* p. 208.

1933 ⋅ The New Mexico State Department of Vocational Education, under the directorship of Brice H. Sewell, launched a training program in Hispanic communities to teach the traditional Hispanic arts of weaving, tanning, leatherwork, furniture making, and ornamental work. The program led to a revival of these arts, but especially of furniture making. Based on the study of original Spanish furniture of the colonial period in New Mexico, the program published manuals and bulletins with detailed illustrations for the design and construction of the furniture.

Wroth, *Furniture from the Hispanic Southwest.*

1938 ⋅ Mexican American sculptor Octavio Medellín became the first U.S. Hispanic artist to join the faculty of a large university when he became a member of the art department of North Texas State University in Denton. In 1945, he took an appointment at Southern Methodist University, Dallas, where he taught until 1966.

Medellín was born in Matehuala, Mexico, in 1907 and immigrated to the United States with his parents as refugees from the Mexican Revolution in 1920. He is considered a member of the first generation of artists with a

Mexican American identity. Medellín's works are inspired by pre- Columbian sculpture; he works in stone and wood.

Quirarte, *Mexican American Artists,* pp. 49–52.

1939 • Patronicio Barela (ca. 1900–1964) became the first Hispanic folk artist to have his works exhibited at a world's fair. The carver of saints, doors, and colonial-style furniture from wood was born in Bisbee, Arizona, and was selected to participate in the Federal Arts Project during the Depression. He came to national attention and his sculptures were selected for exhibit at the 1939 New York World's Fair. Barela was self- taught but is considered by critics to have revealed the inner expression and psychological depth of the figures that he carved in a primitive style.

Meier and Rivera, *Dictionary of Mexican American History,* pp. 34–35.

1940 • *Twenty Centuries of Mexican Art,* the first large-scale and most influential exhibition of Mexican art ever, opened at the Museum of Modern Art in New York.

Griswold et al., *Chicano Art,* p. 208.

1949 • Armando Baeza's sculpture won an art prize in Los Angeles and became the first work by a Mexican American artist to be featured in a national news magazine—*Newsweek.*

Griswold et al., *Chicano Art,* p. 210.

1952 • Puerto Rican painter Rufino Silva was the first Hispanic to become a member of the faculty of the prestigious Art Institute of Chicago. Silva was born in Humacao, Puerto Rico, in 1919 and studied at the Art Institute from 1938 to 1942.

Kanellos, *The Hispanic American Almanac,* p. 480.

1953 • Spanish-born architect José Luis Sert became the first Hispanic to serve as dean of a major school of architecture—the Graduate School of Design at Harvard University. Sert was born and educated in Barcelona, Spain, and in 1939 moved to the United States, where he joined an architectural firm. During his career, he designed important structures not only in the United States but in Brazil, Colombia, and other countries. He is especially known for designing buildings at Harvard and Boston Universities.

Hispanics in U.S. History, p. 31.

1954 • The first annual Mexican American art exhibition was held in Los Angeles.

Griswold et al., *Chicano Art,* p. 210.

1955 • The Institute of Puerto Rican Culture was founded in San Juan to preserve and nurture Puerto Rico's traditional arts and handicrafts. Through its school, workshops, exhibits, festivals, and publications, the institute has preserved and promoted traditional as well as avant-garde arts, from folk dancing to theater and literature, operating annual and biennial festivals in many of the arts. Its founder and first director was the eminent folklorist and professor Dr. Ricardo Alegría. The work of the institute has been essential in the face of the onslaught of U.S. culture, related to Puerto Rico's status as a colony of the United States.

Hispania, 78/4 (December 1995), p. 913.

1956 • Amalia Peláez became the first Hispanic female artist to win a major award in the United States—first prize at the *Gulf Caribbean Art Exhibition* at the Museum of Fine Arts, Houston. Painter and ceramist Peláez was born in 1897 in Yaguajay, Cuba, one of nine children of a country doctor and his wife. She was familiar with the art world, however, because she was the sister of one of Cuba's most famous poets, Julián del Casal. At age fifteen, Peláez began to study painting with Magdalena Peñarredonda. From 1916 to 1924, she studied at the San Alejandro Academy in Havana and also studied with the painter Leopoldo Romañach. She continued her studies in New York at the Art Students' League with George Bridgman, and from 1927 to 1934 she studied in Paris at the Grand Chaumier.

Peláez eventually became a leader, with René Portocarrero and Wilfredo Lam, of the generation that was to bring Cuban painting into the twentieth century. All three insisted on the artist's freedom to reinvent and represent reality. Her solo exhibits included shows in Paris, New York, Havana, and Bogotá. Peláez also won national awards in Havana. Among her most famous paintings is *Hibiscus* (1943), which demonstrates a fusion of native, Creole, and imported elements. Peláez also had a distinguished career as a teacher, illustrator of books and magazines, and ceramist. Peláez died in Havana in 1968.

Kanellos, *Chronology of Hispanic American History,* p. 132.

1963 • Venezuelan American artist Marisol Escobar became the first Hispanic artist to be given a room of her own at a show, *Americans, 1963,* at the Museum of Modern Art in New York. Born in Paris on May 22, 1930, into a wealthy Venezuelan family, Marisol settled in Los Angeles with her father during World War II. After finishing high school in Los Angeles, Marisol studied art at the Académie des Beaux Arts in Paris, at the Art Students' League in New York, and at the New School for Social Research. She became a protégé of Willem de Kooning in New York and began to exhibit in galleries in the late 1950s. By 1961, her work had begun appearing in the Museum of Modern Art and other important places, and *Life* magazine had published photos of her work. Throughout the next three decades, Marisol's fame as a sculptor grew, and in 1991 she was invited to exhibit her sculptures at the National Portrait Gallery in Washington, D.C.

Telgen and Kamp, *Latinas! Women of Achievement,* pp. 231–35.

1965 • The Chicano art movement began when artists became affiliated with César Chávez's efforts to unionize farmworkers. The artists placed

themselves in the service of the effort, creating posters and symbols, painting murals, and illustrating newspapers and publications.
Griswold et al., *Chicano Art,* p. 144.

1967 ⋅ Dominican American fashion designer Oscar de la Renta became the first U.S. Hispanic to win the Coty American Fashion Critics' Award. De la Renta went on to become one of the most important designers in the world.
Tardiff and Mabunda, *Dictionary of Hispanic Biography,* p. 277.

CASA SINGER,
INSTALLATION BY
ANTONIO MARTORELL.

1968 • Puerto Rican painter and graphic artist Antonio Martorell became the first Hispanic to win first prize in illustration from the American Art Institute for illustrating the children's book *ABC de Puerto Rico* by Isabel Freire de Matos and Rubén del Rosario.

Tardiff and Mabunda, *Dictionary of Hispanic Biography,* p. 531.

1968 • The Chicano mural movement began with the works executed by artist Mario Castillo in Chicago and with painter Antonio Bernal's two-panel mural at San Diego's El Centro Cultural. About the same time, artists began executing murals in Austin, Houston, and San Antonio, as well. Inspired by the murals of earlier Mexican master muralists, the movement would take hold throughout the Southwest, the Chicago area, and New York, and would have its greatest activity and exponents in California during the 1970s.

"Barrio Murals in Chicago," *Revista Chicano- Riqueña,* pp. 51–72; Griswold et al., *Chicano Art,* p. 86.

1968 • The first Chicano art galleries were Denver's El Grito de Aztlán Gallery and San Francisco's Galería de la Raza; it was followed in 1969 by the Plaza de la Raza in Los Angeles in 1969. Other Chicano art galleries followed, including La Raza Graphic Center, which opened in San Francisco in 1971. San Diego's El Centro Cultural de la Raza began serving as a gallery in 1970, as well. With the exception of the Denver and the Los Angeles galleries, all of these galleries remain in operation.

Griswold et al, *Chicano Art,* pp. 225–26.

1968 • The first major neighborhood or grassroots Chicano art show was the annual Arte del Barrio show organized by René Yáñez and Ralph Madariaga of the Galería de la Raza in San Francisco.

Griswold et al., *Chicano Art,* p. 168.

1968 • The first major Chicano art group was Oakland's Mexican American Liberation Art Front, founded in 1968. It held its first show of note, *New Symbols for la Nueva Raza,* in 1969.

Griswold et al., *Chicano Art,* p. 223.

1970 • The first annual Chicano art exposition, the Tlacuilo Art Show, was initiated in San Antonio, Texas.

Griswold et al., *Chicano Art,* p. 215.

1971 • The first Puerto Rican mural in the Midwest—perhaps in the continental United States—was *La Crucificación de Pedro Alvizu Campos,* created by the Puerto Rican Art Association in Chicago.

"Barrio Murals in Chicago," *Revista Chicano- Riqueña,* 4/4 (1976), pp. 58–59, 62.

1971 • *Third World Women's Art Exhibit* was the first exhibition of art by Latinas. It was organized by the Galería de la Raza in San Francisco.

Griswold et al., *Chicano Art,* p. 178.

1972 • The first Hispanic performance art group to make living murals was *Asco* (Nausea), founded by Mexican American painters Gronk, Patssi Valdez, Willie Herrón, and by photographer Harry Gamboa. Their street performances, held mostly in East Los Angeles, included Day of the Dead celebrations, war protests, and "instant murals"—parodies of murals in the form of events staged against a wall. In 1972, Asco fused theater with murals and created *Walking Mural,* which seemed to detach itself from the wall. Patssi Valdez played the Virgin of Guadalupe; Gronk was a walking Christmas tree and supported a large masonite board that had figures with sculpted heads and arms projecting from it and flailing as he walked along.

Griswold et al., *Chicano Art,* pp. 148–49; Museum of Fine Arts, Houston, *Hispanic Art in the United States,* pp. 185–88.

1972 • Los Angeles's Self-Help Graphics was founded as a workshop for artists in east Los Angeles through the efforts of Sister Karen Boccalero, a nun, who recognized the talent of youth in the barrio. Over the years, the workshop has grown into one of the most productive and influential training, production, and exhibition spaces for Chicano artists. Self-Help specializes in printmaking, and its workshop allows for community members, whether novices or well-established printmakers, to make multiple-color silk screen prints (serigraphs) of their works. By splitting the run with the artists, Self-Help sustains itself by sales of the prints to galleries and art collectors.

Hispanic, October 1995, pp. 68–72.

1973 • The first truly national exhibition of Mexican American and Chicano art was held on November 10–11, 1973, at Trinity University in San Antonio, Texas. While representative, the short-lived show had little impact on the art scene in the United States.

Griswold et al., *Chicano Art,* p. 169.

1973 • The Mexican Museum, the first museum in the United States to be completely dedicated to collecting and presenting Mexican art, received its charter in San Francisco. It opened its doors to the public with a group exhibition in 1975.

Griswold et al., *Chicano Art,* p 172.

1974 • The first major exhibitions of Chicano art took place at the University of California, Irvine, the Los Angeles County Museum of Art, and several other institutions when the works of the mural-painting group Los Four came indoors. Los Four was the first exhibition to be housed at a large museum such as the Los Angeles County Museum of Art, where it was orga-

~~~~~~

nized by Jane Livingston. The group comprised painters Carlos Almaraz, Frank Romero, Gilbert Luján, and Beto de la Rocha.

Griswold et al., *Chicano Art,* p. 116; Museum of Fine Arts, Houston, *Hispanic Art in the United States,* p. 143.

1974 • The first women's muralist group, Mujeres Muralistas, was formed in San Francisco's Mission District. The original members of the group were Patricia Rodríguez, Consuelo Méndez Castillo, Irene Pérez, and Graciela Carrillo de López. During the next ten years, more than fifty exhibitions of Chicana art were held around the country.

Griswold et al., *Chicano Art,* pp. 167, 178.

1975 • The Association of Hispanic Arts was founded in New York City to offer services to all nonprofit Hispanic arts organizations and individual artists in the United States. It assists in community presentations, maintains a central information office on artists and arts organizations, and publishes the oldest and longest-lasting newsletter on Hispanic arts.

Furtaw, *Hispanic Americans Information Directory,* p. 4.

1976 • Chicana artist Judith Baca conceived of and executed the largest outdoor mural in the world, *The Great Wall of Los Angeles,* a half- mile-long narrative mural on the Tujunga Wash drainage canal in the San Fernando Valley. Its subject is Los Angeles's multiethnic history from Neolithic times until the 1950s. *The Great Wall of Los Angeles* was painted during five summers over the course of nine years ending in 1976. Baca developed the concept, hired the people, and helped raise the money necessary for the project. Using the *Great Wall* project as a model, Baca went on to found the Social and Public Art Resource Center (SPARC) in Venice, California, in 1976. SPARC involves multicultural youth in presenting and preserving murals and public art.

Telgen and Kamp, *Latinas! Women of Achievement,* pp. 28–29.

1976 • *Seventeen Artists, Mexican American, Hispano and Chicano* was the first exhibition of Latino art to travel widely and to be shown in museums in Chicago, San Francisco, Boise, Idaho, and elsewhere. It was organized by Robert Glauber for the Illinois Bell Telephone Company.

Griswold et al., *Chicano Art,* p. 172.

1977 • The first national Chicano arts festival, Canto al Pueblo, was held in Milwaukee, Wisconsin, from April 28–May 9, 1977. Organized by Arnold Vento, Reimundo "Tigre" Pérez, and Ricardo Sánchez, the festival included art exhibitions, art happenings, musical performances, and literary readings.

Griswold et al., *Chicano Art,* p. 171.

1977 • Sculptor Luis Jiménez was the first U.S. Hispanic artist to receive the Hassan Fund Purchase Award from the American Academy and Institute of Arts and Letters. In 1979, he also received a fellowship from the American Academy in Rome.

Museum of Fine Arts, Houston, *Hispanic Art in the United States,* p. 193.

1977 ⬧ The National Endowment for the Arts formed the first National Task Force on Hispanic Arts, chaired by art historian Jacinto Quirarte. The task force helped to create funding opportunities for artists and exhibitions.
Griswold et al., *Chicano Art,* p. 169.

1977 ⬧ The first Latino art exhibition to travel widely and be shown in major museums was *Ancient Roots/New Vision,* organized by Marc Zuver,

VAQUERO, BY LUIS JIMÉNEZ, FEATURED ON THE COVER OF A LATINO LITERARY MAGAZINE.

executive director of Fondo de Cultura in Washington, D.C. The exhibition opened at the Tucson Museum of Art and traveled to Chicago, Albuquerque, Colorado Springs, El Paso, Houston, Los Angeles, New York, San Antonio, and Washington, D.C. It received extensive press coverage in those cities.

Griswold et al., *Chicano Art,* pp. 172–73.

1978 • Mexico-born sculptor Robert Graham became the first Hispanic artist to receive a commission to work on a national monument in Washington, D.C. He and three others were commissioned to create the Franklin Delano Roosevelt Memorial, which has yet to be realized.

Museum of Fine Arts, Houston, *Hispanic Art in the United States,* p. 184.

1981 • Cuban American painter-sculptor-jeweler Pedro Pérez became the first Hispanic artist to receive the Louis Comfort Tiffany Foundation Award.

Museum of Fine Arts, Houston, *Hispanic Art in the United States,* p. 222.

1984 • The Hispanic Designers Association was founded in New York City by Hispanic fashion designers. Each year it organizes a Hispanic Designers Gala Fashion Show and Benefit and recognizes leading designers with awards.

Hispanic Link Weekly Report, 28 August 1995, p. 4.

1985 • The first comprehensive bibliography on Chicano art, *Arte Chicano,* was compiled by Professors Shifra Goldman and Tomás Ybarra- Frausto.

Griswold et al., *Chicano Art,* p. 221.

1987 • The first nationally touring exhibition of U.S. Hispanic art, *Hispanic Art in the United States: Thirty Contemporary Painters and Sculptors,* was launched by the Museum of Fine Arts, Houston, and the Corcoran Gallery in Washington, D.C., under the leadership of Peter Marzio. Some controversy arose about the exhibition, curated by John Beardsley and Jane Livingston, because its curators were neither Hispanic nor specialists in the subject. The exhibition included not only the founding institutions on its itinerary but also major museums in Brooklyn, Los Angeles, Santa Fe, and elsewhere.

Griswold et al., *Chicano Art,* p. 174; Museum of Fine Arts, Houston, *Hispanic Art in the United States.*

1987 • Carolina Herrera became the first Hispanic fashion designer to have her clothes worn by Jacqueline Kennedy Onassis, who, as First Lady, set the standard for American fashion during the 1960s. Kennedy also asked Herrera to create a wedding dress for her daughter, Caroline Kennedy. In 1987, the Venezuela-born Herrera was named Top Hispanic Designer upon receiving the MODA Award. She began her rise to prominence with the founding of her House of Herrera fashion design business in New York City in 1981. She rose to become one of the most successful

Hispanic fashion designers in the United States, eclipsed only by Dominican-born Oscar de la Renta. During the course of her career, she has been named to the Best Dressed Hall of Fame and named one of the Ten Most Elegant Women in the World.

Kanellos, *The Hispanic American Almanac,* p. 728; Tardiff and Mabunda, *Dictionary of Hispanic Biography,* pp. 423–26; Telgen and Kamp, *Latinas! Women of Achievement,* pp.184–85.

CAROLINA HERRERA.

1990 • The first national exhibition of Chicano art to travel to major museums throughout the United States was *Chicano Art: Resistance and Affirmation, 1965–1985,* which included on its three-year itinerary the Wight Art Gallery of the University of California, Los Angeles; the Denver Art Museum; the Albuquerque Art Museum; the San Francisco Museum of Art; the Fresno Art Museum; the Tucson Art Museum; the El Paso Museum of Art; the Bronx Museum of the Arts; and the San Antonio Museum of Art. In addition to showing representative Chicano works, the exhibit's catalog was an effort to write and illustrate the history of the Chicano art movement.
Griswold et al., *Chicano Art.*

1990 • Puerto Rico-born painter Héctor Díaz, from Tacoma, Washington, was included among ten others to be the first American artists invited to exhibit their works in what was then the Soviet Union. Díaz is nationally known for his paintings of nocturnal scenes of New York City neighborhoods. Raised in New York City, Díaz sold his first painting at age fourteen.
Hispanic, December 1995, p. 12.

1991 • Argentine American architect César Pelli became the first U.S. Hispanic to be named by the American Institute of Architects as one of the ten most influential living architects. Pelli has designed both public and private buildings throughout the United States and abroad. Among his most important structures are the San Bernardino City Hall, the Pacific Design Center in Los Angeles, the United States Embassy in Tokyo, and the World Financial Center and Winter Garden at Battery Park in New York, which is considered one of the ten best works of American architecture designed since 1980.
Tardiff and Mabunda, *Dictionary of Hispanic Biography,* p. 661.

1991 • Venezuelan American artist Marisol Escobar became the first U.S. Hispanic sculptor to exhibit her works at the National Portrait Gallery in Washington, D.C. Marisol is considered one of the most important figures in pop sculpture, according to H. Aronson's *History of Modern Art.*
See also Art and Design, 1963.
Telgen and Kamp, *Latinas! Women of Achievement,* p. 235.

1992 • Christy Turlington became the first Hispanic model to join the ranks of the supermodels making more than $1 million per year. The daughter of a Salvadoran immigrant mother and an American pilot, Turlington served as the model for high-powered campaigns for Calvin Klein and Maybelline, among many others, and was featured on the covers of magazines worldwide.
Telgen and Kamp, *Latinas! Women of Achievement,* p. 372.

1993 • Dominican American fashion designer Oscar de la Renta became the first American to lead a French couture business when he was selected to direct the House of Balmain, Paris.
Tardiff and Mabunda, *Dictionary of Hispanic Biography,* p. 277.

HOMENAJE A FRIDA KAHLO, BY IRENE CERVÁNTEZ, FROM CHICANO ART: RESISTANCE AND AFFIRMATION, 1965–1985.

Shattering the Myth:
Plays by Hispanic Women

Selected by Denise Chávez · Edited by Linda Feyder

1994 • The first exhibition of photography from the oldest and largest Spanish-speaking cultures of the United States was held at Houston's FotoFest '94, a citywide international photographic biennial. The exhibition, entitled *American Voices: Latino/Chicano/Hispanic Photography in the U.S.,* featured the works of thirty-nine Latino photographic artists. As part of the historic exhibition, FotoFest sponsored a symposium, "Across Cultures," which brought together artists, curators, and scholars from the United States, Mexico, and the Caribbean. FotoFest is the largest gathering of international photographers in the United States and is one of the largest in the world.

Texas Hispanic, November 1994, p. 43.

1994 • Sculptor of monumental works in fiberglass and epoxy Luis Jiménez became the first U.S. Hispanic artist to be named to an endowed professorship, at the University of Houston. Born in El Paso, Texas, in 1940, Jiménez studied art and then architecture at the University of Texas, where he received his B.A. in fine arts in 1964. Upon graduation he received a grant to study at the National Autonomous University of Mexico. His is one of the most original and innovative approaches to sculpture in the United States; he produces full-color works able to withstand the weather. His pop art sensibility has allowed him to satirize American and Chicano popular culture with surprising humor and pathos in a conventionally stoic medium. Jiménez has received major commissions from cities around the country, and his works are held in some of the most important museums.

Museum of Fine Arts, Houston, *Hispanic Art in the United States,* pp. 191–93; Quirarte, *Mexican American Artists,* pp. 115–20.

1995 • Argentine American architect César Pelli became the first Hispanic architect to receive the gold medal from the American Institute of Architects.

Tardiff and Mabunda, *Dictionary of Hispanic Biography,* p. 662.

1995 • The first major exhibition featuring women artists of Latin America toured major museums in the United States. *Latin American Women Artists, 1915–1995* included works in diverse media by thirty-five artists from eleven different countries. Its itinerary, which lasted until April 29, 1996, included the Milwaukee Art Museum, the Phoenix Art Museum, the Denver Art Museum, and the National Museum of Women in the Arts in Washington, D.C.

Hispanic, July 1995, p. 15.

1996 • Spanish architect Rafael Moneo, who has designed many buildings in the United States, became the first Hispanic to win the major international Pritziker Architecture Prize, given by the Hyatt Foundation and the Pritziker family of Chicago. Among the buildings Moneo has designed are the Davis Museum and the Cultural Center at Wellesley, Massachusetts.

Moneo has also been chosen to design the Beck Building for the Museum of Fine Arts, Houston.

"Museum Architect Wins Award," *Houston Chronicle,* 29 April 1996.

1996 • Carlos Jiménez became the first U.S. Hispanic architect to be selected by the Architectural League of New York for inclusion in *40 Under 40,* a book identifying "design leaders of the next millennium." Jiménez graduated from the University of Houston in 1982 with an award for the best thesis design. Much of his work since graduation has been executed on marginal pieces of urban land and with stringent budgets. Among Jiménez's works is the Junior School and Administration Building of the Glassell School of the Museum of Fine Arts, Houston.

"Leading by Design," *Houston Chronicle Zest Magazine* 17 March 1996, p. 12.

BUSINESS AND COMMERCE

1508 • The first agricultural product introduced to the Americas by the Spaniards was sugar cane. Originally from India, the plant was taken first to Hispaniola and then to the rest of the Americas for its cultivation. The first sugar mill was built in 1508 or 1509 on Hispaniola. The first samples of sugar were sent to Spain about 1515. By 1523, there were twenty-four mills operating on the island.

Kanellos, *Chronology of Hispanic American History,* pp. 24, 65.

1565 • Stock raising and ranching became established under the Spanish around Saint Augustine and Tallahassee, Florida. Most of the cattle were raised for local consumption, but there was enough surplus to make cattle the basis of trade, and smuggling to Cuba began to be instituted. Ranching did not flourish in Florida as it would in California and Texas however. By 1800, the tax rolls showed only thirty-four ranches with some fifteen thousand to twenty thousand cattle.

See also Science and Technology: Agriculture, 1521, 1535, 1539, 1598.

1598 • The leading Spanish colonizer and future governor of the province of New Mexico, Juan de Oñate (ca. 1550–1630), introduced livestock breeding to what would become the American Southwest. He established a livestock industry that would supply the burgeoning silver mining industry in northern New Spain (Mexico), especially around Zacatecas and Guanajuato. There was an intense demand for cattle, horses, and mules, as well as tallow for candles, hides for water and ore bags, clothing, harnesses, hinges, and numerous other items. From New Mexico and western Texas, cattle and livestock ranching spread into the Great Plains and became the basis of much today's livestock industry.

Spain had one of the oldest sheep cultures in the Old World, and it introduced the churro sheep—a small, lean animal that gave coarse wool and could endure long marches and all types of weather. The churro became so acclimated to New Mexico and the Southwest that it became the basis for the large sheep industry that would develop over the centuries. About 1876, fine merino sheep were brought by Anglos from the eastern seaboard and crossed with the churros to produce a hybrid animal that provided a better-quality wool while being ideally acclimated to the environment. By 1880, the Southwest was producing four million pounds of wool per year.

In New Mexico, as elsewhere in the Southwest and the rest of Spanish America, it was the Hispanicized Indians who became the cowboys and shepherds over the centuries, especially since much of ranching originated in and around the missions. The Spaniards also taught the Indians to weave wool, and the Indians—especially Navajo women in the early nineteenth century—labored in the textile industry in New Mexico.

Land grants to individuals, along with grazing rights, also facilitated the development of large cattle and sheep ranches. This was a particular inheritance from the Spaniards and Mexicans for Anglos when they came into the Southwest. A Mexican homestead in the Southwest consisted of 4,470 acres, twenty-eight times the size of an Anglo-American homestead in the Ohio Valley. The Spanish and Mexican land-use system was much better adapted to an arid environment and facilitated the growth of the cattle industry on the open range within that environment.

Rosaldo et al., *Chicano,* pp. 5–8, 13; Slatta, *Cowboys of the Americas,* pp. 20–22.

1663 • Florida-born Tomás Menéndez Márquez inherited his father's cattle ranch in central Florida and built it up over the years into the largest ranch and provider of hides, dried meat, and tallow to the Spanish colonies in

ILLUSTRATION BY THEODORE DE BRY OF INDIANS AT A SUGAR PLANTATION AND MILL IN 1590.

Florida. Menéndez Márquez's products were also exported through shipping to Havana via the Florida port of San Martín. Menéndez Márquez owned his own frigate, with which he brought some of his own goods to market in Havana, returning with extensive trade items to be sold in Florida; his business interests expanded into areas far beyond ranching, including the import of Cuban rum. His fortunes increased further when, in 1684, he was appointed royal *contador,* or accountant- treasurer, for Florida.

La Chua Ranch became the largest cattle ranch on lands that would become the United States, extending from the Saint Johns River westward to the Gulf of Mexico and from Lake George northward to the Santa Fe River. Within its boundaries were contained what is today Ocala, Payne's Prairie, Alachua, Palatka, and Gainesville. The ranch produced more than one-third of Florida's cattle and horses in the late seventeenth century. The ranch met its end when James Moore, with Carolinians and Creek Indians, invaded the Florida peninsula and overran La Chua in 1702, causing the ranch hands to flee and the cattle to become feral.

Henderson and Mormino, *Spanish Pathways in Florida,* pp. 118–39.

1687 • Father Eusebio Kino (1645–1711) established the mission of Nuestra Señora de los Dolores in Arizona, through which he introduced livestock to the Pimería Alta region of southern Arizona and northern Sonora. At this and at least twenty other locations in Arizona, Kino introduced and promoted livestock tending as essential in converting and feeding the Pima Indians. Franciscan missionaries continued to spread ranching and livestock tending throughout missions in Arizona, New Mexico, and California. Under the Spanish and the Mexicans, ranching grew into an important and lucrative business, especially in California.

Slatta, *Cowboys of the Americas,* p. 22.

1690 • An expedition headed by Captain Alonso de León brought livestock to the first Spanish mission in east Texas—San Francisco de los Tejas. This was the beginning of the cattle industry in east Texas, as this and other missions continued to be stocked as well as to raise their own livestock. By 1800, cattle ranching had spread along the Neches and Trinity Rivers.

Slatta, *Cowboys of the Americas,* p. 21.

1721 • The marquis of San Miguel de Aguayo laid the groundwork for ranching along the northern Rio Grande when he brought four hundred sheep and three hundred cattle into south Texas from Nuevo León, Mexico. About 1722, he also introduced large numbers of horses, mules, cattle, and sheep to be ranched at the missions in the San Antonio area.

In 1748, José Escandón brought four thousand colonists into the area, and the expanded population base made livestock raising even more important. In 1757, one José de la Tienda reported more than eighty thousand head of cattle, horses, and mules, and more than 300 thousand sheep and goats in the area. By 1781, nearly all available land grants in Southern Texas had been assigned and nearly all of the lands were in use as ranches.

Chipman, *Spanish Texas, 1519–1821,* pp. 246–47; Simons and Hoyt, *Hispanic Texas,* p. 60.

1750 • The Spanish governor of Texas attempted in vain to license and regulate the illegal trade in cattle between Spanish Texas and French Louisiana: these were the first cattle drives on record. *Vaqueros,* Hispanic cowboys, had been illegally driving cattle from Texas to market in French Louisiana for decades. When Spain acquired Louisiana in 1763, this trade was no longer illegal; however, when the Louisiana Territory passed to the United States in 1803, cattle driving from Texas to Louisiana once again constituted a lucrative smuggling trade. By the late eighteenth century, some fifteen thousand to twenty thousand head of cattle moved eastward to Louisiana each year. By the early 1800s, illegal horse and mule trading also became a lucrative business, and Anglo settlers in the Mississippi Valley provided an expanded market for all Texas livestock.

Slatta, *Cowboys of the Americas,* pp. 19, 22.

1760 • Captain Blas María de la Garza Falcón obtained a grant to 975 thousand acres of land in Southern Texas, which he called Rancho Real de Santa Petronila. In time it would become the largest cattle ranch in the United States—the King Ranch.

Kanellos, *Chronology of Hispanic American History,* p. 57.

1762 • Trade between the British colonies and Cuba was initiated, leading to the establishment of the first communities of Cubans in the United States. During the Seven Years' War, the British occupied Havana, Cuba, for ten months. During that time, Cubans came into contact with soldiers and traders from the British North American colonies, and they discovered the benefits of commercial relations outside of the Spanish Empire. This was to have great influence on the future relations of Cuba and the United States, especially as trading partners. During the first half of the nineteenth century, commercial relations expanded dramatically, leading to the beginnings of Cuban communities in New Orleans, New York, and Philadelphia. Many Cubans immigrated to the United States to pursue higher education. The United States also became a refuge for Cuban dissidents, exiles, and revolutionaries plotting the independence of their homeland. These close relations with the United States led to a strong movement among many Cubans—and even among U.S. politicians—to annex the island to the United States.

Kanellos, *Chronology of Hispanic American History,* p. 57.

1763 • The first successful large-scale merchant and entrepreneur to be born in a mainland area that would become part of the United States was Francisco Javier Sánchez (1736–1807). He became the owner of vast cattle ranches in Florida that stocked the Spanish and British military and governments in Florida, as well as the civilian population of Saint Augustine. He also became the owner and operator of stores, plantations, and ships and engaged in the slave trade—despite his having been married to a mulatto and having cared for his mulatto offspring.

Henderson and Mormino, *Spanish Pathways in Florida,* pp. 168–87.

1769 ◆ Cattle ranching was first introduced to California by Franciscan missionary Father Junípero Serra (1713–1784)with the founding of the mission at San Diego. He proceeded to establish missions and their reliance on livestock tending, ranching, and farming all along the California coast. In 1775 and 1776, Juan Bautista de Anza brought settlers and trailed livestock from Arizona to Monterey and San Francisco in northern California.

Slatta, *Cowboys of the Americas,* p. 22.

1789 ◆ The small-farm land grant in Tubac, Arizona, received from Spain in 1789 by Toribio Otero became the basis generations later for the making of "the cattle king of Tubac," Toribio Otero's great grandson Sabino Otero. On the basis of this initial inherited ranch, Sabino Otero built the largest ranching operation in southern Arizona during the 1870s and 1880s.

Sheridan, *Los Tucsonenses,* pp. 52–53.

1800 ◆ The first major livestock economies flourished in Texas: horse ranching in Nacogdoches, cattle and horse ranching along the Rio Grande Valley and around San Antonio south of La Bahía. Cattle ran free on the open range and were herded and driven to market and slaughtered. The Anglo immigrants who settled in Texas considered these cattle wild and simply

A CATTLE ROUND-UP AT THE SAN GABRIEL MISSION IN EARLY CALIFORNIA.

appropriated them, although they belonged to the Hispanic ranchers and were tended by *vaqueros* (cowboys). They did not *create* a cattle industry, but simply took it over.

Slatta, *Cowboys of the Americas,* p. 19.

1810 ⁕ Hispanic ranchers in California began shipping hides, tallow, and dried beef to South America, providing impetus for expansion of the cattle business. The hide and tallow trade also expanded beginning in 1822, when the Boston markets opened to the Californios; thus the trade with markets in the East far antedates U.S. expansion into California.

Rosaldo et al., *Chicano,* p. 9.

1817 ⁕ Spain became the first European colonial power to outlaw the slave trade in all of its colonies north of the Equator. Spain signed a treaty with England providing for the suppression of the slave trade. This included the selling of slaves in areas that eventually became part of the United States.

Kanellos, *Chronology of Hispanic American History,* p. 73.

1821 ⁕ Under the Mexican Republic, many more land grants were issued for California lands than under Spanish rule; many of these grants became the basis of an ever expanding ranching industry. More than four hundred land grants were issued between 1833 and 1846 for tracts of land ranging from four thousand to one hundred thousand acres. By the time of the U.S. takeover, there were more than eight million acres held by some eight hundred ranchers. Under the United States, the ranching way of life soon succumbed. Most of the large tracts of land fell into the hands of speculators, land plungers, and railroad right-of-way seekers, and prepared the way for the concentration of large land holdings in the hands of a few owners who would become the builders of California's giant agribusiness. By 1889, one-sixth of the farms in the state produced more than two-thirds of the crops.

Rosaldo et al., *Chicano,* p. 159.

1822 ⁕ Hispanic ranchers and missions began exporting hides and tallow to the east coast of the United States after a deal was struck between a British company and Father President Mariano Payeras of La Purísima Concepción Mission to make contracts with individual missions for their hides and tallow. (In the Franciscan missions of California, as well as Arizona, New Mexico, and Texas, Indians herded and slaughtered the cattle and prepared the meat and by-products.) Demand in New England and England for these products became so intense that by the 1830s they became California's principal exports. It is estimated that Boston traders alone may have handled some six million hides and seven thousand tons of tallow from 1826 to 1848.

See also Science and Technology: Agriculture, 1598.

Fontana, *Entrada,* p. 217.

1825 • One of the first women entrepreneurs on the frontier, María Gertrudes Barceló, began operating a game of chance in the Ortiz Mountains of New Mexico. She later opened a gambling casino in Santa Fe; it became one of the most famous establishments of its kind, serving the elite. She invested her profits in trade and merchandise and became very wealthy and even prospered under American occupation.

Tardiff and Mabunda, *Dictionary of Hispanic Biography,* p. 99.

1829 • The new Republic of Mexico abolished slavery. This abolition also affected the Mexican lands to the north, which would eventually become part of the United States.

Kanellos, *Chronology of Hispanic American History,* p. 84.

1830 • The first Longhorn cattle appeared, resulting from the crossbreeding of the Spanish Retinto and animals imported to Texas by Anglo settlers. Immune to tick fever and accustomed to the tough brush country of southern Texas, the Longhorn became the basis for the western livestock indus-

A VAQUERO IN
EARLY CALIFORNIA.

try. After the Civil War, cattle ranching became especially important to the nation; Texas cowboys drove some ten million head of Longhorn north to railheads and markets. Over time, the Longhorn was replaced by many other breeds, but in the initial stages of this important industry, it was the mainstay. Along with the trade in beef, an industry in hides, tallow, and other by-products flourished in coastal "factories" of Texas.

Slatta, *Cowboys of the Americas,* pp. 19–20.

1832 • King Kamehameha III of Hawaii arranged for Mexican *vaqueros* to come to Hawaii from California to teach ranching skills to the Hawaiians; thus the cattle industry was born in the Hawaiian Islands. Cattle had actually been introduced by George Vancouver in 1793 and horses—California mustangs—by Richard J. Cleveland in 1803. The cattle had been allowed to run wild, however, and only in the 1820s had they begun to be hunted for their hides, tallow, and meat. The Hawaiian word for cowboy, *pianolo,* derives from *español.* Many of the techniques and traditions of the Hawaiian ranching industry are owed to the Hispanic cowboy.

1837 • Philip Edwards drove cattle from California north to Oregon, thus opening up the Northwest for ranching, with the help of California *vaqueros.* Ranchers in Oregon established the tradition of employing Mexican American cowboys in the late nineteenth and early twentieth centuries; they came to compose up to half of the cowhands. In 1869, six Mexican American cowboys led by Juan Redón drove three thousand head of cattle for John Devine, who established the largest ranch in Oregon. Redón stayed on to work as Devine's foreman.

Slatta, *Cowboys of the Americas,* p. 167.

1838 • Between 1838 and 1860, Cuba was the world's largest producer of sugar. In 1850, sugar accounted for 83 percent of Cuban exports, most of which was shipped to the United States. By 1860, the island was producing one-half million tons of sugar per year.

Kanellos, *Chronology of Hispanic American History,* p. 91.

1842 • The first real estate mogul in Texas was a Sephardic Jewish banker who brought European immigrants to Texas following the establishment of the Texas Republic. Henry Castro (1786–1862) was a banker in France's Spanish Sephardic community who lent Texas president Sam Houston money for development of the new republic. In addition, Castro entered into a five-year agreement with Houston in 1842 to colonize a land empire west of San Antonio (his contract was later extended another three years). From 1842 to 1847, Castro relocated more than five thousand immigrants, mostly from France and the Rhineland, in twenty-seven ships. Castro received land grants that included Medina County and parts of Frio, McMullen, Zavala, Uvalde, Bexar, and Bandera Counties. He was the founder of the towns of Quihi, Vandenberg, and D'Hanis. The settlers of Castroville named their town in his honor;

this was the county seat of Medina County. Fifteen years after Castro's death (in Monterrey, Mexico), the State of Texas named a stretch of land in the Panhandle Castro County in his honor.

Another Sephardic Jew who became a real estate mogul was Jacob de Córdova, who founded the de Córdova Land Agency and assisted people from the Northeast in relocating to Texas after it had become a state. The largest number of land patents issued by the State of Texas were certificates held or controlled by de Córdova. It was de Córdova and two of his partners who founded and laid out the city of Waco, Texas. To entice Northerners to move to Texas, de Córdova lectured throughout the Northeast. When laying out plots of land for towns, de Córdova's custom was to present free of charge a lot for each religious denomination's construction of a house of worship.

Simonhoff, *Jewish Notables in America, 1776–1865,* pp. 288–91.

1856 • Joaquín Quiroga laid the foundations for the lucrative freighting business in Arizona by carrying the first load of goods from Yuma to Tucson in his fourteen-mule pack train. In the next decades, Mexican entrepreneurs would become the major owners of freighting companies, linking the California coast with the Arizona and New Mexico territories, Baja California, and northern Mexico. They even reached as far east as Missouri. The importance of the freight-hauling business by mule and wagon train only subsided with the introduction of the railroads, and then some of these same entrepreneurs made the transition to hauling freight and people by wagon and stagecoach to secondary and outlying communities. Although Hispanics had followed trails blazed and used by Indians for centuries, they also pioneered most of the techniques and opened most of the trails that would later

A SUGAR REFINERY IN MID-NINETEENTH CENTURY CUBA.

be used for trade and communication during the territorial and early statehood periods. In fact, some of today's major highways run along those routes pioneered for trade by Hispanics and Mexicans.

Sheridan, *Los Tucsonenses,* pp. 43–45.

1866 • Great trail drives northward from Texas began. Ultimately, they resulted in the introduction of cattle ranching to the Great Plains. The U.S. Cavalry's removal of the Indian threat during the 1870s removed the last major barrier to ranching on the northern plains.

Slatta, *Cowboys of the Americas,* p. 25.

LEOPOLDO CARRILLO.

1870 • The first Hispanic urban real estate mogul in Tucson under U.S. rule, and possibly in the entire Southwest was Leopoldo Carrillo, who the 1870 census shows to have been the wealthiest man in Tucson, Arizona. Besides owning rental homes, commercial properties, and farmland, he also owned and operated ice cream parlors, saloons, and even Tucson's first bowling alley. By 1881, he owned nearly one hundred houses in Tucson, making him one of the most prominent landlords.

Sheridan, *Los Tucsonenses,* pp. 50–51.

1875 • Estevan Ochoa (1831–1888) developed his freight business into the largest Hispanic-owned company in Tucson, second only in the overall community to E. N. Fish and Company, handling some $300,000 in transactions per year. By 1880, his Tully, Ochoa and Company was the largest taxpayer in Pima County. Expanding from the long-distance hauling of freight by mule train, he and his partner, Pickney Randolph Tully, went into the mercantile business with stores that depended on freight hauling. Thus, he and his partners were among the first businessmen on the frontier to implement vertical integration. They also invested in mining and raising sheep. At the beginning of the 1880s, they were grazing fifteen thousand sheep and operating a woolen factory; a settlement started at a camp where they raised sheep and eventually became the town of Ochoaville, named in his honor. Ochoa is credited with having introduced to Tucson and its surrounding communities a number of industrial technologies for turning out woolen blankets that had been developed in factories in the eastern United States.

See also Government: Politics, 1875; Education, 1872.

Sheridan, *Los Tucsonenses,* pp. 42–49.

1879 ⬩ Estevan Ochoa became the first Arizona pioneer to plant cotton for commercial purposes. He investigated its potential by planting an acre of Pima cotton and then sending samples back to the eastern United States for testing.

Sheridan, *Los Tucsonenses,* p. 45.

1882 ⬩ Bernabé Robles was the first Hispanic to become a millionaire by taking advantage of the Homestead Act. He and his brother, Jesús, applied for and received two homesteads in southern Arizona and opened a stage station there in 1882. He then founded what became the famous Three Points Ranch. He expanded his holdings and eventually controlled more than one million acres between Florence and the Mexican border. He was one of the most successful cattlemen in Arizona. In 1918, he invested the profits from ranching in urban real estate in the Tucson area. Part of the inheritance he left his children was sixty-five parcels of the most valuable Tucson properties.

Sheridan, *Los Tucsonenses,* p. 97.

1886 ⬩ The first transfer of a whole industry from Latin America to the United States and the subsequent building of a company town occurred when Spanish and Cuban entrepreneurs acquired Florida swampland near Tampa and built a cigar-producing town, Ybor City. In 1880, the population of Tampa was only 721; a decade later the combined population of Tampa and Ybor City was 5,500, and that number tripled by 1900. The first of the entrepreneurs to establish their cigar factories, Vicente Martínez Ybor and Ignacio Haya, hoped to attract a docile workforce (unlike the labor union activists in Cuba), avoid U.S. import tariffs, and get closer to their markets in the

MULE TRAINS IN THE FREIGHTING BUSINESS IN ARIZONA IN 1888.

United States. Also, the Cuban wars for independence were raging and continually disrupting business.

Martínez Ybor, Spanish by birth, had immigrated to Cuba when he was fourteen; after working in cigar factories in Key West and New York, he settled in Tampa and built the world's largest cigar factory in Tampa. The industry in Ybor City grew to ten factories by 1895 and became the principal cigar-producing area in the United States, when cigar-smoking was at its peak. By 1900, there were about 150 cigar factories in West Tampa and Ybor City, producing more than 111 million cigars annually.

Florida Department of State, *Florida Cuban Heritage Trail,* p. 34; Henderson and Mormino, *Spanish Pathways in Florida,* pp. 40–45, 262.

1889 • Mexican immigrant Federico Ronstadt founded a carriage business that became the largest of its kind in Tucson, Arizona, and the surrounding region, including Sonora, Mexico. At its height, Ronstadt's wagon shop and hardware store employed sixty-five people, who, besides repairing vehicles of all kinds, manufactured wagons, buggies, harnesses, and saddles. Ronstadt executed most of the iron forging himself and became known as one of the finest wagon and carriage makers in the Southwest. Ronstadt's business territory extended from California to Sonora, Mexico, where he had agents in Cananea, Nogales, Hermosillo, and Guaymas. By 1910, approximately one-third of his business was transacted south of the border. Ronstadt also marketed nationally known brands of wagons and farm machinery.

Sheridan, *Los Tucsonenses,* pp. 94–95.

DOWNTOWN YBOR CITY
IN THE 1890S.

1968 • Cuban American businesswoman Remedios Díaz-Oliver became the first woman to earn the E Award—Excellence in Export—given by President

Lyndon B. Johnson. Díaz-Oliver was head of the exporting division of the Emmer Glass container business in Miami. Díaz-Oliver went on to found her own company, American International Container, in 1976, and another company, All American Container, in 1991. In 1984, she was named Woman of the Year by the Latin Business and Professional Women Association, and in 1987 she was named Woman of the Year by the U.S. Hispanic Chamber of Commerce.

Tardiff and Mabunda, *Dictionary of Hispanic Biography,* pp. 286–88.

1972 • The American Association of Hispanic Certified Public Accountants was founded to maintain and promote professional and moral standards of Hispanics in the accounting field. The organization assists members in practice development and develops business opportunities in securing government contracts for members. It also sponsors seminars and bestows scholarships.

Furtaw, *Hispanic Americans Information Directory,* p. 1.

1975 • Katherine D. Ortega became the first woman to serve as president of a California bank when she accepted the position of director and president of the Santa Ana State Bank. Ortega later became treasurer of the United States under President Ronald Reagan.

1976 • The Chicana Forum was established with federal funds to enhance the role of Mexican American women in the U.S. economy and the business community.

Griswold et al., *Chicano Art, 1965–1985.*, p. 218.

KATHERINE D. ORTEGA.

1977 • Carlos José Arboleya (1929–) became the first Cuban president and chief executive officer of a major bank in the United States, Barnett Banks of Miami. Prior to that appointment, he had been co-owner, president, and director of Flagler Bank in Miami. Since 1983, he has served as vice chairman of the Barnett Bank of South Florida. Thanks to Arboleya and other Cuban American businessmen and bankers, Miami has become a major banking center for Latin America.

Kanellos, *The Hispanic American Almanac,* p. 317.

1979 • Mexican native Héctor Barreto founded the U.S. Hispanic Chamber of Commerce (USHCC). Barreto worked his way up from digging potatoes and packing meat to running his own companies in Kansas City, including restaurants and import and construction businesses. As president of the USHCC, Barreto worked for greater representation of Hispanics in government and business.

Hispanics in U.S. History, p. 66.

1979 • Humberto Cabañas (1947–) became the first Hispanic chief executive officer of a major corporation in the hospitality industry when he assumed the position of CEO and founding president of Benchmark Hospitality Group in The Woodlands, Texas. He was also the first U.S. Hispanic president of the International Association of Conference Centers, from which he received a distinguished service award in 1988.

Kanellos, *Hispanic American Almanac,* p. 318.

1980 • Frank A. Lorenzo (1940–) became the first U.S. Hispanic to serve as the president of a major national and international airline, Continental Air-

ROBERTO C. GOIZUETA.

lines, headquartered in Houston, Texas. From 1986 to 1990, Lorenzo served as chairman and CEO of Continental. A graduate of the Harvard M.B.A. program, Lorenzo served as president and chairman of the board of Texas International Airlines (TIA) from 1972 to 1980; TIA became the holding company for Continental Airlines. Lorenzo was eventually embattled by strikes and financial problems and was forced to resign.

Kanellos, *The Hispanic American Almanac,* pp. 319–20.

1981 • Roberto C. Goizueta (1931–) became the first U.S. Hispanic to lead one of the largest corporations in the world, Coca-Cola, when he became the company's chief executive officer and chairman of the board. One of the highest-paid CEOs in the United States, the native Cuban started out as a Coca-Cola bottler in Miami after receiving his B.S. degree in Engineering from Yale University in 1953.

Goizueta also sits on the boards of Ford Motor Company, Eastman Kodak, and many other major companies. He was recognized as an immigrant making an outstanding contribution to American society with the Ellis Island Medal of Honor in 1986. In 1984, Goizueta also received the Herbert Hoover Humanitarian Award from the Boys Clubs of America.

Kanellos, *The Hispanic American Almanac,* p. 318.

1983 • California native Luis Nogales, known as one of the most outstanding Hispanic businessmen in the United States, assumed the position of executive vice president for United Press International (UPI), the second-largest news agency in the world. He became the highest-placed Hispanic in the news profession in the United States. Nogales resigned from UPI in 1985 and in 1987 became president of the Univisión television network, a position he kept for only one year.

Tardiff and Mabunda, *Dictionary of Hispanic Biography,* p. 605.

LUIS NOGALES.

1983 • Banker Katherine D. Ortega became the first Hispanic to serve as a commissioner of the Copyright Royalty Tribunal, which determines what royalty fees cable companies and jukebox operators pay throughout the nation.

Telgen and Kamp, *Latinas! Women of Achievement,* p. 293.

1985 • Under the leadership of San Antonio's Rick Bela, the National Hispanic Corporate Council was founded in Washington, D.C., composed of representatives of Fortune 500 companies. Its mission remains the promotion of the value of the Hispanic market in corporate America. The Hispanic community continues as the fastest-growing segment in the United States, with a growth rate five times that of the general population and an estimated annual purchasing power of more than $270 billion.

Hispanic, January/February 1996, p. 88.

1989 • Edgar J. Milán (1934–) became the first New York Puerto Rican to serve as controller and vice president of one of the largest U.S. corporations,

Tenneco. Raised in New York City, where he received a degree in accounting from Hunter College, Milán rose through the ranks of the oil industry, serving in the United States, Canada, England, Peru, and Nicaragua.

Kanellos, *The Hispanic American Almanac,* p. 320.

1990 • Sosa and Associates, the San Antonio advertising agency founded and headed by Lionel Sosa (1939–), became the first Hispanic concern to be

LIONEL SOSA.

named Agency of the Year and the Hottest Agency in the Southwest by *Adweek* magazine. In 1989, Sosa and Associates had billings of $54.8 million. Included among Sosa's clients are American Airlines, Coca-Cola USA, Montgomery Ward, and Western Union. Lionel Sosa has won many other awards, such as the 1988 Gold ADDY from the American Advertising Foundation, 1989 Marketing Person of the Year award, the 1989 Silver Award from the Public Relations Society of America, and the 1990 Entrepreneur of the Year award.

Kanellos, *The Hispanic American Almanac,* pp. 321–22.

1990 • Ramona's Food Products, owned by the former U.S. Treasurer Romana Bañuelos, became the largest Mexican food-processing company in the state of California.

Tardiff and Mabunda, *Dictionary of Hispanic Biography,* p. 97.

1991 • Ignacio Lozano Jr., publisher of Los Angeles's Spanish-language daily newspaper *La Opinión,* became the first Hispanic to receive the Lifetime Achievement Award from the U.S. Small Business Administration. In addition to serving as publisher for the widely circulating newspaper that he inherited from his father, Lozano also served as U.S. ambassador to El Salvador from 1976 to 1977.

Tardiff and Mabunda, *Dictionary of Hispanic Biography,* p. 496.

1992 • Goya Foods became the largest Hispanic-owned company in the United States. After the death of its founder, Prudencio Unanue Ortiz in 1976, his son Joseph A. Unanue took over the chain that his father had built from an importing business. Under Joseph A. Unanue's guidance, the com-

LINDA ALVARADO.

pany grew to sell more than eight hundred products. Its revenue rose to $453 million by 1992, a growth rate of some 12 percent annually. Unanue accomplished this feat mainly by expanding the products offered from those specifically catering to Puerto Ricans and Cubans to include food products appealing to Mexicans and Central Americans, precisely at the time that their populations were growing significantly within the United States.

Tardiff and Mabunda, *Dictionary of Hispanic Biography,* p. 907.

1993 • Linda Alvarado (1951–), president of her own construction company and one of the owners of the Colorado Rockies baseball team, became one of four women to win the Sara Lee Corporation's Frontrunner Award. She was the first Hispanic to receive the honor. Alvarado is also a corporate director at Pitney Bowes and Cyprus Amax Minerals.

See also Sports: Baseball, 1993.

Hispanic Business, October 1994, p. 68.

1995 • Martha S. Tabio became the first Hispanic to be named president of Financial Women International, an organization of ten thousand members worldwide. Since 1987, Tabio has been a senior vice president of Barnett Banks of South Florida.

"About People,"*Hispanic Business,* April 1996, p. 68.

1995 • Arthur C. Martínez became the first Hispanic to lead one of the nation's largest merchandisers, Sears. In August, he became chairman and chief executive officer. Martínez traces his Hispanic heritage to ancestors who immigrated to New Orleans from Spain.

Hispanic Link Weekly Report, 14 August 1995, p. 3.

1995 • María Elena Alvarez became the first Hispanic to serve as the national sales director for Mary Kay Cosmetics.

Hispanic, December 1995, p. 72.

1996 • *Hispanic Business* magazine published its first Hispanic Business Rich List, which documented that there were at least eleven Hispanic entrepreneurs and corporate leaders whose net worth was $100 million or more. At the top of the list as the nation's wealthiest corporate leader was Coca-Cola CEO Roberto C. Goizueta, whose net worth was placed at $574 million. Behind him was Joseph A. Unanue and Family, owners of Goya Foods, with a net worth of $444 million. Of the eleven, one was of Mexican origin, two of Puerto Rican origin, two of Spanish origin, and the rest of Cuban origin.

Hispanic Business, March 1996, p. 18.

1996 • Eduardo Sánchez became the first Hispanic vice president of international relations for one of the world's largest corporations, McDonald's. Sánchez began as a kitchen crew member in Tampa, Florida, in 1976. As vice president, he became responsible for McDonald's in all twenty-one Latin American countries.

Hispanic Link Weekly Report, 22 January 1996, p. 1.

1996 • Barbie Hernández became the first Hispanic president of the Texas Federation of Business and Professional Women's Clubs, which is an advocate for working women in Texas. Hernández is an administrative assistant in the Anheuser-Busch Corporate Relations Office in San Antonio.

Hispanic, September 1996, p. 76.

1996 • Enrique Hernández Jr. was the first Hispanic to be named to the board of directors of the McDonald's Corporation—one of the world's largest corporate entities. Hernández is president and chief executive officer of Inter-Con Security Systems, and principal partner and co-founder of Interspan Communications.

The HACR [Hispanic Association on Corporate Responsibility] Observer, August-September 1996, p. 1.

EDUCATION

1505 • The first elementary school was established in the Americas, in Santo Domingo, for the children of the Spaniards. From then on, elementary schools were included in convents, teaching children reading, writing, arithmetic, and religion. Later, the mission system in the Americas functioned to instruct the children of Indians and mestizos.

Kanellos, *Chronology of Hispanic American History,* p. 24.

1513 • The first school in an area that would become part of the United States was established. The Escuela de Gramática (Grammar School) in Puerto Rico was established at the Cathedral of San Juan by the bishop, Alonso Manso. This secondary school, in which the Latin language, literature, history, science, art, philosophy, and theology were taught, was free of charge to the students. Primary education was soon offered at schools connected to churches.

Dolan and Deck, *Hispanic Catholic Culture in the United States,* p. 296; Kanellos, *Chronology of Hispanic American History,* p. 30.

1513 • The king of Spain issued an edict ordering the teaching of Latin to select Indians. After that, schools for Indians developed and became important, especially in Mexico and Peru where painting, sculpture, and other trades were taught in addition to Latin and religion. Education for the Indians became an important function of the missions from the Floridas to California.

Kanellos, *Chronology of Hispanic American History,* p. 30.

1538 • The first university in the Americas—Saint Thomas Aquinas in the city of Santo Domingo—was founded by the Dominicans. It became a university after having functioned as a Dominican college for years. It is still functioning today as the Autonomous University of Santo Domingo.

Kanellos, *Chronology of Hispanic American History,* p. 38.

1551 • The University of Mexico in Mexico City, the first university in North America, was founded by the Spaniards. The University of San Marcos in Lima, Peru, was founded in the same year. The universities were chartered by the king of Spain in 1551, but the University of Mexico did not actually open its doors until 1553, and the University of San Marcos not until 1572. The latter never had an interruption in its existence and is thus considered the oldest university on the continent. At that time, the universities followed the general models of the University of Salamanca and the University of Alcalá de Henares in Spain, offering humanities, theology, law, and medicine. Latin was the official language used in classes. Some universities taught the indigenous languages for a while. Later, they also taught mathematics and physics. The degrees that were offered were bachelor's, master's (or licentiate), and doctorate. The Jesuits were the most important teaching order in the Americas. During the colonial period, some twenty-five universities, in addition to numerous theological seminaries, were founded by the Spaniards in the Americas.

During the seventeenth century, the University of Mexico had achieved the greatest distinction in the Americas, boasting twenty-three chairs, most of which were in canon law and theology, but others were in medicine, surgery, anatomy, astrology, rhetoric, and the Aztec and Otomí languages. In the last quarter of the seventeenth century, the university held the distinction of being home to the greatest intellectual of the period—the mathematician and historian, Carlos de Sigüenza y Góngora.

Kanellos, *Chronology of Hispanic American History,* p. 42.

1600 ⋅ By 1600, the Spaniards had established the first schools in what later became the United States, at missions in Florida, New Mexico, and Georgia. Later, almost all of the missions in the Southwest would operate schools into the period of U.S. rule.

Kanellos, *Chronology of Hispanic American History,* p. 48.

1612 ⋅ A Franciscan missionary by the name of Francisco Pareja was the first to translate books from a European language (Spanish) into an Indian language in what was to become the United States. Pareja translated books into the Timicuan language from about 1612 to 1627 in what is the present state of Georgia.

Kanellos, *Chronology of Hispanic American History,* p. 48.

1746 ⋅ The first effort to provide a public school outside of the walls of missions took place in Béxar (present-day San Antonio, Texas) in an effort to provide religious education to the children of the villa of San Fernando. This school was short-lived.

Chipman, *Spanish Texas, 1519–1821,* p. 256.

1793 ⋅ Although schooling at missions was firmly established throughout the Spanish colonies, public education was not promoted until almost the nineteenth century. The king of Spain first mandated public education in the Spanish colonies in 1793. High illiteracy among soldiers prompted the king to issue the mandate. The implementation of the mandate did not reach the far northern provinces until the 1800s.

Kanellos, *The Hispanic American Almanac,* p. 291.

1794 • The first public schools in California were established under orders from Spanish governor Diego de Borica. Ten schools in five different cities were built during his term, from 1794 to 1800. The successive governors established more schools during their terms. Most of the schools established during the Spanish period failed, however, for many reasons, including the lack of public education tradition among the settlers, the isolation and sparsity of the population, general indifference, and financial problems.

Kanellos, *The Hispanic American Almanac,* p. 292.

1802 • Spanish governor Juan Bautista Elguezábal, of Texas, issued the first compulsory school attendance law for children up to age twelve. Elguezábal stipulated heavy fines for parents who did not comply.

Chipman, *Spanish Texas, 1519–1821,* p. 257; Kanellos, *The Hispanic American Almanac,* pp. 291–92.

1803 • The Spanish commandant of the first presidios in Texas ordered the founding of schools for the children at the posts that were large enough to afford compensation for a teacher.

Chipman, *Spanish Texas, 1519–1821,* p. 257.

1811 • The first Spanish-language reading textbook for elementary school was published in the United States: *El Director de los niños para aprender a deletrear y leer: método para facilitar los progresos de los niños cuando se mandan por primera vez a la escuela* (The Children's Director for Learning to Spell and Read: Method to Facilitate the Progress of Children When They Are First Sent to School). It was issued in Philadelphia by Mathew Carey.

Online Computer Library Center.

1812 • The first elementary school textbook for learning the Spanish language was published: *El libro primero de los niños, o Nueva cartilla española* (The First Book for Children, or New Spanish Chart), written by Mariano Velásquez de la Cadena and published by La Imprenta Española (The Spanish Press) in New York. Evidently, the book was in widespread use, for it had a new edition as late as 1823 and, presumably, numerous reprints before that date.

Online Computer Library Center.

1825 • Mexican government officials were successful in establishing the first public schools in New Mexico between 1825 and 1827. Eight schools were opened.

Kanellos, *The Hispanic American Almanac,* p. 292.

1827 • Under Mexican rule, the State of Coahuila-Texas formulated a constitution that required all municipalities to establish public schools at the primary level. From 1828 to 1833, many decrees were issued encouraging local authorities to establish schools. Local officials, however, faced many obstacles in establishing schools, including individual and municipal poverty, lack of qualified teachers, and lack of commitment and tradition of education among the common people.

Kanellos, *The Hispanic American Almanac*, p. 292.

1833 • The Mexican state of Coahuila-Texas issued land grants to support local public schools, but the effort was hampered by political unrest in central Mexico.

Kanellos, *The Hispanic American Almanac*, p. 292.

1848 • As American rule took hold in the Southwest after the Mexican War and English-language secular education through public schools expanded, Catholic schools expanded significantly and became the first major imparters of instruction to Hispanics, based on the tradition established by the missions and also based upon segregated population patterns.

Kanellos, *The Hispanic American Almanac*, pp. 292–95.

1851 • Los Angeles city officials enacted the first school ordinance supportive of bilingual education. It provided that "all the rudiments of the English and Spanish languages should be taught" in all the schools subsidized by public funds.

Kanellos, *The Hispanic American Almanac*, p. 297.

1853 • From 1853 to 1874, four Catholic religious orders came to New Mexico to establish and run parochial schools for the predominantly Hispanic population. The Sisters of Loretto, the Christian Brothers, the Sisters of Charity, and the Jesuits established as many as twenty schools in as many towns and cities. The first school the Sisters of Loretta opened was the Academy of Our Lady of Light in Santa Fe. The order went on to establish several other schools throughout the territory. Similar growth took place in Texas and California.

Kanellos, *The Hispanic American Almanac*, p. 293; Rosaldo et al., *Chicano*, p. 89.

1856 • Political leader Antonio Colonel became the first Hispanic to petition a local school board for bilingual education. Colonel promoted the Spanish language because of the economic interests and the public service that could be rendered through its use. Although the petition failed and the Los Angeles school board did not implement bilingual education, his action set an important precedent. Colonel's considerable political and intellectual leadership as an entrepreneur and newspaper publisher contributed to his influence.

Gómez-Quiñones, *Roots of Chicano Politics, 1600–1940*, pp. 232–31.

1859 • The Christian Brothers established the College of San Miguel in Santa Fe, the first college in the territory of New Mexico, principally for the higher education of Hispanics and to produce seminarians from their ranks. They also founded other schools in Las Vegas and Bernalillo, New Mexico, which by 1892 had 350 children enrolled. The college and the schools attracted students from throughout the territories of Arizona, Colorado, and Texas, as well as from northern Mexico.

Rosaldo et al., *Chicano,* p. 89.

ANTONIO CORONEL
IN HIS TWILIGHT
YEARS SURROUNDED
BY HIS MOST
BELOVED POSSESSIONS.

1867 • The establishment of bilingual education in every school with at least twenty-five non-English-speaking children was first mandated in the Colorado territory.

Kanellos, *The Hispanic American Almanac,* p. 297; Kloss, *The American Bilingual Tradition,* p. 25.

1867 • Francisco Solano León was one of a committee of three (along with two Anglos) to organize Tucson's first public school district. The Mexican community supported the establishment and funding of public education in Arizona. The community believed that education was indispensable for Mexicans in the United States and that first and foremost for them was the learning of English. They felt that only through mastering English could they compete with Anglos in the society.

Three years later, Solano León was one of a committee of seventeen Mexicans who lobbied then-governor of Arizona, Richard McCormick, to establish a public school system. The committee comprised wealthy Mexican entrepreneurs, including Estevan Ochoa, who supported McCormick, and he, in turn, pushed for public education and other legislation against discrimination.

See also Education, 1872.

Sheridan, *Los Tucsonenses,* p. 46–47.

1870 • The elites in the Mexican community of Tucson pioneered private, parochial education for their children when wealthy Mexican women were finally successful in convincing the Catholic church to send the Sisters of Saint Joseph to open a Catholic school in Tucson, Arizona—the Academy for Young Ladies. Four years later the male children of the elite were also able to attend their own school, Saint Augustine's Parochial School for Boys.

Sheridan, *Los Tucsonenses,* p. 47.

1872 • Prominent businessman and chairman of the Committee on Public Education of the territorial legislature of Arizona, Esteban Ochoa (1831–1888), introduced the first bill to levy a compulsory property tax to support the first public schools in the territory. Thus, Tucson's first solvent public school was opened in March 1872. By 1875, enrollment had increased so much that a new building was needed; Ochoa donated the lot and supplemented the financing for construction for the new school building.

See also Government: Politics, 1875; Business and Commerce, 1875, 1879.

Sheridan, *Los Tucsonenses,* p. 46.

ESTEBAN OCHOA.

1886 • Mariano Samaniego was appointed a member of the first board of regents for the University of Arizona; he may have been the first Hispanic regent appointed in the United States. Following his appointment, no other Hispanic regent served until modern times. Samaniego was a wealthy businessman and politician and one of the few college graduates on the frontier. He had graduated from Saint Luis University in Missouri in 1862.

Sheridan, *Los Tucsonenses,* pp. 47–48.

1891 • Almado Chávez, the first Hispanic state superintendent of education was elected in New Mexico. He had been speaker of the state legislature in 1884. From 1901 to 1903, he served as the mayor of Santa Fe.

Gómez-Quiñones, *Roots of Chicano Politics, 1600–1940*, p. 258.

1891 • The first Hispanic appointed superintendent of the Tucson, Arizona, schools was Carlos Tully, the only Mexican American ever to hold that office. His tenure lasted from 1891 to 1895.

Sheridan, *Los Tucsonenses*, p. 217.

1894 • Manuel García was the first Mexican American to graduate from the University of Texas.

1930 • Mexican American parents won their first discrimination suit, attacking segregation in the Texas schools in the case of *Salvatierra v. Del Río Independent School.*

See also Government: The Civil Rights Struggle, 1930.

Kanellos, *Chronology of Hispanic American History*, p. 196.

1940 • Ricardo Manzo became the first Mexican public school principal in Tucson, Arizona, in modern times.

Sheridan, *Los Tucsonenses*, p. 218.

1945 • Mexican American parents won their first suit against segregation in California in *Méndez et al. v. Westminster School District et al.* The suit was filed against four Orange County school districts.

See also Government: The Civil Rights Struggle, 1945.

Meier and Rivera, *Dictionary of Mexican American History*, p. 218.

1946 • Upon completing her Ph.D. at Harvard, Rita Ricardo-Campbell became the first woman to teach economics at Harvard University when she accepted an instructorship at that institution. She had been working at the university since 1942 as a teaching and research assistant.

Tardiff and Mabunda, *Dictionary of Hispanic Biography*, p. 736.

1946 • University of New Mexico professor George I. Sánchez organized the First Regional Conference on the Education of Spanish-Speaking People in the Southwest.

Griswold et al., *Chicano Art*, p. 209.

RITA
RICARDO-CAMPBELL.

1958 • Folklorist Américo Paredes published his landmark study, *With His Pistol in His Hand: A Border Ballad and Its Hero,* which became the model for Chicano scholarship for more than twenty years. In his study of the folk ballad, Paredes showed how the analysis of popular culture can lead to the reconstruction of history. His book was also the first Chicano work to become the basis for a film, *The Ballad of Gregorio Cortez,* which was also a landmark in the history of Chicano cinema.

Paredes, *With His Pistol in His Hand.*

1961 • The first organization promoting higher education and providing counseling services for Puerto Ricans in the United States, Aspira, Inc., was founded. In 1958, educator and social worker Antonia Pantoja and others founded the Puerto Rican Forum, the oldest and largest Puerto Rican social service agency in the country. The founding pioneered the Aspira Clubs, which grew into the counseling agency.

Tardiff and Mabunda, *Dictionary of Hispanic Biography,* pp. 652–53.

1963 • The first bilingual education program in public schools during modern times was started in Miami's Coral Way Elementary School with a grant from the Ford Foundation. The experimental program led to Dade County public school's instituting a pioneering bilingual education program, which served as a model for Congress in its 1968 passage of the Bilingual Education Act.

Kloss, *The American Bilingual Tradition;* Meier and Rivera, *Dictionary of Mexican American History,* pp. 39–42.

1964 • Dr. Américo Paredes became the first Hispanic to be elected vice president of the American Folklore Society. The outstanding scholar of folklore of the border and of greater Mexico had also served as president of the Texas Folklore Society from 1961 to 1962.

Tardiff and Mabunda, *Dictionary of Hispanic Biography,* pp. 654–55.

1968 • The first federally mandated bilingual education programs were established with the passage by the U.S. Congress of the Elementary and Secondary Education Act, Title VII, on January 2, 1968. The law mandates that children who speak languages other than English be instructed in two languages and that teachers be trained, materials developed, and research conducted to assist these children in making a rapid transition from the native language to English. Congress appropriated $7.5 million for 1969 to support seventy-six pilot projects serving twenty-seven thousand students. Appropriations for bilingual education expanded rapidly, surpassing the $100 million mark per year by 1978.

Lobbied for and supported by Hispanics from throughout the country, bilingual education has survived in the United States, despite controversy and movements against immigrants and government-funded use of languages other than English.

Kloss, *The American Bilingual Tradition;* Meier and Rivera, *Dictionary of Mexican American History,* pp. 42–46.

1968 • Rita Ricardo-Campbell became the first woman to be appointed senior fellow at Stanford University's Hoover Institution. The professor of economics was also the first woman to teach in the Economics Department of Harvard University. She later became the first woman on the board of directors of two Fortune 500 companies, the Watkins-Johnson Company and the Gillette Company. She also became the only woman to serve on the President's Economic Advisory Board, from 1981 to 1989.

Tardiff and Mabunda, *Dictionary of Hispanic Biography,* pp. 736–37.

1968 • Mexican American students and faculty, led by historian Rodolfo Acuña, founded the first department of Chicano studies in the nation, at California State University at Los Angeles. It has since grown to become the largest department of its kind.

Tardiff and Mabunda, *Dictionary of Hispanic Biography,* p. 4.

1968 • Marta P. Cotera became the first Hispanic to direct the Southwest Educational Development Laboratory in Austin, Texas. A teacher and librarian, Cotera was an activist in the Chicano Movement, one of the first to conduct educational research from a political perspective and promote feminism.

Tardiff and Mabunda, *Dictionary of Hispanic Biography,* p. 252.

1969 • Dr. Américo Paredes became the first Hispanic to serve as editor of the most important scholarly journal of folklore in the United States—the *Journal of American Folklore.* He served as editor until 1973. During this time, Paredes was also one of the first directors of a Mexican American studies program in the United States, at the University of Texas.

Tardiff and Mabunda, *Dictionary of Hispanic Biography,* pp. 654–55.

1970 • At the University of Pittsburgh, scholar Carmelo Mesa Lago founded the *Cuban Studies Newsletter,* which marked the emergence of Cuban studies as an academic discipline.

García, *Havana USA,* p. 204.

1970 • Marta P. Cotera and her husband established the first Mexican American college, Jacinto Treviño College, in Mercedes, Texas, in the Lower Rio Grande Valley. The school, which was affiliated with the Antioch College Graduate School of Education, eventually split off to become Juárez-Lincoln University. The purpose of the now-defunct college was to prepare teachers for bilingual education.

Tardiff and Mabunda, *Dictionary of Hispanic Biography,* p. 252.

1970 • The first university-based Hispanic research center was the Chicano Studies Research Center at the University of California at Los Angeles. The center conducts research and administers a library and a publications program, including the longest running Hispanic academic journal, *Aztlán.*

Furtaw, *Hispanic Americans Information Directory,* p. 142.

1971 • The first Hispanic ethnic studies program in the Midwest was the Center for Chicano-Boricua Studies at Wayne State University in Detroit.

Furtaw, *Hispanic Americans Information Directory,* p. 150.

1971 • The National Association for Chicano Studies was founded to provide services and an annual convention for professors who teach courses related to Chicano themes. Its example was followed in the subsequent founding of similar associations for Puerto Rican and Cuban American studies.

Furtaw, *Hispanic Americans Information Directory,* p. 24.

1971 • Deganawidah-Quetzalcoatl University (DQU), the first Native American and Chicano university, was founded on April 2, 1971, near Davis, California, after a protracted struggle to have the deed transferred from an old army communications center.

Meier and Rivera, *Dictionary of Mexican American History,* p. 117.

1971 • Hispanics won the first suit against school financing through property taxes. In *Serrano v. Priest,* John Serrano sued the California state treasurer, alleging that his son was receiving an inferior education in East Los Angeles because schools were financed by local property taxes. The California courts found in that financing schools through local property taxes did not provide equal protection of the law and, therefore, the financing system had to be changed. Lawsuits that came before the California Supreme Court in 1974 and 1977 resulted in similar findings.

Kanellos, *Chronology of Hispanic American History,* p. 257.

1972 • Aspira, Inc., a national grassroots educational service program brought the first suit against a school district to force it to follow federal guidelines for instituting bilingual education. The suit claimed that tens of thousands of Latino students in the New York City school system were receiving inadequate instruction in their native language.

Meier and Rivera, *Dictionary of Mexican American History,* pp. 39–44.

1972 • Professor Rodolfo Acuña of California State University at Los Angeles wrote and published the first comprehensive history of the Chicano people. The text, which presented the model of Mexican Americans as an internal colony of the United States, became the most widely used Chicano history book in colleges and was published in subsequent editions in 1981 and 1988.

Tardiff and Mabunda, *Dictionary of Hispanic Biography,* p. 4.

1973 • Educator and social worker Antonia Pantoja founded the first university created specifically to serve Puerto Ricans in the United States—

Universidad Boricua. Founded in Washington, D.C., with foundation grants that Pantoja had solicited, the university was designed to provide innovative bilingual, career-oriented programs for professionals, technicians, and other workers. Pantoja served as the institution's first chancellor.

Tardiff and Mabunda, *Dictionary of Hispanic Biography*, p. 653.

1973 • The first Center for Puerto Rican Studies was founded at Hunter College of the City University of New York (CUNY). In addition to coordinating Puerto Rican studies courses for the CUNY system, the center provides seminars and technical services, publishes a journal, and maintains a library and archives.

Furtaw, *Hispanic Americans Information Directory*, p. 134.

1974 • The Latino Institute was founded as the first Hispanic research center in the Midwest, providing research and information on education, housing, voting, economic development, and other topics to schools and government agencies.

Furtaw, *Hispanic Americans Information Directory*, p. 136.

1974 • In *Lau v. Nichols,* the United States Supreme Court held that the San Francisco Unified School District discriminated against a non-English-speaking student, Kinney Lau, by not providing a program to deal with his language problem, thereby depriving him of meaningful participation in school. This decision has served as a cornerstone for the creation and maintenance of bilingual education programs across the country. The Lau decision laid the basis for a new interpretation of equal education opportunity, an interpretation that takes into consideration the linguistic differences of some students and then compares their opportunities to the opportunities given to English-speaking students.

See also Government: The Civil Rights Struggle, 1974.

Kanellos, *Chronology of Hispanic American History,* p. 260; Meier and Rivera, *Dictionary of Mexican American History,* pp. 42–44.

1974 • The U.S. Congress passed the Equal Educational Opportunity Act of 1974 to create equality in public schools by making bilingual education available to Hispanic youth.

Kanellos, *Chronology of Hispanic American History,* p. 260.

1974 • A new Bilingual Education Act was passed by the U.S. Congress. It expanded bilingual education by financing the preparation of bilingual teachers and the development of curriculum.

Kanellos, *Chronology of Hispanic American History,* p. 260.

1974 • On August 29, 1974, Aspira obtained a consent decree mandating bilingual education programs in the New York City schools.

Kanellos, *The Hispanic American Almanac,* pp. 389–90.

1975 • With the support of the Catholic church, the National Hispanic Scholarship was established. It was first national scholarship fund to send Hispanic high school graduates to college.

Dolan and Deck, *Hispanic Catholic Culture in the United States,* p. 150.

1975 • The National Association for Bilingual Education (NABE) was founded to recognize, promote, and publicize bilingual education. Its most important event is its annual convention, which provides seminars, research, and workshops for bilingual teachers throughout the United States. NABE has state and local affiliates that extend its services to teachers, administrators, and communities.

Furtaw, *Hispanic Americans Information Directory,* p. 24.

1975 • The *Cuban Studies Newsletter,* edited at the University of Pittsburgh by Carmelo Mesa Lago, became *Cuban Studies/Estudios Cubanos,* the first journal serving the new academic field of Cuban studies.

García, *Havana USA,* p. 204.

1978 • Dr. Tomás Rivera (1935–1984), the renowned scholar and creative writer, became the first Hispanic chancellor in the University of California system. He served as chancellor of the University of California-Riverside until his death in 1984.

See also Literature, 1971.

Kanellos, *Chronology of Hispanic American History,* p. 208.

TOMÁS RIVERA.

1980 • Sylvia L. Castillo founded the first Hispanic feminist newsletter, *Intercambios Femeniles* (Feminine Exchanges) at Stanford University. Each issue was designed around a theme, such as health or careers in science, and contained statistics, networking lists, and information. The newsletter also profiled successful women and reported on the latest studies of Hispanics.

The newsletter led to the formation of the National Network of Hispanic Women (initially named Hispanic Women in Higher Education), which provided networking and mentoring opportunities for Hispanic women of all ages. The newsletter and the network eventually became independent of Stanford and relocated to Los Angeles.

Tardiff and Mabunda, *Dictionary of Hispanic Biography,* pp. 197–98.

1980 • Texas Tech University broke its long tradition and hired one of its own alumni as president. Lauro F. Cavazos, a medical doctor and researcher, assumed the presidency of the university and of its Health Sci-

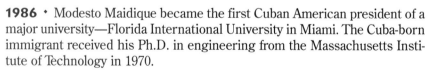

ence Center. Cavazos later became the first Hispanic to be named secretary of Education.

See also Government: Politics, 1988.

Tardiff and Mabunda, *Dictionary of Hispanic Biography,* p. 205.

1981 • Former school principal and supervisor for state and federal education projects, Rita Esquivel, became the first woman assistant superintendent of education for the state of California.

Tardiff and Mabunda, *Dictionary of Hispanic Biography,* p. 314.

1983 • Educator Roberto Cruz founded the first Hispanic university, the National Hispanic University (NHU), in San Jose, California. The four-year, three hundred-student institution offers some five majors, including international business and computer science. Graduates of NHU have a higher-than-average job placement rate and rate of attending graduate school.

Hispanic, March 1996, p. 35.

1984 • Ramón C. Cortines became the first Hispanic to briefly serve as the superintendent of the San Francisco schools. He later served as an assistant secretary in the U.S. Department of Education (1993), and in 1993 became the second Hispanic in history to serve as the chancellor of the New York City public school system.

Tardiff and Mabunda, *Dictionary of Hispanic Biography,* pp. 250–51.

1985 • Linda Chávez was the first Hispanic to become editor of *American Educator,* the quarterly magazine of the American Federation of Teachers. Through her controversial editorials, she caught the eye of conservative politicians, especially as she attacked affirmative action and bilingual education. In 1981, she became a consultant to President Ronald Reagan.

See also Government: Politics, 1985.

Telgen and Kamp, *Latinas! Women of Achievement,* p. 78.

MODESTO MAIDIQUE.

1986 • Modesto Maidique became the first Cuban American president of a major university—Florida International University in Miami. The Cuba-born immigrant received his Ph.D. in engineering from the Massachusetts Institute of Technology in 1970.

Kanellos, *The Hispanic American Almanac,* p. 729.

1986 • Mari-Luci Jaramillo became the first Hispanic to receive the Harvard Graduate School of Education's Anne Roe Award honoring leading educators who have contributed to women's professional growth.

Telgen and Kamp, *Latinas! Women of Achievement,* p. 205.

1987 • Beatriz Angela Ginorio (1947–) became the first Hispanic to direct a national center for research on women—the Northwest Center for Research on Women at the University of Washington, Seattle. Born in Hato

Rey, Puerto Rico, Ginorio received her Ph.D. in psychology from Fordham University, New York City, in 1979, and taught at Bowling Green State University, Bowling Green, Ohio, and the University of Washington, Seattle.

Kanellos, *The Hispanic American Almanac,* p. 361.

1987 • Mari-Luci Jaramillo became the highest ranking Hispanic official at the Educational Testing Service (ETS), one of the largest nonprofit testing corporations in the world. While serving as a vice president for student affairs at the University of New Mexico, Jaramillo was recruited by the ETS to serve as vice president of its San Francisco Bay-area office. In 1992, she was promoted to assistant vice president for field services for the entire ETS; she now administers the ETS's eight U.S. field offices. Jaramillo also served as the U.S. ambassador to Honduras from 1977 to 1980.

Telgen and Kamp, *Latinas! Women of Achievement,* pp. 210–15.

1988 • President Ronald Reagan appointed former president of Texas Tech University, Lauro F. Cavazos (1927–), as the first Hispanic secretary of Education. In 1989, President George Bush reappointed Cavazos to the post. Cavazos was instrumental in having President Bush sign the executive order creating the President's Council on Educational Excellence for Hispanic Americans. Cavazos resigned in December 1990 when he was unable to support many of the president's educational policies.

See also Government: Politics, 1988.

Kanellos, *The Hispanic American Almanac,* p. 277.

1988 • Jaime Escalante became the first Hispanic teacher to be the subject of a Hollywood feature film. *Stand and Deliver* tells the story of how Escalante was able to teach advanced mathematics at Garfield High, an impoverished inner-city school in East Los Angeles, and prepare its students so well that they were admitted to some of the most elite universities in the country to major in math and science. Escalante taught at Garfield from 1974 to 1990. Known as one of the nation's top educators, Escalante received the White House's Hispanic Heritage Award in 1989 and the American Institute for Public Service Jefferson Award in 1990. In 1988, Escalante was the subject of a book that proclaimed his excellence on the national level—*Jaime Escalante: The Best Teacher in America.*

JAIME ESCALANTE.

Kanellos, *The Hispanic American Almanac,* pp. 724–25; Mathews, *Jaime Escalante;* Tardiff and Mabunda, *Dictionary of Hispanic Biography,* pp. 308–11.

1989 • Folklorist Dr. Américo Paredes (1915–) became the first Hispanic scholar to be awarded the prestigious Charles Frankel Prize for his career-long contribution to the humanities by the National Endowment for the Humanities. This is the nation's highest recognition for a humanist.

The famed folklorist, writer, and teacher was born in Brownsville, Texas. He received his B.A., M.A., and Ph.D. degrees from the University of Texas in 1951, 1953, and 1956, respectively. After working at a variety of jobs—

AMÉRICO PAREDES.

including journalist–and serving in the armed forces, Paredes received an advanced education and became one of the most distinguished Hispanic scholars in U.S. history. Paredes has taught at the University of Texas from 1951 on, and is currently professor emeritus of English and anthropology there. He has been instrumental in the development of the field of folklore in academia as well as of the field of Mexican American studies. He has served as president of the American Folklore Society and has been recognized for his leadership internationally.

Besides publishing numerous research articles, Paredes is the author of *With a Pistol in His Hand: A Border Ballad and Its Hero* (1958), *Folktales of Mexico* (1970), *A Texas Mexican Cancionero* (1976), and *Uncle Remus con chile* (Uncle Remus with Chile), 1992. He is also the author of a novel, *George Washington Gomez* (1990), a book of poems, *Between Two Worlds* (1991), and a collection of short stories, *The Hammon and the Beans* (1994).

Kanellos, *Chronology of Hispanic American History,* pp. 173, 274.

ELSA GÓMEZ.

1989 ⋅ Elsa Gómez became the first Hispanic woman to be named president of a four-year liberal arts college when she assumed the position of president of Kean College in New Jersey. The New York City native received her Ph.D. degree in Italian from the University of Texas in 1971. Before becoming president of Kean, she served as dean of arts and sciences at Lock Haven University, Lock Haven, Pennsylvania.

Kanellos, *The Hispanic American Almanac,* p. 727.

1989 ⋅ Educator Rita Esquivel became the first Mexican American woman to head the Office of Bilingual Education and Minority Language Affairs in the U.S. Department of Education. Appointed by President George Bush, she had previously been the first assistant superintendent of education for the state of California.

Tardiff and Mabunda, *Dictionary of Hispanic Biography,* p. 314.

1989 ⋅ Mexican American sociologist Maxine Baca Zinn became the first Hispanic educator to receive the Miller Lecture Award on Women and Social Change, cosponsored by Sociologists for Women in Society and Loyola University in Chicago. A native New Mexican, Baca was named senior research associate at the Julian Samora Institute at Michigan State University in 1990.

Telgen and Kamp, *Latinas! Women of Achievement,* p. 33.

1990 ⋅ The first endowed chair named for a U.S. Hispanic was instituted in the Department of Spanish and Portuguese at the University of Texas. The chair for the study of literature was named for the Texas-born author and academic administrator Tomás Rivera, who died in 1984 while serving as the chancellor of the University of California-Riverside. (The same department that houses this chair had refused to hire him to teach there in his early career.)

See also Education, 1978; Literature, 1970.

Kanellos, *Chronology of Hispanic American History, ,* p. 208.

1990 • Ricardo Fernández became the first president of a college of the City University of New York, Lehman College. The Puerto Rico-born educator had served in a number of administrative positions with the University of Wisconsin and had also served as president of the National Association for Bilingual Education, from 1980 to 1981.

Kanellos, *The Hispanic American Almanac,* p. 725; Tardiff and Mabunda, *Dictionary of Hispanic Biography,* pp. 335–36.

1990 • Joseph A. Fernández became the first Puerto Rican and the first Hispanic to head the New York Public Schools, one of the nation's largest school systems. Born and raised in New York, Fernández received his B.A., M.A., and Ph.D. degrees from the University of Miami. Before becoming the New York superintendent, he served in a similar capacity for the extensive Dade County Public Schools. He served as head of the school system until 1994.

Kanellos, *The Hispanic American Almanac,* p. 725; Tardiff and Mabunda, *Dictionary of Hispanic Biography,* pp. 330–31.

JOSEPH A. FERNÁNDEZ.

1990 • Mari-Luci Jaramillo became the first Hispanic educator to receive the Outstanding Leadership in Education Award from the American Association for Higher Education for her educational leadership in the Hispanic community.

Telgen and Kamp, *Latinas! Women of Achievement,* p. 205.

1991 • The renowned folklorist Dr. Américo Paredes, labor organizer César Chávez, literary critic Dr. Luis Leal, and sociologist Dr. Julián Samora became the first Mexican Americans to be awarded the Aztec Eagle medal by the president of Mexico. The medal is the highest award given by Mexico to a foreigner for contributions to Mexico.

Kanellos, *Chronology of Hispanic American History,* p. 277.

1991 • Professor Julián Samora (1920–) became the first U.S. Hispanic to have a university research center named in his honor—the Julián Samora Center at Michigan State University. The famous sociologist was responsible for preparing a whole generation of Mexican American sociologists at the University of Notre Dame and was one of the first Chicano scholars to conduct research on Mexicans in the Midwest.

Kanellos, *The Hispanic American Almanac,* p. 411.

1991 • Manuel Trinidad Pacheco became the first Hispanic to serve as president of a major research university in the United States when he was sworn in to that position at the University of Arizona.

Born on May 30, 1941, in Rocky Ford, Colorado, Pacheco has dedicated his life to education. He obtained a B.A. degree from New Mexico Highlands University (1962), and M.A. and Ph.D. degrees from Ohio State University (1966 and 1969). Pacheco served as a professor of education and Spanish and as an administrator at various universities and colleges.

Kanellos, *Hispanic American Almanac,* pp. 733–34.

1992 ・ Mexican American sociologist Maxine Baca Zinn became the first Hispanic female educator to be elected to the governing council of the American Sociological Society.

Telgen and Kamp, *Latinas! Women of Achievement,* p. 34.

1993 ・ *The Hispanic American Almanac: A Reference Work on Hispanics of the United States,* edited by scholar Nicolás Kanellos, became the first Hispanic reference work to be named a Best Reference Work for 1993 by the American Library Association (Reference and Adult Section).

Kanellos, *The Hispanic American Almanac.*

1994 ・ The four-volume reference work *Handbook of Hispanic Cultures in the United States,* edited by scholars Nicolás Kanellos of the University of Houston and Claudio Esteva-Fabregat of the University of Barcelona, became the first book by a Hispanic publisher, Arte Público Press, to be named to the list of Outstanding Academic Books by *Choice* magazine. The handbook, which compiles articles by scholars in four areas—literature and art, history, sociology, and anthropology, also became the first Hispanic book to win the American Library Association's Denali Award for Best Reference Work in 1995, as well as being named to the American Library Association's list of Outstanding Reference Sources and the New York Public Library's list of Outstanding Reference Works.

Kanellos and Esteva-Fabregat, *Handbook of Hispanic Cultures in the United States.*

1996 ・ The first Hispanic to direct an academic library in a Texas state university was Gilda Baeza Ortega. Ortega is the director of the Sul Ross University library in Alpine, Texas. With the completion of her Ph.D. degree in library science, she became only the second Hispanic woman in the United States to obtain such a degree in library and information science.

"News and Notes," *Texas Library Journal,* 72/2 (summer 1996), p. 100.

FILM

~~~~~~

1912 • The first actor to establish the stereotype in film of the "Latin lover" was Antonio Moreno, who in 1912 began appearing in films by D. W. Griffith. Born on September 26, 1887, in Madrid, Moreno played a dapper Latin lover in numerous Hollywood silent films and was especially popular during the 1920s, when he played leads opposite such actresses as Gloria Swanson, Greta Garbo, Pola Negri, and Bebe Daniels. His foreign accent limited his career in talkies, where he was seen mainly in character roles.

He appeared in hundreds of films, including: *Voice of the Million, The Musketeers of Pig Alley* (1912); *The Song of the Ghetto, The Loan Shark King, In the Latin Quarter, Sunshine and Shadows* (1914); *The Quality of Mercy, The Gypsy Trail* (1915); *My American Wife, The Spanish Dancer* (1923); *One Year to Live* (1925); *Mare Nostrum, The Temptress* (1926); *Venus of Venice, The Whip Woman* (1928); *Romance of the Rio Grande* (1929); *One Mad Kiss* (1930); *The Bohemian Girl* (1938); *Rose of the Rio Grande* (1938); *Seven Sinners* (1940); *Notorious* (1946); *Captain from Castille* (1947); *Crisis, Dallas* (1950); *Wings of the Hawk* (1953); *Creature from the Black Lagoon* (1954); and *The Searchers* (1956).

Kanellos, *Chronology of Hispanic American History,* p. 121.

1914 • Raoul Walsh became the first Hispanic director in Hollywood when he began work on *The Life of General Villa,* a mixture of staged scenes and authentic footage of Francisco Villa's military campaigns. Walsh went on to direct such silent classics as *The Thief of Bagdad* (1924) and the sound film, *What Price Glory?* He is best known for the series of films he directed for Warner Bros. in the 1930s and 1940s, including *They Died with Their Boots On* and *High Sierra* (1941).

Kanellos, *The Hispanic American Almanac;* Luis Reyes, "Hollywood's Hispanic Heritage," *DGA News,* August-September 1994, p. 18.

1916 • The Puerto Rican film industry was established with the founding of the Sociedad Industrial Cine Puerto Rico in 1916 by Rafael Colorado and Antonio Capellá. The Sociedad produced three films that year; its first film was *Por la Hembra y el Gallo* (For Women and Fighting Cocks).

Kanellos, *The Hispanic American Almanac,* p. 579.

1920 • Juan Emilio Viguié Cajas became the first commercially successful producer of films in Puerto Rico, primarily producing newsreels for continental enterprises such as Pathé, Fox Movietone, and MGM. He also produced many documentaries for private enterprises and for the government.

Kanellos, *The Hispanic American Almanac,* p. 580.

1923 • In 1923, Ramón Novarro (1899–1948) was cast in the leading role in the silent film *The Prisoner of Zenda* and became the first Hispanic matinee idol in the United States. In 1913, Novarro moved to Los Angeles, California, with his family as refugees from the Mexican Revolution. The family experienced abject poverty, which led Novarro to work as a child, including taking small acting and dancing parts on screen and stage.

Largely because of his ability as a dancer, Novarro was cast in the film that would launch his career as a romantic actor, *The Prisoner of Zenda.* Novarro quickly became a success as a romantic matinee idol rivaled only by Rudolph Valentino in sexy Latin- and Arab-lover roles. Among his notable films were *Ben Hur* (1926), *The Student Prince* (1927), *Son of India,* and *Mata Hari* (1932), and *The Cat and the Fiddle* (1934). His last film was *Heller in Pink Tights* (1960).

Novarro was found beaten to death at his home on October 31, 1968.

Kanellos, *Chronology of Hispanic American History,* p. 141.

1925 • The first Hispanic leading lady in Hollywood films, Dolores del Río, made her debut in *Joanne,* which was the first of fifteen silent films she made between 1925 and 1929. Her three most important films were *What Price Glory?, Resurrection,* and *Ramona.* Dolores del Río became one of Hollywood's top ten moneymakers during the 1920s. In 1942, after starring in twenty-three U.S. films, she left the country for Mexico, where she became important in the film industry of her native country.

Born Dolores Asúnsolo y López Negrete to a wealthy family in Durango, Mexico, del Río came to the United States in 1925 at the invitation of Hollywood director Edwin Carewe, who directed her in *Joanne.*

Telgen and Kamp, *Latinas! Women of Achievement,* pp. 103–108.

1926 • Lupe Vélez (1908–1944), the second of two Hispanic leading ladies (Dolores del Río actually had her debut a few months earlier, in 1925) in Hollywood films, made her debut in a film directed by Hal Roach. She became a star the following year as the leading lady in *The Gaucho* opposite Douglas Fairbanks. Known as a fiery leading lady, both in silent and sound films, she later made positive use of her Spanish-accented English to reposition herself as a comedienne in the Mexican Spitfire series.

Her volatile personal life, including a romance with Gary Cooper and marriage to Johnny Weismuller, ended in suicide. Her films included *The Gaucho* (1927), *Stand and Deliver* (1928), *Lady of the Pavements* (1929), *The Squaw Man* and *The Cuban Love Song* (1931), *Hot Pepper* (1933), *The Girl from Mexico* (1939), *Mexican Spitfire* (1940), and *Redhead from Manhattan* (1943).

Kanellos, *The Hispanic American Almanac,* p. 592.

1934 ⬩ Juan Emilio Viguié Cajas's film, *Romance Tropical* (Tropical Romance) was the first Puerto Rican feature film of the sound period. Written by the poet Luis Palés Matos, the film depicts a lovesick young musician who attempts to seek his fortune at sea in a tiny boat.

Kanellos, *The Hispanic American Almanac,* p. 580.

1935 ⬩ Rita Hayworth made her screen debut and was on her way to becoming the first Hispanic sex goddess in Hollywood films. Born as Mar-

DOLORES DEL RÍO.

garita Carmen Cansino in Brooklyn, New York, she was the daughter of Spanish dancer Eduardo Cansino and his Ziegfeld Follies partner Volga Hayworth. By the age of thirteen, Hayworth danced professionally in Mexican night spots in Tijuana and Agua Caliente, where she was eventually noticed by Hollywood scouts. She made her screen debut in 1935, playing bit parts under her real name.

In 1937 she married Edward Judson, under whose guidance she changed her name and was transformed into an auburn-haired sophisticate. For the remainder of the 1930s, Hayworth was confined to leads in B pictures, but throughout much of the 1940s she became the undisputed sex goddess of Hollywood films and the hottest star at Columbia Studios.

Her tempestuous personal life included marriages to Orson Welles, Aly Khan, and singer Dick Haymes. As Rita Cansino, her films included *Under the Pampas Moon, Charlie Chan in Egypt, Dante's Inferno* (1935); *Meet Nero Wolfe* (1936); and *Trouble in Texas, Old Louisiana, Hit the Saddle* (1937). As Rita Hayworth, she acted in *The Shadow* (1937); *Angels Over Broadway* (1940); *The Strawberry Blonde, Blood and Sand* (1941); *Cover Girl* (1944); *Gilda* (1946); *The Lady from Shanghai, The Loves of Carmen* (1948); *Salome, Miss Sadie Thompson* (1953); *Pal Joey* (1957); *Separate Tables* (1958); *They Came to Cordura* (1959); *The Happy Thieves* (1962); *The Money Trap* (1966); *The Wrath of God* (1972); and *Circle* (1976).

See also Film, 1941.

Kanellos, *Chronology of Hispanic American History,* p. 180.

1941 • The first Hispanic actress to be considered a model of American beauty and sensuality was Rita Hayworth, who in 1941 was dubbed "The Great American Love Goddess" by Winthrop Sargent in *Life*. The actress and cabaret dancer Rita Cansino had so successfully molded her identity to the needs of Hollywood that in the early 1940s she was making $6,000 a week as Columbia Pictures's leading actress. This was in contrast to other Hispanic actresses, who were repeatedly cast in the stereotype of the Latin Spitfire.

Telgen and Kamp, *Latinas! Women of Achievement,* pp. 169–73.

JOSÉ FERRER.

1949 • The Puerto Rican government founded a production facility in San Juan to spur the film industry on the island. Administered by the Division de Educación de la Comunidad (Division of Community Education), this unit produced more films than any other entity in Puerto Rico. By 1975, it was able to produce sixty-five shorts and two features.

Kanellos, *The Hispanic American Almanac,* p. 580.

1950 • Puerto Rican actor José Ferrer (1912–1992) became the first U.S. Hispanic to win the Academy Award for Best Actor. Ferrer was one of the most distinguished actors of Hispanic background to have made a career in the mainstream films and on stage in the United States. The star of numerous Hollywood films and of many stage productions was born in Santurce,

Puerto Rico, on January 8, 1912. Raised and educated in Puerto Rico, he graduated from Princeton University in 1933.

As an actor and/or director, his stage credits include *Let's Face It* (1942), *Strange Fruit* (1945), *Design for Living* (1947), *Twentieth Century* (1950), *Stalag 17* (1951), *Man of La Mancha* (1966) and *Cyrano de Bergerac* (1975), among many others. As an actor, director, or producer, he has been associated with some of the most famous Hollywood films, including *Joan of Arc* (1947),

RITA HAYWORTH.

Moulin Rouge (1952), *Caine Mutiny* (1953), *Return to Peyton Place* (1962), *Lawrence of Arabia* (1963), *Ship of Fools* (1966), and others. His awards include the Gold Medal from the American Academy of Arts and Sciences (1949), the Academy Award for Best Actor in *Cyrano de Bergerac* (1950), and induction into the Theater Hall of Fame (1981), among many others.

See also Film, 1952.

Kanellos, *Chronology of Hispanic American History*, p. 167.

1951 • Viguié Film Productions became the first large Puerto Rican film producer. Founded by Juan Emilio Viguié Cajas Jr. and the journalist Manuel R. Navas, the company produced documentaries for both commercial and government use. In 1974, the company changed names and financial backing and became Guastella Film Producers, currently the largest producer in Puerto Rico.

Kanellos, *The Hispanic American Alamanac*, p. 580.

1952 • Actor Anthony Quinn became the first Mexican American to win the Academy Award for best actor for his role as Zapata's brother in *Viva Zapata!*

Born in Chihuahua, Mexico, of Irish-Mexican parentage, Quinn has lived in the United States since childhood. He began his career as a film actor in 1936. Quinn went on to win a second Academy Award for *Lust for Life* (1956), and he began playing leads that emphasized his earthy and exotic qualities. He has appeared in more than one hundred films and has written his autobiography, *The Original Sin* (1972).

Among his many films are *Parole!* (1936); *The Buccaneer, King of Alcatraz* (1938); *Texas Rangers Ride Again* (1940); *Blood and Sand* (1941); *The Ox-Bow Incident, Guadalcanal Diary* (1943); *Back to Bataan* (1945); *California, Sinbad the Sailor, Black Gold* (1947); *The Brave Bulls* (1951), *Viva Zapata!, Against All Flags* (1952); *Ride Vaquero* (1953); *Lust for Life, Man From Del Rio* (1956); *The Black Orchid* (1958); *The Guns of Navarrone, Barabbas* (1961); *Requiem for a Heavyweight, Lawrence of Arabia* (1962); *Zorba the Greek* (1964); *A High Wind in Jamaica* (1965); *The Shoes of the Fisherman, The Magus* (1968); *The Secret of Santa Vittoria* (1969); *The Greek Tycoon, The Children of Sánchez* (1978), *The Salamander* (1981), and *Ghosts Can't Do It, Revenge* (1990).

See also Film, 1956.

Kanellos, *Chronology of Hispanic American History*, p. 172.

1952 • Puerto Rican actor José Ferrer became the Hispanic with most Academy Award nominations (three), when he was nominated for best actor for his role in *Moulin Rouge.*

Kanellos, *Chronology of Hispanic American History*, p. 339.

1956 • Francisco "Chico" Day became the first Hispanic assistant director in Hollywood and the first Hispanic to be inducted into the Directors Guild of America. Born Francisco Alonso in Juárez, Mexico, on October 16, 1907, Chico, as he was affectionately called, was raised in El Paso, Texas, and Los

Angeles, California. He began working in motion pictures as a bit player and extra alongside his older brother, the famed actor Gilbert Roland. In 1956, he became the first assistant director to Cecile B. DeMille on the production of *The Ten Commandments.*

Chico Day went on to be the unit production manager on such films as *The Magnificent Seven, Patton, Hello Dolly,* and *Islands in the Stream.* In 1981, Day was awarded the Frank Capra Achievement Award from the Directors

ANTHONY QUINN IN <u>THE CHILDREN OF SÁNCHEZ.</u>

Guild of America. Today an annual award in his name is given to outstanding Hispanic directors by the Latino Committee of the Directors Guild.

Luis Reyes, "Hollywood's Hispanic Heritage," *DGA News,* August/September 1994, pp. 18–19.

1956 ⬧ Anthony Quinn (1915–), the Irish Mexican actor, became the first Hispanic to win two Academy Awards. His first Oscar was for the role of Emiliano Zapata's brother in *Viva Zapata!* (1952) and the second for his depiction of Vincent Van Gogh in *Lust for Life* (1956). Anthony Quinn has appeared in more than one hundred films, acting in English, Spanish, and Italian.

Kanellos, *Chronology of Hispanic American History,* p. 238.

1961 ⬧ Puerto Rican actress Rita Moreno became the first Hispanic actress to win an Academy Award for best supporting actress. Actress, dancer, and singer Moreno was born Rosita Dolores Alverio in Humacao, Puerto Rico, in 1931. A dancer from childhood, she reached Broadway at thirteen and Hollywood at fourteen.

She won a 1961 Academy Award as best supporting actress for *West Side Story* and has been in several films important for understanding the Hollywood depiction of Hispanics, including *A Medal for Benny* (1954), *The Ring,* and *Popi.* Her other films include *Pagan Love Song* (1950); *Singin' in the Rain* (1952); *Latin Lovers, Fort Vengeance* (1953); *Jivaro, Garden of Evil* (1954); *The King and I, The Vagabond King* (1956); *The Deerslayer* (1957); *West Side Story, Summer and Smoke* (1961); *Marlowe* (1969), *Carnal Knowledge* (1971); *The Ritz* (1976); *The Boss's Son* (1978); *Happy Birthday, Gemini* (1980); *The Four Seasons* (1981); and *Life in the Food Chain* (1991).

Kanellos, *Chronology of Hispanic American History,* p. 199.

RITA MORENO.

1969 • Actor Ricardo Montalbán founded the first organization to promote equal opportunities for Hispanic actors and actresses in Hollywood. The organization was called Nosotros, and it sought to improve the image of Hispanics in the movies and on television. Nosotros sponsored the Golden Eagle Awards to recognize outstanding performances by Hispanics.

Tardiff and Mabunda, *Dictionary of Hispanic Biography*, p. 563.

1971 • The first two Chicano documentary films were made, David García's *Requiem-29,* which described the Chicano moratorium on the Vietnam War, and Jesús Salvador Treviño's *América Tropical,* about the whitewashing of a David Alfaro Siqueiros mural in Los Angeles.

Kanellos, *The Hispanic American Alamanac,* p. 574.

1972 • Jesús Salvador Treviño's documentary film *Yo Soy Chicano* (I Am Chicano) was the first film by a Chicano to be nationally televised. The film dealt with the Chicano Movement, from its pre-Columbian roots to modern activism.

Kanellos, *The Hispanic American Alamanac,* p. 574.

1972 • The feature film based on the Luis Valdez and El Teatro Campesino play *Los Vendidos* was the first nationally televised Chicano feature film. It was a satire of the stereotypes traditionally used to depict Mexicanas and Mexican Americans. *Los Vendidos* may also be considered the first Chicano feature film.

Kanellos, *Hispanic American Almanac,* p. 578.

1975 • The National Latino Communications Center (NLCC) was founded to sponsor Latino-theme programming on television. Initially it was housed

RICARDO MONTALBÁN.

at KCET in Los Angeles but today is a completely independent non-profit corporation. (Its original name was the Latino Consortium.) José Luis Ruiz has served as its executive director since its inception. In addition to producing programming, the NLCC also offers training programs for Latinos in film and television.

1978 • Spanish Cuban cinematographer Nestor Almendros (1930–1993) became the first Hispanic to win the Oscar for best cinematography. A graduate of the University of Havana in philosophy and literature, Almendros began his career in film with an amateur eight-millimeter film with the great Cuban director, Tomás Gutiérrez Alea, in 1950. He later studied film with Hans Richter at the City University of New York and studied cinematography at the Centro Sperimentale di Cinematografia in Rome. In the mid-1960s, he began collaborating regularly with director Eric Rohmer and later with director Francois Truffaut.

He won the Academy Award for cinematography for the 1978 film *Days of Heaven*. Included among his many outstanding films are *The Wild Racers* (U.S., 1968); *Gun Runner* (U.S., 1968); *Ma nuit chez Maud/My Night at Maud's* (France 1969); *L'enfant sauvage/The Wild Child* (France 1970); *Le genou de Claire/Claire's Knee* (France 1971); *L'amour l'aprás-midi/Chloe in the Afternoon* (France 1972); *Chinatown* (1974); *L'histoire d'Adele H./The Story of Adele H.* (France 1975), *Days of Heaven* (U.S., 1978), *Kramer vs. Kramer* (1979), *The Blue Lagoon* (1980), *The Last Metro* (France 1980), *Sophie's Choice* (1982); *Improper Conduct* (1983); *Places in the Heart* (1984); *Heartburn* (1986); and *New York Stories* (1989). Almendros also directed several noteworthy documentaries, including *Improper Conduct* and the anti-Castro film *Nobody Lis-*

NESTOR ALMENDROS.

tened (1988). Almendros was the author of an important autobiographical book on cinematography *Un Homme a la caméra/A Man with a Camera,* published first in French in 1980, and then in English translation in 1984.

Kanellos, *Chronology of Hispanic American History,* pp. 196–97.

1978 • The first Chicano film nominated for an Academy Award was the documentary *Agueda Martínez,* by Esperanza Vázquez and Moctezuma Esparza, which depicts the lifestyle of an elderly woman in northern New Mexico.

Kanellos, *The Hispanic American Alamanac,* p. 574.

1979 • The first Cuban American film comedy—the award-winning *El Super,* based on the play by Iván Acosta—was produced. The film, using the working-class dialect of New York City Cubans, deals with Cuban American culture shock and the adjustment of Cuban exiles to permanent residency in the United States.

Kanellos, *The Hispanic American Alamanac,* p. 568.

1979 • The hit film *El Super* launched the career of Elizabeth Peña, the first Cuban American Hollywood actress in contemporary times. Other films include *Down and Out in Beverly Hills* in 1986, and *La Bamba* in 1987. She has also appeared in numerous television shows and made-for-television movies.

Tardiff and Mabunda, *Dictionary of Hispanic Biography,* pp. 633-34; Telgen and Kamp, *Latinas! Women of Achievement,* p. 298.

ELIZABETH PEÑA.

1981 • *Seguín,* by Jesús Salvador Treviño—the first Chicano western—was filmed, followed by Moctezuma Esparza's *The Ballad of Gregorio Cortez* in 1982. Both films broke the mold of the genre by focusing on the recuperation of lost or suppressed aspects of Chicano history. *Seguín* was the first Hispanic version of the fall of the Alamo since it was first depicted on the screen in 1911, whereas *The Ballad of Gregorio Cortez* dealt with the adventures of a folk hero who was cast as a bandit by Anglo-Texan law.

Kanellos, *The Hispanic American Alamanac,* p. 579.

1984 • Actor César Romero (1907–1994) became the Hispanic actor with the longest, or one of the longest, acting careers in Hollywood films. In 1984, he received an award from the Hollywood International Celebrity Banquet for achieving fifty years in the film industry. That same year he received the Nosotros Golden Eagle for success as a Hispanic in show business. In 1991, this actor who played the suave Latin lover in so many films also won the Imagen Hispanic Media Award for Lifetime Achievement.

Tardiff and Mabunda, *Dictionary of Hispanic Biography,* p. 768.

1985 • Actress Norma Aleandro became the first Hispanic actress to win the Best Actress award at the Cannes Film Festival in the Oscar-winning movie *The Official Story.*

Kanellos, *The Hispanic American Alamanac,* p. 568.

1985 ⋄ Gregory Nava became the first Hispanic screenwriter to have a film nominated for an Academy Award. His highly acclaimed *El Norte* is the story of a peasant couple's journey of immigration to the United States.

Tardiff and Mabunda, *Dictionary of Hispanic Biography,* p. 599.

1987 ⋄ *La Bamba,* the screen biography of rock star Ritchie Valens, written and directed by Luis Valdez, was the first Hollywood film marketed successfully in both English and Spanish versions to audiences in the United States. A record seventy-seven Spanish-language prints were released, and the Hispanic market provided a two-to-one return over mainstream audiences on costs, representing 10 percent of the receipts.

Kanellos, *The Hispanic American Alamanac,* p. 568.

1987 ⋄ Actor José Ferrer became the first Hispanic to receive the National Medal of the Arts.

1988 ⋄ The award-winning film *Stand and Deliver* was the first Hollywood feature film in which virtually the entire film, including scripting, producing, financing, directing, and acting, was conducted by Hispanics. The film presents the inspirational true story of a Bolivian math teacher, Jaime Escalante, in East Los Angeles, who prepares numerous poor, inner city students for college against all odds.

A SCENE FROM GREGORY NAVA'S <u>EL NORTE,</u> WITH DAVID VILLALPANDO AND ZAIDE SILVIA GUTIÉRREZ.

Actor Edward James Olmos was able to provide a second life for the film through massive distribution to educational institutions in the United States, in conjunction with such sponsors as Pepsico.

Kanellos, *The Hispanic American Alamanac,* pp. 567–68.

1988 ⋅ Mexican American filmmaker Jesús Salvador Treviño became the first U.S. Hispanic director to win a Directors Guild of America award for best daytime drama for his film *Gangs*.

Tardiff and Mabunda, *Dictionary of Hispanic Biography,* p. 900.

1990 ⋅ There were finally enough Hispanic directors in Hollywood to not only qualify as members of the Directors Guild of America, but also to found the Latino Committee, whose main purpose was to expand job opportunities

EDWARD JAMES OLMOS.

for Hispanics as directors of Hollywood films. The first members included Bob Burgos, Paul Chávez, Sylvia Morales, Edward James Olmos, José Luis Ruiz, Jesús Treviño, and Luis Valdez. The committee sponsors a variety of events throughout the year, including seminars, screenings, and awards.

1991 • Filmmaker Jesús Salvador Treviño's 1977 feature film *Raíces de Sangre* was the first film by a U.S. Hispanic to be named one of the top twenty-five Latin American films of all time by the Valladolid (Spain) Film Festival.
Tardiff and Mabunda, *Dictionary of Hispanic Biography,* p. 900.

1993 • Film student Robert Rodríguez broke all records by making a critically acclaimed film, *El Mariachi,* on a budget of only $7,000 in an era when films cost millions of dollars to make. Columbia Pictures picked it up, and the movie brought in more than $2 million. *El Mariachi* effectively launched Rodríguez's Hollywood career, and his next film was a fully funded Hollywood production, *Desperado,* starring Antonio Banderas, which opened in 1995 to mixed reviews. For *Desperado,* Rodríguez insisted on an 80 percent Hispanic crew, and the film provided Spanish actor Antonio Banderas with his first American lead. The female lead went to Salma Hayek, the first Mexican actress since Dolores del Río to take the lead in an American film.
Hispanic, July 1995, p. 26; Malbunda and Tardiff, *Dictionary of Hispanic Biography,* p. 763.

1994 • For the first time in history there were enough Hispanic actors and entertainers in film and on television for *Cosmopolitan* magazine to run a feature on them, entitled "Latins in the Limelight." The two-page spread included photos and biographies of Jimmy Smits, Gloria Estefan, Andy García, Raúl Juliá, and Rosie Pérez, among others.
Cosmopolitan, November 1994, pp. 224–25.

1995 • The Gregory Nava film *My Family* had the highest per screen average revenue ($5,375) for all movies released on the weekend of May 5–7, 1995. The importance of this figure is that it brought Hollywood a step further to recognizing the value of producing Hispanic-content films with real Hispanic actors. The year 1995 saw a record number of releases with Hispanic themes, including *The Pérez Family,* Robert Rodríguez's *Desperado, A Walk in the Clouds,* and *Roosters,* which was based on a play by Milcha Sánchez-Scott. For *My Family,* Nava assembled the most prestigious Hispanic cast in film history, which included Jimmy Smits, Esai Morales, and Edward James Olmos. Not only was Hollywood beginning to react to the demographic strength of Hispanics in the United States but to their representing the highest level of video renters among all segments of the society.
Hispanic, July 1995, pp. 22–26.

GOVERNMENT

~~~~~~

LAW

1610 · With the founding of Santa Fe, New Mexico, many Spanish laws governing all facets of life were introduced to what would become the culture of the Southwest. Foremost among those laws were those concerning water and its management; many of these Spanish laws would pass into the legal codes of the United States. In the Spanish and Mexican judicial systems, the rights of the community weighed more heavily than those of the individual concerning the precious resource of water in the arid Southwest. The water in Spanish and Mexican towns and cities was held in trust for the benefit of the entire community. The *cabildo,* the democratically elected town council, held the authority over local water usage. Usually, each pueblo was invested with special rights in respect to water. Title to the water in streams flowing through the pueblo's common lands was reserved to the pueblo and its inhabitants for both domestic and public use, as in parks and for nonagricultural purposes.

The Treaty of Guadalupe Hidalgo passed these rights on to posterity after the Mexican War. The City of Los Angeles, which inherited the pueblo rights, was able to obtain a favorable ruling from the U.S. Supreme Court over a water dispute with landowners of the San Fernando Valley. The court ruled that the city had prior claim to all waters originating within the watershed of the Los Angeles River; thus, the court asserted that pueblo rights took precedence over the common law rights of the landowners.

Meyer, *Water in the Hispanic Southwest,* pp. 156–57; Rosaldo et al., *Chicano,* p. 13.

1681 · The Spanish government issued the first compilation of laws that governed settlement of their colonies in the New World, including those in areas that became the United States. The *Recopilación de las leyes de las Indias* (Compilation of the Laws of the Indies) organized and reduced to a total of sixty-four hundred the laws applicable to its American colonies. By 1635, there had been issued some 400 thousand edicts. The *Recopilación* was reissued with changes in 1774 and revised again in 1791. In these codes and laws, the granting of land and the details of founding of towns were prescribed, including the physical layouts of the towns and the powers of the municipal authorities.

Gómez-Quiñones, *Roots of Chicano Politics, 1600–1940,* p. 18; Kanellos, *Chronology of Hispanic American History,* p. 52.

1767 • Spanish laws governing water usage became the foundation for current Texas law regarding water usage and rights. Spain began making grants of Texas land to colonizers; it is estimated that some twenty-six million of Texas's 170 million acres were granted by Spain and Mexico, and various types of water rights were attached to these land grants. The water rights that go with these grants are covered by Texas law but determined by the terms of the original grants. After the founding of the Republic of Texas in 1836 and then the later admission of Texas as a state to the union, the Spanish and Mexican laws regarding water usage were incorporated into the state constitution. This Spanish heritage was the basis of the Irrigation Act of 1852, which is the basis for Texas statutory irrigation law.

Dobkins, *The Spanish Element in Texas Water Law,* pp. ix-x, 124–25.

1810 • The first Spanish translation of the U.S. Constitution was effected by Joseph Manuel Villavicencio and published in Philadelphia. The U.S. Constitution served as a model for the newly emerging states gaining their independence from Spain in the rest of the Hemisphere.

Online Computer Library Center.

1839 • Texas adopted the first Homestead Law in the United States on January 26, 1839. The principle of protecting certain pieces of personal property from creditors has its roots in Castilian practices that date to the thirteenth century and passed into Texas law from the Hispano-Mexican legal codes. This made it possible for a debtor to protect the principal residence of the family from seizure by creditors; it also protected other basic items, such as clothing and implements of trade needed for the debtor to make a living. Today, Texas continues to have one of the strongest property exemption laws of any state. Texas also accepted the Mexican and Spanish land use system via this law, which called for large tracts of land with access to water that could be used for ranching cattle and sheep.

Chipman, *Spanish Texas, 1519–1821,* pp. 253–54; McKnight, *The Spanish Elements in Modern Texas Law,* p. 9; Rosaldo et al., *Chicano,* p. 13.

1840 • The Texas legislature adopted the Hispano-Mexican system of a single court rather than continuing the dual court system (courts of law and courts of equity) of Anglo-American law. Under the Hispanic system, all issues could be considered simultaneously rather than divided between two jurisdictions. Thus, the Republic of Texas became the first English-speaking country to adopt a permanent and full unitary system of justice. This system passed into Texas law after it became a state.

Chipman, *Spanish Texas, 1519–1821,* pp. 250–51.

1840 • The Texas legislature adopted from the Hispanic legal system the requirement that a person be sued in the locale in which he resides, for his convenience. This principle passed into Texas state law.

Chipman, *Spanish Texas, 1519–1821,* p. 251.

1840 • The legislature of the Republic of Texas adopted and subsequently passed on to the state legal code the Spanish legal concept of community property. Husband and wife were to share equally in the profits and fruits of their marriage. Under Anglo-American law, however, property belonged exclusively to the husband, and on the death of her spouse, the wife was protected only by a life interest in one-third of the lands of her deceased spouse. The Republic of Texas recognized this inequity and specifically excluded the Anglo-American law of matrimonial property. The previously Hispanic provinces of Texas and Louisiana were the first to protect wives through common-law statues.

    Today, community property law is prevalent in states that have a Hispanic heritage: Texas, Louisiana, New Mexico, Arizona, Nevada, and California. It has also been pointed out that even the right to file a joint income tax return derives from the Spanish principle.

Chipman, *Spanish Texas, 1519–1821,* p. 253; McKnight, *The Spanish Elements in Modern Texas Law,* p. 8; Rosaldo et al., *Chicano,* pp. 13–14.

1840 • The legal code of Texas incorporated the Spanish concept of "independent executor" in relation to probate matters (i.e., wills). This did away with the Anglo-American legal practice that allowed executors to obtain court orders to perform acts not specifically called for in the testament. Placing confidence in an executor was more expedient and saved legal expenses both for the legal system and the individuals involved. This Spanish judicial procedure later spread from Texas to Arizona, Washington, Idaho, and some ten other states as provisions of the Uniform Probate Code.

Chipman, *Spanish Texas, 1519–1821,* p. 251.

1841 • Numerous principles of Spanish family law were incorporated into the legal code of Texas, covering the rights of partners in marriage as well as the adoption of children. Included among these principles was the protection of the rights of parties in a common-law relationship. Furthermore, children of such marriages, even if the marriages were declared invalid later, were considered legitimate and a fair division of the profits of marriage resulted. This legitimation of children is still part of Texas family law today.

Chipman, *Spanish Texas, 1519–1821,* p. 252.

1849 • At the California constitutional convention, Anglos resisted giving the vote to Indians, blacks, and mestizos. Largely through the leadership of Pablo de la Guerra and other Hispanic delegates, however, the convention came to an agreement that any man who had been considered a Mexican citizen, regardless of race, would be so considered under the constitution of California. This was the first time that a state constitution defined citizenship based on the inclusiveness of all races, as was practiced in Mexico. However, those blacks and Indians who had not been Mexicans would be excluded.

Gómez-Quiñones, *Roots of Chicano Politics, 1600–1940,* pp. 226–27.

1849 • The California state constitution required that all laws be printed in English and Spanish. However, disenfranchisement of the Spanish- speaking population progressed over the years in California as the legislature mandated English-only ballots, enacted English literacy requirements, and, in 1890, amended the constitution to declare English the official language of the state.

Gómez-Quiñones, *Roots of Chicano Politics, 1600–1940,* p. 228; Kanellos, *The Hispanic American Almanac,* p. 296.

1849 • The California legislature adopted Anglo-American law, except for the community property system as prescribed by Hispanic legal tradition. The American regimes in both Texas and Louisiana also adopted the Hispanic community property system.

Joseph McKnight, "Law without Lawyers on the Hispano Mexican Frontier," *The West Texas Historical Association Year Book,* 64 (1990), pp. 51–65.

1850 • Texas reinstated in its legal code the Spanish principle of adoption for children, after it had been dropped ten years earlier under the new legal code of the Republic of Texas. The concept of adoption was not recognized in English law, and Anglo-American law continued this glaring gap. Because of numerous petitions for specific rulings on adoptions during the years of the republic and early statehood of Texas, the legislature decided to reinstate the Hispanic concept of adoption, including the right of adopted children to inherit their adopted parents's estates. In Texas, as in the Hispanic world, the rights of an adopted child became the same as those of biological children, and they could still claim inheritance from their natural parents. After Mississippi, Texas was the second Anglo- American state to permanently recognize and codify adoption.

Chipman, *Spanish Texas, 1519–1821,* pp. 252–53; McKnight, *The Spanish Elements in Modern Texas Law,* p. 7.

1856 • Mariano Vallejo, a Californio leader and the mayor of Sonoma, met with President Abraham Lincoln in Washington, D.C., to discuss the issue of expropriation of Californio lands by Anglos. This may have been the first meeting between a Mexican American political leader and a president of the United States.

Gómez-Quiñones, *Roots of Chicano Politics, 1600–1940,* p. 230.

1875 • The constitution of the state of Colorado specifically protected the civil rights of Spanish-speaking citizens and called for all laws to be published in both English and Spanish. The constitution itself was drafted in both languages.

Kanellos, *The Hispanic American Almanac,* p. 278.

1916 • The first state constitution was written specifically protecting the rights of citizens to speak and vote in Spanish. Article 7 of the New Mexico

Constitution provides that the "right of any citizen to vote, hold office, or sit upon juries, shall never be restricted, abridged or impaired on account of religion, race, language or color, or inability to speak, read or write the English or Spanish languages." The constitution, under Article 2, specifically incorporated the rights of the people of New Mexico under the Treaty of Guadalupe Hidalgo, which was a product of the war with Mexico. In addition, the state was officially bilingual, as provided for by its constitution: "All laws passed by the Legislature shall be published in both the English and Spanish languages." The legislature was also mandated to provide funds for the training of teachers to be proficient in both English and Spanish (Article 12). Article 12 also prohibited segregation of the children of Spanish descent.

Gómez-Quiñones, *Roots of Chicano Politics, 1600–1940*, pp. 325–28.

1968 • The first federal law mandating bilingual education, the Bilingual Education Act, which became Title VII of the Elementary and Secondary Education Act, was sponsored by Senators Joseph M. Montoya of New Mexico and Ralph Yarborough of Texas. The law authorized grants to local school districts to develop and implement instruction of all subjects in both languages until the limited-English-speaking child was able to continue his or her education in English. It also called for teaching the history and culture associated with the native language.

Vigil, *Los Patrones*, pp. 157–63.

1974 • Senator Joseph P. Montoya was one of the authors of a new Bilingual Education Act, which expanded bilingual education by financing the preparation of bilingual teachers and the development of curricula.

Vigil, *Los Patrones*, pp. 157–63.

POLITICS

1539 • Hernando de Soto (ca. 1500–1542) led some six hundred soldiers, priests, and followers into Florida and built a winter camp on the site of today's city of Tallahassee, making it the oldest known European building site in what has become the United States. Excavations at Tallahassee's Lafayette Street have uncovered some of the remains of that camp.

Henderson and Mormino, *Spanish Pathways in Florida*, p. 87.

1560 • The Spanish founded Santa Elena in what is today the state of South Carolina; it was the first European settlement in what became the continental United States. Both Santa Elena and Saint Augustine predate Jamestown, which was founded in 1607 by the British, and the arrival of the Mayflower in 1620. Santa Elena did not last as a settlement.

Kanellos, *Chronology of Hispanic American History,* p. 45.

1565 • The first permanent town settlement and government (not counting Native American settlements, of course) in what became the continental United States was San Agustín (Saint Augustine), Florida, founded by Pedro Menéndez de Avilés on the eastern Florida coast. It served to protect Spanish shipping around the islands of the Caribbean. (The English did not establish the town of Jamestown in Virginia until 1607.)

During the seventeenth century, the city of Saint Augustine and other areas of Florida received a considerable amount of migration from Spain

PEDRO MENÉNDEZ
DE AVILÉS.

and the Spanish Caribbean. The population of Saint Augustine grew to two thousand by the turn of the eighteenth century. The city was afforded more security by the building of the San Marcos Fort, begun in 1672 and finished in 1756.

In 1763, the region of the Florida peninsula, called Eastern Florida—as opposed to Western Florida, which ranged from the Georgia coast to the Mississippi River—came under British control as a result of the Treaty of Paris. This included Saint Augustine. In 1783, under the Treaty of Versailles, Eastern Florida was returned to Spain. It remained a possession of Spain until 1821, when it was surrendered to the United States.

Cruz, *Let There Be Towns,* p. 19; Kanellos, *Chronology of Hispanic American History,* p. 45.

1565 • With the founding of Saint Augustine, the Spanish system of local government was instituted in the continental United States; it would be extended to all new towns and municipalities founded over the next two centuries. The system included an elected town council (*cabildo*) and an elected mayor (*alcalde*); thus, the first democratic municipal elections in what would become the continental United States were introduced by the Spanish-mestizo colonizers. (However, the Spanish Crown had the power to confirm or nullify the elections.) Among the rights of citizens (*fueros*) was that of holding open town meetings (*cabildo abierto*) for the discussion of issues affecting the community and for decision making regarding the issues; these represented the first town meetings in what would become the United States.

The roots of the cabildo abierto lay in the rights of medieval Spanish towns. Typically, the town councils on the Spanish frontier consisted of four annually elected councilmen (*regidores*). The council selected two magistrates (*alcaldes ordinarios*) to preside over the cabildo and to try local cases, one citizen to serve as a constable (*alguacil*), one as a city clerk (*escribano*), and another as a royal standard bearer (*alférez real*). In addition to executing local governance, the cabildos came to serve as advisory boards for the governors of the provinces, and they served as spokesmen for the community to the authorities of the church, the higher government, and the royalty.

In the larger municipalities, such as San Antonio, alcalde held court daily except for Sundays; in frontier municipalities, the judges convened the court whenever it was needed. The first lawyers in what became the United States date to this period, and in the later colonial period the first public defenders were appointed by the cabildos at city expense to serve citizens who could not afford legal fees. The cabildo also appointed a *fiel exector,* a person in charge of weights and measures, thus regulating the marketplace, and a person in charge of surveying lands. All of these positions and institutions were the first of their kind in areas that became the United States.

In the Southwest, another type of governing organization was the local ditch *acequia* association, which is extant today in some parts of New Mexico. These associations maintained and governed the use of the irrigation systems, which were essential to the agriculture and economy of each of the villages. Representatives were elected to a commission and a supervisor administered the flow and usage of the water on an equitable basis.

Cruz, *Let There Be Towns*, pp. 74–76, 133–34, 148–51; Gómez-Quiñones, *Roots of Chicano Politics, 1600–1940*, pp. 24–25, 40.

1598 • On April 30, 1598, Don Juan de Oñate (ca. 1550–1630) took formal possession of what would become the province of New Mexico in a pass on the Rio Grande dividing New Spain (Mexico) from what would eventually become the southwestern United States. The pass would serve as a weigh station for colonizers traveling north into the new province; it eventually became the town of El Paso, today a large city in Texas that still serves as a vital commercial link between Mexico and the United States.

Cruz, *Let There Be Towns*, pp. 36–37.

1598 • On July 15, 1598, Juan de Oñate founded the first town in what would become the southwestern United States and became the first governor of what would soon be the Spanish colonial province of New Mexico. He chose a site known as Caypa on the east bank of the Rio Grande by a friendly Indian pueblo and christened the town San Juan de los Caballeros. Three years later, he founded another town across the river from San Juan, baptized it San Gabriel, and set up his governor's residency there.

Cruz, *Let There Be Towns*, pp. 19–22.

1610 • Under orders from Don Luis de Velasco, viceroy of New Spain, Juan de Oñate founded the capital of the province of New Mexico in Santa Fe. This became the first capital on what would later be U.S. soil. The founding of Santa Fe was carried out according to the Spanish Ordinances of 1573,

PALACE OF THE GOVERNORS, SANTA FE.

calling for the establishment of a mayor (*alcalde*) and council (*cabildo*) elected by the citizens, a municipal court, a constable, and a clerk.

Cruz, *Let There Be Towns,* pp. 19–29.

1690 ⋄ On May 24, 1690, the first permanent Spanish settlement in Texas, San Francisco de los Tejas, was founded near the Neches River by Father Massanet and Father Fontcubierta.

Kanellos, *Chronology of Hispanic American History,* p. 52.

1691 ⋄ Father Eusebio Kino (1645–1711), an untiring Jesuit missionary, made the first inroads into Arizona. By 1700, Kino had established a mission at San Xavier del Bac, near present-day Tucson. He later established other missions in Arizona, including Nuestra Señora de los Dolores, Santa Gertrudis de Saric, San José de Imuris, Nuestra Señora de los Remedios, and San Cayetano de Tumacácori.

Kanellos, *Chronology of Hispanic American History,* p. 52.

1691 ⋄ Domingo Terán de los Ríos was named the first governor of the province of Texas. As a response to French exploration and incursions, Spain decided to rapidly settle Texas. Terán de los Ríos was empowered to establish eight missions among the Indian nations in east Texas.

Kanellos, *Chronology of Hispanic American History,* p. 52.

1716 ⋄ San Antonio was founded in 1716 by Alonso de Alarcón. It became the most important and most prosperous settlement in Texas. During the 1730s and the 1740s, missions spread from eastern Texas westward. The

THE SPANISH
GOVERNOR'S PALACE.

eastern Texas missions had been partially abandoned and moved to San Antonio, with San Antonio de Valero, San Juan Capistrano, San Francisco de la Espada, and Purísima Concepción being established along the San Antonio River. The area developed into an important center for trade.

Kanellos, *Chronology of Hispanic American History,* p. 53.

1761 • The province of Alta California was founded through the leadership of José de Gálvez, who, besides convincing the Crown to colonize the area,

JUNÍPERO SERRA.

also outfitted two ships, which occupied the port of San Diego in April. After establishing missions and settlements in San Diego, Gaspar de Pórtola and Father Junípero Serra set out for Monterey Bay in July. After discovering San Francisco Bay, they reached Monterey Bay in March 1770.

Kanellos, *Chronology of Hispanic American History,* p. 57.

1766 • Antonio de Ulloa became the first governor of Louisiana under Spanish rule. Spanish dominion lasted until 1803.

Fontana, *Entrada,* p. 115.

1769 • On July 3, 1769, Fray Junípero Serra (1713–1784) established the first mission of Alta California in what would become San Diego; the colonization of California had begun. Serra eventually founded ten missions, traveled more than ten thousand miles, and converted close to sixty-eight hundred Indians.

Kanellos, *Chronology of Hispanic American History,* p. 58.

1773 • The first European settlements in Alaska were established by the Spanish. Spanish expeditions began to explore the Canadian coast up into Alaska over the next few years, making contact with Russians. Their explorations eventually led to the establishment of a base at Nutka on the coast of Vancouver Island. This was the only European outpost in the expanse from San Francisco to Alaska.

In 1789, Spanish soldiers arrested several English sailors who arrived at Nutka, which provoked protests and threats from the British government. The Nutka Convention of 1879 resulted in abandonment of the base by the Spanish. The convention specified that all nations would be allowed to engage in trade on the coast of "Columbia," but no nation would be allowed to erect any establishments in the area.

Kanellos, *Chronology of Hispanic American History,* p. 58.

1776 • On September 17, 1776, José Moraga, a lieutenant in Juan Bautista de Anza's colonizing mission to Alta California consisting of twenty families (240 people), 700 horses, and 350 cattle, founded San Francisco. In 1777, the governor of Alta California, Felipe de Neve, established his capital in Monterey and also founded the village of San José with some of the settlers brought by Moraga. In 1781, De Neve went south with other settlers and established Nuestra Señora la Reina de los Angeles de Porciúncula (Los Angeles).

Kanellos, *Chronology of Hispanic American History,* pp. 58–59.

1779 • The first Hispanic of African heritage became a high official in the colonial system. Antonio Gil y Barbo, a mulatto, was named lieutenant governor of Texas under Spanish rule. He led colonists in resettling Nacogdoches, which had been abandoned earlier.

Gómez-Quiñones, *Roots of Chicano Politics, 1600–1940,* p. 45.

1822 • Joseph Hernández (1793–1857), from the territory of Florida, was elected the first Hispanic representative to the U.S. Congress. He was the son of Spanish immigrants who had settled in Florida in 1768. Two years later, Hernández, a Whig Party member, was elected president of the legislative council of Florida. Hernández ran unsuccessfully for the U.S. Senate in 1845. No Hispanic held a national office for another thirty years.

Hispanics in U.S. History, p. 70.

1822 • The first empire in North America was proclaimed. A former royalist soldier, Agustín de Iturbide, proclaimed himself emperor of Mexico shortly after Mexico won its independence from Spain, but he was forced to abdicate in 1823 by General Antonio López de Santa Anna.

Kanellos, *Chronology of Hispanic America History,* p. 78.

1832 • Pío de Jesús Pico became the first governor of African heritage in North America. Born on May 5, 1801, at San Gabriel Mission, Pico, who was a mulatto, also had the distinction of being the last governor of California under Mexican rule.

As a young man he became a successful businessman in Los Angeles. In 1828, he was elected to the territorial legislature and assumed grand stature as a southern Californio political leader. From January to February 1832, he was governor briefly but then became the civilian administrator of the San Luis Rey Mission. In 1845, he once again became governor, this time at the seat in Los Angeles instead of at Monterey. He was attacked on various occasions for land grants that he made and for his sale of mission lands.

When the Americans invaded, Pico at first offered some resistance, but soon fled to Baja California. After signing a peace treaty, Pico returned to California and assumed the peaceful life of a rancher. He, like many other Californios, lost all of his lands to mortgage companies when he had to raise funds to defend the titles to the properties from squatters and other usurpers.

Under American rule, Pico continued his interest in politics, serving on the Los Angeles City Council and as the Los Angeles County tax assessor. He also owned a large hotel, the Pico House, which still stands in downtown Los Angeles. Pico died penniless on September 11, 1894.

Kanellos, *Chronology of Hispanic American History,* pp. 65–66.

1836 • Politician and statesman Lorenzo de Zavala, one of the main leaders of the revolt against the central government in Mexico, became the first vice president of the Republic of Texas.

Meier and Rivera, *Dictionary of Mexican American History,* p. 374.

1852 · Manuel Requena (1802–1876) was elected to the first Los Angeles County Board of Supervisors. In 1850, he had been elected to the city council, eventually serving a total of six terms, most of the time as president of the council.

Kanellos, *The Hispanic American Almanac,* p. 281.

1853 · The second Hispanic to serve in the U.S. House of Representatives was the first elected representative of the New Mexico Territory, José Manuel Gallegos (1815–?). An ordained priest who had studied under Antonio José Martínez, Gallegos ministered to the San Juan Pueblo and was later transferred to Albuquerque. Gallegos became a delegate to the New Mexican assembly in 1843, when the province still belonged to Mexico.

In 1851, under U.S. rule, he was elected to the territorial senate and two years later became a representative to the U.S. Congress, despite his inability to speak English. While in his second term in Congress, Gallegos was unseated (in 1856) by the House as a result of appeals from Miguel A. Otero, who had opposed Gallegos in the close election. Gallegos returned to New Mexico and continued his political career, serving as the Speaker of the New Mexico House from 1860 to 1862. In 1870, he again won a seat in the U.S. Congress and served until 1873.

See also Religion, 1857.

Gómez-Quiñones, *Roots of Chicano Politics, 1600–1940,* p. 240; Meier and Rivera, *Dictionary of Mexican American History,* pp. 141–42.

1856 · When the Los Angeles mayor resigned, Manuel Requena, serving as president of the city council, became mayor until an election was held

GOVERNOR PÍO PICO.

eleven days later. For a brief time, then, he was the only Mexican American to serve as mayor of Los Angeles under U.S. rule.

Kanellos, *The Hispanic American Almanac*, p. 281.

1875 • Romualdo Pacheco (1831–1899) became the first Hispanic governor of California under U.S. rule. After being elected to the lieutenant governorship in 1871, Pacheco succeeded to the position of governor when Gov-

GOVERNOR ROMUALDO PACHECO.

ernor Newton Booth was elected to the Senate in 1875. After serving for nine months, Pacheco failed to even gain the Republican nomination for governor in the next election.

Pacheco was the son of a Mexican army officer from Guadalajara; he was raised in Hawaii, where he received his English-language education. After the Mexican War, he supervised his family's ranch in San Luis Obispo and entered politics. He was first elected to the California assembly in 1853; he won a seat in the state senate in 1858 and then won the lieutenant governorship in 1871. After serving as governor, he served two terms in the U.S. House of Representatives, between 1878 and 1882.

Gómez-Quiñones, *Roots of Chicano Politics, 1600–1940*, p. 256; Meier and Rivera, *Dictionary of Mexican American History*, p. 268.

1875 • Casimiro Barela was the only Hispanic elected as a delegate to the state constitutional convention of Colorado. Barela secured a provision in the state constitution protecting the civil rights of the Spanish- speaking citizens as well as a rule providing for the publication of laws in Spanish, English, and German. The state constitution was written and published in both languages. In 1876, he was elected a state senator from Colorado; he served until 1916.

A native of New Mexico whose family had moved to Colorado in 1867, Barela held various other elected posts before becoming a state senator. While serving in politics, he kept up his interests in banking and other businesses and became one of the wealthiest men in the state.

Gómez-Quiñones, *Roots of Chicano Politics, 1600–1940*, pp. 265–66; Kanellos, *The Hispanic American Almanac*, p. 278.

1875 • Four years after Tucson was incorporated as a city (in 1871), its first Hispanic mayor was elected. Estevan Ochoa (1831–1888), a wealthy freighter, was the only Mexican mayor of Tucson elected following the Gadsden Purchase in 1854.

From a wealthy Chihuahua family, Ochoa became a loyal American, so loyal in fact that he fiercely opposed the Confederacy. He grew up learning the freighting business and developing bilingual-bicultural skills that allowed him to prosper in business both in the United States and Mexico as well as to win the confidence of both the Anglo and Mexican electorates in Tucson. During the 1860s and 1870s, he served in the territorial legislature and on the city council.

See also Business and Commerce, 1875 and 1879; Education, 1872.

Gómez-Quiñones, *Roots of Chicano Politics, 1600–1940*, p. 268.

1877 • Romualdo Pacheco became the first Hispanic regular member of the U.S. House of Representatives and served until 1882. Elected as a Republican, Pacheco's Democratic opponent contested the election and was seated in his place on February 7, 1878. Pacheco again ran for the position in 1878 and was elected again; this time, he served out his term and another full term until 1833. In 1890, he was named minister plenipotentiary to Central America by President Benjamin Harrison.

Dictionary of the United States Congress, p. 1418.

1890 • Félix Martínez Jr. founded the first Hispanic third party in U.S. history. The New Mexico businessman and newspaper publisher, after breaking with the Democratic Party, ran in 1890 and 1892 as a candidate of El Partido del Pueblo Unido (The United People's Party) and won a seat on the territorial council in the second election. In addition, the party swept all offices in San Miguel County in 1890. The principal issues of the party were land tenure and the common people's mistreatment by the dominant political leaders, both Anglo and Mexican.

In 1899, Martínez moved to El Paso, Texas, where he furthered his business and publishing interests and was later appointed by President William Howard Taft as U.S. Commissioner General to South America.

See also Government: The Civil Rights Struggle, 1889.

Gómez-Quiñones, *Roots of Chicano Politics, 1600–1940,* p. 281; Meier and Rivera, *Dictionary of Mexican American History,* pp. 213–14, 270.

1897 • President William McKinley's appointment made Miguel A. Otero Jr. (1859–1944) the youngest and only Hispanic governor of the New Mexico Territory. He served until January 1907. In 1917, Otero was appointed U.S. marshall of the Panama Canal Zone by President Woodrow Wilson.

Otero was a politician and businessman born in Albuquerque, New Mexico, into the distinguished family of his father and namesake, Miguel A. Otero Sr., an outstanding business and political figure. Educated in Saint Louis, Annapolis, and at Notre Dame University, the younger Otero developed his business acumen in the offices of his father's company, Otero, Sellar & Company, which served him well when he took the major role in the firm after his father's death.

With significant business interests in mining, ranching, real estate, and banking, Otero entered politics as a Republican. During the course of his early career, he held various elected and appointed positions and was even a candidate for the Republican vice presidential nomination in 1894. In 1897, Otero was appointed by President William McKinley to the governorship of the New Mexico Territory. Because he opposed President Theodore Roosevelt's National Forest Project, Otero was not reappointed to a second term as governor.

At this point, Otero switched to the Democratic Party. Under President Woodrow Wilson, Otero was appointed U.S. marshall of the Panama Canal Zone in 1917. Otero remained active in politics in the 1920s. He also found time during his busy career to author various memoirs of historical value: *My Life on the Frontier, 1864–1882* (1935), *My Life on the Frontier, 1882–1897* (1939), and *My Nine Years as Governor of the Territory of New Mexico, 1897–1906* (1940). Four years after the publication of his last book, Otero died in Albuquerque, at the age of eighty-four.

Kanellos *Chronology of Hispanic American History,* p. 103–104; Meier and Rivera, *Dictionary of Mexican American History,* pp. 267–68.

1913 · Ladislao Lázaro (1872–1927) became Louisiana's first Hispanic congressman. A medical doctor, Lázaro had served in the Louisiana state senate from 1908 to 1912. Lázaro served eight successive terms in the U.S. Congress, until his death in 1927.

Dictionary of the United States Congress, p. 882.

LADISLAO LÁZARO.

1916 ◆ Ezequiel Cabeza de Vaca became the first Mexican American governor of the State of New Mexico.

Kanellos, *Chronology of Hispanic American History,* p. 174.

1923 ◆ Soledad C. Chacón became the first Hispanic woman to win a state office; the Mexican American was elected New Mexico's secretary of state.

OCTAVIANO LARRAZOLO.

In the 1930s, she was followed in that office by other women: Marguerita Baca and Elizabeth González.

Gómez-Quiñones, *Roots of Chicano Politics, 1600–1940,* p. 358.

1928 • Octaviano Larrazolo (1859–1930) was the first Hispanic to become a U. S. senator. The native of Allende, Chihuahua, Mexico, was elected to complete the term of A. A. Jones, a New Mexico senator who died in office. Larrazolo graduated from Saint Michael's College in Arizona and had worked as a teacher and principal of an elementary school in Texas when he was appointed in 1885 as clerk of the U.S. District and Circuit Courts in El Paso. In Texas, he was also elected district attorney twice and served on the school board. He was an early, strong advocate for Mexican American civil rights.

Larrazolo's political career rose and, after moving to New Mexico in 1895, continued until he became governor of the state and a U.S. congressman in 1927. Larrazolo is said to have been a gifted orator in both English and Spanish. Larrazolo was elected to the U.S. Senate again in 1929, but did not complete the term because of poor health.

Córdova and Judah, *Octaviano Larrazolo,* pp. 16–21, 22–28; Gómez-Quiñones, *Roots of Chicano Politics, 1600–1940,* pp. 330–31; Rosales, *Chicano! History of the Mexican American Civil Rights Movement,* p. 109.

1932 • Benjamin Nathan Cardozo (1887–1938), of the famed Sephardic Jewish family which dated back to colonial days, was the first Hispanic named to the Supreme Court of the United States.

Born in New York City, Cardozo received his legal training at Columbia University. He was elected judge of the New York Supreme Court in 1914 and in 1915 became an associate justice of the New York Court of Appeals. He became chief justice of that court in 1927. Cardozo was named by President Franklin Delano Roosevelt to the United States Supreme Court in 1932.

Cardozo became known as the most influential liberal justice of his times. Part of his reputation came from his opinions on legal questions, especially those dealing with public welfare and Roosevelt's New Deal. One of his most noteworthy opinions was that upholding the Social Security Act. Many of Cardozo's ideas were fully expressed in his writings. He was the author of such important books as *The Nature of the Judicial Process* (1921), *The Growth of the Law* (1924), and *The Paradoxes of Legal Science* (1928).

Encarta '95 Encyclopedia.

1935 • Dennis Chávez (1888–1962) became the first Hispanic elected to the United States Senate. Born to a poor family in a village to the west of Albuquerque, New Mexico, Chávez attended school in Albuquerque, but was forced to drop out of school to work. Chávez continued his education on his own and eventually enrolled in law school; he graduated with a law degree from Georgetown University in 1920. He returned to New Mexico, established a private practice, and ran for office.

In 1930, he won a seat in the House of Representatives; that was followed by his election to the Senate in 1935, where the Democrat was a

staunch supporter of education and civil rights. In all, Chávez was elected
to the Senate five times.

Kanellos, *The Hispanic American Almanac,* p. 269.

1946 ⋆ Jesús T. Piñero became the first native Puerto Rican to be appointed governor of Puerto Rico. He was appointed by President Harry S Truman.

Kanellos, *Chronology of Hispanic American History,* pp. 224–25.

DENNIS CHÁVEZ.

1946 • Felisa Rincón de Gautier became the first woman to serve as mayor of San Juan, the capital of Puerto Rico. If Puerto Rico, which was under American rule, is considered part of the United States, then she was the first female mayor of a major American city. As mayor, Rincón de Gautier was a populist who opened the doors of city government to the people. She was so beloved that she served until 1969 and was named one of the one hundred outstanding women of the world.

Hispanics in U.S. History, p. 46.

1949 • The first native governor of Puerto Rico under American rule was Luis Muñoz Marín (1898–1980). Muñoz Marín received his early education on the island and then attended Georgetown University, where he studied journalism and also earned a degree in law. Besides developing his career as a politician, Muñoz Marín worked as a journalist, serving as publisher of the *Revista de Indians* (Review of the Indies) and editor of various newspapers, including *EL Imparcial* (The Imparcial), *El Batey* (The Beaten Ground), and *La Democracia* (Democracy).

GOVERNOR LUIS
MUÑOZ MARÍN.

Muñoz Marín also served as secretary to the resident commissioner for Puerto Rico in Washington, D.C. (1916–1918). He was a labor organizer, served in the secretariat of the Pan American Union, was first elected to the Puerto Rican senate in 1932, and founded the Popular Democratic Party in 1940. In 1941, he was elected president of the senate. He served as the first governor of Puerto Rico from 1949 to 1965 and was one of the principal architects of the Commonwealth of Puerto Rico, a political and governmental organization that established Puerto Rico as a Free Associated State of the United States—a contradiction in terms that really was a liberal definition of a colony. He was also a chief architect of Operation Bootstrap, a program that offered tax incentives for American industries to locate in Puerto Rico and thus contribute to the economic development of the island.

Muñoz spearheaded many reforms and programs that improved the economy, the transportation infrastructure, and the educational and health delivery systems in Puerto Rico. One constant criticism, however, has been that much of the success of his programs and the improvement of the Puerto Rican economy has come at the high cost of shifting its working-class population to the urban centers of the United States, most notably New York City and surrounding areas.

Muñoz Marín died of a heart attack on April 30, 1980.

Kanellos, *Chronology of Hispanic American History,* pp. 212–28; Muñoz Marín, *Memorias: Autobiografía pública.*

1949 • Edward R. Roybal (1915–) became the first Mexican American to be elected to the Los Angeles City Council since 1881. A representative from East Los Angeles, his election was very much a part of the effort by returning Mexican American veterans of World War II to get representation.

Born into a middle-class Mexican American family in Albuquerque, New Mexico, Roybal began his education in the Los Angeles public schools after his parents moved there. After attending the University of California and Southwestern University, Roybal became a health care educator in the 1930s. He served in World War II and has returned to Los Angeles to continue his profession, when a group of Mexican American citizens approached him about running for city council. He was successful on his second attempt.

See also Government: The Civil Rights Struggle, 1949.

Kanellos, *Chronology of Hispanic American History,* pp. 174, 245; Rosales, *Chicano! History of the Mexican American Civil Rights Movement,* p. 106.

1951 • President Harry S Truman appointed the first Hispanic to the U.S. Court of Appeals for the Second Circuit—Judge Harold R. Medina Sr. (1888–1991). Born in Brooklyn, New York, of Mexican American and Dutch American parents, Medina graduated from Princeton University with honors in 1909 and received his law degree from Columbia University Law School in 1912. In 1918, Medina formed his own law firm and specialized in appeals. The most famous case argued by Medina was the Cramer treason case during World War II. Medina won the case on appeal to the U.S. Supreme Court. After World War II, Medina was appointed to the U.S. District Court for the District of New York.

Kanellos, *Hispanic American Almanac,* p. 253.

1951 • Adam Díaz became the first Mexican American to serve on the Phoenix, Arizona, City Council.

Rosales, *Chicano! History of the Mexican American Civil Rights Movement,* p. 106.

1954 • The first Hispanic appointed to the Democratic National Committee was Dr. Héctor García Pérez (1914–).

Kanellos, *Chronology of Hispanic American History,* pp. 169, 248.

1956 • San Antonio native Henry B. González (1916–) became the first Mexican American to be elected to the Texas state senate in 110 years. Similar to his previous advocacy on the San Antonio City Council, González was a champion of civil rights for minorities.

González was born in San Antonio into a family of refugees from the Mexican Revolution who stressed education and intellectual pursuits. After graduating from the University of Texas, González went on to get his law degree from Saint Mary's University in San Antonio in 1943. His first elected office was that of city councilman in 1953.

Meier and Rivera, *Dictionary of Mexican American History,* p. 148; Rodríguez, *Henry B. González;* Rosales, *Chicano! History of the Mexican American Civil Rights Movement,* p. 107.

HENRY B. GONZÁLEZ.

1957 • One of the most significant electoral gains for Mexican Americans was the election of Raymond Telles as mayor of El Paso, Texas. Telles had served as El Paso county clerk since 1948. Telles's election signified that Mexican Americans could vote as a bloc if the candidate was one of their own. Although more than half of El Paso's population was Mexican American, low voter registration meant that Telles had to carry a sizable percentage of the white vote, which he did by carrying on a campaign that minimized racial and ethnic differences.

Rosales, *Chicano! History of the Mexican American Civil Rights Movement,* p. 107.

1961 • President John F. Kennedy appointed the first Hispanic judge to the U.S. District Court for the Southern District of Texas. Judge Reynaldo G. Garza (1915–), the son of Mexican immigrants, was born in Brownsville, Texas, and attended the University of Texas, where he received his law degree in 1901. In 1974, he became the chief judge of the U.S. District Court of the Southern District of Texas.

Kanellos, *The Hispanic American Almanac,* p. 252.

1961 • Henry B. González was elected to the U.S. Congress, becoming the first Texan of Mexican American descent to serve in the U.S. House of Representatives. He has served there ever since, becoming one of the longest tenured representatives in U.S. history. He has been a staunch protector of civil rights, adequate housing, and adult education, among many other causes.

Kanellos, *The Hispanic American Almanac,* p. 262.

1961 • Teodoro Moscoso became the first Puerto Rican to be appointed an ambassador of the United States. President John F. Kennedy named the former pharmacist to the post of ambassador to Venezuela on March 29, 1961. Moscoso only served for a few months. Based on his success in Venezuela, President Kennedy named him to the position of coordinator for the Alliance for Progress, a ten-year, multibillion-dollar cooperative enterprise for the social and economic development of Latin America.

Moscoso was born to Puerto Rican parents in Barcelona, Spain, but grew up in Ponce, Puerto Rico, where he followed in his father's footsteps to run the family pharmacy. He found his way into politics in Puerto Rico, where he distinguished himself in the economic development program known as Operation Bootstrap.

EDWARD R. ROYBAL.

Charles Moritz, *Current Biography Yearbook, 1963,* pp. 283–85.

1962 • Edward R. Roybal became the first Mexican American from the Twenty-fifth District of California elected to the U.S. Congress, where he served for more than three decades. During his tenure in Congress, Roybal worked for social and economic reform. In 1967, he introduced legislation that became the first bilingual education act. In 1982, as chairman of the Congressional Hispanic Caucus, he led the opposition to sanctions against employers for hiring undocumented workers, which ultimately was enacted as the Immigration Reform and Control Act of 1986.

Kanellos, *The Hispanic American Almanac,* p. 264–65.

1964 • Governor Edmund G. Brown appointed the first Mexican judge, Philip Newman (1916–) to a Los Angeles municipal judgeship, where he remained until his retirement in 1982. Newman's family fled Mexico during the Mexican Revolution; his father went to night school and became a lawyer. His son followed in his footsteps.

Kanellos, *The Hispanic American Almanac*, p. 254.

1967 • Dr. Héctor Pérez García became the first Hispanic to become an alternate delegate to the United Nations with the rank of ambassador. He was appointed by President Lyndon B. Johnson.

Alex Avila, "Freedom Fighter: Dr. Héctor P. García, Founder of the American G.I. Forum," *Hispanic*, January/February 1996, pp. 18–22; Kanellos, *Chronology of Hispanic American History*, pp. 169, 248.

1968 • The National Council of La Raza (formerly Southwest Council of La Raza) was founded as an umbrella organization working for civil rights and economic opportunities for Hispanics. The council provides technical assistance to community-based organizations and lobbies on behalf of Hispanic civil rights and for economic opportunities for Hispanics.

Furtaw, *Hispanic Americans Information Directory*, p. 29.

1969 • Under the sponsorship of Congressman Edward Roybal, the first cabinet-level committee on opportunities for Spanish-speaking people was founded.

Meier and Rivera, *Dictionary of Mexican American History*, p. 309.

HERMAN BADILLO

1970 • Herman Badillo (1929–) became the first Puerto Rican ever elected as a voting member of Congress. Orphaned in Puerto Rico, he was sent to New York to live with relatives in 1940. He acquired all of his education in city schools, earning his bachelor's degree at City College and his law degree at Brooklyn Law School. Badillo entered politics in 1961, losing in a run for state assembly. He later made a strong showing in a race for mayor and finally became a congressman in 1970, eventually serving four terms.

Kanellos, *The Hispanic American Almanac*, pp. 265–66.

1970 • José Angel Gutiérrez (1944–) and others founded the first successful third party in Texas, La Raza Unida (The United Race), which was also the first Mexican American political party in Texas. He and two other Chicanos were elected to the Crystal City city council. In 1974, Gutiérrez was elected judge of Zavala County, a position from which he resigned in 1981. La Raza Unida won some initial victories, especially in Texas towns and counties densely populated with Mexican Americans, but by the 1980s much of its pioneering reforms were absorbed by the Democratic Party, which finally became more open to Mexican Americans in Texas and other southwestern states.

Meier and Rivera, *Dictionary of Mexican American History,* pp. 157–58, 294–96; Pendas and Ring, *Toward Chicano Power.*

1970 • Hispanic voters won their first write-in campaign when La Raza Unida Party was denied access to the La Salle County, Texas, ballot. La Raza Unida Party candidate Roel Rodríguez was elected county commissioner.

Meier and Rivera, *Dictionary of Mexican American History,* p. 294.

1971 • Phillip V. Sánchez (1929–), the son of Mexican immigrants, became the first Hispanic to direct the Office of Economic opportunity. He was appointed by President Richard M. Nixon.

Meier and Rivera, *Dictionary of Mexican American History,* p. 318.

1971 • Henry G. Cisneros (1947–), the future mayor of San Antonio, became the youngest White House fellow in history. A San Antonio native, Cisneros received a B.A. and an M.A. in urban planning just prior to serving as a fellow. When his fellowship year terminated, Cisneros earned a second M.A. in public administration at Harvard University. He then went on to earn a Ph.D. in public administration at George Washington University.

See also Government: Politics, 1981, 1992, 1993.

Kanellos, *The Hispanic American Almanac,* p. 279.

1971 • The first National Council of La Raza Women conference was held in San Antonio, Texas, with six hundred delegates attending.

Griswold et al., *Chicano Art,* p. 216.

1972 • Ramona Acosta Bañuelos (1925–) became the first Hispanic treasurer of the United States. Born in Miami, Arizona, Bañuelos was forcefully deported with her parents during the Depression. In 1944, she resettled in Los Angeles and soon thereafter founded a tortilla factory. By 1969, she was named Outstanding Businesswoman of the Year in Los Angeles. She was sworn in as treasurer on December 17, 1971.

Meier and Rivera, *Dictionary of Mexican American History,* p. 33.

1972 • Roberto Mondragón (1940–) became the first Hispanic vice chairman of the Democratic National Committee. Born in La Loma, New Mexico, Mondragón had served in his state senate and as lieutenant governor of New Mexico.

Meier and Rivera, *Dictionary of Mexican American History,* p. 236–37.

1972 • La Raza Unida Party candidate gubernatorial candidate, Ramsey Muñiz, won 6 percent of the total votes, causing the first election of a Texas governor, Dolph Briscoe, by less than a majority vote.

Meier and Rivera, *Dictionary of Mexican American History,* p. 295.

1972 • The Cuban American Legal Defense and Education Fund was founded to ensure equal opportunity and legal treatment for Cuban Americans and Hispanics in the fields of education, employment, housing, politics, and justice.

Furtaw, *Hispanic Americans Information Directory,* p. 11.

1972 • The Puerto Rican Legal Defense and Education Fund was founded to protect and promote the civil rights of Puerto Ricans and other Latinos and to increase the number of minority lawyers who can serve their communities.

Furtaw, *Hispanic Americans Information Directory,* p. 38.

1973 • Puerto Rican Maurice Ferré (1935–) became the first Hispanic mayor of Miami. His election as mayor was a sign of the emergence of a Latino voting bloc in Miami. Ferré was reelected five times but ultimately lost in 1985 to a Cuba-born candidate. During his tenure he presided over the city's growth as an important center of international trade and banking.

The wealthy businessman's electoral career had started in the mid-1960s with his election to the Miami City Council; he later served in the state legislature.

Henderson and Mormino, *Spanish Pathways in Florida,* pp. 305, 308, 310–15.

1973 • By this date there were sufficient numbers of Mexican Americans in command executive positions in police forces to merit the founding of the Mexican American Police Command Officers Association. In 1984, the organization became national and changed its name to Hispanic American Police Command Officers Association. It is the oldest advocacy group for Hispanic executives in law enforcement and criminal justice.

Hispanic, January/February 1996, p. 88.

1974 • Jerry Apodaca (1934–) became the first Hispanic governor of New Mexico in fifty years. After his term as governor, President Jimmy Carter appointed him chairman of the President's Council on Physical Fitness and Sports. Born and raised in Las Cruces, Apodaca entered politics in 1966 as a Democratic state senator.

Kanellos, *The Hispanic American Almanac,* pp. 277–78.

1974 • President Gerald Ford appointed the first Hispanic special assistant to the president, Fernando E. Cabeza de Baca (1937–) of New Mexico. In the 1960s and 1970s, Cabeza de Baca held high-ranking positions with the New Mexico Department of Transportation, the Civil Service Commission and the Department of Health, Education, and Welfare. When Ford selected him for special assistant, Cabeza de Baca was serving as the chairman of the Federal Regional Council for the Western States.

Kanellos, *The Hispanic American Almanac,* pp. 276–77.

1975 • Raúl Castro (1916–) became the first Hispanic governor of Arizona. Born on June 12, 1916, in Cananea, Mexico, he moved as a child with his poverty-stricken parents to Pertleville, Arizona, where he became the family's wage earner after his father died. Despite working as a migrant laborer, miner, and rancher, he was able to earn a degree from Arizona State College in 1939 and went to Washington, D.C., to work for the State Department. He returned to Arizona in 1946 and earned a law degree from the University of Arizona in 1949.

He entered politics and served in various elected positions. In 1964, he was appointed ambassador to El Salvador and, in 1968, ambassador to Bolivia. He ran unsuccessfully for governor in 1970 but was victorious in 1974. In 1977, he resigned from his office to serve as ambassador to Argentina.

Meier and Rivera, *Dictionary of Mexican American History,* pp. 72–73; Unterburger, *Who's Who among Hispanic Americans.*

1976 • Judge Luis Rovirá became the first Hispanic appointed to the Colorado Supreme Court. Born in San Juan, Puerto Rico, in 1923, Rovirá obtained his bachelor's and law degrees from the University of Colorado.

Kanellos, *The Hispanic American Almanac,* p. 256.

1976 • Largely through the efforts of New York congressman Herman Badillo, the Congressional Hispanic Caucus was organized. This signified that for the first time there were enough Hispanic congressional representatives to have a caucus—a total of five. The caucus is dedicated to voicing and advancing, through the legislative process, issues affecting Hispanic Americans in the United States and its territories.

Enciso et al., *The History of the Congressional Hispanic Caucus,* p. 7.

1977 • Mari-Luci Jaramillo (1928–) became the first Hispanic woman to be named an ambassador. The native of Las Vegas, New Mexico, and education professor at the University of New Mexico was appointed by President Jimmy Carter as ambassador to Honduras.

MARI-LUCI JARAMILLO.

Born into a poor family in Las Vegas, New Mexico, on June 19, 1928, Jaramillo became an outstanding student but went on to receive a college education only after her three children were old enough to allow her to continue studying. She also held jobs while studying and raising a family.

In 1955, Jaramillo obtained her degree in education from New Mexico Highlands University and became a teacher. She later worked her way up into university teaching, and through her involvement in international education, she came to the attention of President Jimmy Carter, who named her to an ambassadorship. In 1990, the Mexican American Women's National Association honored her with the Primera Award as the first Hispanic woman to be appointed an ambassador.

Meier and Rivera, *Dictionary of Mexican American History,* p. 176; Telgen and Kamp, *Latinas! Women of Achievement,* pp. 210–15.

1977 • Leonel Castillo (1939–) became the first Hispanic to direct the U.S. Immigration and Naturalization Service. Born in Victoria, Texas, Castillo received his B.A. from Saint Mary's University in San Antonio and his M.S.W. from the University of Pittsburgh in 1967. After graduating from Saint Mary's in 1961, Castillo served in the Peace Corps in the Philippines from 1961 to 1965. After the Peace Corps, Castillo returned to Houston and, in 1970, won a surprise victory in the race for city comptroller against a twenty-five-year incumbent. In 1974, he was named treasurer of the Texas Democratic Party.

Kanellos, *The Hispanic American Almanac,* p. 276; Meier and Rivera, *Dictionary of Mexican American History,* p. 72.

1977 • Lawyer Grace Olivárez was the first Hispanic to serve as director of the Community Services Administration, under President Jimmy Carter. She was the highest-ranking Hispanic female in the Carter administration.

Telgen and Kamp, *Latinas! Women of Achievement,* p. 288.

1977 • The Congressional Hispanic Caucus was founded. The privately funded caucus brings attention to all governmental issues of concern to Hispanics.

Kanellos, *Chronology of Hispanic American History,* p. 261.

1977 • The Hispanic political party, La Raza Unida, scored its first victory outside of its Mexican American power base with the election of candidate Frank Shaffer-Corona to the District of Columbia school board.

Meier and Rivera, *Dictionary of Mexican American History,* p. 295.

1978 • Congressman Herman Badillo of New York resigned his congressional seat to become the first Puerto Rican appointed as deputy mayor of New York City, under Mayor Edward Koch.

Kanellos, *The Hispanic American Almanac,* pp. 265–66.

1978 • U.S. Congressman Eligio "Kika" de la Garza became the first Mexican American to receive the Aztec Eagle, the highest award given to a foreigner by the Mexican government. De la Garza was born in Mercedes, Texas, in 1927 and went on to serve in the U.S. Congress from 1964 to 1980.

Meier and Rivera, *Dictionary of Mexican American History,* p. 117.

1978 • Polly Baca-Barragán became the first Hispanic woman elected to the Colorado state senate. Born in LaSalle, Colorado, in 1941, Baca-Barragán was director of Spanish Speaking Affairs for the Democratic National Committee from 1971 to 1972. In 1974, she was elected to the Colorado legislature. She was elected to the state senate in 1978 and was reelected in 1982.

Kanellos, *The Hispanic American Almanac,* p. 278.

HISPANIC JUDGES IN STATE COURTS

COURT	HIGHEST (A)	INTERM (B)	TRIAL (C)	MUNICIPAL (D)	MAGISTRATE/JOP (E)	OTHER (F)
AL	0	0	1	0	0	0
AK	0	0	1	0	0	0
AZ	0	20	42	18	19	0
CA	0	30	86	41	0	9
CO	1	1	14	3	0	1
DC	0	0	3	0	0	0
FL	0	0	25	0	0	0
HI	0	0	1	0	0	0
IL	0	0	16	0	0	0
IN	0	0	2	0	0	0
KS	0	0	1	0	0	0
LA	0	0	4	0	0	0
MD	0	0	1	0	0	0
MI	1	0	2	0	0	1
MN	0	0	2	0	0	0
MO	0	0	1	0	0	0
MT	0	0	1	0	1	0
NV	0	0	7	0	2	0
NJ	0	0	13	5	0	0
NM	1	4	86	35	18	1
NY	0	1	25	11	0	0
OH	0	0	2	0	0	0
OR	0	0	1	0	0	0
PA	0	0	2	0	0	0
TX	2	3	280	93	114	0
UT	0	0	1	0	0	0
VA	0	0	1	0	0	0
WA	0	0	4	0	0	0
TOTAL	**5**	**14**	**625**	**206**	**154**	**12**

Source: Hispanic National Bar Association Nationwide Summary of Hispanics in the State Judiciary (1992). This summary excludes judges sitting in Puerto Rico courts.

A. Judges in state courts of last resort; in most states, such courts are called supreme courts
B. State appellate or intermediate court judges
C. State judges in trial courts or general jurisdiction
D. Municipal or metropolitan court judges
E. Local magistrates, or justices of the peace

1978 • La Raza Unida Party's gubernatorial candidate, Mario Compeán, polled 2 percent of the vote, thus influencing the election of the first Republican governor in Texas in more than one hundred years.

Meier and Rivera, *Dictionary of Mexican American History,* p. 295.

1978 • The Hispanic National Bar Association was founded.

Hispanic Business, September 1996, p. 68.

1979 • President Jimmy Carter appointed the first native Puerto Rican, José A. Cabranés (1940–), to the federal court within the continental United States. Born in Mayagüez, Puerto Rico, Cabranés moved as a child with his family to New York City. He attended public schools and graduated from Columbia College in 1961 and from the Yale University Law School in 1965; he received his LL.M. degree from the University of Cambridge in England in 1967.

Cabranés practiced law and also taught at Rutgers University Law School in New Jersey. He served on the President's Commission on Mental Health from 1977 to 1978 and in a variety of other governmental advisory positions. In 1979, President Carter appointed Cabranés to the U.S. District Court for the District of Connecticut.

In 1988, U.S. Supreme Court Chief Justice William H. Renquist named Judge Cabranés as one of five federal judges for the fifteen-member Federal Court Study Committee, created by an act of Congress "to examine problems facing the federal courts and develop a long-range plan for the future of the federal judiciary."

Kanellos, *The Hispanic American Almanac,* pp. 250–51.

1979 • President Jimmy Carter appointed the first Hispanic judge to the U.S. Court of Appeals for the Fifth District, Judge Reynaldo G. Garza, who was also the first Mexican American appointed to the federal bench, in 1961.

See also Government: Politics, 1961.

Kanellos, *The Hispanic American Almanac,* p. 252.

1979 • President Jimmy Carter appointed the first Hispanic secretary of the U.S. Navy, Edward Hidalgo (1912–), a native of Mexico City.

See also The Military, 1979.

Kanellos, *The Hispanic American Almanac,* p. 277.

1980 • President Jimmy Carter named Julián Nava (1927–) U.S. ambassador to Mexico. Nava thus became the first Mexican American to serve in that position.

Born in Mexico, but raised in East Los Angeles, Nava had previously created a successful career as an educator, author, and politician. After receiving his doctorate in history from Harvard University in 1955, Nava taught at the University of Puerto Rico and later at California State College at Northridge. He served on the Los Angeles school board for various terms and wrote books on Mexican American history.

Meier and Rivera, *Dictionary of Mexican American History,* p. 252.

1980 • President Jimmy Carter appointed Hipólito Frank García (1925–) the first Hispanic to the U.S. District Court for the Western District of Texas, making him the first Hispanic to serve in that position. He served from 1964 to 1980 as a Texas county court judge. He graduated from the Saint Mary's University Law School in 1951.

Kanellos, *The Hispanic American Almanac,* p. 252.

1981 • Henry G. Cisneros (1947–) became the first modern-day Hispanic mayor of San Antonio, Texas, the nation's ninth largest city. Born in a Mexican barrio of San Antonio, the son of a civil servant, Cisneros was educated in the city's parochial schools and attended Texas Agricultural and Mechanical University, where he received a B.A. and then a master's degree in urban planning in 1970. In 1971, Cisneros moved to Washington, D.C., where he worked for the National League of Cities and began full-time graduate studies in public administration at George Washington University. At age twenty-two, Cisneros became the youngest White House Fellow in U.S. history. When his fellowship ended, he earned a second master's degree, in public administration, at Harvard University. He went on to complete his work at George Washington University and received a Ph.D. in public administration. He then returned to San Antonio to teach government at the University of Texas.

In 1975, Cisneros ran for the city council on the Good Government League ticket and won. He gained a reputation as a bright young politician, and in 1977 he was reelected by a landslide. In 1981, Cisneros was elected mayor of San Antonio with 62 percent of the vote. In 1983, he was reelected with 94 percent of the vote, again reelected in 1985 with 72 percent, and reelected in 1987 with twice as many votes as his closest opponent. Cisneros did not thereafter seek reelection as mayor.

Kanellos, *Chronology of Hispanic American History,* pp. 226, 279.

1981 • President Ronald Reagan appointed the first Hispanic deputy director of the Peace Corps, war hero Everett Alvarez Jr. (1937–). At the time he was serving in the capacity of deputy administrator of the Veterans Administration.

See also Military, 1973 and 1981.

Kanellos, *The Hispanic American Almanac,* p. 275.

1981 • Wealthy Cuban businessmen formed the first organization to influence United States policy through lobbying and financial contributions to campaigns: the Cuban American Foundation (CANF). It established its center in Washington, D.C., under the chairmanship of Jorge Mas Canosa. The CANF began influencing U.S. policy toward Cuba principally through its political action committee (PAC), Free Cuba, which donated to the campaign funds of congressmen and senators who maintained a hard line toward Castro's Cuba. The CANF also became a principal lobbyist for the establishment by the U.S. government of Radio Martí, a radio station founded to broadcast news and features to Cuba and serve as a supplement to the censored or ideologically biased transmissions that characterized the Cuban broadcast media.

García, *Havana USA*, pp. 147–48.

1982 • Cruz Reynoso (1931–) became the first Hispanic appointed to the Supreme Court of California. The Mexican American born in Brea, California, is the son of farmworker parents. He received his law degree from the University of California Law School in 1958 and immediately entered private practice. He worked in the government in the 1960s both in California and Washington, D.C. After serving as the director of the California Rural Legal Assistance program, in 1972 he accepted a teaching position at the University of New Mexico Law School. In 1976, he was appointed to the California Court of Appeals in Sacramento, and in 1982 Governor Jerry Brown appointed him to the California Supreme Court, where he served until 1986. In 1990, he was appointed to the law faculty at the University of California.

Kanellos, *The Hispanic American Almanac*, pp. 255–56.

1982 • Dorothy Comstock Riley (1924–) became the first Hispanic female state supreme court judge. Born to Hispanic parents in Detroit, Michigan, Riley attended Wayne State University, where she received both her B.A. and her law degree. After a career in private practice, including running her own firm, Riley sat on the Michigan Court of Appeals from 1976 to 1982, when she was elevated to the Michigan Supreme Court as an associate justice.

See also Government: Politics, 1987.

Kanellos, *The Hispanic American Almanac*, p. 256.

1982 • Gloria Molina (1948–) of Los Angeles became the first Hispanic woman ever to be elected to the California state legislature. She continued her political career in 1987 by being elected to the Los Angeles City Council, on which she served until she was elected to the Los Angeles County Board of Supervisors in 1991.

The daughter of Mexican immigrants, Molina grew up in the Los Angeles area. Although she became the principal provider for her family when her father became ill, she was able to finish her college education at California State College in Los Angeles.

Kanellos, *The Hispanic American Almanac*, p. 280.

1982 • The United States Hispanic Leadership Conference was founded.

Hispanic, September 1996, p. 80.

1983 • Federico Peña (1947–) became the first Hispanic mayor of Denver, Colorado, one of the nation's major cities. At age thirty-six, Pena was elected Denver's thirty-seventh mayor and was reelected to a second term in 1987. At the time he entered office, he was among the youngest chief executives in Denver history. Mayor Peña's efforts to strengthen Denver's economy placed the city in the national spotlight. The U.S. Conference of Mayors selected Denver over one hundred other cities as the winner of its prestigious City Liveability Award.

Kanellos, *Chronology of Hispanic American History,* p. 226.

1984 ⬩ President Ronald Reagan appointed the first Hispanic to the Eastern District Court of California, Edward J. García (1928–). Previously, García served as the district attorney for Sacramento County. He received his law degree from McGeorge School of Law in 1958.

Kanellos, *The Hispanic American Almanac,* p. 252.

1985 ⬩ Miami elected its first Cuba-born mayor, Xavier Suárez (1949–). By then, Hispanics controlled three of five seats on the city commission and held many of the city's most important administrative and patronage positions.

Born in Las Villas, Cuba, the son of a university professor, Suárez moved as an exile to Washington, D.C., with his family in 1961. After studying law and public policy at Harvard University, Suárez moved to Miami to become involved in politics. After unsuccessfully challenging Maurice Ferré for the office of mayor in 1983, he was finally successful by creating coalitions of blacks, Anglos, and Hispanics.

Henderson and Mormino, *Spanish Pathways in Florida,* pp. 314–22.

1985 ⬩ Mexican American Frances García became the first Hispanic woman mayor in the Midwest when she took office in Hutchinson, Kansas. Hutchinson had a population of forty-one thousand, of which only 2 percent were Hispanic.

Tardiff and Mabunda, *Dictionary of Hispanic Biography,* pp. 368–69.

1985 ⬩ New Mexican Linda Chávez became the first Hispanic to serve as director of the White House Office of Public Liaison, a position that made her the highest-ranking woman in the Reagan administration.

See also Education, 1981.

Telgen and Kamp, *Latinas! Women of Achievement,* p. 79.

1987 ⬩ Chief Justice of the U.S. Supreme Court William H. Renquist appointed Reynaldo G. Garza as the first Hispanic judge to the Temporary Emergency Court of Appeals of the United States. Garza later became the chief judge of that court.

Kanellos, *The Hispanic American Almanac,* p. 252.

1987 ⬩ Tampa native Bob Martínez became the first Catholic and first Hispanic to be elected governor of Florida.

Tardiff and Mabunda, *Dictionary of Hispanic Biography,* p. 527.

1987 ⬩ Judge Dorothy Comstock Riley, born to Hispanic parents in Detroit, Michigan, was named chief justice of the Michigan Supreme Court.

Kanellos, *The Hispanic American Almanac,* p. 256.

GOVERNOR BOB
MARTÍNEZ.

1987 ⬩ Gloria Molina became the first Mexican American woman ever elected to the Los Angeles City Council.

Tardiff and Mabunda, *Dictionary of Hispanic Biography,* p. 559.

1988 ⬩ President Ronald Reagan appointed Dr. Lauro F. Cavazos, the former president of Texas Tech University, to the cabinet post of secretary of

LINDA CHÁVEZ.

Education. He became the first Hispanic to hold the post and the first Hispanic ever to become a member of the presidential cabinet.

See also Education, 1988.

Kanellos, *The Hispanic American Almanac,* p. 277.

1989 • For the first time in history, a Cuban American was elected to the U.S. Congress. Miami's Ileana Ros-Lehtinen (1952–) was also the first Hispanic woman to become a congresswoman. Ros-Lehtinen received bachelor's and master's degrees from Florida International University in Miami and went on to teach in her own private school. In 1982, she was elected to the Florida legislature as a Republican. She was elected to the Florida state senate in 1986.

Kanellos, *The Hispanic American Almanac,* pp. 264–65; Telgen and Kamp, *Latinas! Women of Achievement,* pp. 327–31.

ILEANA ROS-LEHTINEN.

1989 • President George Bush appointed the first Hispanic secretary of the Interior, Manuel Luján Jr. The Santa Fe, New Mexico, native had served as a Republican congressman from 1969 to 1989 and, at the time of his appointment was the ranking minority member of the House Interior Committee.

Kanellos, *The Hispanic American Almanac,* p. 273.

1989 • Cari M. Domínguez (1949–) was appointed by President George Bush as the director of the Office of Federal Contract Compliance Programs of the U.S. Department of Labor. She was the first Hispanic to hold this position. As the director, she is responsible for enforcement of federal mandates prohibiting discrimination and requiring affirmative action in the employment and advancement of the persons with disabilities, women, minorities, and veterans.

Domínguez had joined the Office of Federal Contract Compliance Programs in 1974, but had left in 1984 to become a vice president of a bank in San Francisco.

Kanellos, *The Hispanic American Almanac,* p. 272.

1989 • The first Hispanic to be appointed chief of police of a major metropolitan police department was Philip Arreola when he assumed the leadership of the Milwaukee Police Department.

Born on February 4, 1940, in Acambaro, Guanajuato, Mexico, Arreola had previously served as chief of the Port Huron Police Department in Michigan. Arreola's education includes a bachelor of science (cum laude) degree and a law degree from Wayne State University, conferred in 1974 and 1985, respectively. He is also a graduate of the FBI National Academy (1977) and was a fellow of the Harvard University School of Law (1970–71).

Kanellos, *The Hispanic American Almanac,* p. 718.

1989 • Raymond E. Orozco became the first fire commissioner of a major metropolitan fire department when he assumed the leadership of the Chica-

RAYMOND OROZCO.

go Fire Department. Born in Chicago, Illinois, on December 7, 1933, Orozco rose through the ranks to become chief.

Kanellos, *The Hispanic American Almanac,* p. 732.

1990 ‣ Ecuadoran American lawyer Lourdes Baird became U.S. attorney for the Central District of California, the largest federal district in the nation. In that position she would oversee the work of 150 attorneys.

Born on May 12, 1935, in Quito, Ecuador, Baird was educated in a Catholic school for girls in Los Angeles. She married a businessman and raised children, becoming a lawyer later in life, in 1977. By 1986, she had become a judge in East Los Angeles Municipal Court. She became a Los Angeles Superior Court judge in 1988 until her appointment as U.S. attorney.

ANTONIA C. NOVELLO.

Tardiff and Mabunda, *Dictionary of Hispanic Biography,* pp. 85–86; Telgen and Kamp, *Latinas! Women of Achievement,* pp. 45–50.

1990 ‣ President George Bush appointed the first woman and the first Hispanic Surgeon General of the United States, Antonia C. Novello (1944–). Born in Fajardo, Puerto Rico, Novello received her B.A. (1965) and M.D. (1970) degrees from the University of Puerto Rico. She received a master's degree in public health from Johns Hopkins University in 1982. Novello joined the U.S. Public Health Service in 1978 and served in various capacities at the National Institutes of Health, including serving as deputy director of the National Institute of Child Health and Human Development.

Kanellos, *The Hispanic American Almanac,* p. 274.

1990 • Judge Luis Rovirá became the first Hispanic to serve as chief justice of the Colorado Supreme Court.

Kanellos, *The Hispanic American Almanac,* p. 256.

1990 • Governor James Florio of New Jersey appointed the first Hispanic to the cabinet post of public advocate and public defender, Wilfredo Caraballo (1947–). Caraballo was born in Yabucoa, Puerto Rico, and grew up in New York City, where he received a law degree from New York University in 1974. He then rose to the position of associate dean at Seton Hall Law School in New Jersey.

Kanellos, *The Hispanic American Almanac,* p. 242.

1990 • President George Bush appointed the first Hispanic assistant attorney general of the United States, Jimmy Gurulé of Utah. Before joining the Department of Justice, Gurulé was an associate professor of law at Notre Dame University Law School and was a former president of the Hispanic National Bar Association. He became the highest-ranking Hispanic in the history of the Department of Justice.

Kanellos, *The Hispanic American Almanac,* pp. 272–73.

1990 • Ana Sol Gutiérrez became the first Hispanic ever to win an elected position in the state of Maryland. The native of El Salvador ran successfully for a seat on the Board of Education of Montgomery County, one of Maryland's most affluent counties.

Kanellos, *The Hispanic American Almanac,* pp. 279–80.

1991 • Gloria Molina became the first woman ever elected to the Los Angeles County Board of Supervisors. She was the first Hispanic since 1875 to serve in that position.

Tardiff and Mabunda, *Dictionary of Hispanic Biography*, p. 560.

1991 • Leo M. Romero (1943–) became the first Hispanic dean of a law school in the United States. He has taught law at Dickinson University Law School, the University of Oregon Law School, and the University of New Mexico Law School, where he is dean. He received his law degree from Washington University Law School in Saint Louis and his LL.M. from Georgetown University Law School in Washington, D.C.

Kanellos, *The Hispanic American Almanac,* p. 244.

ED PASTOR.

1991 • Ed Pastor (1943–) became Arizona's first Hispanic congressman when he was appointed and then elected to fill the House seat vacated by Morris K. Udall. The former chemistry teacher and lawyer began his political career when elected to the Maricopa County board of supervisors in 1977. The only Democratic district in Arizona, represented by Pastor, is 45 percent Hispanic.

"New Members, New Districts," *Congressional Quarterly,* 50/14 (7 November 1992), p. 52.

1991 • President George Bush appointed the first Hispanic director of the Office of National Drug Control Policy, Robert Martínez (1934–), the former governor of Florida. The Tampa native was elected governor in 1988, and during his tenure as governor, President Ronald Reagan named Martínez to the White House Conference on a Drug-Free America.

Kanellos, *The Hispanic American Almanac,* p. 274.

1992 • Henry Bonilla was the first Hispanic from Texas to be elected as a Republican to the U.S. Congress. The San Antonio native had previously spent most of his career in television news when he was elected to represent Texas's Twenty-third District, the largest in Texas, accounting for more than 22 percent of the total square miles of the state and larger than every state east of the Mississippi. Bonilla's tenure has been marked by awards from health and small business organizations, such as the U.S. Chamber of Commerce (1996), the National Association of Community Health Centers (1995), and the American Heart Association of Texas (1994), for his protection of their interests.

HENRY BONILLA.

1992 • Henry G. Cisneros was named by President Bill Clinton to the cabinet position of secretary of Housing and Urban Development and became the first Hispanic to hold that post.

Kanellos, *Chronology of Hispanic American History,* p. 279.

1992 • Federico Peña was named by President Bill Clinton to the cabinet position of secretary of Transportation, and became the first Hispanic to hold that post.

Kanellos, *Chronology of Hispanic American History,* p. 279.

1992 • Brooklyn's Nydia Margarita Velázquez (1953–) became the first Puerto Rican woman and the second Hispanic woman to be elected to the U.S. Congress. Born and raised in Puerto Rico, Velázquez received her B.A. from the University of Puerto Rico and her M.A. in political science from New York University. From 1984 to 1986, Velázquez served on the New York City Council. In 1986, she became the director of the Migration Division of the Commonwealth of Puerto Rico.

NYDIA VELÁSQUEZ.

"Loyalty and Labor: Nydia Margarita Velázquez," *New York Times,* 16 September 1992, p. B6; Tardiff and Mabunda, *Dictionary of Hispanic Biography,* pp. 939–42.

1992 • Lucille Roybal-Allard became the first Mexican American woman to be elected to the U.S. House of Representatives, representing Los Angeles's Thirty-third Congressional District, which was previously represented by her father, Edward Roybal.

Telgen and Kamp, *Latinas! Women of Achievement,* pp. 333–37.

1992 • Aeronautical engineer Ana Sol Gutiérrez became the first Hispanic elected to a board of education in the state of Maryland and the first Salvadoran American ever elected to a public office in the United States.

LUCILLE ROYBAL-ALLARD.   Tardiff and Mabunda, *Dictionary of Hispanic Biography,* p. 410.

1993 • At the 103rd Congress, there were more Hispanic representatives than ever before in history. There were eight new Hispanic members of the House of Representatives, for a total of seventeen. In addition, there were two nonvoting members from Puerto Rico and one from the Virgin Islands.

1994 • Judge Sylvia García became the first Hispanic female judge to direct a major municipal court system. She serves as director and presiding judge of the Houston Municipal Courts. Born on September 6, 1950, in San Diego, Texas, García received her law degree from the Thurgood Marshall School of Law at Texas Southern University. García is active in many Hispanic and women's organizations in Texas.

Texas Hispanic, 5/26 (1995), p. 53.

1994 • Nora Linares was the first Hispanic to direct a state lottery when she became executive director of the Texas Lottery Commission. Linares directed the lottery from its founding to its becoming the largest and most successful in the United States. The San Antonio native is a graduate of Southwest Texas State University.

Texas Hispanic, 5/26 (1995), p. 55.

1994 • Attorney Eva Plaza became the highest-ranking Hispanic woman in the Justice Department when she was appointed deputy assistant attorney general in the Clinton administration. Plaza was raised and educated in El Paso, Texas. She is a graduate of the University of California Boalt Hall School of Law.

Hispanic, August 1995, p. 9.

1995 • Dr. Dianne Mendoza Galaviz was appointed director of the Division of Tourism for the Texas Department of Commerce. The Laredo native received her Ph.D. from the University of Texas at Austin.

Texas Hispanic, 5/26 (1995), p. 52.

1995 • Raquel Rodríguez, an attorney with Florida's large law firm of Greenberg Traurig, became the first Hispanic to serve as the chairperson of the American Bar Association's (ABA) Young Lawyers Division. The ABA is the second largest professional organization in the world.

Hispanic, December 1995, p. 72.

1995 • Lawyer Tony Alvarado became the first Hispanic president of the State Bar Association of Texas. The Mexican American lawyer is a native of Laredo.

1995 • Captain Juan Jorge of the detective bureau of the Harris County Sheriff's Department, Texas (which includes the city of Houston), was promoted to major, making him the highest ranking officer in the sheriff's department since its inception in 1836. He is also believed to have been the first Hispanic captain in the department's history.

Houston Chronicle, 6 July 1995, p. A21.

1996 • John M. Bernal became the first Hispanic (the first Mexican American) to head the International Boundary and Water Commission in its 106-year history. This U.S. federal agency was created to handle boundary and water disputes between the United States and Mexico. The Tucson engineer was appointed to the post by President Bill Clinton.

Hispanic, March 1996, p. 9.

1996 • The first Hispanic was named to direct a presidential election advertising campaign. Cuban American Alex Castellanos was selected by Republican presidential nominee Bob Dole to lead his advertising campaign against incumbent president Bill Clinton.

Born in Havana, Castellanos fled Cuba with his parents at age six. They settled in North Carolina, where Castellanos attended the University of North Carolina. He dropped out during his senior year to work on the Ronald Reagan campaign and has been involved in Republican Party politics ever since. He was widely credited with inventing a lucrative direct-mail operation for Senator Jesse Helms in the late 1970s and continued putting successful campaigns together for the conservative senator.

Time, 16 September 1996, p. 44.

1996 • The first national Hispanic March for Justice took place in Washington, D.C., on October 12, 1996, to protest attacks on affirmative action, immigration, the minimum wage, welfare, and education. Some 100 thousand Hispanic marchers took part. The event was coordinated by Coordinadora '96, directed by Juan José Gutiérrez.

Hispanic Link Weekly Report, 23 September 1996, p. 1; "We Want to Be Heard, Respected," *Houston Chronicle,* 13 October 1996, pp. A1, A27.

1996 • Democrat Carlos "Cruz" Bustamante became the first Hispanic elected speaker in the California Assembly. Thirteen of the eighty assembly members are Hispanic. As speaker, Bustamante became one of the three most powerful elected officials in state government—the other two are leader of the senate and governor. Bustamante is the son of a barber and grandson of emigrants from Mexico.

Hispanic, December 1996, pp. 8–9; UPI, December 17, 1996.

1996 • Art Torres became the first Hispanic to chair the California Democratic Party.

"One Hundred Influentials," *Hispanic Business,* October 1996, p. 72.

1997 • Former Denver mayor Federico Peña became the first Hispanic to serve as the secretary of Energy. The new energy czar had previously served as secretary of Transportation during President Bill Clinton's first term.

1997 • Loretta Sánchez became the first Mexican American U.S. congresswoman. She was elected in a very close race in one of the nation's most conservative districts—Orange County, California.

Hispanic, December 1996, pp. 8–9.

THE CIVIL RIGHTS STRUGGLE

1687 • The first of what would become a consistent stream of runaway slaves from the British Carolinas took refuge in Spanish Florida. From that point on, Spanish Florida, and Saint Augustine in particular, would become a well-known haven for escaped slaves from the British colonies on the North American mainland. Eight men, three women and a three-year-old child had escaped from British Georgia by boat and were accepted in Saint Augustine, where they were given work and instruction in the Catholic religion. One year later, the slaves were claimed, but the Spanish governor in Saint Augustine refused to return them, since they had gainful employment, were now Catholics, and had married locally.

Henderson and Mormino, *Spanish Pathways in Florida,* p. 192.

1693 • Sanctuary for runaway slaves as a state policy in the Americas became official. King Charles III of Spain issued an edict stating that runaway slaves would be given their liberty "so that by their example and my liberality others will do the same." This stimulated the flow of runaway slaves from the British southern colonies into Florida. The British opposed this policy and in 1728 attacked Saint Augustine in retaliation. Black soldiers fought so bravely in defending the town that the governor freed all slaves who were soldiers and abolished the slave market.

Henderson and Mormino, *Spanish Pathways in Florida,* p. 192.

1728 • Saint Augustine was the first town in what became the United States to abolish its slave market. This was in partial recognition of black Spanish militia who had defended the town so bravely against British invaders from Georgia.

Henderson and Mormino, *Spanish Pathways in Florida,* p. 192.

1738 • The first free black community in what became the mainland United States was established at Fort Mose in Spanish Florida. Made up of free black families and escaped slaves from the British Carolinas and Georgia, Fort Mose was established north of Saint Augustine as a first line of defense against invading British soldiers and escaped-slave hunters.

Many of the colonists of Florida were free black craftsmen and black soldiers in the Spanish army. Under Spanish law and practice, slaves had certain rights, and Spanish culture and the Catholic church were more inclined to release slaves than were British culture and Protestant religions. A black militia was present in Florida by the seventeenth century, with both free and enslaved blacks serving as soldiers and officers. By the late seventeenth century, slaves in southern British colonies became fully aware of the advantages of escaping to Florida and living under Spanish rule. The first of these fugitives had arrived in Saint Augustine in 1687.

In 1738, the governor of Florida decreed that all fugitives from South Carolina would be guaranteed their freedom in Florida and he authorized the establishment of the village of Gracia Real de Santa Teresa de Mose as their home. Initially, thirty-eight men and their families moved in, but the village soon grew much larger and a small fort was built. A 1759 census showed that sixty-seven people lived in twenty-two houses in the community.

Henderson and Mormino, *Spanish Pathways in Florida,* pp. 188–203.

1855 • Mariano G. Vallejo (1808–1890), who became one of the first Californios to be elected to the state legislature and then to the state senate, was also one of the first Californios to have his extensive land grants validated, in 1855. But his happiness was short-lived, because squatters and speculators appealed the court decision all the way up to the U.S. Supreme Court, which invalidated his title to the large Soscol land grant. In addition to the land, much of the family wealth was lost in defending his rights to the grant in court. Vallejo thus became one of the first of a long line of Hispanics and Mexicans in the southwestern states and territories to lose their lands in similar processes. When he died, he only owned 280 acres.

Meier and Rivera, *Dictionary of Mexican American History,* pp. 361–62.

1863 • Chipita Rodríguez (?–1863) became the only woman legally hanged in Texas history. Found guilty of having murdered a horse trader, John Savage, Rodríguez was hanged, despite the jury's recommendation for mercy because the evidence against her was weak and because of her tender age.

The first woman hanged in California was Josefa Segovia, who during the gold rush killed an Anglo man who had made advances to her; she was hanged despite being pregnant.

Gómez-Quiñones, *Roots of Chicano Politics, 1600–1940,* p. 246; Meier and Rivera, *Dictionary of Mexican American History,* pp. 305–6.

FORT MOSE, 1760.

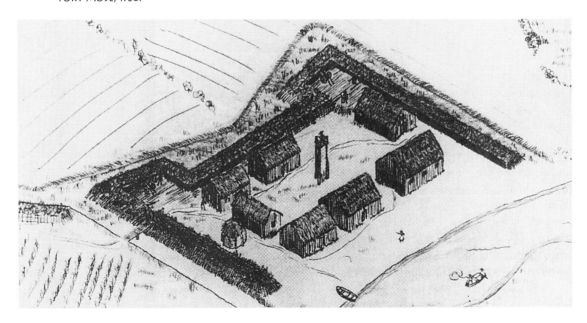

1868 • The Fourteenth Amendment to the U.S. Constitution was adopted, declaring all people of Hispanic origin born in the United States U.S. citizens.

Kanellos, *Chronology of Hispanic American History,* p. 108.

1872 • Puerto Rican representatives in the Spanish Cortes won equal civil rights for the colony. From this date forward, both Cuba and Puerto Rico began enjoying greater freedom and autonomy under Spanish rule.

Kanellos, *Chronology of Hispanic American History,* p. 111.

1877 • Puerto Rican patriot and poet Lola Rodríguez de Tió became the first Hispanic woman to be sent into political exile for her leadership in the Puerto Rican independence movement from Spain.

Born on September 14, 1843, in San Germán, Rodríguez de Tió received an education at religious schools and from private tutors. In 1865, she married Bonocio Tió, a journalist who shared Rodríguez de Tió's desire for Puerto Rican independence, and they held literary and political meetings regularly at their home in Mayagüez. In 1868, she wrote the lyrics to what would become the Puerto Rican national hymn, "La Borinqueña."

In 1877, the government exiled Rodríguez de Tió; she and her family took refuge in Venezuela for three years and then returned to Puerto Rico. In 1889, she was exiled once again, this time to Cuba, where she continued her revolutionary activities until 1895, when she was again exiled. This time she took up residence in New York and again continued to conspire with the leading revolutionaries for Puerto Rican and Cuban independence.

In 1899, after the Spanish American War, she returned to a hero's reception in Cuba. She remained in Cuba and began to work on fashioning a new society, one in which women would have greater liberty and opportunity. In 1910, she was elected a member of the Cuban Academy of Arts and Letters. Lola Rodríguez de Tió was a romantic poet, as her three books of poems readily attest: *Mis cantares* (My Songs), 1876; *Claros y nieblas* (Clarities and Cloudiness), 1885; and *Mi libro de Cuba* (My Book of Cuba).

Rodríguez de Tió was a beloved patriotic and literary figure, as well as an early feminist, in both Puerto Rico and Cuba. She died on November 10, 1924, in Cuba.

Kanellos, *Chronology of Hispanic American History,* p. 93.

1883 • An early fight, possibly the first in the Southwest, against segregation in Texas took place when a veteran, Juan Cárdenas, organized a successful protest against prohibiting the use of a dance floor to Mexicans in San Pedro Park, San Antonio.

Gómez-Quiñones, *Roots of Chicano Politics, 1600–1940,* p. 270.

1889 • The first underground guerrilla movement to protect the rights of native New Mexicans was founded. It was called Las Gorras Blancas (The White Caps). Bands of Mexican Americans wearing white caps or masks would sally out at night to pull down fences, destroy crops, burn buildings, tear up tracks on the Atchison, Topeka, and Santa Fe and even shoot people to stem the tide of Anglo-American encroachment on common land and abuse of the natural resources.

LOLA RODRÍGUEZ DE TIÓ.

Beginning in Las Vegas, New Mexico, but growing throughout San Miguel County and to other parts of the territory, the movement, made up of poor Hispanos, was principally aimed at protecting land use and ownership by the Mexican Americans and fighting the disruption of their traditional lifestyle. The nearly two years of activity of Las Gorras Blancas represented the most widespread, well-organized and effective resistance to Anglo-American control during territorial days, and the movement did succeed in temporarily halting the Anglo advance. In addition, the agitation created by the White Caps led to the formation of the first Hispanic third party in U.S. history: El Partido del Pueblo Unido (The United People's Party).

One man who served as a catalyst for the movement was Juan José Herrera, a union organizer for the Knights of Labor, who was able to use the labor association as a base for organizing the disaffected native New Mexicans. He established twenty local assemblies in San Miguel County, rallying the members's opposition to land speculation and large landowners. It is believed that Las Gorras Blancas was the clandestine, militant arm of the Knights of Labor assemblies in New Mexico. Local bands of Las Gorras Blancas continued to ride at least until 1926.

See also Government: Politics, 1890; Labor, 1888.

Rosaldo et al., *Chicano,* pp. 128–33.

1894 • The Alianza Hispano Americana, one of the first Hispanic civil rights organizations, was founded in Tucson, Arizona, and quickly spread throughout the Southwest. The Alianza originally was a mutualist society, or alliance of mutualist societies, that was organized along masonic lines through the leadership of Carlos Velasco, editor of the Tucson newspaper, *El Fronterizo* (The Frontier), as well as some forty-eight other prominent Mexican citizens of Tucson. At first, the organization was directed by middle- and upper-class businessmen and intellectuals, who realized that Mexicans were losing political and economic power as Anglos flooded into Arizona with the coming of the railroads. They were also responding to extensive discrimination and nativist attacks perpetrated by such organizations as the American Protective Association.

Over the years, the Alianza included more working-class Mexicans and became involved more in the protection of civil rights and in furthering the rights of workers. In the 1890s and 1900s, numerous Alianza members were successfully elected to office. By 1930, it had spread throughout the Southwest and had grown to include more than seventeen thousand members. In the post-World War II period, the organization became very active in protecting the civil rights of Mexican Americans. Today, it still counts over three hundred chapters in its membership.

Gómez-Quiñones, *Roots of Chicano Politics, 1600–1940,* pp. 284–85; Kanellos, *Chronology of Hispanic American History,* pp. 187, 229; Sheridan, *Los Tucsonenses,* pp. 108–10, 112–16.

1911 ✦ The first large convention of Mexicans for action against social injustice, El Primer Congreso Mexicanista (The First Mexicanist Congress), was held in Laredo, Texas, on September 14–20, 1911, led by Nicasio Idar, editor and publisher of *La crónica* newspaper. Several women were prominent in shaping the policies of the Primer Congreso, including Hortencia Moncayo and Soledad Flores de la Peña. The program created both an agenda for labor organization and for protection of civil rights of Mexicans and Mexican Amer-

CARLOS VELASCO,
NEWSPAPER PUBLISHER
AND FOUNDER OF LA
ALIANZA HISPANO
AMERICANA.

icans in the United States, through such strategies as organizing and joining trade unions, soliciting the support of the Mexican consular system, having schools that taught in Spanish and taught Mexican culture, improving the plight of Mexican women in the United States, and other strategies to protect Mexican lives and economic interests. The Congress concluded by establishing an ongoing organization, La Liga Mexicanista (The Mexicanist League).

Gómez-Quiñones, *Roots of Chicano Politics, 1600–1940,* pp. 314–23.

1915 • The first widespread plot to overthrow U.S. rule of the territories taken from Mexico—including Arizona, California, Colorado, New Mexico, and Texas—and create a separate republic was uncovered. The Plan de San Diego, supposedly organized in San Diego, Texas, was a reaction against civil rights abuses and expropriation of lands from Mexicans in Texas, and called for an armed revolt. The plan also included clauses addressed to the African American, Indian, and Asian population, in which provision for their liberation was made.

There were, in fact, a series of raids, destruction of bridges and encounters with the Texas Rangers that were effected by bands of armed riders in the lower Rio Grande Valley. But in all, the plan and its promoters remained cloaked in secrecy, and not much is known to this date about the perpetrators.

Gómez-Quiñones, *Roots of Chicano Politics, 1600–1940,* pp. 347–49; Rosaldo et al., *Chicano,* p.124.

1917 • Puerto Ricans, who had existed under the military rule of the United States since the end of the Spanish American War, became citizens of the United States with the passage of the Jones Act by the U.S. Congress. While the island of Puerto Rico remained a colony of the United States and had very limited self-determination, individual Puerto Ricans were entitled to the full civil rights enjoyed by any other U.S. citizens—except islanders then, as now, were not entitled to elected representation in Congress.

Kanellos, *The Hispanic American Almanac,* pp. 231–36.

1920 • One of the first Mexican American civil rights organizations founded in Texas was the Order of the Sons of America, which existed in the early 1920s, and had been organized by Luz Sáenz, a teacher and World War I veteran. The organization, made up mostly of U.S.-born members, concentrated on encouraging naturalization and participation in U.S. institutions for all Mexicans.

Rosales, *Chicano! History of the Mexican American Civil Rights Movement,* pp. 90–91.

1921 • One of the first organizations comprising both Hispanics and Anglos to combat discrimination was San Antonio's Pan American Round Table, which was made up of businessmen who promoted a positive image for Hispanics and fought anti-Latin American attitudes. The organization was founded by Ricardo Arenales.

Rosales, *Chicano! History of the Mexican American Civil Rights Movement,* p. 91.

1924 • The first battle against segregation of Mexicans in the Midwest was fought in the Argentine, Kansas, schools. Mexican parents and the Mexican consul protested when white parents petitioned the local school board to separate the Mexican children from theirs. The result was only a partial victory: Mexican children were allowed to attend high school with whites, but segregation was maintained in the elementary schools.

Rosales, *Chicano! History of the Mexican American Civil Rights Movement,* p. 71.

1926 • Mexican women in Los Angeles founded the first civil rights organization operated by Hispanic women, La Sociedad de Madres Mexicanas (The Society of Mexican Mothers). The SMM's purpose was to help finance the legal defense of compatriots facing civil or criminal charges. The SMM often held fund-raising events in local theaters, and its members were known for bringing toiletries and sundries to the Mexican prisoners in city and county jails; they also provided contacts and communication with the families of the incarcerated, most of whom still resided in Mexico.

Balderrama and Rodríguez, *Decade of Betrayal,* pp. 42–43.

1929 • The largest and longest-lasting Hispanic civil rights organization, League of United Latin American Citizens (LULAC), was founded in Texas. LULAC was founded as a mainly middle-class organization that only accepted citizens for membership. Among its most important goals was to fight segregation; another main concern was discrimination in the judicial system. A constant issue for LULAC was equal treatment under the law for Mexicans and Mexican Americans.

Rosales, *Chicano! History of the Mexican American Civil Rights Movement,* pp. 93–97.

ORDER OF THE SONS OF AMERICA, COUNCIL NO. 4, CORPUS CHRISTI, 1927.

1929 • Mexican parents won the first battle to stop a local school board from segregating their children with blacks in the De Olivera Elementary School in San Bernardino, California. They did not accept the rationale given by County Superintendent of Public Instructions Ida Collins, that the purpose for the separation was to help the children learn English.

Rosales, *Chicano! History of the Mexican American Civil Rights Movement,* p. 71.

1929 • Mexican Americans María and Pedro Hernández founded one of the earliest Hispanic civil rights organizations, Orden de Caballeros de América (Order of the Knights of America). This was the first Hispanic civil rights organization that had a specifically feminist viewpoint.

Tardiff and Mabunda, *Dictionary of Hispanic Biography,* p. 422.

1930 • Mexican American parents, through the League of United Latin American Citizens (LULAC) support, won their first discrimination suit, attacking segregation in the Texas schools in the case of *Salvatierra v. Del Río Independent School District,* brought by Jesús Salvatierra against the Del Rio, Texas, school district. The courts found that Mexican American children had been segregated without regard to individual ability; they said that the only legitimate use of segregation should be for special education. The case put an end to the practice of labeling certain schools Mexican, but in most instances segregation did not end, just the naming of the school.

Kanellos, *Chronology of Hispanic American History,* p. 196.

1930 • Parents successfully desegregated the schools in Lemon Grove, California, via a court suit; this was the first desegregation victory in Cali-

NINTH ANNUAL
LULAC CONVENTION,
HOUSTON, TEXAS, 1937.

fornia for Mexican Americans. It was heard at about the same time as the Salvatierra case.

See also Government: The Civil Rights Struggle, 1930.

Gómez-Quiñones, *Roots of Chicano Politics, 1600–1940,* p. 374.

1932 • The first significant civil rights organization of high school and college youth was formed, the Mexican American Movement (MAM). With the support of Protestant church affiliates and the Young Men's Christian Association (YMCA), young Los Angeles Mexican Americans banded together to lead the way to obtaining a secure and respected place in the society through Americanization. They especially believed that discrimination would disappear through education. Some of MAM's most dynamic leadership came from its female members, such as Dora Ibáñez, who encouraged Mexican American women to strive for education and professional careers.

Gómez-Quiñones, *Roots of Chicano Politics, 1600–1940,* pp. 391–97; Rosales, *Chicano! History of the Mexican American Civil Rights Movement,* pp. 100–102.

1932 • For the first time, concerted action by the Mexican community resulted in the freeing of what the community believed was an innocent Mexican immigrant convicted of a crime. The freeing of Alfredo Grijalva, who had been sentenced to life in prison for the murder of an Arizona patrolman, became a celebrated cause for many Mexican community organizations, Mexican consuls, and the Grijalva Defense Fund.

Various other cases of unjustly sentenced and even executed Mexican immigrants had been lost, such as those of Francisco Rodríguez and Aurelio Pompa. But a committee of both Mexicans and Anglos, including the treasurer of the Alianza Hispano Americana, was finally able to convince the state parole board to free Grijalva. Three years later Grijalva and eight other Mexican prisoners were released from the state prison at Florence.

Sheridan *Los Tucsonenses,* pp. 174–75.

1939 • El Congreso Nacional del Pueblo de Habla Hispana (The National Congress of Spanish-Speaking Peoples) was founded; it was the first national effort to bring together Hispanic workers from diverse ethnic backgrounds: Cubans and Spaniards from Florida, Puerto Ricans from New York, Mexicans and Mexican Americans from the Southwest, and other groups. The prime mover in bringing the diverse Hispanic labor and community organizations together and in founding the congress was Luisa Moreno, who developed the organization under the auspices of the Congress of Industrial Organizations (CIO).

The result of the first national convention of the Congress, held in Los Angeles in 1939, was that Spanish-speaking people in the United States began to realize that they constituted a national minority whose civil and labor rights were being violated consistently across the country. Another important result of the convention was a highlighting of the role of Hispanic women, who had been leaders in organizing the congress and the convention.

See also Labor, 1939.

García, *Memories of Chicano History,* pp. 109–113.

1944 • Senator Dennis Chávez introduced the first Fair Employment Practices Bill, which prohibited discrimination because of race, creed, or national origin. Although the bill was voted down by the conservative majority, it was an important predecessor of the 1964 Civil Rights Act. Chávez consistently promoted and supported civil rights legislation in Congress.

See also Government: Politics, 1935.

Kanellos, *The Hispanic American Almanac,* p. 269.

1944 • Wage discrimination in the mining industry, which paid Mexicans a lower, "Mexican rate," was finally recognized by the government and abolished.

See also Labor, 1944.

McWilliams, *North from Mexico,* pp. 197–98.

1945 • Mexican American parents in California won their first suit against segregation of Mexican children on constitutional grounds in *Méndez et al. v. Westminster School District et al.* against four Orange County school districts. The parents argued that the districts were depriving the students of due process and equal protection under the law. Although the school districts appealed the decision to the higher courts, the lower court decision was upheld in 1947 in the Ninth Circuit Court in San Francisco. Some five thousand Mexican American children were affected. The case set an important precedent for National Association for the Advancement of Colored People (NAACP) lawyers arguing the historic case *Brown v. Board of Education* in 1964.

Meier and Rivera, *Dictionary of Mexican American History,* p. 218; Rosales, *Chicano! History of the Mexican American Civil Rights Movement,* pp. 104–105.

1947 • The Community Services Organization (CSO) was founded; it was the first predominantly Hispanic civil rights group to adopt the tactics that would characterize American civil rights movements in the post-World War II period and would form the backbone of the Chicano Movement.

Mainly made up of Mexican Americans, many of its leaders were trained in the dramatic, confrontational tactics developed by Saul Alinsky and his Industrial Areas Foundation: mass demonstrations, picketing, confronting those in "the system" for its malfunction. Alinsky, in fact, hired César Chávez and Fred Ross to organize the CSO. Other important Mexican American leaders who would make history in the struggles of future decades became involved, notably Dolores Huerta and Tony Ríos. The CSO also obtained the support of the Catholic church. The CSO's first major victory came in 1949, when it organized and led the movement to elect Edward Roybal to the Los Angeles City Council.

Beyond the political realm, the CSO concentrated on neighborhood services and community health issues. To effect these ends, they organized door-to-door in working-class and lower-middle-class neighborhoods, with many women in leadership positions. César Chávez was later successful in taking many of the tactics and philosophy of the CSO and the Industrial Areas Foundation into the struggle to unionize farm workers.

See also Government: Politics, 1949; Labor, 1965.

García, *Memories of Chicano History,* pp. 163–68.

1954 • *Hernández v. Texas* was the first Mexican American discrimination case to reach the U.S. Supreme Court. The suit against Texas claimed that Pete Hernández, a convicted murderer, had been denied equal protection under the law because he had faced a jury that did not include Mexican Americans. The court found that Jackson County, Texas, had not chosen a Mexican American juror in twenty-five years, despite its having a Mexican American population of 14 percent. This was also the first case before the U.S. Supreme Court that was argued by Mexican American attorneys: Carlos Cadena and Gus García.

The decision also was the first to recognize Hispanics as a separate class of people suffering profound discrimination. Previously, Hispanics were officially recognized as "white" and, therefore, not a separate, minority class. The 1954 decision paved the way for Hispanic Americans to use legal means to attack all types of discrimination throughout the United States.

Kanellos, *The Hispanic American Almanac,* p. 237; Meier and Rivera, *Dictionary of Mexican American History,* pp. 160–61; Rosales, *Chicano! History of the Mexican American Civil Rights Movement,* p. 108.

1954 • Puerto Rican nationalists, frustrated at their inability to gain recognition and support for the movement for Puerto Rican independence from the United States, committed one of the first acts of political terrorism when they attacked the U.S. Congress. The nationalists, headed by Lolita Lebrón, attacked the U.S. House of Representatives in order to bring national attention to the colonial status of Puerto Rico. Five congressmen were shot. Lebrón and her followers, including Ramón Cancel Miranda, Irving Flores, and Oscar Collazo, were arrested, tried, and convicted. Lebrón subsequently spent twenty-five years in federal prison without recanting and became a heroine and martyr of the independence movement.

Kanellos, *Chronology of Hispanic American History*, pp. 236–37; Zavala and Rodríguez, *The Intellectual Roots of Independence*, p. 7.

1957 • The National Puerto Rican Forum was founded in New York City.

Kanellos, *Chronology of Hispanic American History*, p. 240.

1959 • The first Mexican American civil rights organization to acknowledge racism as the major enemy confronting Hispanics—the Mexican American Political Association (MAPA)—was founded in southern California and spread rapidly throughout the Southwest. Among its main organizers were Edward Roybal, who later became the first Hispanic in modern times elected to the Los Angeles City Council, and labor organizer Bert Corona.

Rosales, *Chicano! History of the Mexican American Civil Rights Movement*, p. 111.

1960 • Vicente Treviño Ximenes (1919–), a research economist and politician from Texas, received the United Nations Human Rights Award.

Meier and Rivera, *Dictionary of Mexican American History*, pp. 371–72.

1960 • For the first time in history, Mexican Americans had become a sizable portion of the voting population, and they organized extensive support for the Kennedy-Johnson ticket in the national elections. Mexican American political and labor organizers throughout the Southwest established Viva Kennedy Clubs to help deliver the presidential victory to Kennedy. Before this, Mexican Americans had been taken for granted as a modest part of the Democratic Party.

The success of the Kennedy-Johnson ticket was also seen by Mexican Americans as an ethnic victory. As a result of representing the voting margin putting John F. Kennedy and Lyndon B. Johnson into office, Mexican Americans and Hispanics made many civil rights gains and won a greater representation in government during the Kennedy and Johnson administrations than ever before.

Rosales, *Chicano! History of the Mexican American Civil Rights Movement*, p. 111.

1963 • In Crystal City, Texas, where Mexican Americans made up 85 percent of the population, the community ousted five Anglo city council members and elected five Mexican Americans. The slate of Mexican Americans had defeated the old Anglo establishment that had been in power since the town's founding in 1907. Crystal City became the only community in the Southwest where Anglos had been ousted from decades of rule. This was the first time that Hispanic political action had had such a success in the United States.

With the assistance of the Teamsters Union at the local Del Monte cannery and the Political Association of Spanish-Speaking Organizations, the new city government made important positive reforms, but Anglo resistance and factionalism made the job difficult.

A second revolt took place in 1969 and led to greater, more successful reforms. As a result of this revolt and a protest against discrimination in the

Crystal City schools, a political party was formed, La Raza Unida, which expanded quickly throughout Texas under the leadership of José Angel Gutiérrez. Crystal City became the first city in the United States to have a Chicano third party controlling the local government. Later on, La Raza Unida gained control of the government of Zavala County and made inroads into other areas. By 1981, however, the party was in decline, especially as the Democratic Party began to make reforms and become more inclusive of

RODOLFO "CORKY" GONZALES.

Mexican Americans and their issues. La Raza Unida and Crystal City are important historically for bringing about political change and forcing the two-party system in the United States to take Hispanics into account.

Kanellos, *Chronology of Hispanic American History,* p. 246; Rosaldo et al., *Chicano,* pp. 303–26; Rosales, *Chicano! History of the Mexican American Civil Rights Movement,* pp. 228–47.

1964 • The Supreme Court reversed the conviction for murder of Daniel Escobedo, ruling that the police had violated his constitutional rights by refusing his request to see a lawyer before he confessed. The landmark decision established a suspect's right to legal counsel during questioning and laid the foundation for the Miranda decision two years later that required police to inform suspects of their rights.

Houston Chronicle, 9 September 1996, p. A2.

1965 • Popular singer Joan Baez founded the Institute for the Study of Nonviolence, in Carmel Valley, California.

Tardiff and Mabunda, *Dictionary of Hispanic Biography,* p. 82.

1966 • Rodolfo "Corky" Gonzales founded the Crusade for Justice in Denver, Colorado. It was one of the most militant Chicano civil rights organizations.

Rosales, *Chicano! History of the Mexican American Civil Rights Movement,* pp. 175–82.

1967 • President Lyndon B. Johnson established the first Inter-Agency Committee on Mexican American Affairs and appointed Vicente Treviño Ximenes (1919–), a research economist and politician, as its chair. The committee was established to coordinate the programs in federal departments that affected Mexican Americans. As a result, more Mexican Americans were recruited for

SWEARING IN OF VICENTE TREVIÑO XIMENES, WITH PRESIDENT LYNDON B. JOHNSON. PHOTO BY YOICHI OKAMOTO.

government positions, and more agencies were set up to provide services to the Hispanic community under the War on Poverty than ever before in history.

The committee was the result of Mexicans having registered their largest vote in history in the 1964 presidential elections, voting solidly for LBJ. The establishment of the committee was more specifically a result of President Johnson's 1966 meeting in the White House with a committee of Mexican American representatives. He became the first U.S. president to hold such a meeting.

García, *Memories of Chicano History,* pp. 218–21; Meier and Rivera, *Dictionary of Mexican American History,* p. 372.

1967 • Reies López Tijerina and his Alianza Federal de Mercedes (Federal Land Grant Alliance) members raided and took over the Rio Arriba County Courthouse in Tierra Amarilla, New Mexico, to dramatize the plight of New Mexican small farmers attempting to recover their families's Spanish-Mexican land grants. The event became a landmark in the development of the Chicano civil rights movement and Tijerina a symbol of the civil disobedience that would force authorities to react to demands. Eventually the Alianza waned as Tijerina and some of his followers were arrested and sentenced to prison terms for their illegal acts, which were among the most militant of the Chicano Movement.

Rosaldo et al.,*Chicano,* pp. 267–77; Rosales, *Chicano! History of the Mexican American Civil Rights Movement,* pp. 153–70.

1967 • Young, well-educated Mexican Americans in San Antonio, Texas, founded the Mexican American Youth Organization (MAYO), whose chapters would spread throughout Texas and become the basis for the creation of the first Hispanic third party in the twentieth century: La Raza Unida Party. Under the leadership of José Angel Gutiérrez and other graduate students, MAYO chapters sprung up on college campuses throughout the state. Its program included ousting Anglos from economic and political control. One of the first battles won was the taking over of the school board in Crystal City in the 1970 elections under the banner of La Raza Unida Party.

Rosaldo et al., *Chicano,* pp. 314–26; Rosales, *Chicano! History of the Mexican American Civil Rights Movement,* pp. 228–47.

1968 • The first national legal fund to pursue protection of the civil rights of Mexican Americans was founded, the Mexican American Legal Defense and Education Fund (MALDEF). Founded by lawyers Pete Tijerina and Gregory Luna with funding from the Ford Foundation, MALDEF has filed and won some of the most important suits in education and political representation in the history of Mexican American civil rights. Pete Tijerina served as its first director.

Rosales, *Chicano! History of the Mexican American Civil Rights Movement,* p. 265.

1969 • The first National Chicano Youth Liberation Conference was held in Denver, Colorado. The historic meeting, sponsored by Denver's Crusade for Justice under the leadership of Rodolfo "Corky" Gonzales, brought Mexican

American activist youth together from throughout the Southwest to plan a coordinated civil rights strategy. The conference drafted and issued a spiritual plan for Chicano nationalism, El Plan Espiritual de Aztlán (The Spiritual Plan of Aztlán), using the name of the mythic place of origin, Aztlán, of the Aztec tribes, which corresponded roughly to the five Southwestern states where the majority of Chicanos live. The plan emphasized cultural pride and the need for self-determination. The conference also called for the creation of a Chicano political party; it called for making La Raza Unida, which had been organized in Texas, into a national third party.

García, *Memories of Chicano History,* p. 264; Rosales, *Chicano! History of the Mexican American Civil Rights Movement,* pp. 210, 228, 230.

1969 • The Young Lords Party, the first militant politicized street gang made up of Puerto Rican youth, was founded in New York City. Similar to the Black Panthers, the party soon spread to other cities in the Northeast and to Chicago.

Kanellos, *Chronology of Hispanic American History,* p. 254.

1969 • Nosotros, a Hollywood-based organization of Hispanic actors and other film media people, was created to advocate for more positive portrayal of Hispanics in film and television and to integrate the movie and television industries. Its first president and guiding force was actor Ricardo Montalbán.

Kanellos, *The Hispanic American Almanac,* p. 573.

1970 • The first national march to protest the disproportionately high casualty rate among Mexican Americans serving in Vietnam while the community's civil rights were being denied at home took place in Los Angeles, California. The National Chicano Moratorium on the Vietnam War drew between twenty and thirty thousand marchers from throughout the Southwest, making it the largest public demonstration in U.S. Hispanic history. The principal organizer of the event was a young graduate of University of California-Los Angeles (UCLA) who had served as student body president, Rosalío Muñoz. Unfortunately, police, the California National Guard, and other law enforcement agencies severely repressed the march by rioting and dispersing the crowd. Numerous protesters were injured, and the leading Chicano journalist, Rubén Salazar, was killed when he was struck by a tear gas canister shot into a bar. The moratorium became a watershed in the Chicano civil rights movement, and Salazar was erected as a martyr.

García, *Memories of Chicano History,* pp. 275–79; Rosales, *Chicano! History of the Mexican American Civil Rights Movement,* pp. 197–208.

1971 • Hispanics win the first suit against schools being financed through property taxes. In *Serrano v. Priest,* John Serrano sued the California state treasurer, alleging that his son was receiving an inferior education in East Los Angeles because schools were financed by local property taxes. The California courts found in August—and in April 1974 and December 1977 (California Supreme Court)—financing schools through local property taxes did not provide equal education opportunities and, therefore, the financing system had to be changed. After that, the state legislature mandated that income taxes be used for financing education.

Kanellos, *Chronology of Hispanic American History,* p. 257.

1972 • Mexican American voters replaced an all Anglo-American city council for the first time in California history, in the small predominantly Mexican American town of Parlier, where discrimination against them had run high.

Meier and Rivera, *Dictionary of Mexican American History,* p. 270.

VILMA MARTÍNEZ.

1972 • Lawyers Vilma Martínez and Graciela Olivárez became the first women to join the board of the Mexican American Legal Defense and Education Fund (MALDEF). In 1973, Martínez became the first woman to serve as its president and general counsel. During her presidency, one of Martínez's major accomplishments was her campaign toward expanding the U.S. Voting Rights Act, which, since its passage in 1965, had only applied to blacks and Puerto Ricans. Thanks to her coalition building and concerted pressure levied by organizations that she mobilized, Congress extended the act to Mexican Americans in 1975. Martínez was also successful in spearheading efforts to guarantee bilingual education for non-English- speaking children in public schools, which was secured in 1974.

Telgen and Kamp, *Latinas! Women of Achievement,* pp. 241–46.

1972 • The National Conference on Puerto Rican Women was founded in Washington, D.C.

Kanellos, *Chronology of Hispanic American History,* p. 257.

1972 • National Image, Inc., was founded in Washington, D.C., by federal employees to end employment discrimination against Mexican Americans. The organization now works to combat discrimination against all Hispanics.

Kanellos, *Chronology of Hispanic American History,* p. 257.

1973 • The right of the Puerto Rican people to decide their own future as a nation was approved by the United Nations. In 1973, the United Nations officially recognized Puerto Rico as a colony of the United States. This finding by the United Nations was of great support to the independence movement on the island and in the United States.

Kanellos, *Chronology of Hispanic American History,* p. 259.

1974 • The U.S. Congress passed the Equal Educational Opportunity Act of 1974 to create equality in public schools by making bilingual education available to Hispanic youths. According to the framers of the act, equal education means more than equal facilities and equal access to teachers. Students who have trouble with the English language must be given programs to help them overcome their difficulties with English.

See also Education, 1968.

Kanellos, *Chronology of Hispanic American History,* p. 260.

1974 • The first large Hispanic voter registration organization was founded, the Southwest Voter Registration Education Project, which has registered more than two million Hispanics to vote over the last twenty years. Centered in San Antonio, Texas, the project has offices throughout the Southwest and has made significant strides in empowering Hispanics to vote, having conducted more than eighteen hundred voter registration drives in fourteen states. In addition, the organization has been instrumental in the formation of voting districts with majority Hispanic populations. Its founder and first director, Willie Velásquez (1944–1988), was its initial driving force; he laid the groundwork for the organization's outstanding success.

"New Mission, New Leaders for Hispanics," *Houston Chronicle,* 7 January 1996, pp. A23–24; Rosales, *Chicano! History of the Mexican American Civil Rights Movement,* pp. 264, 266.

1975 • Thanks to the lobbying efforts of the Mexican American Legal Defense and Education Fund (MALDEF), under the directorship of Vilma Martínez, the U.S. Congress voted to expand the U.S. Voting Rights Act to include Mexican Americans. The original act, passed in 1965, had only applied to blacks and Puerto Ricans. The act also made bilingual ballots a requirement in certain locations of the United States.

Tardiff and Mabunda, *Dictionary of Hispanic Biography,* p, 529.

1975 • The Congressional Hispanic Caucus was founded to offer Hispanic congressmen and senators the opportunity to identify and further interests of Hispanics in the United States. The caucus also strives to strengthen the roles of Hispanics at all levels of government. It publishes the monthly *Legislative Review.*

Kanellos, *The Hispanic American Almanac,* pp. 259, 387, 390.

1976 • Attorney Vilma Martínez was the first Hispanic to win the Jefferson Award for public service from the American Institute in recognition of her pioneering work in civil rights as director of the Mexican American Legal Defense and Education Fund (MALDEF).

Tardiff and Mabunda, *Dictionary of Hispanic Biography,* p. 530; Telgen and Kamp, *Latinas! Women of Achievement,* pp. 241–46.

1978 • On the initiative of Cuba, the status of Puerto Rico's relationship to the United States was discussed at the United Nations, with the world body declaring Puerto Rico a colony of the United States, under which the Puerto Rican people do not enjoy the full rights of citizenship.

Zavala and Rodríguez, *The Intellectual Roots of Independence,* p. 9.

1979 • Singer Joan Baez founded Humanitas International, in Menlo Park, California. Humanitas promoted human rights, disarmament, and nonviolence through seminars and other educational opportunities. Baez served as its president until the organization's demise in 1992.

Tardiff and Mabunda, *Dictionary of Hispanic Biography,* p. 83.

1982 • Through the work of the Mexican American Legal Defense and Education Fund (MALDEF), the *Plyler v. Doe* case was won, giving the children of undocumented workers in Texas the right to free public education. Before this decision, Texas required tuition of $1,000 for each undocumented child.

Tardiff and Mabunda, *Dictionary of Hispanic Biography,* p. 529.

1983 • After passage of the Voting Rights Act Amendments of 1982, one of the first cases to challenge vote dilution of minorities was *Velásquez v. City of Abilene* in 1983. Prominent Judge Reynaldo G. Garza delivered the opinion of the U.S. Court of Appeals for the Fifth Circuit, stating that the intention of Congress was clear in cases of vote dilution. He ruled that the City of Abilene's use of at-large voting, bloc voting, and other voting mechanisms resulted in vote dilution and had a discriminatory effect on Hispanic American voters in the city.

Kanellos, *The Hispanic American Almanac,* p. 259.

1984 • Héctor García Pérez (1914–) became the first Hispanic to be awarded the United States of America Medal of Freedom for his years of work on behalf of civil rights for Hispanics. Born in Llera, Tamaulipas, Mexico, García was educated in the United States after his parents immigrated to Texas. He received his B.A. in 1936 and his M.D. in 1940, both from the University of Texas. During World War II he served with distinction in the Army Medical Corps, earning the Bronze Star and six battle stars. At the end of the war, he opened a medical practice in Corpus Christi and, outraged at the refusal of local authorities to bury a Mexican American veteran in the city cemetery, he organized the American G.I. Forum, which is still one of the largest and most influential Hispanic civil rights organizations.

In 1967, President Lyndon B. Johnson named García alternate delegate to the United Nations with the rank of ambassador, and he also appointed him the first Mexican American member of the United States Commission on Civil Rights. In 1965, the president of Panama awarded García the Order of Vasco Núñez de Balboa in recognition of his services to humanity. In 1984, he was awarded the United States of America Medal of Freedom.

Kanellos, *Chronology of Hispanic American History,* pp. 169–70.

1984 • Ernesto J. Cortés Jr. became the first community organizer to receive the MacArthur Fellowship, commonly known as the "genius" fellowship, for his more than twenty years dedicated to organizing grassroots communities to empower them to make changes in the structure of authority in their schools and communities. After receiving training at the Industrial Areas Foundation in 1973, Cortés went on to organize Communities Organized for Public Service in his native San Antonio. He later created grassroots organizations and movements in Los Angeles, Houston, El Paso, Dallas, Tucson, Phoenix, Albuquerque, New Orleans, and other cities in the Southwest, and built them into a network.

Today he is the Southwest director for the Industrial Areas Foundation. Thanks to his efforts, government has been more responsive to providing services for poor people, and educational access and achievement has improved for low-income neighborhoods because of the concerted community organizing and pressure exerted by the organizations he pioneered. Cortés is a member of the Carnegie Task Force on Learning in the Primary Grades, the Pew Forum for K-12 Education Reform, and the Aspen Institute Domestic Strategy Group.

1986 • The U.S. Congress enacted the Immigration and Control Act, which created an alien legalization program that affected hundreds of thousands of Hispanic undocumented workers, curtailing abuses of employers who took advantage of them and relieving their flight from authorities. Legal status was given to applicants who held illegal status in the United States before January 1, 1982, until the time of application. The bill also called for sanctions against employers of undocumented workers.

Kanellos, *Chronology of Hispanic American History,* pp. 272–73.

1991 • As a result of the Voting Rights Act, its 1982 amendments, and the cases of *Velásquez v. City of Abilene* and *Jones v. City of Lubbock,* for the first time in history the city of Abilene, Texas, elected two Hispanics to its city council in 1991 and the City of Lubbock elected one. The act and these court cases resulted in many Hispanics being elected to local positions throughout the United States.

See also Government: The Civil Rights Struggle, 1983.

Kanellos, *The Hispanic American Almanac,* p. 259.

1992 • The U.S. Congress passed the Voters Assistance Act of 1992, which made bilingual voting information readily available.

Kanellos, *Chronology of Hispanic American History,* p. 278.

1994 • The Mexican American Legal Defense and Education Fund (MALDEF) and a coalition of other civil rights organizations were successful in curtailing the effects of a voter referendum in California, Proposition 187, which banned undocumented immigrants and their children from receiving public education and social services.

Kanellos, *Chronology of Hispanic American History,* p. 282.

1995 • The Presidential Medal of Freedom was awarded posthumously to Willie Velásquez, the founder and director of the Southwest Voter Registration Education Project. The medal, which is the nation's highest civilian honor, was presented by President Bill Clinton to Velásquez's widow in recognition of the deceased activist's lifetime commitment and contributions

WILLIE VELÁSQUEZ.

to democracy. Willie Velásquez is recognized as the single most influential organizer of Hispanics on the road to political power and representation.

In an effort to continue the legacy of Velásquez, the Southwest Voter Registration and Education Project committed itself to the most ambitious registration goal in history: one million new Latino voters for the general elections in November 1996.

Southwest Voter Research Notes, (fall 1995/winter 1996), p. 1.

1995 ⬥ Anita Pérez Ferguson became the first Hispanic to serve as president of the National Women's Political Caucus.

1995 ⬥ Consumer and civil rights advocate Helen Gonzales became the highest-ranked Hispanic in the National Gay and Lesbian Task Force when she assumed the duties of director of public policy. Gonzales previously served as staff advocate at the National Consumer Law Center and associate counsel for the Mexican American Legal Defense and Education Fund (MALDEF).

Hispanic Link Weekly Report, 14 August 1995, p. 1.

1995 ⬥ The Democrats in Congress launched a newsline for Spanish-language radio and television. The newsline is coordinated out of the offices of Representative Gene Green of Houston, Texas, where articles are assembled and translated.

Houston Chronicle, 18 June 1995, p. A18.

1996 ⬥ Antonia Pantoja, educator and founder of Aspira, which counsels and provides support services for students on their way to higher education, became the first Hispanic woman to receive the Medal of Freedom, which was presented by President Bill Clinton.

Born and raised in Puerto Rico but active as a community organizer in the United States—principally in New York City and Washington, D.C.—Pantoja received the award for promoting community development. In 1991, she also received the John W. Gardner Leadership Award from the independent sector.

Houston Chronicle, 10 September 1996, p. A2.

LABOR

~~~~~~

1883 • The first Hispanic labor organizing activity recorded in U.S. history was Juan Gómez's organizing of cowboys in the Panhandle of Texas. He led several hundred cowboys on strike against ranch owners.

McWilliams, *North from Mexico,* p. 190.

1886 • The first Hispanic female labor leader came to the fore at the Haymarket Square riots in Chicago. She was Lucy Gonzáles Parsons, the well-known socialist and working-class activist from San Antonio, Texas. For more than fifty years, she worked to build socialist organizations among laborers in urban areas of the United States.

Gómez-Quiñones, *Roots of Chicano Politics, 1600–1940,* p. 287.

1888 • The Caballeros de Labor, one of the first Hispanic labor unions to serve the Southwest, was founded in San Miguel County, New Mexico, under the leadership of Juan José Herrera, a district organizer for the Knights of Labor (a nationwide union founded in Philadelphia in 1869). Although it was a labor union, it was never chartered by the Knights of Labor, possibly because most of its efforts were directed at fighting Anglo-American land-grabbing.

See also Government: The Civil Rights Struggle, 1889.

Meier and Rivera, *Dictionary of Mexican American History,* p. 60; Rosaldo et al., *Chicano,* pp. 131–32.

1899 • Santiago Yglesias Pantín (1870–1939) moved to Puerto Rico, where he became the first labor organizer under U.S. rule. Yglesias Pantín was born in La Coruña, Spain, where he received an elementary education and became a carpenter. He relocated to Cuba, where he became active in organizing labor through the Círculo de Trabajadores de la Habana (Havana Workers's Circle) from 1889 to 1896. In 1899, he moved to Puerto Rico, where he was instrumental in organizing the Partido Obrero Social (Workers's Social Party) and later became an organizer for the American Federation of Labor for Puerto Rico and Cuba.

In 1917, Yglesias Pantín founded the Federación Libre de Trabajadores de Puerto Rico (Free Federation of Puerto Rican Workers) and the Socialist Party. From 1917 to 1933, Yglesias Pantín served as a legislator in the Puerto Rican senate. From 1925 to 1933, he served as secretary of the Federación Panamericana de Trabajo (Panamerican Federation of Labor). In 1932 and 1936, he was elected resident commissioner to represent Puerto Rico in Washington, D.C.

During his years as a labor organizer, Yglesias Pantín also founded and directed three newspapers: *El Porvenir Social* (The Future of Society, 1898); *La Unión Obrera* (Worker Unity, 1903); and *Justicia* (Justice). He died on December 16, 1939, in Washington, D.C.

Kanellos, *Chronology of Hispanic American History*, p. 140.

1899 ⋅ The first large strike in the cigar industry occurred in Ybor City (Tampa), Florida, where Spanish and Cuban entrepreneurs had relocated their industry in 1886, in part to avoid labor unrest and organizing. The cigar industry relied on extensive manual, but skilled, labor by tobacco rollers. The cigar workers were among the most radicalized and educated, through a system whereby they supported professional *lectores,* or readers, who read to them throughout the day from world literature and newspapers while they hand-rolled cigars at their tables. The cigar rollers developed the strongest unions of any Hispanic workers and became the most influenced by socialist ideology. They struck again in 1901, 1910, 1920, and 1931.

Henderson and Mormino, *Spanish Pathways in Florida,* pp. 40–45.

1900 ⋅ At the turn of the twentieth century, American railway companies began recruiting Mexican workers at El Paso, Texas, for six-month contracts to work in the construction of lines in the North. The most active recruiters and employers of Mexican labor were the Southern Pacific Railroad and the Atchison, Topeka and Santa Fe, which heavily recruited workers to lay track in California. It is estimated that some sixteen thousand Mexicans were working on the railroads in the Southwest and West by 1908. The importation of Mexican labor by the railroads reached its peak between 1910 and 1912. During World War I, thousands of Mexican workers were brought to the Midwest to construct railways there. During World War II, the Bracero Program authorized further recruitment of Mexican workers for the railroads; during the war more than eighty thousand Mexican nationals were employed on some thirty American railroads. More than half of these worked on the Southern Pacific and Santa Fe lines. By April 1946, all of the Bracero Program workers were repatriated.

Kanellos, *Chronology of Hispanic American History*, p. 144.

1901 · The American Federation of Labor (AFL) broke its pattern of exclusion of nonwhites by allowing affiliation of the Federación Libre de Trabajadores (Workers's Labor Federation).

Kanellos, *Chronology of Hispanic American History,* p. 146.

1903 · One of the earliest and most important copper mine strikes in the Southwest occurred during the first two weeks in June 1903 in Arizona, when mostly Mexican and Mexican American workers walked out. Although the territorial legislature had reduced the work day from ten to eight hours and prohibited the mines from cutting wages, mining officials at Clifton, Morenci, and Metcalf reduced their workers's wages. A few thousand miners walked out in protest; 80 to 90 percent of them were Mexicans, whom the unions had resolved not to organize, for they had been characterized as taking work away from Americans. Despite the absence of unions, the Mexicans were well organized, with the help of mutual aid societies, and withstood hundreds of national guardsmen, Arizona Rangers, and federal troops. But the Clifton-Morenci strike failed because Anglo workers did not join the Mexicans in the walk-out and because a flood wreaked havoc in Clifton on June 9.

Rosales, *Chicano! History of the Mexican American Civil Rights Movement,* pp. 115–17.

1903 · More than twelve hundred Mexican and Japanese farmworkers organized the first farmworker union, the Japanese-Mexican Labor Association (JMLA), during February, in Oxnard, California. It was also the first to win a strike against the strong agricultural industry in California.

MEXICAN MINERS
IN ARIZONA IN THE
EARLY 1900S.

The rapid development of the sugar beet industry in Ventura County, with its dependence on cheap seasonal labor amid the highly racist European American society that had moved into the area, resulted in unfair and racist labor practices by the contractors and the association of farmers and refiners. The banding together of the Japanese and Mexican farmworkers marked the first time in history that two ethnic groups united when faced with Anglo-American discrimination and labor exploitation. Their founding of the union was not an easy task, given the enormous linguistic and cultural barriers that the organizers had to overcome.

The JMLA press release about the history-making strike spoke eloquently to the relationship of the workers to the industry owners and managers: "Many of us have families, were born in the country, and are lawfully seeking to protect the only property that we have—our labor. It is just as necessary for the welfare of the valley that we get a decent living wage, as it is that the machines in the great sugar factory be properly oiled—if the machine stops, the wealth of the valley stops, and likewise if the laborers are not given a decent wage, they too, must stop work and the whole people of the country will suffer with them."

By the first week in March, the JMLA had recruited more than twelve hundred workers—over 90 percent of the entire sugar beet work force. Despite strikebreaking efforts, violence, and repression by the industry owners supported by the judicial system, the JMLA won an overwhelming victory and ended the strike on March 30. Because of the success of the JMLA, labor unions began to rethink their policy of not organizing nonwhite labor or farm labor. One of the important benefits for Mexican workers was

MEXICAN WORKERS BAILING HAY IN THE SAN GABRIEL VALLEY, 1890S.

that they learned some doctrines and techniques from the Wobblies (members of the labor organization and Industrial Workers of the World) that were involved and were able to apply them in their own Mexican unions.

Almaguer, *Racial Fault Lines,* pp. 183–203; Jamieson, *Labor Unionism in American Agriculture,* pp. 76–77; Kushner, *Long Road to Delano,* pp. 20–21; McWilliams, *North from Mexico,* p. 190; Rosales, *Chicano! History of the Mexican American Civil Rights Movement,* p. 117.

1905 • San Antonio labor organizer Lucy Gonzales Parsons was one of the prominent founders of the Wobblies, the International Workers of the World. Gonzales Parsons, wife of the slain Haymarket Square labor leader Albert R. Parsons, took part in the leadership of the Wobblies's founding convention in Chicago in 1905. Furthermore, Gonzales Parsons urged solidarity with embattled Russian workers, who were on the verge of their first revolution. The Wobblies pledged nondiscrimination against workers of other races or immigrants to the United States, unlike other unions, which actively discriminated.

Kushner, *Long Road to Delano,* pp. 39–42.

1907 • Luisa Capetillo became the first Puerto Rican woman to be a leader in the labor movement, with her participation in a strike of tobacco factories in Arecibo, Puerto Rico. She joined the Federation of Free Workers and, in 1910, she founded the newspaper *La mujer* (The Woman). For the next two decades she was active as an organizer in New York, Florida, and again in Puerto Rico. She is also known as one of Puerto Rico's first feminists.

Tardiff and Mabunda, *Dictionary of Hispanic Biography,* p. 166.

1910 • The first strikes in the railroad industry led by Mexicans were a series of strikes that led to the bombing of the *Los Angeles Times* building. The wave of strikes was initiated when Mexicans working on the city's street railroad system walked out.

McWilliams, *North from Mexico,* p. 190.

1915 • Labor organizer and feminist Luisa Capetillo (1880?–1922) became known as the first woman in Puerto Rico to wear slacks in public, as an exterior sign of her rebellion. In addition to becoming one of the first female labor organizers in Puerto Rico, she was probably the first feminist, in the modern sense of the term.

Capetillo was born in Arecibo in 1880 or 1882. She received her early education in a private school, where she won prizes in grammar, history, and geography. Shortly after graduating, she worked as a journalist and labor organizer. In 1912, she lived in New York City and, in 1913, she moved to Ybor City, Florida, to organize cigar workers.

From 1914 to 1915, she lived in Cuba, presumably continuing her organizing among cigar workers. Thereafter, she returned to Puerto Rico and became involved in the labor and feminist movements as a socialist. She was particularly outstanding in militating for women's suffrage. She advocated free love, had children out of wedlock, and she worked for a society without social classes. She was the founder and editor of the magazine *La mujer* (Woman) and wrote various books: *Ensayos libertarios* (Libertarian Essays), 1909; *La humanidad en el futuro* (Humanity in the Future), 1910; *Mi opinión sobre las libertades, derechos y deberes de la mujer* (My Opinion on the Liberties, Rights and Duties of Women), 1911; and *Influencia de las ideas modernas* (The Influence of Modern Ideas, 1916). She died of tuberculosis in Río Piedras, Puerto Rico, in 1922.

Kanellos, *Chronology of Hispanic American History,* p. 117.

1922 • The first strikes of grape pickers unsuccessfully attempting to organize a union took place in Fresno, California. A three-day celebration in honor of Mexican independence turned into a union-organizing activity, but the effort ultimately failed. A small union was organized by Mexicans in the cantaloupe fields of Brawley as another early attempt at creating a farmworker union.

Jamieson, *Labor Unionism in American Agriculture,* p. 76; McWilliams, *North from Mexico,* pp. 190–91.

1927 • The first large-scale effort to organize and consolidate Mexican workers took place at a meeting of federated Mexican societies in Los Angeles. The result was the Confederación de Uniones Obreras Mexicanas (Federation of Mexican Worker Unions—CUOM), which was joined by more than twenty unions representing both agricultural and industrial workers throughout southern California. By May 1929, the federation had some three thousand members organized in twenty locals throughout the region; but because many of its members were migrants without a stable residential base, the union had difficulties in surviving. The first strike called by the union, in the Imperial Valley, was broken by arrests and deportation of Mexican workers. Two years later, the union struck again by surprise, and the growers were forced to settle.

Gómez-Quiñones, *Roots of Chicano Politics, 1600–1940,* p. 381; Jamieson, *Labor Unionism in American Agriculture,* pp. 76–77; Kushner, *Long Road to Delano,* pp. 55–56; McWilliams, *North from Mexico,* p. 191; Rosales, *Chicano! History of the Mexican American Civil Rights Movement,* pp. 119–20.

1928 • The first union to organize farmworkers in the Imperial Valley, California, was one formed under the leadership of the Mexican vice-consul in Calexico—Union of the United Workers of the Imperial Valley. The Imperial Valley Cantaloupe Workers's strike was the first attempt at work stoppage by Mexican farmworkers in modern California. The vice-consul, Carlos Ariza, had been called upon so often to intervene in labor disputes that he thought establishing a union might be a solution. The strike was broken easily, primarily through threats and violence. Most growers agreed to pay the fifteen cents per crate wage requested by the workers, however, the growers did not recognize the union as a bargaining agent.

Rosaldo et al., *Chicano,* pp. 181–82, 185–92; Rosales, *Chicano! History of the Mexican American Civil Rights Movement,* p. 120.

1931 • The first labor strike in the United States over a cultural issue took place in Ybor City (Tampa), Florida, when the owners of the cigar factories abolished the *lectores* (readers), who read aloud all day from a wide variety of books and periodicals to help cigar rollers pass the time in their boring manual task. The owners accused the *lectores* of radicalizing the workers and replaced them with radios; the workers walked out but the owners were victorious. The demand for cigars had fallen greatly due to the massive change by Americans to smoking cigarettes. The cigar industry was beginning to decline.

Henderson and Mormino, *Spanish Pathways in Florida,* p. 42.

1933 • The El Monte Berry strike in 1933, possibly the largest agricultural strike thus far, was led by Mexican unions in California. In June, members of the Mexican Farm Labor Union, an affiliate of the Confederación de Uniones Obreras Mexicanas (CUOM) officially sanctioned the strike and called for a minimum wage of twenty-five cents per hour. The strike spread from Los Angeles County to Orange County, and the union grew rapidly. In June, the strike ended with the concession of a small increase in wages and recognition of the Confederación. That same year, the confederation became the largest and most active agricultural union in California.

In 1935, the Confederación was responsible for six of the eighteen strikes in California agriculture and was also effective in winning negotiations without striking. In 1936, it was a leader in establishing the Federation of Agricultural Workers Union of America. By the end of the 1930s, however, the confederation's power had waned in the face of increased resistance from the growers, legislators, jurisdictional disputes between the American Federation of Labor and the Congress of Industrial Organization, and a surplus of workers.

Kanellos, *Chronology of Hispanic American History,* p. 201; Kushner, *Long Road to Delano,* pp. 68–76; McWilliams, *North from Mexico,* p. 191.

1933 • In October 1933, Mexican farmworkers struck the cotton industry in the counties of the Central Valley, California. The San Joaquin cotton strike was the largest and best organized of labor actions initiated by the radical Cannery and Agricultural Workers Industrial Union in the 1930s. Some twelve thousand to eighteen thousand pickers walked out, demanding a raise from sixty cents to one dollar a pound for picked cotton. Growers and vigilante groups attempted to repress the strike violently and, in fact, killed two strikers and wounded various others. California Governor James Rolf called in the National Guard and established a fact-finding board, which eventually created the basis for a compromise: seventy-five cents per pound and a condemnation of the growers for violation of the strikers's civil rights.

Jamieson, *Labor Unionism in American Agriculture,* pp. 100–105; Kanellos, *Chronology of Hispanic American History,* pp. 203–204; Kushner, *Long Road to Delano,* pp. 57–70.

1933 • Mexican working women as a group became very active for the first time in organizing workers in the garment industry. Rose Pessota recruited heavily among Mexican women for the International Ladies' Garment Workers Union (ILGWU), which in 1933 launched a massive strike that brought garment production to a halt in Los Angeles. The strike prevailed despite harassment by city officials spurred on by the sweatshop owners. The union prevailed, and a contract was signed with a number of shops for an increase in wages.

Rosales, *Chicano! History of the Mexican American Civil Rights Movement,* p. 119.

1933 • Mexican and Mexican American workers in Texas organized one of the broadest unions in the history of Hispanic labor in the United States, La Asociación de Jornaleros (The Journeymen's Association), which represented everything from hatmakers to farmworkers. But the union's very diversity was the cause of its failure and it died after Texas Rangers arrested leaders of a strike in the onion fields of Laredo in 1934.

Rosales, *Chicano! History of the Mexican American Civil Rights Movement,* p. 121.

1934 • Mexican sheepshearers went on strike for the first time in west Texas.

McWilliams, *North from Mexico,* p. 194.

1935 • By 1935, the most effective agricultural labor unions were those organized among Mexican farmworkers. Most of the membership of the Cannery and Agricultural Industrial Union (C&AIU) had been Mexican since 1933. What was learned through the C&AIU was applied to the other Mexican unions that existed. The Confederación de Uniones de Campesinos y Obreros Mexicanos del Estado de California (Federation of Mexican Farmworker and Industrial Worker Unions of California) became the most active farmworker organization in the state. The federation, which had developed out of the general strike in strawberries, celery, and other crops during June 1933, by now claimed ten thousand members. It coordinated its strategies with the C&AIU and carried out at least one strike under a united front with its partner.

1935 • The Liga Obrera de Habla Española (Spanish-Speaking Labor League) was organized in Gallup, New Mexico, among coal miners in an effort to save miners arrested and/or charged with a variety of offenses stemming from their long-lasting strike against the Gallup-American Company (a subsidiary of Kennecott Copper Company). Jesús Pallares, a miner originally from Chihuahua, was the main organizer. With some eight thousand members, the league succeeded in forcing the authorities to abandon criminal syndicalism proceedings and won relief rights for the strikers. The personal price for this victory was the one paid by Pallares—and often meted out to Mexican-origin organizers—when he was arrested and deported.

McWilliams, *North from Mexico,* p. 195; Rosales, *Chicano! History of the Mexican American Civil Rights Movement,* p.122.

1936 • Mexican workers struck the celery fields in southern California, which led to police violently attacking and suppressing two thousand strikers with a force of fifteen hundred armed men. Injured strikers were refused aid at local hospitals and taxpayer dollars were employed by local authorities to hire field agents to visit growers and urge them not to settle. The growers themselves spent thousands of dollars in hiring armed guards from a local strikebreaking detective agency.

McWilliams, *North from Mexico,* p. 192.

1936 • Some twenty-five hundred Mexican farmworkers tied up a $20- million citrus crop in Orange County, California, for several weeks with a strike. More than four hundred special armed guards were recruited. Some two hundred arrested strikers were formally arraigned in an outdoor bullpen that served as a courtroom. Orange County remained in a state of virtual siege for several weeks as local newspapers celebrated the vigilantism used against the farmworkers on strike.

McWilliams, *North from Mexico,* pp. 192–93.

1937 • Bert Corona became one of the founders of the International Longshoremen's and Warehousemen's Union (ILWU), serving as the secretary of Local 26. From there, Corona became the leading Hispanic voice in mainstream labor unions and in creating a place for Hispanics in the American labor movement.

García, *Memories of Chicano History,* p. 89.

1937 • Mexican workers had increasingly been recruited for the steel and automobile industries in the Midwest. Mexicans and Mexican Americans were among the most militant members of the Steel Workers Organizing Committee in the Chicago area. Their involvement meant that Mexicans were finding that racially mixed organizing was becoming a better solution to improving their lot as workers. Mexicans participated significantly in the Little Steel Strike of 1937, one of the most famous events in the labor history of the United States. In this strike, workers from throughout the Midwest walked off the job, including thousands of Mexicans, who also suffered heavy losses and injuries in the famed Republic Steel Massacre.

Rosales, *Chicano! History of the Mexican American Civil Rights Movement,* p. 122.

1938 • Luisa Moreno, a Guatemalan immigrant who came to the United States as a child and was educated at the College of the Holy Names in Oakland, California, became the first Hispanic vice president of a major labor union, the United Cannery, Agricultural, Packing, and Allied Workers of America (UCAPAWA). Moreno had broad experience in organizing tobacco workers in Florida, factory workers in New York City, cane workers in Louisiana, cotton pickers in Texas, and sugar beet workers in Colorado.

While she was organizing cannery workers in California, she developed the idea to create a national congress of Hispanic workers and communities, which she was able to accomplish under the auspices of the Congress of Industrial Organizations (CIO) and with many other union organizers, especially women. She was a leader in bringing the UCAPAWA to giant canneries in California, such as Calpak, Del Monte, Campbell, and Libby.

During the McCarthy era, Moreno was severely persecuted for her politics and her labor activities. She was ordered to face a deportation hearing and, rather than let the authorities create negative publicity for the unions, she went into exile in Guatemala voluntarily. In Guatemala, she supported the democratic government of Jacobo Arbenz before he was overthrown. After the triumph of the Communist revolution in Cuba, she went there to work in the educational system. Moreno died in Guatemala in 1992.

See also Labor, 1939.

García, *Memories of Chicano History,* pp. 116–20; Kushner, *Long Road to Delano,* pp. 89–94.

1938 • The first large Mexican and Mexican American agricultural workers strike in Texas occurred in the pecan shelling plants of San Antonio. Since the late nineteenth century, the Texas pecan industry had been centered in San Antonio and had traditionally used predominantly Mexican American labor. Paying only two or three cents a pound for shelling pecans, the industry rejected the National Recovery Administration's higher- wage code.

By 1937, various unions had made incursions into the pecan industry and, in January 1938, announcement of a 15 percent wage cut led to spontaneous strikes throughout the industry. Fully half of all the pecan workers in some 130 plants walked out. More than one thousand pickets were arrested, and tear gas was used against picketing strikers six times within the first two weeks of the strike. A Mexican American pecan sheller, Emma Tenayuca, emerged as a leader. Known as La Pasionaria because of her fervor, Tenayuca joined the Communist Party, because she believed that it was the only entity willing to help the shellers.

The strike and the management's reaction to it became increasingly strife-ridden. More than one thousand out of six thousand strikers were arrested, and much violence was employed against the strikers. In March, the strike was settled through arbitration; the union was recognized, but there was a 7.5 percent decrease in wages.

This decision was rendered moot in October when the Fair Labor Standards Act enforced a twenty-five cents per hour minimum wage. This was stimulus for the industry to mechanize and eventually reduce its labor force drastically. When the dispute began in 1938, the Southern Pecan Shelling Company had employed some ten thousand workers; by 1941, the company had only six hundred employees.

Kanellos, *Chronology of Hispanic American History,* p. 210; Rosaldo et al., *Chicano,* pp. 192–202; Rosales, *Chicano! History of the Mexican American Civil Rights Movement,* pp. 121–22.

1939 • El Congreso Nacional del Pueblo de Habla Hispana (National Congress of Spanish-Speaking Peoples) was founded. It was the first national effort to bring together Hispanic workers from diverse ethnic backgrounds—Cubans and Spaniards from Florida, Puerto Ricans from New York, Mexicans and Mexican Americans from the Southwest.

The prime mover in bringing the diverse Hispanic labor and community organizations together and in founding the congress was Luisa Moreno, who developed the organization under the auspices of the Congress of Industrial Organizations (CIO). Moreno developed her idea for a national Hispanic civil rights and labor organization while working for the United Cannery, Agricultural, Packing, and Allied Workers of America (UCAPAWA). The first convention of the Congress was held in Los Angeles in April 1939, with a wide variety of labor people, educators, religious leaders, and community organizers attending. Anglo representatives from CIO unions also attended, as well as representatives from the movie industry and from African American organizations. The result of the convention and the organization of the Congress itself was that Spanish-speaking people in the United States began to realize that they constituted a national minority whose civil and labor rights were being violated consistently across the country.

Another important result of the convention was a highlighting of the role of Hispanic women, who had been leaders in organizing the Congress and the convention. In addition to Luisa Moreno, Josefina Fierro took a notable leadership role in including regional leaders, such as Linda Silva and Marta Casares. Fierro became the key administrator of the Congress as executive secretary.

PECAN SHELLERS IN SAN ANTONIO DURING THE 1930S.

World War II led to the demise of the Congress, when the organization restricted its civil rights protests in order to support the war effort; it also lost numerous members to enlistment in the armed services. Although the organization attempted its revival after the war, McCarthyism and political persecution led to leaders, such as Moreno and Fierro, going into voluntary exile rather than being grilled by the House Un-American Activities Committee or being deported.

García, *Memories of Chicano History*, pp. 109–16; Rosales, *Chicano! History of the Mexican American Civil Rights Movement*, pp. 123–24.

1939 ⋅ The celebrated organizer of the San Antonio pecan shellers strike, Emma Tenayuca, along with Homer Brooks, published the first document analyzing the condition of Mexican workers in the United States from a worker's point of view, "The Mexican Question in the Southwest." Although Tenayuca and Brooks were both Communists, they described the distinctive commonality of Mexican people in the Southwest because of class and cultural oppression. The document promoted the enlistment of Mexican workers in labor unions and the Communist Party.

Gómez-Quiñones, *Roots of Chicano Politics, 1600–1940*, p. 393.

CA. 1940 ⋅ The Committee on Spanish-Speaking Workers, founded and headed by Luisa Moreno, was the first, or one of the first, to function within a mainstream labor union. It operated during the 1940s within the California Congress of Industrial Organization (CIO) to combat discrimination against Hispanics.

García, *Memories of Chicano History*, p. 105.

1944 ⋅ Wage discrimination in the mining industry, which paid Mexicans a lower, "Mexican rate," was finally recognized by the government and abolished. The International Union of Mine, Mill, and Smelter Workers-CIO proved its charges before the National War Labor Board that three large mining companies classified employees as "Anglo-American males" and "other employees." Included in the latter classification were all females, Latin Americans, Negroes, Filipinos, and Indians. If a Mexican with no experience was hired, he was classified as a "common laborer" and paid $5.21 per hour; an Anglo with no experience was classified "helper" and paid $6.36. In addition, "other employees" rarely got wage increases, thus receiving their initial rate of pay for as long as ten years. The board ordered the elimination of the discriminatory rates. Nevertheless, workers had to strike throughout the Southwest in 1946 because the companies had been stalling in implementing the labor board's orders.

McWilliams, *North from Mexico*, pp. 197–98.

1950 ⋅ The Salt of the Earth Strike was the first major strike conducted by women and children. From October 1950 until January 1952 the predominantly Mexican Mine-Mill Workers Union struck the mines in southern New

Mexico. A local judge issued an injunction prohibiting the mine workers from picketing the mines, but the women's auxiliary of the union continued to picket and organize, quite often with their children at their sides and in their arms, and suffering abuse, violence, and arrest. The strike ended when the union was able to obtain minor concessions. In addition to the importance of the leadership role taken by women, the strike was historically important because it focused on the pattern of discrimination against Mexican workers that prevailed throughout the Southwest.

García, *Memories of Chicano History*, pp. 174–75.

1951 · In California, the first union of Mexican immigrant workers was founded, La Hermandad Mexicana Nacional (The Mexican National Brotherhood). The lead organizers, Phil and Alberto Usquiano, organized a quasi union made up of a large membership of undocumented workers who were, for the most part, members of the Carpenters Union or the Laborers Union. The hermandad was organized in response to the Immigration and Naturalization Service's program to cancel work visas of Mexican nationals.

García, *Memories of Chicano History*, pp. 290–91.

1956 · California union organizer Ernesto Galarza published the first exposé of abuses in the Bracero Program and the inhuman conditions under which growers employed Mexican farmworkers. *Strangers in Our Fields,* published by the Joint U.S.-Mexico Trade Union Committee, was so successful that it went through two editions for a total of ten thousand copies, and it was condensed in three national magazines, receiving widespread publicity. Galarza's book even spurred the American Federation of Labor and Congress of Industrial Organizations(AFL-CIO) to begin supporting the unionization of farmworkers by granting $25,000 to Galarza's National Agricultural Workers Union. The book was one of the most damaging documents to the visitor worker program so favored by California agribusiness and helped to force both the United States and Mexico to allow the program to expire in 1964. The termination of the Bracero Program, in turn, led to the successful unionizing of farmworkers that began in 1965 under the leadership of César Chávez and what would become the United Farm Workers Union.

Rosaldo et al., *Chicano*, pp. 286–87; Rosales, *Chicano! History of the Mexican American Civil Rights Movement.*

1962 · César Chávez (1927–1993) began organizing the first successful farmworkers union in U.S. history. Born near Yuma, Arizona, to a family of migrant farmworkers, Chávez attended nearly thirty schools, eventually achieving a seventh-grade education. During World War II he served in the U.S. Navy, after which he returned to migrant farm labor.

He eventually settled down in 1948 in the barrio of Sal Si Puedes (Get Out If You Can) in San Jose, California. It was in San Jose that he began working for the Community Services Organization (CSO) as a community organizer. By 1958, he had become general director of the CSO in California and Arizona. In 1962, wishing to organize farmworkers, he resigned the CSO directorship and moved to Delano, California, where he became the head of the United Farmworkers Organizing Committee, which today has become the United Farm Workers, AFL-CIO.

CÉSAR CHÁVEZ ON THE PICKET LINE DURING THE NATIONAL GRAPE BOYCOTT.

From 1965 on, Chávez and his fledgling union embarked on a number of history-making strikes and national boycotts of agricultural products that have become the most successful in the history of farm labor in the United States. Due principally to the efforts of Chávez and his organization, the California legislature passed the California Labor Relations Act in 1975, which provides secret ballot union elections for farmworkers. Also because of his efforts, there have been many improvements in wage, health, and housing conditions for farmworkers in California and Arizona.

Chávez was known as a selfless and spiritual leader of farmworkers everywhere, bringing their plight to national attention through media appearances and interviews, hunger strikes, and well-organized boycotts. In 1993, Chávez died of a heart attack near the place of his birth. In 1994, President Bill Clinton bestowed the United States Medal of Freedom upon him posthumously; he became the first Hispanic to win the award for labor-organizing activities.

See also Labor, 1965.

Griswold and García, *César Chávez,* pp. 22–40; Kanellos, *Chronology of Hispanic American History,* pp. 187, 245, 250; Kushner, *Long Road to Delano,* pp. 106–114; Rosaldo et al., *Chicano,* pp. 170–73.

1965 • The largest and most important farmworker union was founded in Delano, California, under the leadership of César Chávez, who led his organization into a strike started by Filipino grape pickers in Delano. Chávez and his United Farm Workers (UFW) successfully converted the strike into one of the most significant movements for social justice for farmworkers, especially the Mexican/Mexican American farmworkers who formed the majority of pickers.

From this humble beginning, the UFW was able to develop into the largest union of agricultural workers through more than a decade of struggles, national boycotts, court cases, and legislative action in California. From table grapes, the labor actions spread to lettuce and other crops and eventually successfully won concessions and contracts on wages, working conditions, safe use of pesticides, and the right to unionize and strike. In his pacifist tactics, hunger strikes, and crusades, Cesar Chávez enlisted and received the support of national politicians, such as Robert F. Kennedy, the Catholic Conference of Bishops, and, eventually organized labor. When Chávez died in 1993, he was mourned in the United States as a national hero.

See also Government: The Civil Rights Struggle, 1947.

Griswold and García, *César Chávez,* pp. 41–58; Kanellos, *Chronology of Hispanic American History,* p. 250.

1965 • Dolores Huerta became the first female leader of a farmworker union. She cofounded the United Farm Workers with César Chávez and became its contract negotiator. Both Huerta and Chávez had worked with the Community Services Organization (CSO), a Mexican American self-help organization, as organizers and had unsuccessfully tried to bring it into farm labor organizing. Huerta and Chávez resigned and moved to Delano, California in 1962 to start the United Farm Workers Organizing Committee. In 1965, Huerta became the unmovable contract negotiator for the new union and its strike.

Born on April 10, 1930, in Dawson, New Mexico, Huerta came from a middle-class background, learning organizational skills from her mother and her stepfather, who owned and administered two restaurants in California. Her divorced and estranged father, however, lived as an impoverished farmworker; Huerta's accompanying him in his migrations and in labor camps sensitized her to the conditions faced by agricultural workers. She became further politicized working as a teacher of very poor children and then became swept up in the growing Chicano Movement, so much so that she joined the CSO, becoming its lobbyist in Sacramento. Over the years, Huerta has been the most successful contract negotiator, lobbyist, and one of the most important fund-raisers for the union.

Telgen and Kamp, *Latinas! Women of Achievement,* pp. 193–99.

1965 ⋅ The most important and long-standing Hispanic theater, El Teatro Campesino, was founded as a labor theater in the agricultural fields, under the directorship of Luis Valdez.

See also Theater, 1965.

Kanellos, *Chronology of Hispanic American History,* p. 248.

1969 ⋅ Screen actor Ricardo Montalbán founded the first organization, Nosotros, to promote equal opportunity for Hispanic actors and technicians in the motion picture and television industries. The organization also had as a mission the improvement of the image of Hispanics on the screen.

Meier and Rivera, *Dictionary of Mexican American History,* p. 237.

1974 ⋅ Continued strikes and boycotts by the Mexican American-led United Farm Workers Association (UFWA) resulted for the first time in California history in a prounion legislative act: the California Agriculture Labor Relations Act. After prolonged strikes and national boycotts, the UFWA, under the leadership of César Chávez, signed contracts with most of the Central Valley table grape growers of California and immediately chose the Salinas Valley lettuce growers for the organization's next labor action. In response, some seventy growers signed "sweetheart" contracts with the International Brotherhood of Teamsters. Despite the Teamster contracts, some seven thousand farmworkers struck in August. In September, UFWA launched a national boycott of lettuce.

Strikes and lettuce and grape boycotts continued—as did the jurisdictional battle with the Teamsters—through 1974, when newly elected Governor Jerry Brown pioneered passage of the California Agriculture Labor Relations Act. Under this legislation, union elections could be held by workers; the result was that the UFWA won 65 percent of the elections and regained many lost contracts. In 1977, the UFWA-Teamsters dispute was resolved, but the lettuce boycott did not end until February 1978. Definitive victory at unionizing the lettuce fields, for the first time, came in September 1979, when the UFW successfully signed contracts with major lettuce farmers in the state.

Kanellos, *Chronology of Hispanic American History,* p. 256.

1974 • Through implementing a strike in 1972 and a national boycott, the heavily Mexican/Mexican American Amalgamated Clothing Workers of America succeeded in unionizing the workers of the Farah Manufacturing Company in El Paso, Texas.

Kanellos, *Chronology of Hispanic American History,* p. 258.

1983 • Mexican American lawyer Patricia Díaz Dennis became the first Hispanic woman and only the second female to serve on the National Labor Relations Board. She was appointed by President Ronald Reagan after she had developed a background of representing television management in labor issues.

Tardiff and Mabunda, *Dictionary of Hispanic Biography,* p. 285.

1989 • Dennis Rivera was the first Hispanic elected president of the 1199 National Health and Human Services Employees Union, which has a membership of some 117 thousand workers, primarily residing in New York and New Jersey. As president, Rivera became one of the nation's most respected and powerful labor leaders.

Rivera has been a leader in signing up new members during a time when unions in the United States have waned. He has also been successful in making the union's political action department a powerhouse, especially in registering voters. Rivera is the only Hispanic who serves on the board of the Children's Defense Fund, and he has served as the chairperson of the Rainbow Coalition since 1993.

Born in Arecibo, Puerto Rico, in 1950, Rivera was active in Puerto Rico in the antiwar movement and became president of the local chapter of the Independence Party by the time he was twenty. He was hired as a union organizer in New York in 1976 and eventually worked his way up to the presidency.

Hispanic, March 1994, pp. 14–18.

1989 • Mexican American labor leader María Elena Durazo became the first woman to head a major union in the city of Los Angeles, the Hotel and Restaurant Employees Local 11, a union with a 70 percent Hispanic membership. She presides over an organization of thirteen thousand members and a staff of thirty-five.

Tardiff and Mabunda, *Dictionary of Hispanic Biography,* pp. 301–302.

1993 • The César Chávez Legacy Award was established by the César Chávez Foundation in honor of the deceased farmworker union organizer. The award was founded to honor those whose own lives reflect the same determination, spirit, and vision that Chávez taught through the example of his life. The award is given in three categories—legacy, freedom, and friendship—and has honored such people as Ethel Kennedy, Gloria Molina, and Edward James Olmos.

Hispanic, March 1996, p. 8.

1995 ⋅ Linda Chávez Thompson became the highest-ranking Hispanic in the history of the Congress of Industrial Organizations (CIO) when she assumed the position of executive vice president of the combined AFL (American Federation of Labor)and CIO (the AFL-CIO). She had been elected national vice president in 1993 and became the first Latina to serve on the executive council of the union.

Hispanic, August 1995, p. 10.

LITERATURE

1598 • In the mission to colonize New Mexico led by Juan de Oñate (ca. 1550–1630), there were literary men who imported the first European-style drama and poetry to an area that would become part of the United States. Among his men was an amateur playwright, Captain Marcos Farfán de los Godos, who wrote a play based on their colonizing adventure that the soldiers performed. This was the first play in a European language written and performed in what became the present-day United States. The soldiers also had in their repertoire the folk play, often performed on horseback, entitled *Los moros y los cristianos* (The Moors and the Christians), which dramatized the reconquest of the Spanish peninsula from the Moors during the Crusades. Finally, the poet Gaspar Pérez de Villagrá, also one of Oñate's soldiers, penned an epic poem memorializing the expedition, *La conquista de la Nueva Méjico* (The Conquest of New Mexico), which was later published in Spain and, considered an important literary work in the Hispanic world, is still studied today. This was the first or one of the first epics written in a European language in the New World.

Kanellos, *Chronology of Hispanic American History,* p. 47.

1654 • The first Spanish-speaking community in the northeast of what would become the United States was a colony of Sephardic Jews who established an oral and literary tradition that was unbroken until the present day.

Kanellos, *The Hispanic American Almanac,* p. 413.

1732 • Miguel de Quintana, a New Mexico peasant, became the first writer in the history of the Southwest to be tried by the Inquisition. The poet's verses came under suspicion and, on March 17, 1732, formal charges were made against Quintana to the Holy Office in Santa Fe, whereupon depositions and evidence were collected and sent to Mexico City. On May 22, 1734, the Inquisition office in Mexico City ruled that it did not have enough evidence to prosecute Quintana, although it advised that he be "examined for lesions of the head and questioned intensively regarding his claim to a divine inspiration behind his writing." The case was reopened in 1735, resulting in warnings being leveled at Quintana from the Mexico City offices, but the case was closed abruptly in 1737.

Gallegos, *Literacy, Education, and Society in New Mexico 1693–1821*, pp. 70–73.

1776 ◆ Probably the first documented library (other than private libraries) in New Mexico and much of the Southwest was in existence and use by this date, at the Santo Domingo mission, according to a report by Fray Anasta-

TITLE PAGE OF VILLAGRÁ'S EPIC OF THE COLONIZATION OF NEW MEXICO.

cio Domínguez who was studying the schools and churches in New Mexico. The catalog listed some 256 titles, but this number did not include sets and duplicates, which were extensive.

Gallegos, *Literacy, Education, and Society in New Mexico 1693–1821,* pp. 53–54.

1803 • The first literary work in the Spanish language published in the United States was José Agustín Caballero's *Sermón fúnebre en elogio del excelentísimo señor Don Christóbal Colón* (Funereal Sermon in Eulogy of That Excellent Gentleman Don Christopher Columbus), issued in Philadelphia by printers Eaken & Mecum.

Online Computer Library Center

1808 • The first book of exile literature, a popular Hispanic genre in the United States during the next two centuries, was *España ensangrentada . . .* (Bloodied Spain), written anonymously by "Viejo castizo español" (an old Spaniard of pure blood), and published in New Orleans. It was written in protest of the French invasion of Spain and of Napoleon's puppet Francisco Godoy.

Online Computer Library Center.

1811 • The first Spanish-language novel published in the United States was Atanasio Céspedes y Monroy's *La paisana virtuosa* (The Virtuous Countrywoman), issued by Mathew Carey in Philadelphia. That same year, Carey issued another novel by Céspedes, *La presumida orgullosa* (The Presumptuously Proud Woman).

Online Computer Library Center.

1817 • The first Spanish-language autobiography published in the United States was that of a nun in Colombia, Francisca Josefa de la Concepción de Castillo's *Vida de la V. M. Francisca Josefa de la Concepción* (Life of . . .), published in Philadelphia by T. H. Palmer, who specialized in publishing Spanish-language books.

Online Computer Library Center.

1821 • The first great eulogy by a Hispanic recorded in history was that of Captain Jacob de la Motta (1821–1877), a Sephardic Jewish doctor who resided in Charleston but gave the speech in New York on the death of the famed Reverend Gershom Mendes Seixas, also a Sephardic Jew. The eulogy was of particular relevance to Hispanic Jews in that it compared the freedom that Jews encountered in the United States with their persecution in Europe. Many of Charleston's Jews were immigrants or descended from immigrants who had to leave Spain and Portugal when they were persecuted by the Inquisition. Like de la Motta, who was a medical doctor and army surgeon who had served with distinction in the War of 1812, many of the Sephardics became founding and leading citizens in South Carolina and Georgia (which had originally belonged to Spain). So effective and moving was de la Motta's eulogy that two former U.S. presidents, James Madison and Thomas Jefferson, congratulated him on it in writing.

See also Science and Technology: Physical and Social Sciences, 1807 and 1836.
Simonhoff, *Jewish Notables in America, 1776–1865,* pp. 189–92.

1822 ✦ The first anthology of Spanish literature, *Extractos de los más célebres escritores y poetas españoles* (Excerpts from the Most Celebrated Spanish Writers and Poets), was published in Baltimore for use as a textbook in St. Mary's School.
Online Computer Library Center.

FÉLIX VARELA.

1824 ✦ In Philadelphia, the first philosophical work by the great Cuban patriot, novelist, journalist, and Catholic priest Félix Varela (1778–1853), *Lecciones de filosofía* (1818, Lessons in Philosophy) was published. Varela was the first Catholic vicar of New York and one of the leaders of the Cuban independence movement.
Cortina and Leal, "Introducción," in Felix Varela, *Jicoténcal,* p. xi.

1825 ✦ The first collection of poems by an Hispanic writer *Poesías de José María Heredia,* by Cuban exile José María Heredia (1803–1839), was published in New York. Heredia, who produced most of his poems in the United States, is considered to be one of the greatest poets of Spanish America.
Online Computer Library Center.

1826 ✦ The first Hispanic novel written and published in the United States, *Jicoténcal,* attributed to Cuban philosopher Félix Varela (1778–1853), was issued in Philadelphia. The novel relates the wars of Spanish conquest over the Indians of Mexico and, thus, indirectly supported the Cuban independence movement by equating Spanish Americans with the Indians. The novel, which was first published anonymously, was also the first historical novel ever written in the Spanish language. The historical genre entered Hispanic literature through the influence of Sir Walter Scott and James Fenimore Cooper.
Varela, *Jicoténcal.*

1828 ✦ The first collection of poetry by a Mexican author published in the United States, *Poesías de un mexicano* (The Poems of a Mexican), by Anastasio María de Ochoa y Acuña, was issued in New York.
Online Computer Library Center.

1828 ✦ The first collection of Spanish Golden Age plays to be read and studied as literature in U.S. colleges and universities was compiled and published in Boston by Francis Sales. *Selección de obras maestras dramáticas por Calderón de la Barca, Lope de Vega y Moreto* (A Selection of Dramatic Master Works by . . .) included plays by three of the greatest playwrights of

Spain's theatrical flowering in the seventeenth century. This anthology and others that followed helped to canonize these authors in the American college curriculum. During the 1820s, Sales published a number of anthologies and collections of Spanish literature.

Online Computer Library Center.

1834 • Lorenzo de Zavala (1788–1836) wrote and published the first book of travel literature by a Hispanic touring the United States, *Viage a los Estados Unidos de America* (Voyage to the United States of America). Zavala, a Mexican citizen, later became important in the Texas Revolution and became a vice president of the Texas Republic. That same year, another travel book written by a Mexican author, *Viage por los Estados Unidos del Norte* (Voyage to the United States of the North), by Rafael Reynal, was published in the United States in Cincinnati.

Online Computer Library Center.

1840 • The first edition by a mainstream publisher of Spanish Golden Age playwrights, *Obras maestras de Lope de Vega y Calderón de la Barca* (Master Works by . . .), published in New York by Henry Holt, was issued for use in the study of Spanish literature in U.S. colleges and universities.

Online Computer Library Center.

1858 • The first autobiography written by a Mexican American in the English language was Juan Nepomuceno Seguín's *The Personal Memoirs of John N. Seguín,* by the embattled and disenchanted political figure of the Texas Republic and former mayor of San Antonio. Seguín was born on October 27, 1806, and became a politician and one of the founders of the Republic of Texas. Born into a prominent family of French extraction in San Antonio, Texas, by the age of eighteen he had been elected mayor of San Antonio. One of the developers of a nationalist spirit in Texas, Seguín led Texans in opposition to the centrist government of Antonio López de Santa Anna in the 1830s.

JUAN NEPOMUCENO SEGUÍN.

In the struggle for independence from Mexico, Seguín served as a captain in the Texas cavalry, eventually achieving the rank of lieutenant colonel. After the war of independence, Seguín once again served at the head of San Antonio government, but this time as commander. In 1838, he was elected to the Texas senate, and in 1840 again to the mayoralty of San Antonio. He was active in defending Tejanos against profiteering Anglos that were rushing into the state to make their fortune at all costs. Unjustly accusing him of favoring invading Mexican forces and betraying the Santa Fe Expedition to foment revolt in New Mexico against Mexico, Anglos forced Seguín to resign as mayor in April 1842. He moved with his family across the Río Grande into Mexico in fear of reprisals. In Mexico, he was jailed and forced to serve in the Mexican army, including in battle against the United States during the Mexico War. In 1848, he once again moved to Texas, only to return to live out his days in Nuevo Laredo, Mexico, from 1867 until his death in 1890.

Tardiff and Mabunda, *Dictionary of Hispanic Biography,* p. 836.

1858 • The first anthology of Hispanic exile literature, *El laúd del desterrado* (The Lute of the Exiled), was published in New York by a group of Cuban exile poets and included the works of José María Heredia, Miguel Teurbe Tolón, Juan Clemente Zenea, and others. The anthology was an important indication that these writers were aware of the whole tradition of Hispanic literary exile and established political exile as one of the bases for literary creation by Hispanics in the United States to the present.

Matías Montes Huidobro, ed., *El laud del desterrado.*

1872 • The first novel written and published in English by a Hispanic of the United States was by María Amparo Ruiz de Burton (1832–1895), a domestic novel entitled *Who Would Have Thought It?* Originally published anonymously, the novel reconstructs antebellum and Civil War society in the North and engages the dominant U.S. myths of American exceptionalism, egalitarianism, and consensus, offering an acerbic critique of opportunism and hypocrisy as it represents northern racism and U.S. imperialism. The novel was the first by a U.S. Hispanic to address the disenfranchised status of women.

Ruiz de Burton, *Who Would Have Thought It?*

1881 • The first fictional narrative written and published in English from the perspective of the conquered Mexican population of the Southwest was *The Squatter and the Don* by María Amparo Ruiz de Burton (1832–1895); it was self-published under the pseudonym C. Loyal in San Francisco. The novel documents the loss of lands to squatters and banking and railroad interests in southern California shortly after statehood. Ruiz de Burton was a member of the landed gentry in southern California and she witnessed the disintegration of the old order, shifts in power relations, and the rapid capitalist development of the California Territory, all of which led to the disruption of everyday life for the Californios. In *The Squatter and the Don,* a historical romance, Ruiz de Burton laments land loss and calls for justice and redress of grievances. The novel questions U.S. expansionism, the rise of corporate monopolies and their power over government policy.

Kanellos, *The Hispanic American Almanac,* p. 414; Ruiz de Burton, *The Squatter and the Don.*

GEORGE SANTAYANA.

1881 • The first Spanish-language novel written and published in the Southwest was Manuel M. Salazar's romantic adventure novel, *La historia de un caminante, o Gervacio y Aurora* (The History of a Traveler on Foot, or Gervasio and Aurora), which created a colorful picture of pastoral life in New Mexico at the time.

Kanellos, *The Hispanic American Almanac,* p. 414.

1889 • Spanish-born philosopher George Santayana (1863–1952) became the first Hispanic philosopher and writer to receive a Ph.D. from Harvard. He went on to become a noted poet, philosopher, and professor in the United States and Europe. He published his first book, *The Sense of Beauty* on aesthetics, in 1896. In 1890, he was named assistant professor in the philosophy department at Harvard and in 1890 published his first book of poems, *Lucifer: A Theological Tragedy.*

Tardiff and Mabunda, *Dictionary of Hispanic Biography,* p. 824.

1915 • The first novel of the Mexican Revolution, *Los de abajo* (The Under-dogs), by Mariano Azuela, was published in El Paso, Texas,. It was the first and most important in a long line of novels of revolution published in exile and is also an important work in the history of Hispanic exile literature. Mariano Azuela, one of Mexico's greatest novelists and chroniclers of the Mexican Revolution, was born on January 1, 1873, in Lagos de Moreno, Jalisco, Mexico. Educated as a physician (University of Guadalajara, M.D., 1898), Azuela actually developed his career as a writer while practicing medicine until his death of a heart attack on March 1, 1952. Azuela's early career as a writer, in fact, was developed while participating in the revolution firsthand as a physician in the army of Francisco "Pancho" Villa.

Azuela wrote more than forty novels, most of them based on Mexico's political life from the point of view of a skeptic and critic bent on reforming social and political life in his native land. In many of his works, he documents the loss or corruption of the ideals that were fought for during the revolution. True to his immediate appreciation of social reality, Azuela's keen ear for dialogue and deft appropriation of characters from social reality contributed a recognition of grassroots Mexican culture that had not really appeared in Mexican letters before, especially within the context of political analysis through literature.

True to a tradition of Hispanic literature in exile, Azuela's greatest and most renowned novel, *Los de abajo,* was written while he was a fugitive in El Paso, Texas. In *Los de abajo,* Azuela examines the revolution through the eyes of a common soldier and comes to condemn the uncontrollable whirl-wind of violence that the revolution had become. But Azuela's condemnation was a pointed indictment of the forces of corruption and greed in converting the revolution into the murderer of those it was meant to protect and vindicate, such as the rural, grass-roots protagonist who is ultimately killed on the very spot where his involvement in the struggle began.

Throughout his career, Azuela was a productive novelist. His other works include *María Luisa* (1907), *Los fracasados* (The Failures, 1908), *Mala yerba* (1909; translated as *Marcela: A Mexican Love Story* in 1932) *Andrés Pérez* (1911), *Sin amor* (Without Love, 1912), *Los caciques* (1917; translated as *The Bosses* in 1956), *Las moscas* (1918; translated as *The Flies* in 1956), *Las tribulaciones de una familia decente* (1918; translated as *The Trials of a Respectable Family* in 1963), and many others.

Kanellos, *Chronology of Hispanic American History,* p. 172.

1916 • The first literary book to be published by a Dominican author in the United States was *El nacimiento de Dionisos* (The Birth of Dionysus) by Pedro Henríquez Ureña (1884–1946). At the time, Henríquez Ureña was the editor of the New York newspaper *Las novedades* (The News); he also was a brilliant teacher and literary critic.

Kanellos, *The Hispanic American Almanac,* p. 419.

1917 • The first immigration novel published in the United States was written by Colombian immigrant Alirio Díaz Guerra (1862–?). *Lucas Guevara* is the story of a young South American student who immigrates to the grand metropolis of New York, becomes disillusioned, and commits suicide.

Kanellos, *The Hispanic American Almanac,* p. 419.

1927 • Poet-philosopher George Santayana was the first U.S. Hispanic to be awarded the Gold Medal from the Royal Society of Literature in London.

Tardiff and Mabunda, *Dictionary of Hispanic Biography,* p. 824.

1929 • Poet-philosopher George Santayana became the first U.S. Hispanic poet to be offered a chair at a major university: the prestigious Norton Chair of Poetry at Harvard. He did not accept because he had given up teaching.

Tardiff and Mabunda, *Dictionary of Hispanic Biography,* p. 824.

1935 • The first novel written by a U.S. Hispanic to be nominated for the Pulitzer Prize was George Santayana's *The Last Puritan: A Memoir in the Form of a Novel.*

Tardiff and Mabunda, *Dictionary of Hispanic Biography,* p. 824.

1939 • Brother Angélico Chávez (1910–) published his first book of poetry, *Clothed with the Sun,* and eventually became the greatest religious poet among Hispanics in the United States. Born on April 10 in Wagon Mound, New Mexico, he was raised in Mora and attended St. Francis Seminary in Cincinnati, Ohio, and colleges in the Midwest. Chávez is the author of some twenty books, and he is also a historian of his order and of the Catholic church in New Mexico. What unifies Chávez's large output as a poet and historian is his interest in New Mexico's past and his own Catholicism.

Beginning as a religious poet, he later took an interest in historical fiction and, finally, in the history of the region itself, as in his most famous historical essay, *My Penitente Land: Reflections on Spanish New Mexico* (1947). Chávez's reputation as a creative writer rests upon an important body of poetic works that includes *Clothed with the Sun* (1939), *Eleven Lady Lyrics and Other Poems* (1945), *The Single Rose; The Rose Unica and Commentary of Fray Manuel de Santa Clara* (1948), and *The Virgin of Port Lligat* (1959). Although Chávez's poetry and all of his works are grounded in New Mexican Catholicism, his poems are not local color pieces celebrating New Mexico's picturesque landscape; instead they depict Chávez's inner life.

Dictionary of Literary Biography, Volume 82: *Chicano Writers,* pp. 86–90; Kanellos, *Chronology of Hispanic American History,* pp. 162, 176.

1945 • Chilean Gabriela Mistral (1889–1957) became Latin America's first Nobel Prize winner, for poetry. After becoming a Nobel laureate, she spent many years in the United States as an ambassador to the League of Nations and the United Nations for Chile.

Mistral was born in Vicuña, Chile, and trained as a teacher. As she became well known in the world of letters, she left teaching to serve as a consul and later as an ambassador. As Latin America's first Nobel laureate, she traveled extensively throughout the Americas and became known as a great humanitarian, an active promoter of public education, and a wonderful speaker. Her poetry reveals Mistral as a great humanitarian of broad erudition in world literature and the classics. But her overriding theme was always love. Her work was also rooted in a deep religiosity and the condition and circumstances of women, spanning the gamut of preoccupations from maternity to sterility. Mistral's first book, *Desolación* (Desolation), was published in New York by the Hispanic Institute in 1922. Of her twenty-some books of poetry, *Desolación* and *Tala* (1938) are considered her best works. She died in Hempstead, New York, on January 10, 1957.

GABRIELA MISTRAL, WINNER OF THE NOBEL PRIZE FOR LITERATURE.

Kanellos, *Chronology of Hispanic American History,* p. 122; Ryan, *Hispanic Writers,* pp. 222–23.

1958 • Novelist Floyd Salas (1931–) became the first U.S. Hispanic writer to receive a Rockefeller grant to study creative writing at the prestigious Centro Mexicano de Escritores in Mexico City. Upon returning to California from Mexico, Salas worked on Bay Area campuses as a creative writing instructor and became active in the campus protest movement, as well as immersed in the drug and hippie subcultures. These experiences became grist for his novels *What Now My Love?* (1970) and *State of Emergency* (1996). His first published book, *Tattoo the Wicked Cross* (1967), was made possible by his winning the prestigious Joseph Henry Jackson Award and a Eugene F. Saxton Fellowship, on the basis of early drafts of that novel.

FLOYD SALAS.

Tattoo the Wicked Cross is an exposé of the brutality of juvenile jail as seen by a street youth (*pachuco*) who is raped and abused; the brutalized protagonist ends up committing murder. The raw power and passion of Salas's narration left reviewers believing that Salas had experienced this brutality firsthand, but he actually based the story on tales he had heard. The overwhelming acclaim the novel received from reviewers projected Salas into a resplendent career. The *Saturday Review of Literature* gave the most important canonizing response to *Tattoo:* "One of the best and certainly one of the most important first novels published in the last ten years."

Kanellos, *The Hispanic Literary Companion,* p. 293.

1959 • José Antonio Villarreal (1924–) published what is considered to be the first Chicano novel in contemporary times. *Pocho,* a developmental novel in which the protagonist has a classic identity crisis, was also the first Chicano novel to be published by a major commercial house, Doubleday.

Dictionary of Literary Biography, Volume 82: *Chicano Writers,* pp. 282–88.

1962 • Nuyorican writer Piri Thomas was the first Hispanic writer to receive a grant from the Louis M. Rabinowitz Foundation. The grant enabled him to finish writing his groundbreaking autobiography, *Down These Mean Streets* (1967). The work that launched Nuyorican literature, *Down These Mean Streets* was also the first agonizing tale of the search for identity among conflicting cultural, racial, ethnic, and linguistic alternatives presented to Latinos in general and to Afro-Hispanic peoples in the United States in particular. It was such a milestone that the Nuyorican and Latino literature that followed it either continued its themes or totally rejected its poetic mélange of street language and psychodrama as a naive and unsophisticated cry out of the culture of poverty.

Thomas was born John Peter Thomas on September 30, 1928, in New York City's Harlem Hospital to a light-skinned Puerto Rican mother and an Afro-Cuban of the working class. In his upbringing he experienced racism in the most intimate of settings when his siblings's lighter skin was preferred over his obviously dark African inheritance. This prejudice, of course, presented one of the principal causes for anguish in his life and is reflected in his books. When his family attempted to escape the ills of the city by moving to Babylon, Long Island, he again faced rejection at school and in the neighborhood because of his skin color. In part, this is the subject of his second book, *Savior, Savior, Hold My Hand,* which also deals with the hypocrisy he faced while working with a Christian church.

Thomas grew up on the streets of Spanish Harlem, where he became involved in gang activity and criminality. In 1950, he participated in an armed robbery of a nightclub that left him and a policeman wounded; he was sentenced to and served seven years in jail, the subject of his *Seven Long Times* (1974). While in prison, Thomas became part of the black pride movement, converted to Islam, earned a G.E.D. and began writing. As a former convict, in 1962 he was befriended by an editor from Knopf and supported by a grant for five years from the Louis M. Rabinowitz Foundation, with which he was able to produce the modern classic autobiography that forever changed his life and the trajectory of Latino and ethnic literatures in the United States.

Kanellos, *The Hispanic Literary Companion,* pp. 327–28.

1963 • Jose Yglesias became the first Cuban American creative writer to be published by a mainstream press with the publication of *A Wake in Ybor City,* based on the Cuban Spanish community in Tampa, Florida. Yglesias is one of the pioneers of Hispanic literature in English; it could also be said that he is the first writer with a Cuban American consciousness. For more than thirty years, he wrote novels and stories based on Hispanic life in the United States, and he saw them published by some of the largest and most respected publishing houses in the country.

Yglesias was born in the cigar-making community of Ybor City, on November 29, 1919. He was the child of a Cuban mother and a Spanish father, who returned home to Galicia when Yglesias was only a child. Among the cigar rollers, a proud and intellectual lot, he learned about Hispanic litera-

JOSE YGLESIAS.

ture, history, and politics—interests that would inform his fiction and nonfiction writing his entire life. Like the tobacco workers, Yglesias was largely self-educated. Two days after graduating from high school, he went to New York City. After serving in the U.S. Navy during World War II, he attended Black Mountain College for one year (1946–47). He returned to New York City, married and began a family while working for a pharmaceutical company, where he eventually became an executive.

During the 1950s, Yglesias began writing reviews and articles for magazines and in 1963 saw his first novel published. *A Wake in Ybor City,* like most first novels, is highly autobiographical. Yglesias soon became a full-time writer of stories for such magazines as the *New Yorker, Esquire,* the *Atlantic,* the *Nation* and the *Sunday New York Times Magazine;* novels that deal mostly with Hispanics in the United States; and journalistic books about such topics as Franco's Spain and Castro's Cuba. Two of his stories were included in *Best American Stories* and form a part of his posthumous collection *The Guns in the Closet* (1996). In all, he wrote ten books of fiction, three of which were published posthumously. He died of cancer in December 1995.

Kanellos, *The Hispanic Literary Companion,* pp. 389–90.

1964 • The first literary magazine founded by Cuban exiles from the Cuban Revolution, *Cuadernos desterrados* (Exiled Notebooks), was established in Miami, Florida.

García, *Havana USA,* p. 262.

1965 • Ediciones Universal, the first and largest publishing house to serve the Cuban refugee community was founded in Miami, Florida, by Juan Manuel Salvat. It publishes the works of leading émigré scholars and literary figures. It was not until the 1970s and 1980s that other Cuban and Cuban American publishing houses began to appear, such as Editorial SIBI, Editorial Persona, Editorial Arcos, and Linden Lane Press.

García, *Havana USA,* p. 195.

1966 • San Antonio Texas poet Angela de Hoyos became the first U.S. Hispanic poet to win international recognition by winning the Bronze Medal of Honor (poetry) from Centro Studi e Scambi Internazionale (CSSI), Rome, Italy, 1966. She also won the Silver Medal of Honor (literature), CSSI, in 1967; the Diploma di Benemerenza (literature), CSSI, 1968; the Diploma di Benemerenza (poetry), CSSI, 1969 and 1970; and the Distinguished Service Citation, World Poetry Society Intercontinental, India, 1970.

Angela de Hoyos is a pioneer of modern Chicano poetry; when there was little opportunity for her works to be published and recognized in the United States, she began disseminating her poetry internationally. Finally, in the early 1970s as the Chicano literary movement was peaking, her work became part of the basis for Chicano literary flowering. She was the first of the women poets to gather a following in the movement, and became an inspiration for other early writers, such as Evangelina Vigil- Piñón, who followed in her path.

Tardiff and Mabunda, *Dictionary of Hispanic Biography,* p. 274.

1967 ⬧ Rodolfo "Corky" Gonzales, founder of a militant Chicano civil rights organization, the Crusade for Justice, wrote and published the first Chicano epic poem, *I Am Joaquín/Yo Soy Joaquín,* which influenced the development

COVER OF <u>YO SOY JOAQUÍN,</u> BY RODOLFO "CORKY" GONZALES.

of Chicano literature and the nationalist ideology. The poem was widely read and emulated, and was even the basis of a film created by El Teatro Campesino and narrated by Luis Valdez.

Rosales, *Chicano! The History of the Mexican American Civil Rights Movement*, pp. 180, 217.

1967 · The most influential Chicano magazine, *El grito* (The Shout), was founded in Berkeley, California, by two University of California professors, Octavio Romano and Herminio Ríos. *El grito* and the publishing house *Editorial Quinto Sol* (Fifth Sun), which they established in 1968, launched the careers of the most important writers of the Chicano movement, such as Alurista, Tomás Rivera, Rudolfo Anaya, and Rolando Hinojosa, as well as defined Chicano literature and established the canons of that literature by publishing those works that best exemplified Chicano culture, language, themes, and styles.

The very name of the publishing house emphasized its Mexican/Aztec identity, as well as the Spanish language; the "quinto sol" referred to Aztec belief in a period of cultural flowering that would take place sometime in the future, in a fifth age, which conveniently coincided with the rise of Chicano culture. In its publications there was a definite insistence on working-class and rural culture, as exemplified in the works of Rivera, Anaya, and Hinojosa, and there was also a promotion of works written bilingually or in dialect.

Kanellos, *The Hispanic American Almanac*, p. 422.

1969 · Nuyorican poet Victor Hernández Cruz became the first U.S. Hispanic poet to be published by a mainstream publishing house when Random House issued his *Snaps*. Cruz is the Nuyorican poet who was discovered as a precocious street poet while still in high school in New York; he has become the most recognized and acclaimed Hispanic poet by the mainstream. Despite his early acceptance into creative writing circles, culminating with *Life* magazine's canonizing him in 1981 as one of the twenty-five best American poets, Hernández Cruz has resisted estheticism and academic writing to remain very much an oral poet, a jazz poet, a poet of the people and popular traditions, a bilingual poet, a poet of intuition and tremendous insight.

Victor Hernández Cruz was born on February 6, 1949, in Aguas Buenas, Puerto Rico. He moved with his family to New York's Spanish Harlem at the age of five. Cruz attended Benjamin Franklin High School, where he began writing poetry. In the years following graduation, his poetry began to appear in *Evergreen Review, New York Review of Books,* and many other magazines. Beginning in 1970, he worked with poetry-in-the-schools programs in New York, such as the Teachers and Writers Collaborative.

In 1973, Cruz left New York and took up residence in San Francisco, where he worked for the U.S. Postal Service and served as a visiting poet at area colleges. From 1973 to 1975, he took up the life of the traveling troubadour, covering the full expanse of the United States from Alaska and Hawaii to Puerto Rico reading and performing his works while also continuing to write. Thereafter, he alternated living in San Francisco and Puerto Rico, dedicating himself mostly to writing and accepting engagements nationally to read from his works. Hernández Cruz received fellowships from the National Endowment for the Arts and the Guggenheim Foundation in 1980 and 1991, respectively.

Victor Hernández Cruz's poetry books include *Papo Got His Gun* (1966), *Snaps* (1969), *Mainland* (1973), *Tropicalization* (1976), *By Lingual Wholes* (1982), and *Rhythm, Content and Flavor* (1989).

Kanellos, *The Hispanic American Almanac*, pp. 447–48.

1969 • Editorial Quinto Sol published the first (or one of the first) anthologies of Chicano literature, *El Espejo/The Mirror,* edited by Octavio Romano-V. It included the works of such notable and still studied authors as Alurista, Miguel Méndez, and Tomás Rivera.

Griswold et al., *Chicano Art,* p. 215.

1970 • Editorial Quinto Sol established the first national award for Chicano literature, Premio Quinto Sol. The Premio included a $1,000 prize and publication of the winning book manuscript. The first three years, the prize went to books that are still seen as exemplary Chicano novels: Tomás Rivera's *. . . y no se lo tragó la tierra/ . . . And the Earth Did Not Part,* Rudolfo Anaya's *Bless Me Ultima* and Rolando Hinojosa's *Estampas del Valle y otras obras/Sketches of the Valley and Other Works.*

Kanellos, *The Hispanic American Almanac,* p. 423.

1970 • Texas novelist Tomás Rivera won the first national award for Chicano literature, Premio Quinto Sol, for his novel of migrant worker life *. . . y no se lo tragó la tierra / . . . And the Earth Did Not Part.*

Kanellos, *The Hispanic American Almanac,* p. 424.

1971 • Rudolfo Anaya's novel *Bless Me, Ultima,* the second winner of the Premio Quinto Sol, became the best-selling Chicano novel, selling more than one million copies over a twenty-year period according to the publishers. A straightforward narrative written in poetic and clear English, the novel is about a boy's coming of age in rural New Mexico and having to mediate the competing Indian and Spanish traditions of his maternal and paternal heritages. *Bless Me, Ultima* was the first U.S. Hispanic book to reach a broad segment of non-Hispanic readers.

Kanellos, *The Hispanic American Almanac,* p. 424.

1971 • Celedonio González became the first writer in exile from Castro's Cuba to change the focus from the political situation in Cuba to the development of Cuban culture in the United States in his novel *Los primos* (The Cousins). In this and following novels, he not only examined culture shock and conflict between Cubans and Americans but also treated a very taboo topic: criticism of the economic system of the United States, especially in its exploitation of Cuban workers. González was the first writer to present readers with Cubans who did not see themselves as Americans but who were also conscious that Cuba was no longer theirs. This was an intermediate step to the development of a Cuban American literature in the English language.

Kanellos, *The Hispanic American Almanac,* p. 441.

1971 • *Floricanto en Aztlán,* by Alurista, became the first Chicano poetry book to be published by a university, the University of California, Los Angeles, through its Chicano Studies Publications. The book was highly influential in integrating pre-Columbian culture and symbolism into rising Chicano nationalism. It was also an exemplary model of bilingualism in poetry.

Griswold et al., *Chicano Art,* p. 217.

1972 • The first journal for the study and promotion of Puerto Rican culture of the mainland United States, *The Rican Journal,* was founded and published by a Northeastern Illinois University sociology professor, Samuel Betances, in Chicago. In addition to publishing social science articles, the journal published original literature by Nuyoricans.

Kanellos, *The Hispanic American Almanac,* pp. 434–35.

1972 • Festival Floricanto, the first national Chicano literature festival, was held in Los Angeles.

Griswold et al., *Chicano Art,* p. 217.

1973 • The first national magazine of U.S. Hispanic literature, *Revista Chicano-Riqueña* (The Chicano-Rican Review), was founded at Indiana University Northwest in Gary, Indiana, by coeditors Nicolás Kanellos and Luis Dávila. Over the years, the magazine which is still published today under the title *The Americas Review* at the University of Houston, has promoted a pan-Hispanic culture in the United States and launched the careers of most of the important writers of Hispanic literature, including Lorna Dee Cervantes, Sandra Cisneros, Ana Castillo, and many others. In 1979, the magazine founded its own literary press, Arte Público Press, which grew to be the largest noncommercial publisher of literature in the United States.

Kanellos, *The Hispanic American Almanac,* p. 427.

NICHOLASA MOHR.
PHOTO BY PHIL CANTOR.

1973 • Nicholasa Mohr (1935–) became the first U.S. Hispanic woman in modern times to have her literary works published by the major commercial publishing houses, and she has developed the longest career as a creative writer for these publishing houses than any other Hispanic female writer. Only Jose Yglesias has published more works than she and for a longer period of time. Mohr's books for such publishers as Dell/Dial, Harper & Row, and Bantam, in both the adult and children's literature categories, have won numerous awards and outstanding reviews. Part and parcel of her work is the experience of growing up female, Hispanic, and a minority in New York City.

Born November 1, 1935, in New York City, Nicholasa Mohr was raised in Spanish Harlem. Educated in New York City schools, she finally escaped poverty after graduating from the Pratt Center for Contemporary Printmaking in 1969. From that date until the publication of her first book, *Nilda* (1973), Mohr developed a successful career as a graphic artist.

Nilda, a novel that traces the life of a young Puerto Rican girl confronting prejudice and coming of age during World War II, won the Jane Addams Children's Book Award and was selected by *School Library Journal* as a Best Book of the Year. It was the first book by a U.S. Hispanic author to be so honored. The Society of Illustrators presented Mohr with a citation of merit for the book's jacket design. After *Nilda's* success, Mohr was able to produce numerous stories, scripts, and the following titles: *El Bronx Remembered* (1975), *In Nueva York* (1977), *Felita* (1979), *Rituals of Survival: A Woman's Portfolio* (1985), *Going Home* (1986), and others.

Kanellos, *Chronology of Hispanic American History,* p. 258; Telgen and Kamp, *Latinas! Women of Achievement,* pp. 247–54.

1973 • Ricardo Sánchez (1941–1995) became the first Chicano poet to have a book published by a mainstream commercial publishing house when Anchor/Doubleday issued his *Canto y grito mi liberación* (I Sing and Shout for My Liberation). It was also the first bilingual poetry book published by a major commercial publisher. Ricardo Sánchez was one of the most prolific Chicano poets, one of the first creators of a bilingual literary style, and one of the first to be identified with the Chicano movement. He was a tireless and popular oral performer and social activist whose creative power expressed itself in innovative uses of both Spanish and English in poetry, frequently through the creation of interlingual neologisms and abrupt linguistic contrasts. His verse is as overwhelming in sheer power as was the his strong and aggressive personality, which was forged in hard prison labor.

Ricardo Sánchez was born the youngest of thirteen children in the notorious Barrio del Diablo (Devil's Neighborhood) in El Paso, Texas. He received his early education there and became a high school drop-out, an army enlistee, and later a repeat offender sentenced to prison terms in Soledad Prison in California and Ramsey Prison Farm Number One in Texas. At these institutions he began his literary career before his last parole in 1969. Much of his early life experience of oppressive poverty and overwhelming racism, as well as his suffering in prisons and his self-education and rise to a high level of political and social consciousness, is chronicled in his poetry, which, although very lyrical, is the most autobiographical of all the Hispanic poets. Sánchez always envisioned himself participating, in fact leading, a sociopolitical consciousness-raising movement. His many travels and itinerant lifestyle—always in search of a permanent job in academia—resulted in his functioning as a troubadour-model for the developing Chicano literary movement. His poetry announced and exemplified the authenticity of a bilingual writing style that had roots in oral tradition and community concerns.

Dictionary of Literary Biography, Volume 82: *Chicano Writers,* pp. 239–45.

1973 • Poet-novelist Floyd Salas became the first Hispanic writer to serve as the statewide coordinator of poetry in the schools of California.

Tardiff and Mabunda, *Dictionary of Hispanic Biography,* p. 793.

1974 • Estela Portillo Trambley became the first woman to win the national award for Chicano literature, Premio Quinto Sol, for her collection of short stories, *Rain of Scorpions*. Her winning marked the ascendancy of Mexican American women into the Chicano literary movement, which had been so dominated by males.

Kanellos, *The Hispanic American Almanac,* p. 426.

1974 • A group of young and radical Cuban émigrés founded the first pro-Cuban Revolution magazine in the United States: *Areíto*. Headed by Lourdes Casal, the magazine supported the Cuban government, which it stated had created a more egalitarian society. The magazine's stance prompted the defection of various sponsors and hostile reaction from the Cuban refugee press and intellectuals. Despite the hostility, *Areíto* survived well into the 1980s.

García, *Havana USA,* pp. 201–203.

1975 • The first anthology of Nuyorican literature, *Nuyorican Poetry: An Anthology of Puerto Rican Words and Feelings,* was compiled by Miguel Algarín and Miguel Piñero. Algarín owned and administered the Nuyorican Poets Cafe, which promoted the distinct identity of Puerto Ricans born or raised on the mainland, and Piñero was the first Nuyorican writer to gain national acclaim with his play *Short Eyes*.

See also Theater, 1973.

Kanellos, *The Hispanic Literary Companion,* pp. 244–46.

1975 • New York Puerto Rican novelist Nicholasa Mohr's second book, *El Bronx Remembered,* was awarded the *New York Times*'s Outstanding Book Award in teenage fiction and received the Best Book Award from the *School Library Journal*. *El Bronx Remembered* was also a National Book Award finalist in children's literature.

Telgen and Kamp, *Latinas! Women of Achievement,* p. 252.

1975 • Chicano poet Gary Soto became the first Hispanic writer to win the nationally prestigious Academy of American Poets Prize. That same year, he won the *Nation*'s Discovery Award. Soto is a prolific poet and writer of books for children and young adults.

Kanellos, *The Hispanic American Almanac,* p. 429.

1975 • Alejandro Morales became the first Chicano novelist to have a book published in Spanish in Mexico. The publication of *Caras viejas y vino nuevo* (Old Faces and New Wine) was an important landmark in Mexico's recognition of Mexican Americans and their culture.

Kanellos, *The Hispanic American Almanac,* pp. 454–55.

1976 • The first literary magazine founded by Cuban exile writers outside of Miami *Exilio,* was founded. It was published in New York until 1973 by Víctor Batista Falla and Raimundo Fernández Bonilla. Other magazines followed, such as Ediciones Universal's *Revista Alacrán Azul* (1970), *Caribe* (1975–80), and *Escandalar* (1978–82).

García, *Havana USA,* p. 195.

ROLANDO HINOJOSA.

1976 • Rolando Hinojosa became the first U.S. Hispanic writer and the first American to win the prestigious international award Premio Casa de las Américas (House of the Americas Prize) from Cuba for his novel *Klail City y sus alrededores* (Klail City and Surroundings). He was the first Chicano novelist to win an international award.

Kanellos, *The Hispanic American Almanac,* pp. 425–26.

1976 • Gary Soto became the first U.S. Hispanic writer to win the United States Award of the International Poetry Forum for his book *The Elements of San Joaquin.*

Fernández, *Twenty-five Years of Hispanic Literature in the United States,* p. 14.

1977 • Nicholasa Mohr's third book, *In Nueva York,* was the first Hispanic title to be named Notable Trade Book in the Field of Social Studies by the joint committee of the National Council for Social Studies and the Children's Book Council.

Telgen and Kamp, *Latinas! Women of Achievement,* p. 252.

1977 • San Antonio poet Evangelina Vigil-Piñón became the first Hispanic writer to win the National Literary Contest of the Coordinating Council of Literary Magazines for work published in a small magazine. Vigil-Piñón is the Chicano poet who has most sensitively portrayed and celebrated working-class culture. She is also one of the leading exponents of bilingual code-switching in poetry—for Vigil-Piñón as natural a transference from English to Spanish and back as conversation at the kitchen table. Working at the center of U.S. Hispanic literature as the poetry editor for the leading Hispanic literary magazine, *The Americas Review,* Vigil-Piñón has also been a leader in the Hispanic women's movement as an anthologizer, speaker, and host of writers on tour.

Kanellos, *The Hispanic Literary Companion,* p. 358–60.

1978 • The group of young Cuban émigrés publishing the pro–Cuban Revolution magazine *Areíto* in New York published their first anthology, *Contra viento y marea* (Against Wind and Waves), in Cuba. The writings of these refugees, who had been forced to accompany their parents into exile from Cuba at an early age, recounted their experiences as refugees in a foreign culture and their allegiance to Communist Cuba. In 1978, the anthology was awarded Cuba's highest literary award, one regarded as one of the most distinguished in all of Spanish America: Premio Casa de las Américas (House of the Americas Prize).

García, *Havana USA,* p. 201.

1978 ⋅ Puerto Rican novelist and short story writer José Luis González became the first U.S. Hispanic writer to win Mexico's most prestigious literary award, the Xavier Viallurrutia Prize for Fiction, for his novel *Balada de otro tiempo* (Ballad of Another Time), which is set to the background of the U.S. invasion of Puerto Rico during the Spanish-American War.

Kanellos, *Chronology of Hispanic American History,* p. 262.

1978 ⋅ Poet Gary Soto's book *The Tale of Sunlight* became the first book by a Hispanic poet to be nominated for the Pulitzer Prize. It was also the first Hispanic poetry book to be nominated for the National Book Award.

Tardiff and Mabunda, *Dictionary of Hispanic Biography,* p. 866.

1979 ⋅ The oldest and largest publisher of U.S. Hispanic literature, Arte Público Press, was founded at the University of Houston by Nicolás Kanellos, a professor and founder-editor of *Revista Chicano-Riqueña,* the oldest Hispanic literary magazine in the United States. Over the years, the press won numerous awards and launched the careers of most of the prominent U.S. Hispanic writers. By the early 1990s, the press had become the largest noncommercial publisher of literature in the United States, issuing more than thirty titles per year. The first book published by Arte Público Press was Tato Laviera's groundbreaking collection of poems *La Carreta Made a U-Turn.*

Kanellos, *The Hispanic American Almanac,* p. 427.

1979 ⋅ Arte Público Press organized the First National Latino Book Fair in Chicago, Illinois. In addition to exhibiting and selling books by the few Hispanic presses and magazines that existed in the United States at that time, the book fair featured readings by some of the most important writers of the period, such as Ana Castillo, Lorna Dee Cervantes, Sandra Cisneros, Abelardo Delgado, Sandra María Esteves, Tato Laviera, and Rolando Hinojosa.

Kanellos, *The Hispanic American Almanac,* pp. 437–38.

1979 ⋅ Nicolás Kanellos, editor of *Revista Chicano-Riqueña* literary magazine, became the first Hispanic to receive the $5,000 award for Outstanding Editor from the Coordinating Council of Literary Magazines. *Revista Chicano-Riqueña* was and continues to be the leading magazine of U.S. Hispanic literature.

1980 • Prize-winning novelist Rudolfo Anaya was the first Hispanic novelist to receive a gubernatorial award, the New Mexico Governor's Award for Excellence. Anaya is the author of one of the most celebrated novels of U.S. Hispanic literature, *Bless Me, Ultima* (1972). Anaya was born on October 30, 1937, in the village of Pastura, New Mexico, in surroundings similar to those celebrated in his famous novel about growing up in the rural culture of New Mexico. He attended public schools in Santa Rosa and Albuquerque and earned both his B.A. (1963) and his M.A. (1968) in English from the University of New Mexico. In 1972, he also earned an M.A. in guidance and counseling from the same university. From 1963 to 1970, he taught in the public schools, but in 1974 he became a member of the English department of the University of New Mexico.

With the success of his writing career, Anaya rose to become the head of the creative writing program at the University of New Mexico. Included among his many awards are an honorary doctorate from the University of Albuquerque, the New Mexico Governor's Award for Excellence, the President's National Salute to American Poets and Writers in 1980, and the Premio Quinto Sol in 1972 for *Bless Me, Ultima*. Anaya is also a fellow of the National Endowment for the Arts and the Kellogg Foundation, through whose auspices he has been able to travel to China and other countries for study.

Kanellos, *The Hispanic Literary Companion,* pp. 41–42; *Dictionary of Literary Biography,* Volume 82: *Chicano Writers,* pp. 24–35.

1980 • Mexican American poet Luis Omar Salinas became the first Hispanic writer to win the Stanley Kunitz Poetry Prize and the Earl Lyon Award for his collection *Afternoon of the Unreal.* Salinas is one of the most beloved and enduring poets to emerge from the Chicano literary movement. His productivity has spanned the entire contemporary movement, with his first poems appearing in newspapers, magazines, and anthologies about the time when the first Chicano literary magazines and presses were being founded in the late 1960s. He always provided a broadly romantic and highly lyric inspiration to Chicanos in search of roots, rather than solely basing his works in the sociopolitical reality of ethnic minority struggle.

Highly influenced by Spain's Federico García Lorca and Chile's Pablo Neruda, Salinas has created a somewhat surreal, thoughtful, and very personal ongoing text in what otherwise has been the development of an epic and communal literature. Salinas has said that his poetic ideal is to "somehow come to terms with the tragic and through the tragic gain a vision which transcends this world in some way."

Tardiff and Mabunda, *Dictionary of Hispanic Biography,* pp. 795–96.

1981 • Jesús Abraham "Tato" Laviera became the fist Hispanic author to win the American Book Award of the Before Columbus Foundation, which recognizes and promotes multicultural literature. Laviera is the best-selling Hispanic poet of the United States, and he bears the distinction of still having all of his books in print. Born September 5, 1950, in Santurce, Puerto Rico, he migrated to New York City at the age of ten with his family, which settled in a poor area of the Lower East Side. After finding himself in an alien society and with practically no English, Laviera was able to adjust and eventually graduate high school as an honor student. Despite having no other degrees, his intelligence, aggressiveness, and thorough knowledge of his community led to his developing a career in the administration of social service agencies.

After the publication of his first book, *La Carreta Made a U-Turn* (1979), Laviera gave up administrative work to dedicate his time to writing. Since 1980, Laviera's career has included not only writing but touring nationally as a performer of his poetry, directing plays he has written and producing cultural events. In 1980, he was received by President Jimmy Carter at the White House Gathering of American Poets. In 1981, his second book, *Enclave,* was the recipient of the American Book Award.

Kanellos, *The Hispanic American Almanac,* pp. 435–39, 452–53.

1981 • Lorna Dee Cervantes's *Emplumada* became the first Hispanic poetry book to be published by a university press, the University of Pittsburgh Press, in its prestigious Pitt Poetry Series.

Griswold et al., *Chicano Art,* p. 220.

1981 • Cherrie Moraga and Gloria Anzaldúa, two Chicana lesbian writers, became the first to compile an anthology of the literature and thought of women of color, *This Bridge Called My Back: Writings by Radical Women of Color.* The book has become the most famous and best-selling anthology of its kind and it has inspired a movement of Hispanic feminist and lesbian writers.

Kanellos, *The Hispanic American Almanac,* p. 454.

1981 • New York poet Sandra María Esteves's *Yerba buena* (Mint) was the first Hispanic book to win the award for Best Small Press Publication. Esteves, the daughter of Puerto Rican and Dominican parents, is one of the leading exponents of bilingual feminist poetry; she is also one of the most noted oral performers of poetry. Her other works include *Tropical Rains: A Bilingual Downpour* (1984) and *Bluestown Mockingbird Mambo* (1990).

Telgen and Kamp, *Latinas! Women of Achievement,* pp. 121–23.

SANDRA MARÍA ESTEVES.

1981 • Victor Hernández Cruz became the first U.S. Hispanic poet to be canonized as one of the few great American poets when the April 1981 issue of *Life* magazine proclaimed him a national treasure by including him among a handful of outstanding American poets—without making reference to his race or ethnicity.

Kanellos, *The Hispanic American Almanac,* pp. 447–48.

1983 • Poet Evangelina Vigil-Piñón became the first Hispanic female writer to win the American Book Award from the Before Columbus Foundation for her *Thirty an' Seen a Lot.* Vigil-Piñón was born in San Antonio, Texas, on November 19, 1949, the second of ten children of a very poor family that lived for years in public housing. In her later childhood years, Vigil lived with her maternal grandmother and uncle, from whom she learned much of the oral lore that has become such an important basis for poetry; but Vigil-Piñón's mother was also an avid reader who gave her daughter a love of books. From her grandmother, she learned "to observe and listen for words of wisdom which come only with experience." And, indeed, the predominant narrator in her first full-length collection of poems, *Thirty an' Seen a Lot* (1982), is that of the acute but anonymous observer, the observer of the life of working-class people in her beloved West Side barrio of San Antonio, the recorder of their language and diction, their proverbs and music, their joys and sorrows.

Despite the apparently natural vernacular of her writing, Vigil- Piñón's poetry is the product of great craftsmanship, obtained through extensive reading and self-education as well as through formal study. She obtained a B.A. in English from the University of Houston in 1974 and took post-graduate courses at various institutions afterward. She also has served as an adjunct faculty member for the University of Houston since the mid-1980s.

Dictionary of Literary Biography, Volume 122: *Chicano Writers,* pp. 306–12; Kanellos, *The Hispanic Literary Companion,* p. 358–60.

1983 ⬥ *Revista Mariel,* the first magazine published by Cuban refugees from the Mariel Boatlift, was founded. Established in Miami initially by Reinaldo Arenas, Roberto Valero, and Juan Abreu, it was later moved to New York and specialized in publishing the works of authors who had been silenced by the Castro regime, as had its leading editor and literary figure, Reinaldo Arenas.

García, *Havana USA,* p. 195.

1983 ⬥ Texas Mexican American writer Lionel G. García was the first Hispanic to win the PEN Southwest Award, for his novel *Leaving Home.* García went on to become the first and only Hispanic author to win the two other major awards for fiction in the Southwest: the Southwest Book Award of the Southwest Booksellers Association and the Texas Institute of Letters Award for Fiction for his 1989 novel, *Hardscrub.*

García is a novelist who has created some of the most memorable characters in Chicano literature in a style that is well steeped in the traditions of Texas tall-tale and Mexican American folk narrative. Born in San Diego, Texas, on August 20, 1935, García grew up in an environment in which Mexican Americans were the majority population in his small town and on the ranches where he worked and played. In order to make a living, García became a veterinarian, but always practiced his first love: storytelling and writing. In 1983 he won the PEN Southwest Discovery Award for his novel in progress, *Leaving Home,* which was published in 1985. This and his second novel, *A Shroud in the Family* (1987), draw heavily on his family experiences and small-town background; both are set in a quaint village very much like San Diego, Texas, where he grew up, and follow the antics of children similar to those friends and family members that surrounded him as a child—they reappear again in his collection of autobiographical stories, *I Can Hear the Cowbell Ring* (1994).

García's prize-winning novel *Hardscrub* (1989) is a departure from his former works; it is a realistically drawn chronicle of the life of an Anglo child in an abusive family relationship. It won the Award for the Best Novel and the Southwest Booksellers Association Prize for Fiction.

Dictionary of Literary Biography, Volume 82: *Chicano Writers,* pp. 123–24.

1983 • Luis Omar Salinas became the first Hispanic writer to win the General Electric Foundation Younger Writers Award, in recognition for poems he published in the literary magazine *Revista Chicano-Riqueña.*

Tardiff and Mabunda, *Dictionary of Hispanic Biography,* pp. 785–86.

1983 • Nicolás Kanellos, founder and publisher of Arte Püblico Press, became the first U.S. Hispanic publisher ever to be inducted into the international writers organization PEN.

Unterburger, *Who's Who among Hispanic Americans,* p. 355.

1984 • El Paso poet Pat Mora's first collection of poems, *Chants,* was the first Hispanic book to win the Southwest Book Award, given by the Border Regional Library Association. *Chants* is a celebration of women and the culture of the United States-Mexican border. Pat Mora has developed the broadest audiences for her poetry of all of the Hispanic poets in the United States. Her clean, crisp narrative style and the healing, all-embracing messages in her verse have allowed her poetry to reach out to both adults and young people. In fact, Mora's poems have been reprinted in more elementary, middle, and high school textbooks than any other Hispanic poet's of the United States.

Pat Mora was born and raised in El Paso, Texas. She attended the El Paso public schools and received all of her higher education in this border city, including a B.A. and an M.A. in English from the University of Texas at El Paso. After graduating from college in 1963, she worked as an English teacher in the El Paso public schools and the El Paso Community College; eventually she made her way back to the University of Texas at El Paso as an instructor and, from 1981 to 1988, served as a university administrator and museum director. Mora began publishing poetry in little magazines, such as *The Americas Review* in the late 1970s and early 1980s as part of the first wave of Chicana writers to grab the reins of the Chicano literary movement and assume its leadership. It was her first books of poetry, however, that firmly established her reputation as a lyric shaman and celebrant of biculturalism. For *Chants* (1984) and for *Borders* (1986), Mora received Southwest Book Awards, critical acclaim, and entry into the college and high school curricula. Her publication in 1991 of *Communion* consolidated her dominant themes and solidified her reputation in academia.

Telgen and Kamp, *Latinas! Women of Achievement,* pp. 255–60.

1985 • Nicholasa Mohr's collection of feminist short stories, *Rituals of Survival: A Woman's Portfolio,* became the first Hispanic book to receive a legislative commendation, from the New York state legislature.

Telgen and Kamp, *Latinas! Women of Achievement,* p. 253.

1985 • Oscar Hijuelos, who later won a Pulitzer Prize, became the first U.S. Hispanic writer to win the prestigious American Academy in Rome Fellowship from the American Academy and the Institute for Arts and Letters.

Kanellos, *The Hispanic Literary Companion,* p. 117.

1986 • *The Americas Review* (formerly *Revista Chicano- Riqueña*) became the first Hispanic magazine ever to win the Citation of Achievement from the Coordinating Council of Literary Magazines. *The Americas Review* went on to win the citation again in 1987.

Kanellos, *The Hispanic Literary Companion,* p. xx.

1986 • Dominican American novelist and poet Julia Alvarez became the first Hispanic female writer to win the General Electric Foundation Award for Young Writers. The daughter of Dominican immigrants, Alvarez is the author of novels and poetry about growing up biculturally in the United States and also teaches creative writing at Middlebury College, Middlebury, Vermont. Her most successful work is a novel, *How the García Girls Lost Their Accent,* published in 1991.

Telgen and Kamp, *Latinas! Women of Achievement,* pp. 19–24.

1986 • Michael Nava published his first novel, *The Little Death,* thus becoming the creator of the first Hispanic gay detective series. As of 1996, six novels have been published in the series that features gay detective Henry Ríos.

Publishers Weekly, 30 September 1996, p. 49.

1988 • Poet Pat Mora was the first Hispanic writer to be named to the *El Paso Herald Post* Writers Hall of Fame. An El Paso native who had won two Southwest Book Awards, Mora was also inducted into the Texas Institute of Letters the same year.

Telgen and Kamp, *Latinas! Women of Achievement,* p. 258.

1988 • Arte Público Press was named one of four finalists for the *Boston Globe* Small Press Grand Prize. It was the only Hispanic press to ever progress that far in the competition.

Kanellos, *The Hispanic Literary Companion,* p. xx.

1988 • Nicolás Kanellos, the founder and publisher of Arte Público Press, became the first Hispanic publisher ever to be honored with the Hispanic Heritage Award for Literature, presented at the White House by President Ronald Reagan.

Unterburger, *Who's Who among Hispanic Americans,* p. 355.

1989 • Poet Carolina Hospital compiled the first anthology of Cuban American literature, *Cuban American Writers: Los Atrevidos,* thus announcing the birth and acceptance of Cuban American literature, rather than a literature of exile and immigration. Carolina Hospital has been in the forefront of developing a Cuban American aesthetic in literature. Not only does her poetry demonstrate the particular bilingual-bicultural nature of Cubans developing their literary sensibility in the United States, but her editorial work has helped to announce and define this aesthetic.

CAROLINA HOSPITAL.
PHOTO BY PHIL ROCHE.

Born in Havana just two years before the triumph of the revolution, she accompanied her family into exile in 1961 and was raised and educated in Florida. Like so many other children of exiles who had no say in their being transported into another culture and raised in an educational system that utilized a language different from that of the home, she became part of a generation of young people who knew only the United States as home but were constantly encouraged by parents and relatives to identify with an island of the past that they could only re-create in their imagination. The tensions between the U.S. reality and a mythic Cuba formed by the nostalgia of exiles, between the institutional English and Anglo-American culture of the outside world and the nurturing Spanish of the home and tradition, between growing up as an immigrant rather than viewing life as an exile dominate the works of Carolina Hospital and the generation of writers that she identified in her groundbreaking anthology.

Kanellos, *The Hispanic Literary Companion,* pp. 138–39.

1989 • Short story writer and novelist Helena María Viramontes became the first Hispanic to win the Storytelling Award of the Sundance Institute, the famed workshop for screenwriters. Viramontes is one of the most distinguished craftspeople of short fiction that Hispanic literature has produced. Her writing career began while she was still young and affiliated with one of the most avant-garde Chicano magazines, the streetwise *ChismeArte,* for which she served as literary editor. The magazine was emblematic of her own writing style, still very much in touch with her upbringing on the streets of East Los Angeles, very hip and polished owing to her college education and her studies in creative writing and film. She is the author of two books, *The Moths and Other Stories* (1985) and *Under the Feet of Jesus* (1995).

Dictionary of Literary Biography, Volume 122: *Chicano Writers,* pp. 322–28; Kanellos, *The Hispanic Literary Companion,* pp. 383–84.

1989 • The first Hispanic book to win the title Outstanding Book in the Humanities was *European Perspectives on Hispanic Literature of the United States,* edited by Genvieve Fabre and published by Arte Público Press.

Fabre, *European Perspectives on Hispanic Literature of the United States.*

1989 • The first television documentary on Hispanic literature of the United States, *Birthwrite: Growing Up Hispanic,* directed by Jesús Treviño, was aired by the Public Broadcasting Service.

Kanellos, *The Hispanic American Almanac,* p. 439.

1989 • Nicolás Kanellos, publisher of Arte Público Press, became the first publisher to be honored with the American Book Award in the publisher-editor category of the Before Columbus Foundation. Arte Público Press, founded by Kanellos in 1979, is the largest Hispanic book publisher in the United States and has accrued more awards and launched more Hispanic authors into mainstream acceptance than any other press.

Unterburger, *Who's Who among Hispanic Americans,* p. 355.

1990 • The first major textbook of Chicano literature for high schools, *Mexican American Literature,* edited by Charles Tatum, was published by the educational publishing giant Harcourt Brace Jovanovich. The publication marked not only the institutionalization of Chicano literature but also the growth of the Mexican American school population.

Kanellos, *The Hispanic American Almanac,* p. 428.

1990 • Poet-novelist Judith Ortiz Cofer became the first Hispanic writer to receive a Special Citation in the PEN Martha Albrand Award competition for *Silent Dancing: A Partial Remembrance of a Puerto Rican Childhood* (1990), a collection of autobiographical essays and poems. The book was also awarded the Pushcart Prize in the essay category, it was selected for the New York Public Library System List of Best Books for the Teen Age, and the title essay was chosen by Joyce Carol Oates for *The Best American Essays* (1991).

Kanellos, *The Hispanic Literary Companion,* pp. 231–32.

1990 • The first Hispanic novel to become a National Book Award finalist was Elena Castedo's *Paradise,* published by Warner Books.

Fernández, *Twenty-five Years of Hispanic Literature in the United States,* p. 13.

1991 • Oscar Hijuelos (1951–) became the first Hispanic writer to win the Pulitzer Prize for fiction. Born to Cuban American working-class parents in New York City, Hijuelos was educated in public schools and obtained a B.A. in 1975 and an M.A. in 1976, both in English, from City College of the City University of New York. Hijuelos is one of the few Hispanic writers to have formally studied creative writing and to have broken into the Anglo-dominated creative writing circles, participating in prestigious workshops, such as the Breadloaf Writers Conference, and benefiting from highly competitive fellowships, such as the American Academy in Rome Fellowship from the American Academy and the Institute for Arts and Letters (1985), the National Endowment for the Arts Fellowship (1985) and the Guggenheim Fellowship (1990).

Hijuelos is the author of various short stories and three novels, *Our House in the Last World* (1983), *The Mambo Kings Play Songs of Love* (1989), and *The Fourteen Sisters of Emilio Montez O'Brien* (1993). *The Mambo Kings Play Songs of Love,* the winner of the Pulitzer Prize, is more than just a story of immigration. It examines a period in time when Hispanic culture was highly visible in the United States and was able to influence American popular culture: the 1950s during the height of the mambo craze and the overwhelming success of Desi Arnaz's television show, *I Love Lucy.* Written in a poetic but almost documentary style, the novel follows two brothers who are musicians trying to ride the crest of the Latin music wave. While providing a picture of one segment of American life never seen before in English-language fiction, the novel also indicts womanizing and alcoholism.

Kanellos, *Chronology of Hispanic American History,* pp. 231, 276.

1991 • Victor Villaseñor's family autobiography, *Rain of Gold,* became the first book published by a Hispanic press, Arte Público Press, to make it onto the best-seller lists in the United States.

Kanellos, *Chronology of Hispanic American History,* pp. 214, 259.

1991 • *How the García Girls Lost Their Accent,* by Julia Alvarez became the first novel by a Dominican American author to join the current of Hispanic ethnic novels being issued by mainstream presses.

Tardiff and Mabunda, *Dictionary of Hispanic Biography,* pp. 33–34.

1991 • Publishing giant Random House issued a collection of essays and short stories, Sandra Cisneros's *Woman Hollering Creek and Other Stories,* and then also reissued her two previous titles, *The House on Mango Street* and *My Wicked Wicked Ways.* Cisneros thus became the first Chicana to be supported by the commercial establishment.

Dictionary of Literary Biography, Volume 82: *Chicano Writers,* pp.77–81.

1991 • *Intaglio: A Novel in Six Stories,* by Roberto Fernández, became the first Hispanic book to win the Minority Publishers Exchange Award for fiction.

Kanellos, *Hispanic American Literature,* p. 128.

LUCHA CORPI.

1992 • Mexican American novelist Lucha Corpi became the first Hispanic writer to win the PEN Oakland Josephine Miles Award for her *Eulogy for a Brown Angel,* in which Corpi created the astute Chicana detective Gloria Damasco, who unravels the mysterious assassination of a young boy during the protest activities of the 1970 Chicano Moratorium against the Vietnam War. Described as a feminist detective novel, *Eulogy* is fast-paced, suspenseful, and packed with an assortment of interesting characters. The feminist protagonist, Gloria Damasco, is somewhat of a clairvoyant who is able to use more than reason and logic in solving a very puzzling crime. In addition to the PEN Oakland award, *Eulogy* also received the Multicultural Publishers Exchange Best Book of Fiction award. In 1995, Gloria Damasco returned in a mystery set against the background of the United Farm Workers movement in California, *Cactus Blood.*

Dictionary of Literary Biography, Volume 82: *Chicano Writers,* pp. 91–98; Kanellos, *The Hispanic Literary Companion,* pp. 49–51.

SANDRA CISNEROS.

1992 • Mexican American poet Lorna Dee Cervantes became the first Hispanic writer to win the prestigious Paterson Poetry Prize for her second book, *From the Cables of Genocide: Poems of Love and Hunger.* It was also awarded the Latin American Writers Institute Award that same year. Cervantes is the most celebrated Hispanic female poet of the United States. Although she is the author of only two books, the result of some twenty-five years of work, Cervantes's poems are so finely crafted and insightful of Mex-

LORNA DEE CERVANTES.

ican American and women's cultures that they are the most reprinted in anthologies and textbooks of any Hispanic woman writer.

Of Mexican and Amerindian ancestry, poet Lorna Dee Cervantes was born into a very poor family in the Mission District of San Francisco, California. Despite this poverty, she was able to discover the world of books at a very early age. Cervantes began writing poetry when she was six years old; poems written when she was fourteen were eventually published in a magazine after she had established her career as a writer. In 1990, she left her Ph.D. studies in philosophy and aesthetics at the University of California, Santa Cruz, before finishing her dissertation. She then went on to teach creative writing at the University of Colorado in Boulder.

Cervantes's early career as a poet achieved recognition in 1974 when her work was published in *Revista Chicano-Riqueña*. She was one of the first Chicana poets to achieve publication and quickly assumed leadership in the literary movement by founding and editing a literary magazine, *Mango,* out of San Jose, California. Her work was quickly circulated throughout the Chicano literary movement and soon began to appear in anthologies and textbooks nationwide. Many of these early movement poems, poems dealing with identity and roots, became part of *Emplumada* (Plumed, 1981), Cervantes's first collection of poems, published in the prestigious University of Pittsburgh Press Poetry Series. The predominant themes include culture conflict, oppression of women and minorities and alienation from one's roots. Cervantes's poetry is very well crafted and has the distinction of using highly lyrical language while at the same time being direct and powerful.

Cervantes's second book, *From the Cables of Genocide: Poems of Love and Hunger,* which is very much the work of a mature poet, deals with the great themes of life, death, social conflict, and poverty.

Telgen and Kamp, *Latinas! Women of Achievement,* pp. 67–70.

1992 • Mexican American Jungian psychologist Clarissa Pinkola Estés became the first U.S. Hispanic author to have her book, *Women Who Run with the Wolves: Myths and Stories of the Wild Women Archtype,* make the *New York Times* best-seller list. Making the list just five weeks after its publication. The book also remained on the list longer than any other book written by a Hispanic. *Women Who Run with the Wolves* contains original stories, folktales, myths and legends by Estés, along with psychoanalytic commentary based on women's lives. *Hispanic* magazine hailed it as a "feminine manifesto for all women, regardless of age, race, creed, or religion, to return to their wild roots." Estés founded and directs the C. P. Estés Guadalupe Foundation, which has as one of its missions the broadcasting of strengthening stories, via shortwave radio, to trouble spots around the world. In 1994, Estés was awarded the Associated Catholic Church Press Award for Writing, and in 1995 she won the National Association for the Advancement of Psychoanalysis Gradiva Award.

Tardiff and Mabunds, *Dictionary of Hispanic Biography,* p. 318; Telgen and Kamp, *Latinas! Women of Achievement,* pp. 115–20.

1992 • Cristina García is the first Cuban American woman to experience mainstream success as a novelist in the United States, through the publication of her first novel *Dreaming in Cuban,* issued by Knopf. Her journalistic background and her interest in politics led her into the world of writing and the examination of her Cuban American circumstances, which have been so shaped by the political history of the United States and Cuba.

Cristina García was born in Havana, Cuba, on July 4, 1958, and immigrated to the United States when her parents went into exile after the triumph of the Cuban Revolution. García was an excellent student and was able to attend elite American universities; she graduated from Barnard College with a degree in political science in 1979 and from the Johns Hopkins University with a master's in Latin American studies. She was able to land a coveted job as a reporter and researcher with *Time* magazine, where she was able to hone her writing skills. She quickly ascended to bureau chief and correspondent at *Time,* but left the magazine in 1990 to pursue her career as a creative writer. Her highly acclaimed novel was the first one authored by a woman to give insight into the psychology of the generation of Cubans born or raised in the United States who grew up under the looming myth of the splendors of the island in the past and the evils of Castro, a group, however, that never really had firsthand knowledge of their parents's homeland. In addition, the novel closely examines women's perspective on the dilemma of living between two cultures.

Kanellos, *The Hispanic Literary Companion,* pp. 93–95.

1993 • Mexican American poet Luis Rodríguez's memoir of life on the streets, *Always Running,* became the first Hispanic book to win the Carl Sandburg Award for Non-Fiction. It also won the *Chicago Sun-Times* First Prose Book Award in 1994.

Tardiff and Mabunda, *Dictionary of Hispanic Biography,* p. 760.

1993 • *Heartbeat Drumbeat,* by Irene Beltrán Hernández, became the first Hispanic book to win the Benjamin Franklin Award for Juvenile-Young Adult Fiction.

Hernández, *Heartbeat Drumbeat.*

1993 • Novelist Sandra Benítez became the first Hispanic writer to win the Barnes & Noble Discovery Great New Writers Award for her first novel, *A Place Where the Sea Remembers.*

Hispanic Business, October 1994, p. 72.

1993 • Poet Gustavo Pérez Firmat was the first to provide a theoretical base for Cuban American culture with his book-length essay *Life on the Hyphen: The Cuban-American Way.*

Pérez-Firmat, *Life on the Hyphen.*

1994 ⁕ Puerto Rican novelist, short story writer, and poet Judith Ortiz Cofer was the first U.S. Hispanic to win the O. Henry Prize for the short story. That same year, she also won the Anisfield-Wolf Award in Race Relations for her novel *The Latin Deli*. Among her other important works are *Silent Dancing: A Partial Remembrance of a Puerto Rican Childhood* and *Line of the Sun*.

Tardiff and Mabunda *Dictionary of Hispanic Biography*, p. 236; Telgen and Kamp, *Latinas! Women of Achievement*, pp. 89–92.

1994 ⁕ Graciela Limón's novel *In Search of Bernabé* and José Bareiro's novel *The Indian Chronicles* became the first U.S. Hispanic literary works to be chosen as finalists for the *Los Angeles Times* Book Award.

Kanellos, *The Hispanic Literary Companion*, pp. 153–65.

1994 ⁕ Puerto Rican poet Gloria Vando's book *Promesas: A Geography of the Impossible* became the first Hispanic book to win the Thorpe Menn Award for literary achievement. Gloria Vando is also the editor-publisher of *Helicon Nine* magazine and Helicon Nine Books, which publish of feminist literature.

Vando, *Promesas*.

1995 ⁕ Pat Mora's *The Desert Is My Mother/El desierto es mi madre* a poetry-picture book for children, became the first Hispanic book to win the Stepping Stones Award for children's environmental literature.

Kanellos, *The Hispanic Literary Companion*, p. 226.

1995 ⁕ Mexican American poet and novelist Sandra Cisneros became the first Hispanic writer to win the prestigious MacArthur Award. Cisneros is the short story writer, essayist, and poet who has brought Chicana writing into the mainstream of literary feminism. She is also the first Chicana writer to be published and promoted by mainstream commercial publishing houses. Born on December 20, 1954, in Chicago into a Mexican American working-class family, Cisneros nevertheless benefited from a private education, graduating with a B.A. in English from Loyola University (1976) and later with an M.F.A. in creative writing from the prestigious Iowa Workshop (1978).

Cisneros's first and only novel, *The House on Mango Street* (1983), remains her most important contribution in that it captures the hopes, desires, and disillusionment of a young female writer growing up in the city. In *Mango Street,* Esperanza Cordero functions in a similar manner to the unidentified narrator in Tomás Rivera's classic *. . . y no se lo tragó la tierra* (. . . and the Earth Did Not Devour Him), observing the behavior and attitudes of the people who populate their environments. In Esperanza's urban Chicago world, children naively internalize the attitudes about gender and class of their adult Latino models; however, somehow the spirit of independence and creativity grows in Esperanza and leads her to escape the barrio in search of a house of her own—her own personality and identity, presumably through literature. For *Mango Street,* Cisneros was awarded the American Book Award (1985), and she began touring college campuses for readings. Her other awards include a Dobie-Paisano Fellowship (1986) and NEA Writing Fellowships in fiction and poetry (1982, 1990).

In 1991 publishing giant Random House issued a collection of essays and short stories, *Woman Hollering Creek and Other Stories,* neither of which surpassed the critical acclaim of *Mango Street,* which had assumed a secure place in college and high school curricula. Random House then reissued her two previous titles—*The House on Mango Street* and *My Wicked Wicked Ways;* Cisneros became one of the very few Hispanic writers of the United States to be supported by the commercial establishment.

Dictionary of Literary Biography, Volume 122: *Chicano Writers,* pp. 77–81.

1995 • Lionel G. García became the first Hispanic writer to win first place in the Texas Playwright Festival for his play *An Acorn on the Moon,* produced by Stages Repertory Theatre in 1995.

Kanellos, *The Hispanic Literary Companion,* p. 101.

1995 • Tina Juárez's historical novel *Call No Man Master* was the first Hispanic book to win the Austin Writer's League Violet Crown Book Award and the Presidio La Bahía Award, the latter presented by the Sons of the Republic of Texas.

Juárez, *Call No Man Master.*

1996 • Puerto Rican novelist Alba Ambert became the first Hispanic author to win the Carey McWilliams Award for Multicultural Literature, presented by the *Multicultural Review,* for her novel *A Perfect Silence.* Alba Ambert creates penetrating psychological narrative in fiction, much of which is based on her rise from abject poverty in Puerto Rico to literary acclaim. A poet and scholarly writer as well, Ambert combines lyrical and rhapsodic narrative style with minute attention to detail.

ALBA AMBERT.

Born and raised in an infamous slum in San Juan, Puerto Rico, Alba Ambert was one of those "scholarship" children who through force of will and extraordinary intelligence are able to pull themselves up out of adversity and not only make something of themselves but also contribute greatly to humanity. Ambert followed a roundabout route to becoming a barrio teacher in Boston, and later a successful creative writer. She studied philosophy at the University of Puerto Rico, graduating with a B.A. in 1974 with great distinction; thereafter Ambert received M.A. and Ed.D. degrees in psycholinguistics from Harvard University in 1975 and 1980, respectively. Not only was Ambert a bilingual teacher, but she also specialized in the teaching of bilingual special education students, curriculum writing, and theory, and some of this experience and study is reflected in the scholarly books that she has written.

In 1986, Ambert began teaching and researching in Europe, which also gave her time to devote to her creative writing. Always interested in poetry and writing since her childhood, Ambert began publishing her poetry in Europe and then in the United States. But a milestone in her career was the writing of her highly autobiographical novel, *A Perfect Silence,* which charts the protagonist's psychological struggles in resolving her previous poverty-stricken life with her highly successful intellectual career.

Kanellos, *The Hispanic Literary Companion,* pp. 22–23.

1996 • Initiative, courage and inventiveness are what win the day in Ofelia Dumas Lachtman's novel *The Girl from Playa Blanca,* which received critical acclaim and was the first Hispanic book to win the Benjamin Franklin Award for Young Adult Literature. This exciting book follows a teenager and her little brother from her Mexican seaside village to Los Angeles in search of her father, who has disappeared while working to support his two children back in Mexico. The young protagonist unravels the mystery behind a major crime and not only succeeds in finding her father in the grand metropolis but also falls in love along the way.

Kanellos, *The Hispanic Literary Companion,* pp. 64–66.

1996 • Novelist Isabel Allende, an emigrant from Chile, became the first Hispanic writer to win the prestigious Harold Washington Award for Literature, presented in Chicago on May 3. The next day, she received an honorary doctorate from Columbia College in Chicago. Allende, who began writing late in life after working as a journalist in exile in Venezuela, is the foremost female exponent of magic realism in narrative. Her most important novel is *La casa de los espíritus* (The House of the Spirits).

Chicago Tribune, 4 May 1996.

1996 • Junot Díaz became the first Dominican American author to be "discovered" by a major publisher with his book of short stories, *Drown,* published by Putnam's Riverhead Books. Díaz received the greatest reception of any new Hispanic author ever, with articles appearing in *Newsweek* and other mass-market publications. Díaz, who was born in the Dominican Republic, received his B.A. from Rutgers University and his M.F.A. in creative writing from Cornell.

Newsweek, January 1996.

1996 • Author Judith Ortiz Cofer and illustrator Susan Guevara became the first to win the new Pura Belpré Award for Hispanic children's literature, presented by REFORMA, the Hispanic librarian's organization of the American Library Association.

Hispanic Link Weekly Report, 9 September 1996, p. 1.

MEDIA

PRINT MEDIA

1513 • Explorer Juan Ponce de León's search for the land of Bimini, described to him by the natives of Puerto Rico, took him to Florida, where he explored most of the coastal regions up to Apalachi Bay and some of the interior. At the time, there were an estimated 100 thousand natives living there. This was the first introduction of a written language into what would become the mainland United States. Juan Ponce de León recorded his travels in his diaries. From this point on, the history of literacy, books, and writing in what was to become the United States, was developed by Spanish, mestizo, and mulatto missionaries, soldiers, and settlers. From then on there were civil, military, and ecclesiastical records in what eventually would become the southern and southwestern United States. Of course, this was followed by the importation of books, the penning of original historical and creative writing, the use of the printing press, and the publication of newspapers and other written products.

Kanellos, *Chronology of Hispanic American History,* p. 30.

1533 • The printing press was brought to the Americas, namely to Mexico City. The printer was one Esteban Martín. By the mid-sixteenth century, seven printers were operating in Mexico City, issuing everything from contracts and religious books to public notices and literary works. Among the first books printed were catechisms, religious books, grammars of the indigenous languages, dictionaries, and some technical and scientific books.

Kanellos, *Chronology of Hispanic American History,* pp. 35–36.

1642 • The first library in Puerto Rico was established at the Convent of San Francisco.

Kanellos, *Chronology of Hispanic American History,* p. 48.

1699 • The first book published in Spanish in what would become the United States was Cotton Mather's *La fe del Christiano* (The Christian Faith), a translation of his work in English, published in Boston by B. Green and J. Allen. It was published to be sent to the Spanish, "so that they would open their eyes and be converted from darkness and the power of Satan to God," Mather said.

Online Computer Library Center.

1722 • *La gaceta de México* (The Mexico Gazette) became the first newspaper in the Americas. Shortly thereafter, others appeared in Guatemala, Lima, Buenos Aires, and elsewhere. The history of journalism in North America began here.

Kanellos, *Chronology of Hispanic American History,* p. 54.

1779 • The first history of colonial Texas was written by a Franciscan missionary, Juan Agustín Morfi. Morfi's *History of Texas, 1673–1779* documented the life of the missions, villages, and presidios using his service there.

Jenkins, *Basic Texas Books,* p. 387.

CA. 1780 • Revolutionary War hero and Sephardic Jew (originally from Spain), Benjamin Nones became the first official interpreter of Spanish and French (Nones had lived in exile in Bordeaux, France) for the United States government.

Simonhoff, *Jewish Notables in America, 1776–1865* p. 101.

1791 • Jacob Newton Cardozo (1786–1875), son of a Sephardic Jewish immigrant and American Revolutionary War hero, was the first Hispanic to become an editor of a newspaper, Charleston's *Southern Patriot.* In 1823, Cardozo was able to buy the newspaper and became its publisher. Cardozo also became a respected author and expert on commerce and finance with the publication of his book *Notes on Political Economy,* published in 1826. But it was as an editor that Cardozo made his greatest contribution, editing *The Southern Patriot* until 1845 and, later, newspapers in Mobile, Alabama, and Atlanta, Georgia.

Simonhoff, *Jewish Notables in America, 1776–1865,* pp. 264–67.

1793 • The first book published by a Hispanic printer/publisher in the United States was W. H. Dilworth's *The Complete Letter Writer, or Young Secretary's Instructor,* issued by Benjamin Gómez in New York. Gómez was the first Hispanic publisher and printer on record in the United States. He was the great grandson of underground Sephardic Jews from Madrid, Spain, who fled to France, then to Canada, and finally to New York to escape persecution during the Inquisition.

Although Gómez belonged to the wealthiest Jewish (and Spanish) family in the United States, he chose to go into the book trade and issued mostly works in English, some of them of great importance to the history of literature in the United States: John Bunyon's *Pilgrim's Progress;* Blackstone's *Commentaries;* and Fielding's *Tom Jones.*

Simonhoff, *Jewish Notables in America, 1776–1865,* pp. 112–16.

1795 • The first book written and published by a Hispanic in the United States was Hipólito San Joseph Giral del Pino's *A New Spanish Grammar,* published in Philadelphia by Colerick and Hunter. The book also included an English grammar for the use of Spaniards.

Online Computer Library Center.

1798 • The first printed book in the southern part of what would become the United States was Louisiana governor Gayoso de Lemos's *Deseando mantener el buen orden y tranquilidad pública . . .* (Wishing to Maintain Good Order and Public Tranquility), issued in New Orleans. It was also the first bilingual publication in what would become the United States, with Spanish and French parallel columns.

Online Computer Library Center.

1806 • The first newspaper in Puerto Rico was *La gaceta de Puerto Rico* (The Puerto Rican Gazette), which was a government organ.

Kanellos, *Chronology of Hispanic American History,* p.68.

1808 • The first Spanish-language newspaper was founded in the United States—New Orleans's *El Misisipí.* Shortly thereafter other newspapers were founded: Nacogdoches, Texas's *La Gaceta de Texas* (The Texas Gazette) in 1813, and New York's *El Mensajero Semanal* (The Weekly Messenger) in 1828. Hundreds of Spanish-language newspapers were subsequently founded in Hispanic communities throughout the Southwest, Louisiana, Florida, and the Northeast in the years to come.

During the nineteenth century, the newspapers were the principal vehicle for the publication of literature; they functioned not only to facilitate business and publish news but also to entertain and reinforce the Spanish language and Hispanic culture. They flourished especially in the first half of the twentieth century and provided news and advertising of importance to Hispanics, as well as the cultural information and reinforcement that helped them to preserve their identity and protect their civil rights. They are once again flourishing today.

Kanellos, *Chronology of Hispanic American History,* p. 68.

1823 • The first Spanish-English bilingual newspaper, *El Correo de Texas/The Texas Courier,* was published in San Antonio by the Texas Government Printing House.

Online Computer Library Center.

1836 • *Crepúsculo de la Libertad* (The Dawn of Liberty) became the first newspaper published in New Mexico. Published by Antonio Barrera in Santa Fe, it was printed by Jesús Baca. After the newspaper folded that same year, the historically important priest, Father Antonio José Martínez, bought the press to print school manuals and pamphlets for his parish.

Meier and Rivera, *Dictionary of Mexican American History,* p. 110.

1902 • The first Hispanic journalist to pay with his life for exposing corruption through investigative reporting was Narciso Gener Gonzales, the son of a Cuban immigrant. Gonzales founded *The State* newspaper in Charleston, South Carolina, in 1881; and in his editorials, he crusaded for women's right to vote and against child labor and the lynching of blacks. He also attacked corrupt politicians, one of the worst of which was the governor of South Carolina Jim Tillman.

In 1902, Tillman lost the gubernatorial election and blamed Gonzales for his defeat. In retaliation, Tillman confronted Gonzales on a busy street and shot him dead. Tillman was exonerated at his trial by jury, which found the shooting to be "justifiable" because of the injury to Tillman's reputation.

Hispanics in U.S. History, p. 12.

1904 • Teacher, poet Sara Estela Ramírez became the first Hispanic woman to publish and edit a newspaper, *Aurora,* in Laredo. She also edited *La corregidora* (The Corrector), named for an important heroine of Mexican independence from Spain. Ramírez, an important activist for workers's and women's rights, was followed by other editor-publishers in Texas, such as Jovita Idar and Andrea and Beatriz Villarreal.

Kanellos, The Hispanic American Almanac, p. 414.

HARRY CAICEDO.

1958 • Harry Caicedo became the first Hispanic chief of the news bureau for a major U.S. daily newspaper on assuming that role for the *Miami Herald.* Born in New York City on April 1, 1928, the son of Colombian parents, Caicedo received his bachelor's degree in journalism from the University of Missouri in 1954.

Kanellos, The Hispanic American Almanac, p. 720.

1959 • Miami's *Patria* became the first newspaper founded by Cuban refugees from the Cuban Revolution.

García, Havana USA, p. 261.

1965 • Journalist Rubén Salazar was promoted to foreign correspondent for the *Los Angeles Times,* thus becoming the first Mexican American to hold such a position at a major newspaper. He covered the U.S. invasion of the Dominican Republic that year and was one of two *Times* correspondents in Vietnam during the period of increased U.S. involvement in that war. Later, he was named *Times* bureau chief in Mexico City, covering Mexico, Cuba, and Central America.

Hispanic Link Weekly Report, 14 August 1995, p. 2.

1971 • REFORMA (National Association to Promote Library Services to the Spanish-speaking) was founded. REFORMA provides a newsletter, an annual meeting and awards to librarians interested in serving the Spanish- speaking.

Furtaw, Hispanic Americans Information Directory, p. 38.

1976 ✦ The *Miami Herald* became the first major daily to publish a Spanish-language insert in its issues, entitled *El Herald*. By 1979, *El Herald* was delivered to more than seventy-six thousand households.

García, *Havana USA,* p. 105.

1982 ✦ The National Association of Hispanic Publications was founded to represent some one hundred Hispanic newspapers and magazines being published in the United States. The organization promotes Hispanic print media as a valuable means of communication and encourages recruitment and training of Hispanics as print journalists.

Furtaw, *Hispanic Americans Information Directory,* p. 25.

1984 ✦ Journalist Harry Caicedo became the founding editor of the nation's first Hispanic mass-circulation magazine, *Vista,* which was distributed as a Sunday supplement in major daily newspapers.

Kanellos, *The Hispanic American Almanac,* p. 720.

1986 ✦ Mexican American lawyer Patricia Díaz Dennis became the first Hispanic woman and only the second female to serve on the Federal Communications Commission. She was appointed by President Ronald Reagan. Prior to her appointment, she had served in management of ABC-TV in Hollywood, California, and on the National Labor Relations Board.

Tardiff and Mabunda, *Dictionary of Hispanic Biography,* p. 285.

1987 ✦ Newspaper publisher Knight-Ridder became the first U.S. media corporation to launch a Spanish-language daily newspaper, *El Nuevo Herald,* which grew out of the Spanish-language insert published by the *Miami Herald.*

García, *Havana USA,* p. 105.

1989 ✦ Mónica Lozano became the first Hispanic woman to be named publisher of a Spanish-language daily newspaper in the United States, when she assumed the position of associate publisher of *La Opinión,* which was founded in Los Angeles by her grandfather in 1926. *La Opinión* is one of three major Spanish-language dailies publishing in the United States today. The other two are New York's *El Diario-La Prensa* and Miami's *El Nuevo Herald.* In 1991, Lozano was named publisher of the widely read and respected weekly Spanish-language newspaper, *El Eco del Valle.*

Telgen and Kamp, *Latinas! Women of Achievement.*

1990 ✦ Roberto Suárez (1928–) became the first Hispanic to head a major-city daily newspaper, as president of *The Miami Herald.* He also became publisher of the Spanish-language daily that is the *Herald*'s subsidiary, *El Nuevo Heraldo.* Born in Havana, Cuba, Suárez received his primary and secondary education there and went on to study economics and finance at Vil-

ROBERTO SUÁREZ.

lanova University, where he graduated with a B.S. in 1949. He joined the *Herald* staff in 1962 as a mailer and worked his way up.

Kanellos, *The Hispanic American Almanac*, p. 739.

1990 • Elizabeth Martínez became the first Hispanic to serve as the director of the Los Angeles County Public Library system. In that capacity, she revitalized the county's sixty-three branches and supervised the construction of twenty-three new branches, including the central library built at a cost of $214 million.

Born on April 14, 1943, in Pomona, California, where she grew up in the poorest part of town, Martínez fell in love with books and spent all the time she could reading in the local library. She graduated from the University of California-Los Angeles in 1965 with a degree in Latin American studies and in 1966 secured her master's degree in library science from the University of Southern California. She further studied management, earning certificates in 1978 and 1986.

In 1966, the year Martínez obtained her library science degree, there were only five Mexican American librarians in the country. She joined the Los Angeles library system and worked her way up through the ranks, recruiting Hispanic librarians along the way. She has also mentored many librarians, taught at universities and published articles on library management and on racism. In 1993, Martínez was honored with the PEN West Freedom to Write Award.

Telgen and Kamp, *Latinas! Women of Achievement*, pp. 237–40.

1992 • Mónica Lozano, associate publisher of Los Angeles's *La Opinión* newspaper, was the first Hispanic woman to receive the National Organization of Women (NOW) Legal Defense and Education Fund award for her contributions as a woman in media.

Telgen and Kamp, *Latinas! Women of Achievement*, p. 218.

1995 • The first magazine dedicated exclusively to reviewing books by and about Hispanics of the United States, *The Latino Book Review,* was founded at the State University of New York at Albany by Professor Edna Acosta-Belén.

The Latino Book Review, 1/1 (1995).

1995 • Alma Guillermo Prieto became the first Hispanic journalist to win the prestigious MacArthur Foundation Fellowship. Guillermo Prieto is a writer for *New Yorker* magazine; her writings document modern Latin America. In 1983, as a *New York Times* writer, she was one of the first to report on military massacres of civilians in El Salvador.

Hispanic Link Weekly Report, 19 June 1995, p. 2; 26 June 1995, p. 3.

1996 • *Hispanic Business* was the first Hispanic magazine to win a Maggie Award for Best Business and Finance Magazine by the Western Publications Association. The seventeen-year-old publication has a circulation of 200 thousand.

Hispanic Link Weekly Report, 13 May 1996, p. 8.

1996 • For the first time in U.S. publishing history, mainstream popular magazines began targeting Hispanic readers in the United States. (Previously, such magazines as *Selecciones de Readers' Digest* and *Cosmopolitan,* in Spanish, were targeted more to readers in the Spanish American countries and Spain.) Time-Warner Communications launched *People en Español* and Essence Communications launched *Latina,* specifically targeted at Hispanic women in the United States. Also *Newsweek en Español* became the first mainstream news magazine to enter this market. These publications joined a host of other periodicals that targeted Hispanics in both languages—some 230 magazines being distributed in the United States.

"Whose Media Is This Anyway?" *Hispanic,* December 1996, pp. 53–58.

1996 • Miguel Laosa became the first Hispanic to serve as publisher of a major city English-language daily newspaper, the *American Statesman* (circulation 190 thousand), in Austin, Texas. He is the former president of Cox Arizona Publications.

"100 Influentials," *Hispanic Business,* October 1996, p. 62.

RADIO

1924 • Pedro J. González started the first Spanish-language radio program in the United States. Between 1924 and 1934, González aired his show, *Los Madrugadores* (The Early Risers) on brokered air time from Los Angeles station KMPC each day from 4:00 A.M. to 6:00 A.M. The program, broadcast with 100-thousand-watt power, could be heard throughout the Southwest.

Gutiérrez and Schement. *Spanish-Language Radio in the Southwestern United States,* pp. 56–58; Kanellos, *The Hispanic American Almanac,* pp. 645–47; Schement and Flores, "The Origins of Spanish-Language Radio."

1939 • The first Spanish-language radio network, International Broadcasting Company (IBC), was established to supply Spanish-language programming across the country. IBC was founded in El Paso, Texas. It is estimated that by 1941, IBC and other radio networks were supplying 264 hours of programming per week.

Gutiérrez and Schement. *Spanish-Language Radio in the Southwestern United States,* pp. 56–58; Kanellos, *The Hispanic American Almanac,* p. 647; Schement and Flores, "The Origins of Spanish-Language Radio."

1946 • Raúl Cortez established the first full-time Spanish-language radio station in a major market: 100-thousand-watt KCOR in San Antonio, Texas. Nine years later, Cortez expanded into Spanish-language television.

Gutiérrez and Schement. *Spanish-Language Radio in the Southwestern United States,* pp. 56–58; Kanellos, *The Hispanic American Almanac,* p. 647; Schement and Flores, "The Origins of Spanish-Language Radio."

1973 ⋅ Caballero Spanish Media was founded in New York City and eventually became the largest Hispanic radio advertising agency, with sales reaching as high as $26 million in 1994. Founded by Cuban immigrant Eduardo Caballero, the media company began selling syndicated Spanish movies and television advertising in 1973 and switched exclusively to airtime sales for Spanish-language radio in 1975. The first major advertiser Caballero landed was Colgate Palmolive. Caballero opened six other offices

PEDRO J. GONZÁLEZ'S SINGING GROUP FOR HIS RADIO SHOW, <u>LOS MADRUGADORES.</u>

in cities with large Hispanic populations. Today, Caballero works with about 130 Spanish-language stations, whose listeners account for 90 percent of the Hispanic radio audience in the United States.

Hispanic, September 1995, pp. 30–31.

1976 • The first Spanish-language news service, Spanish Information Systems, was founded in Dallas, Texas. The service provides news in Spanish via satellite to radio and television stations nationwide.

Kanellos, *The Hispanic American Almanac,* p. 651.

1983 • Cuban immigrant Raúl Alarcón bought radio station WSKQ- AM in New York and founded Spanish Broadcasting Systems, which grew into the largest Hispanic-owned media entity in the United States, with revenues of approximately $94 million by 1994. By 1990, the Alarcón family had acquired and was operating six stations in Florida, Los Angeles, and New York. Their KLAZ-FM became the first Spanish-language station in Los Angeles to hit number one, in 1993. Their WSJQ-AM became the first Spanish-language station to break into the top three in New York City in 1995.

Hispanic, September 1995, p. 30.

1983 • The United Farm Workers Union established Radio Campesina, the first radio station for farmworkers. Its initial station was established in Woodhead, California, but today affiliates exist in Bakersfield, California, and in Phoenix, Arizona. The format of the Radio Campesina is entirely in Spanish, and the programming is approximately 70 percent music and 30 percent educational programs. It is estimated that its audience comprises some 600 thousand people in the San Joaquin Valley and 400 thousand in the Phoenix area.

Hispanic, March 1996, p. 8.

1985 • After extensive lobbying by the Cuban American National Foundation (CANF), directed by Jorge Mas Canosa, the U.S. Congress founded Radio Martí, a radio station designed to broadcast news, features, and entertainment to Cuba in order to counter the censored or ideologically biased broadcast media run by the Castro regime. Funded at an estimated $10 million to $12 million per year, it was established on Marathon Key, Florida. The radio station has an immediate impact; it is believed that because of its series on AIDS, the Cuban government was forced to acknowledge and address this important health issue.

García, *Havana USA,* pp. 147–48; Tardiff and Mabunda, *Dictionary of Hispanic Biography,* p. 533.

1986 • María Hinojosa became the first Hispanic in broadcast journalism to win a Silver Cindy Award for her work on the National Public Radio pro-

MARÍA HINOJOSA.

gram *Immigration and Detention*. Born on July 2, 1961, in Mexico City, Hinojosa was raised in the Chicago area. While a student at Barnard, Hinojosa entered the field of radio by founding a Latino radio show at Columbia University; she went on to become the program director for the radio station. When she graduated magna cum laude in 1985, she became an intern at National Public Radio and nine months later was hired as a production assistant. She has gone on to become a leading socially responsible Latino radio journalist and a published author.

Telgen and Kamp, *Latinas! Women of Achievement*, pp. 187–92.

1989 • María Hinojosa became the first Hispanic journalist to win the Corporation for Public Broadcasting Silver Award; she won the award for her piece "Day of the Dead."

Telgen and Kamp, *Latinas! Women of Achievement*, p. 190.

1990 • María Hinojosa became the first Hispanic to win a Silver Award in the International Radio Festival of New York. She won for "Drug Family."

Telgen and Kamp, *Latinas! Women of Achievement*, p. 190.

1991 • The first Hispanic-owned-and-operated radio network, Hispano U.S.A., was created, providing programming via satellite to eighteen stations in the Southwest, California, and Florida.

Kanellos, *The Hispanic American Almanac*, p. 652.

1991 • Public radio journalist María Hinojosa became the first Hispanic to win the first place award from the New York Newswomen's Club, for "Crews," a program about youth gangs, which later inspired her book. It also won Top Story and First Place Radio Award from the National Association of Hispanic Journalists. That same year, Hinojosa also won a first place award from the Associated Press for her coverage of South African leader Nelson Mandela's trip to New York City.

Telgen and Kamp, *Latinas! Women of Distinction*, pp. 190–91.

1992 • Amado Bustos bought 92.1 KSZA-FM in Sacramento, which grew into the Spanish Radio Network, the nation's largest Hispanic-owned satellite radio network, earning revenues of $4.5 million by 1994. Born in Michoacán, Mexico, Bustos came to the United States as a child and worked as a farm laborer. After earning a college degree, he worked as a teacher and then decided to try radio. After succeeding with his first station, he acquired others in California and Arizona and decided to link them into a satellite-based network. In addition to reaching listeners all over California and Arizona, Spanish Radio Network reaches another 500 thousand in Mexico.

Hispanic, September 1995, p. 30.

1993 • Public radio journalist María Hinojosa was the first Hispanic radio journalist to win the Deadline Award from the New York Society of Professional Journalists.

Telgen and Kamp, *Latinas! Women of Achievement*, p. 191.

1993 • Spanish Broadcasting Systems station KLAZ-FM became the first Spanish-language station in Los Angeles to hit number one, in 1993. Spanish Broadcasting Systems is the largest Hispanic-owned media entity.

See also Media: Radio, 1983.

Hispanic, September 1995, p. 30.

1995 • Public radio journalist María Hinojosa became the first Hispanic journalist to win the prestigious Robert F. Kennedy Award for her piece "Jail as a Right of Passage." The Hispanic Association for Media Arts and Sciences won the Outstanding Body of Work for Radio award.

Telgen and Kamp, *Latinas! Women of Achievement*, p. 191.

1995 • Spanish Broadcasting Systems station WSJQ-AM became the first Spanish-language station to break into the top three in New York City. Spanish Broadcasting Systems is the nation's largest Hispanic-owned media firm.

See also Media: Radio, 1983.

Hispanic, September 1995, p. 30.

1996 • *Universo,* the daily Spanish-language astronomy radio program, became the most widely syndicated Spanish-language radio program in the United States, airing on 150 stations in twenty-eight of the top thirty U.S. Hispanic markets. The second most syndicated Spanish-language program is *CNN Noticias,* the news program. The Spanish-language astronomy program is produced by the University of Texas McDonald Observatory as part of its program to keep students in school and interested in the sciences. Production and distribution are made possible by grants from the National Science Foundation and the National Aeronautics and Space Administration (NASA).

Press Release supplied by University of Texas McDonald Observatory, 20 September 1996.

1997 • The Hispanic Radio Network (HRN) became the first Hispanic media entity to win the 1996 Population Institute Global Media Award in Excellence. HRN won the award for its program *Buscando la Belleza* (Searching for Beauty), which informs listeners on a wide range of educational subjects. HRN is the only Hispanic-owned national Spanish radio network in the United States. It produces and syndicates programs that air on more than 165 stations.

Hispanic Link Weekly Report, 13 January 1997, p. 8.

TELEVISION

1951 • *Buscando Estrellas* (Looking for Stars), thought to be the first Spanish-language television program in the United States, began broadcasting from San Antonio, Texas. Produced and hosted by José Pérez del Río, the show was a weekly entertainment variety and talent-search program. Its production and broadcasting rotated every thirteen weeks to three other Texas cities: Corpus Christi, Harlingen, and Laredo.

Between 1956 and 1961, Pérez del Río also produced *Cine en Español,* which featured old films from Spain, Mexico, and Argentina.

Kanellos, *The Hispanic American Almanac,* p. 653.

1952 • The record-breaking sitcom, *I Love Lucy* was the first television comedy to feature a Hispanic as a star, Desi Arnaz. Eventually lasting nine years, Arnaz and Lucille Ball modified the Latin lover and dumb blonde stereotypes to capture the attention of television audiences, who were also engaged by the slightly titillating undercurrent of a mixed marriage between an Anglo and a Hispanic who played and sang Afro-Cuban music. The formula pairing a White Anglo-Saxon Protestant (WASP) and a minority or outcast has been duplicated on television to this date through such programs as *Chico and the Man, Who's the Boss?* and *The Nanny.* Under the direction of famed bandleader and minor movie star Desi Arnaz, Desilu Productions was formed and grew into a major television studio. *I Love Lucy* can still be seen in black-and-white reruns in many parts of the United States.

Pérez-Firmat, *Life on the Hyphen,* pp. 48–52.

1955 • KCOR-TV, the first Spanish-language television station in the United States opened for business in San Antonio, Texas.

Kanellos, *The Hispanic American Almanac,* pp. 652–53.

1956 • The first Hispanic dancer to be featured in television variety shows was Broadway star Chita Rivera, who began appearing on all the leading television variety shows, including *The Garry Moore Show, The Ed Sullivan Show, The Arthur Godfrey Show, The Sid Caesar Show,* and others. This was at a time when practically the only shows featuring Latinos were *I Love Lucy* and *The Cisco Kid.*

See also Theater, 1952.

Telgen and Kamp, *Latinas! Women of Achievement,* p. 315.

1961 • Emilio Azcárraga Vidaurreta, the most prominent media magnate in Mexico, and René Anselmo, along with a group of minority investors, founded the first national Spanish-language television network, Spanish International Network (SIN). At that time, most of the programming was purchased from Televisa, Azcárraga's company in Mexico. When the network started using satellites in 1976, SIN programs were being disseminated to Spanish language communities around the world. By 1979, SIN was feeding more than sixty-four hours of programming to eight affiliates in the United States by Westar satellite, fifty hours of which came from Televisa. The remainder originated in the United States or was imported from Venezuela, Spain, Argentina, or Brazil. The network feed consisted primarily of *novelas* (soap operas), variety shows, and the news from Mexico City.

Kanellos, *The Hispanic American Almanac*, p. 654.

1971 • Journalist and lawyer Geraldo Miguel Rivera became the first Hispanic to win the New York State Associated Press Broadcaster Association Award, for his investigative series *Drug Crisis in East Harlem*. He also became the first Hispanic to be named Broadcaster of the Year; he was named to this honor again in 1972 and 1974.

See also Media: Television, 1987.

Tardiff and Mabunda, *Dictionary of Hispanic Biography*, p. 746.

1976 • Spanish International Network (SIN) became the first major broadcasting company, preceding CBS, ABC, and NBC, to distribute programming directly to its affiliates via domestic satellites. SIN signals reached the San Antonio station from Mexico City by terrestrial microwave and from there were distributed by the Westar satellite.

Kanellos, *The Hispanic American Almanac*, pp. 654–55.

1978 • Cuba-born Luis Santeiro became the first Hispanic screenwriter and producer to work for the most important children's television show in

LUIS SANTEIRO.

history, *Sesame Street.* Over the course of his career there, he has won six Emmy Awards.

Kanellos, *The Hispanic American Almanac,* p. 738.

1979 • Spanish International Network (SIN) became the first Spanish-language network to pay cable franchise operators to carry its satellite signals. Today, SIN's successor, Univisión, is carried by more than 570 cable operators. Univisión is the largest Spanish-language network serving the United States and extends to Spanish-language communities around the world.

Kanellos, *The Hispanic American Almanac,* p. 655–62.

1982 • Teresa Rodríguez became Spanish-language network television's first Hispanic female newscaster for Univisión's predecessor, SIN.

Hispanic, July 1994, p. 54.

1984 • The Los Angeles Fox affiliate KTLA became the first station in the country to transmit a Spanish-language track via audio channel; and in 1985 the station hired Analía Sarno-Riggle to be the Spanish interpreter of the *News at Ten.* She developed an accurate technique to provide Spanish-speaking viewers with an adequate simultaneous representation of what they were getting on the screen.

Kanellos, *The Hispanic American Almanac,/i>, pp. 672–73.*

1984 • NBC became the first major network to offer a news anchor position to a Hispanic. Teresa Rodríguez of Univisión, was offered the position once held by Connie Chung in hosting *Sunrise.* Rodríguez reportedly turned down the job because she did not want to be separated from her family in Miami. As of 1994, NBC was the only network to have a Latina as a full-time anchor—Jackie Nespral. Nespral is also a Cuban American residing in Miami; she commutes to New York at least three times a week to work at the network.

Hispanic, July 1994, p. 54.

1985 • Puerto Rican dancer and Broadway star Chita Rivera became the first Hispanic woman to be named to the Television Academy Hall of Fame. Rivera was one of the most popular dancers ever featured on such classic television variety shows as *The Garry Moore Show, The Ed Sullivan Show, The Arthur Godfrey Show* and *The Sid Caesar Show.*

See also Theater, 1952.

Tardiff and Mabunda, *Dictionary of Hispanic Biography,* p. 739; Telgen and Kamp, *Latinas! Women of Achievement,* pp. 313–19.

1987 • Geraldo Miguel Rivera (1943–) became the first Hispanic to host a nationally syndicated talk show, *Geraldo.* Rivera, a journalist and television personality, was born in New York City. He studied at the University of Arizona and Brooklyn Law School and received a law degree from the University of Pennsylvania and a degree in journalism from Columbia University. Rivera went on to become one of the nation's most celebrated and respected investigative television journalists, writing and producing various award-winning documentaries. He has won a Peabody Award and ten Emmys for distinguished broadcast journalism. After beginning his career as a reporter for WABC-TV in New York in 1970, he went on to become a reporter, producer, and host for various television news and entertainment shows. Today, Rivera is one of the most visible and successful Hispanics in media and entertainment.

Kanellos, *Chronology of Hispanic American History,* pp. 221, 274.

1989 • Home Box Office's Selecciones en Español (Selections in Spanish) became the first U.S. cable network to provide to cable subscribers the option of Spanish-language audio for the telecast of motion pictures and some sporting events. The service was the idea of Lara Concepción, a native of Mexico, who persuaded HBO to address the important Hispanic market. By the end of 1989, HBO was offering an average of twenty dubbed movies per month; and by 1991, Selecciones en Español was carried by 182 cable operators in the United States. Following up on its U.S. success with Selecciones, in 1991 HBO launched HBO-Olé pay-TV service in Latin America and the Caribbean Basin, which allows cable subscribers in more than twenty Latin American countries prompt access in Spanish to HBO programs.

Kanellos, *The Hispanic American Almanac,* pp. 671–72.

1990 • Radio journalist María Hinojosa became the first Hispanic to host a prime-time public affairs television news show in New York City, with WNYC Television's *New York Hotline.*

See also Media: Radio, 1986.

Telgen and Kamp, *Latinas! Women of Achievement,* p. 190.

1990 • Jesús Garza Rapport founded International TeleMúsica, the first show featuring international music videos primarily in the Spanish language, entertainment news, promotions, and lifestyle segments. The programs are produced in Hollywood, using various California settings. The program reaches its targeted youth audience throughout the Western Hemisphere on the Spanish International Network (SIN) network via satellites and affiliates.

Kanellos, *The Hispanic American Almanac,* p. 670.

1991 • Giselle Fernández became the first Hispanic to anchor a national morning news and features television show, *CBS This Morning.* Born on May 15, 1961, in Mexico City, at the age of four Fernández and her family moved to East Los Angeles, where her father was a flamenco dancer and her mother a university professor. She graduated with a degree in journalism from the University of Southern California in 1983. Her first job in television news was as a reporter in Colorado Springs, Colorado. She was working as a weeknight anchor in a Miami station in 1989 when the CBS network offered her the anchor position.

Telgen and Kamp, *Latinas! Women of Achievement*, pp. 133–35.

1991 ᛫ Sonia Manzano became the first Hispanic scriptwriter for educational television to be honored by the Congressional Hispanic Caucus. Manzano, who has a master's degree in education and a bachelor's degree in

GISELLE FERNÁNDEZ.

drama, had served for more than ten years as an actress and scriptwriter for the leading children's program in the United States, *Sesame Street.*

Telgen and Kamp, *Latinas! Women of Achievement,* pp. 227–29.

1991 • Univisión network's *El Show de Cristina* became the first Spanish-language talk show to win an Emmy. Rated number one in daytime television and among the top ten Spanish-language programs in the United States, the show is produced and hosted by Cristina Saralegui, former *Cosmopolitan-en-Español* editor.

Telgen and Kamp, *Latinas! Women of Achievement,* p. 345–46.

1992 • Giselle Fernández became the first Hispanic to become a correspondent on a major network national evening news program, the *CBS Evening News.*

Telgen and Kamp, *Latinas! Women of Achievement,* p. 134.

1992 • Nelly Galán, president of Galán Entertainment (a production company fully funded by Fox Television and devoted to the production of Latino-theme projects), cofounded HBO's Latino Division, Tropix. One of her first projects to air was *Loco Slam,* a highly popular series of stand-up comedy specials in English featuring Latino comedians.

La Smithsonian, 1/1 (1995), p. 7.

1992 • Viva Television Network became the first Latino-owned national cable television network in the United States.

Kanellos, *The Hispanic American Almanac,* pp. 670–71.

1994 • The first Spanish-language national sports network, La Cadena Deportiva Nacional, was launched as a subsidiary of the Prime Ticket Network. It began in 1993 as a southwestern network; it was carried successfully in 750 thousand homes in the Southwest.

Hispanic, July 1994, p. 9.

1995 • After considerable pressure (ABC was the focus of an ongoing boycott by the National Hispanic Media Coalition) was applied to the television networks to hire Latino talent and improve the portrayal of Latinos on the screen, ABC became the first network in history to create a program to recruit Latino writers to work on prime-time shows. As part of the ABC Latino Freelance Writers Project, ABC issued a call for any Latino who had previously written for or sold written material to any production company to submit scripts. The project was cosponsored by the Writers Guild of America.

Hispanic Link Weekly Report, 19 June 1995, p. 8; 26 June 1995, p. 4.

1996 • José Díaz-Balart became the first Hispanic anchor of a morning network news program, *CBS This Morning*. Díaz-Balart had previously served as anchor for an NBC-owned station in Miami. Before that, he was bureau chief in Washington, D.C., for the Spanish-language network Telemundo.

Hispanic Link Weekly Report, 13 May 1996, p. 8.

1996 • HTV, the twenty-four-hour, all Spanish-language music network launched in August 1995, became the first music channel to be carried by

NELLY GALÁN.

SCOLA, a nonprofit educational service that reaches five million subscribers in the United States and Canada at educational institutions and through cable systems. In addition, HTV is distributed to more than four million homes in Venezuela, Ecuador, Nicaragua, Spain, and Portugal. The new music network was created by Robert Behar and Daniel Sawicki, partners in Hero Communications of Florida, Inc.

Hispanic Business, April 1996, p. 66.

1996 • Telemundo became the first Spanish-language network to enter into a coproduction agreement with a foreign company. Telemundo Group established a first-of-its-kind agreement with the Mexican network Televisión Azteca to co-produce programming, with an emphasis on Spanish-language soap operas, for an international audience. The organizations share facilities and talent and each other's markets as they compete with Mexico-based giant Televisa.

Hispanic Business, June 1996, p. 150.

1996 • The Cisneros Group and Playboy Enterprises launched the first Spanish-language channels for adult entertainment—PlayboyTV/Latin America and AdulTV/Latin America; both channels are offered on Galaxy Latin America's DIRECTV satellite service.

Hispanic Media Update, 23 October 1996, p. 3.

1996 • Soledad O'Brien became the first Hispanic to host an interactive cable on-line news program, *The Site,* which is a joint venture of NBC News and Microsoft Corporation. O'Brien discusses technology issues in the daily program. A national total of 22.5 million cable subscribers can view the program nightly. O'Brien is the daughter of a Cuban mother and an Australian father. Born and raised in St. James, Long Island, O'Brien is a graduate of Harvard University and is the winner of an Emmy award for her work as co-host of The Discovery Channel's *The Know Zone.*

"Soledad O'Brien, Host of MSNBC's *The Site,*" *Hispanic,* October 1996, pp. 9–10.

1997 • Cable News Network (CNN) launched the first twenty-four-hour Spanish-language news channel for Latin America. The initiative came under the directorship of Carlos I. Díaz, present of Turner International Latin America, Atlanta, Georgia.

"100 Influentials," *Hispanic Business,* October 1996, p. 58.

THE MILITARY

1600 • The first black militia was formed in what later became the United States. Many of the colonists of Florida were free black craftsmen and black soldiers in the Spanish army; under Spanish law and practice, slaves had certain rights, and Spanish culture and the Catholic Church were more encouraging to releasing slaves than was British culture and Protestant religions. A black militia was present in Florida by the seventeenth century, with both free and enslaved blacks serving as soldiers and officers.

Henderson and Mormino, *Spanish Pathways in Florida,* p. 192.

1738 • The first black commander of a Spanish regiment in lands that would become part of the United States was a runaway slave by the name of Francisco Menéndez. Originally a Mandingo from West Africa, Menéndez escaped from English slavery in the Carolinas. After he assisted Yamassee Indians in battle, they helped him to reach the sanctuary for runaway slaves in Saint Augustine, Florida. He was betrayed by an Indian and sold into Spanish slavery as a soldier. He became an officer while still a slave, and in 1738 he was freed and made commander of the all-black regiment of soldiers at Fort Mose, just north of Saint Augustine. Captain Menéndez held the position until 1763, when Florida became a British colony and the inhabitants of Fort Mose were evacuated to Cuba.

Henderson and Mormino, *Spanish Pathways in Florida,* pp. 118–200.

1776 • One of the first Hispanic heroes of the American Revolution was Francisco de Miranda (1756–1816). Miranda was an early activist for independence of the Spanish American colonies.

Born in Venezuela, Miranda became a soldier in the Spanish army and later participated in the War of Independence of the thirteen British colonies in North America; he had also participated in the French Revolution. Inspired by all of those ideas associated with "liberty, fraternity, equality," Miranda in 1797 founded the American Lodge in London, whose members swore their allegiance to democracy and were to work for the independence of the Spanish American colonies.

In 1806, Miranda tried to liberate Venezuela by embarking from New York with a group of 200 soldiers. When they disembarked in Coro, Venezuela, they did not find the necessary support and the mission failed. Miranda returned to England and from there prepared the liberation of his country with Simón Bolívar. When Miranda returned to Venezuela in 1810, he was arrested and sent to Spain, where he died in jail on July, 14, 1816, in Cádiz.

Kanellos, *Chronology of Hispanic American History,* pp. 56, 64.

A DRAWING OF FREE BLACK SOLDIERS IN HAVANA, 1795.

1776 · The first Sephardic Jewish hero of the American Revolution was Francis Salvador, a Charleston, South Carolina, financier. Salvador, who was from a refugee family that abandoned Spain because of persecution by the Inquisition, in 1776 led his men against Tories and their Indian allies. Found still alive, but scalped, Salvador is reputed to have asked before dying whether the enemy was beaten. The answer was "Yes."

Simonhoff, *Jewish Notables in America, 1776–1865*, pp.1–4.

FRANCISCO
DE MIRANDA.

1779 • One of the first, if not *the* first, Hispanic Revolutionary War heroes was Jorge Farragut, a seaman born on the Spanish island of Minorca who joined the South Carolina navy as a lieutenant and fought at the battle of Savannah (1779) and at the second defense of Charleston (1780), where he was captured. After being freed, Farragut joined the Continental army and earned the rank of major. He was the father of the first Hispanic U.S. admiral, David Farragut.

Hispanics in U.S. History, pp. 54, 56; Secretary of Defense, *Hispanics in America's Defense,* p. 9.

1779 • One of the first Hispanic Revolutionary War heroes was Louisiana governor Bernardo de Gálvez, who engaged British forces repeatedly for three years along the Gulf of Mexico, destroying their forts, capturing Mobile and Pensacola, and rendering great support to the Continental army. Gálvez's victory at Pensacola, in particular, made the American victory at Yorktown possible. His most important feat took place in 1781, when as brigadier general, he took Mobile and Pensacola from the English to return these territories to Spanish dominion and to assist George Washington's forces in the War of Independence from England. This strategy forced the British army to fight on two fronts. The Spanish also opened a route to supply Washington's army with money, food, and weapons. As a result of this support of the Americans, Western Florida came under the dominion of Spain again through the Treaty of Versailles.

Hispanics in U.S. History, p. 54.

1811 • The first martyr for Mexican independence from areas that would become the United States was Juan Bautista Casas, a captain in the militia who led a revolt in San Antonio, Texas, against the Spanish governor, Colonel Manuel de Salcedo. Casas seized the governor and officials, proclaiming support for Mexico's revolution and appointing himself as the Mexican governor of Texas. Casas was captured and executed by Spanish soldiers, and his head was exhibited at the central plaza as a warning to other sympathizers of the revolution led by Miguel Hidalgo. Texas submitted to the Spanish throne again by March 1811.

Gómez-Quiñones, *Roots of Chicano Politics, 1600–1940,* pp. 48, 77–79.

1812 • The first hero in the struggle for Mexican independence from Spain in areas that would become the United States was Bernardo Gutiérrez de Lara, who in June 1812 led his men in taking the towns of Nacogdoches and Salcedo from the royalist garrison. Gutiérrez also sent emissaries to other parts of Texas and to the Rio Grande Valley to spread the word of the revolution.

Gómez-Quiñones, *Roots of Chicano Politics, 1600–1940,* pp. 81–83.

1840 • The first Hispanic to lead a secessionist movement in the area that would soon become the Republic of Texas was Texan José Antonio Canales. On January 14, 1840, in San Patricio, Texas, General Canales and a mixed bag of Texas-Mexico forces, including Juan Nepomuceno Seguín, proclaimed the independence of the Republic of the Río Grande, to be made up of southern Texas and the Mexican state of Tamaulipas. In the following months,

Canales's forces were successful in capturing Laredo, a number of border towns, and Ciudad Victoria, the capital of Tamaulipas. In Canales's attempts to capture Saltillo, most of his troops went over to the Mexican government side, and the remaining soldiers were forced to withdraw to Texas. Canales finally surrendered to the government in November, and thus ended the northern secessionist effort.

Kanellos, *Chronology of Hispanic American History,* pp. 92–93.

BERNARDO DE GÁLVEZ.

1859 • The first man to organize an armed protest by Texas Mexicans against the abuses of Anglos and the power structure they had instituted after the Mexican War (1846–1848) was Juan Nepomuceno Cortina, who was a military man most of his life and precipitated the "Cortina War." He was at one time or another a rancher, social bandit, and Mexican governor.

Cortina was born in Camargo, on the Mexican side of the Rio Grande River on May 16, 1824. He was raised in a family of Mexican landowners, but after fighting against the United States in the Mexican War, he purchased and settled on a ranch near Brownsville, Texas. Recognizing the discrimination that Mexicans faced after the war, Cortina struck out against injustice when he wounded a Brownsville deputy sheriff who was mistreating a Mexican vagrant. He escaped across the border to avoid arrest and possibly death, whereupon he became a folk hero to the oppressed Mexican population in Texas. He soon led a large force of rebels who crossed the border at Matamoros and took over the city of Brownsville, raising the flag of Mexico over it. As a result of this and other actions, Cortina faced responses from local militia, the Texas Rangers, and the U.S. Army.

In mid-1860, Cortina was again forced to retreat across the border. In Mexico, he distinguished himself as an officer in Tamaulipas fighting against the French intervention. During this time, he became acting governor of Tamaulipas for a short term, and he was promoted by President Benito Juárez to general. During the American Civil War, he fought on the side of the North. In the mid-1870s he incurred political disfavor in Mexico and was arrested for cattle rustling. After a pardon, under General Porfirio Díaz, he returned to the border for a short period but was arrested again and spent most of his remaining years under local arrest in Mexico City. He died in 1892.

Rosales, *Chicano! History of the Mexican American Civil Rights Movement,* pp. 8–10.

1862 • The first Hispanic spy for the United States was Captain Román Antonio Baca, an officer in the New Mexico Volunteers, a unit that was incorporated into the Union forces during the Civil War.

Crocchiola, *The Civil War in New Mexico;* Secretary of Defense, *Hispanics in America's Defense,* p. 16.

1863 • The U.S. government authorized the formation of the first Hispanic battalion during the Civil War. The First Battalion of Native Cavalry was formed to take advantage of the extraordinary horsemanship of the Mexican Americans of California, under the command of Major Salvador Vallejo. Approximately 470 Mexican Americans served in the four companies of the battalion throughout California and Arizona.

Crocchiola, *The Civil War in New Mexico;* Meier and Rivera, *Dictionary of Mexican American History,* p. 93; Secretary of Defense, *Hispanics in America's Defense,* p. 14.

1864 • Diego Archuleta (1814–1884) became the first Hispanic brigadier general of the United States, commanding the New Mexico militia during the Civil War. Archuleta was born into a prominent New Mexico family and was educated in Durango, Mexico. From 1843 to 1845, he served in the Mexican National Congress as a delegate from New Mexico. After the conquest of New Mexico by the United States, Archuleta took part in two unsuccessful

GENERAL JUAN
NEPOMUCENO CORTINA.

rebellions, in 1846 and 1847. After the Mexican-American War (1846–1848), Archuleta took the oath of allegiance to the United States, served in the state assembly, and became a brigadier general for the Union. In 1857, he was appointed a U.S. Indian agent, a position to which he was reappointed by President Abraham Lincoln after the Civil War.

Kanellos, *The Hispanic American Almanac,* pp. 275–76.

1864 ⬩ The first Hispanic female spy in U.S. history was the Cuban-born woman who disguised herself as a Confederate soldier and served as Lieutenant Harry Buford. Loretta Janet Vásquez left her married domestic life in San Antonio, Texas, without her husband's knowledge and fought at such battles as Bull Run, Ball's Bluff, and Fort Donelson. After her female identity had been detected twice and she was discharged, she began her life as a spy, for the Confederacy, working in male and female guise. The real-life existence of Vásquez is reported in her published autobiography; some scholars believe the work is apocryphal and that Vásquez was a figment of a male author's literary imagination.

Secretary of Defense, *Hispanics in America's Defense,* p. 20.

1864 ⬩ The first surgeon general of the Confederate States was Sephardic Jew David Camden DeLeón of Charleston. Known as the "Fighting Doctor," DeLeón enlisted in the army after graduating with a degree in medicine from the University of Pennsylvania in 1836. He was sent to the Florida tropics to treat the sick and wounded soldiers of the Seminole Wars. Later he became a hero at the Battle of Chapultepec in the Mexican War when, without any military training, he jumped into the trenches and turned the tide of battle in favor of the United States.

When the Confederacy seceded from the Union, Major DeLeón left the Union to join the Confederate army despite the pleading of his former commander, Zachary Taylor. President Jefferson Davis assigned DeLeón the important task of organizing the medical department of the Confederate army. DeLeón became the first surgeon general of the Confederacy. He also served in the field and in hospitals in various capacities until the end of the war.

After the defeat of the Confederacy, DeLeón moved to Mexico. At the request of President Ulysses S. Grant, he eventually returned to the United States and settled in New Mexico to practice medicine.

See also Science and Technology: Physical and Social Sciences, 1836.

Simonhoff, *Jewish Notables in America, 1776–1865,* pp. 297–300.

1865 ⬩ The first Hispanic Medal of Honor winner was Philip Bazaar, a seaman born in Chile, South America, who on January 15, 1865, courageously engaged in an assault on a fort from a six-man boat.

Secretary of Defense, *Hispanics in America's Defense,* p. 50.

1866 • The first admiral of the U.S. Navy, David G. Farragut (1801–1872), was commissioned on July 26, 1866. The son of a Spanish immigrant who served in the South Carolina navy during the War of Independence, Farragut was appointed a midshipman at the age of nine. As a commander during the Civil War, Farragut was engaged in numerous battles, including the capture of New Orleans, Vicksburg, and Mobile. It was after the tremendous victory that he had led at Mobile Bay—where he is reported to have said, "Damn the torpedoes! Full speed ahead!"—that he was commissioned admiral. In today's navy, the guided missile destroyer USS *Farragut* bears his name.

Gleiter and Thompson, *David Farragut;* Secretary of Defense, *Hispanics in America's Defense,* pp. 17–18, 86.

1915 • Luis R. Esteves was the first Puerto Rican to graduate from the United States Military Academy at West Point. Born in Aguadilla, Puerto Rico, in 1893, before the American occupation, he obtained his elementary and secondary education under American military rule of the island and, without his parents's knowledge, took the test and was admitted to West Point. After graduating, Esteves rose through the ranks to become a brigadier general in 1937. In 1919, he organized the first Puerto Rican National Guard, commanding its first battalion and its first regiment. General Esteves died on March 12, 1958.

Secretary of Defense, *Hispanics in America's Defense,* p. 93.

1918 • The first Hispanic soldier to be awarded with the Distinguished Service Cross was Private Marcelino Serna, of Albuquerque, New Mexico, who on September 12, 1918, single-handedly captured twenty-four German soldiers. The Albuquerque native was not recommended for a Medal of Honor because he was only a "buck" private and could not read or write English well enough to sign reports.

Secretary of Defense, *Hispanics in America's Defense,* p. 25.

1943 • The first Hispanic Medal of Honor winner of World War II was Private José P. Martínez, who took part in the American invasion of the Aleutian Islands in May 1943. The Taos, New Mexico native led his outnumbered platoon in fighting Japanese soldiers in their trenches and was finally mortally wounded in his valiant attacks. A Disabled American Veterans chapter in Colorado and an American Legion post in California are named in his honor.

Secretary of Defense, *Hispanics in America's Defense,* p. 28.

1944 • Guy Gabaldón (1927–), a Mexican American born in Los Angeles who was adopted by a Japanese American family, became a war hero at the battle for Saipan Island. He is the first Hispanic whose military heroism became the subject of a Hollywood film, *Hell to Eternity*. In 1970, Gabaldón returned his Navy Cross and Purple Heart to the government in protest of discrimination against minorities in the United States.

Meier and Rivera, *Dictionary of Mexican American History,* pp. 139–40.

1952 • The first Hispanic flying ace was Colonel Manuel J. Fernández Jr., who from September 1952 to May 1953 during the Korean War flew 125 combat missions in the F-86, engaging Communist MIG aircraft. On his fifth victory, he became an "ace" and ended the war with 14.5 "kills" to his credit. His 14.5 air victories placed him sixtieth among the top U.S. Air Force aces of the two world wars and the Korean War combined.

Secretary of Defense, *Hispanics in America's Defense,* p. 35.

1963 • *Among the Valiant* became the first book to document the heroism and valor of Mexican Americans in the armed services during World War II. Its author, Raúl Morín (1913–1967), a commercial artist from Lockhart, Texas, was denied publication of the book for ten years until the American G.I. Forum backed its publication and distribution. After the book's successful publication, Morín remained active in Mexican American and Democratic political organizations and in veterans affairs. In 1968, a veterans's memorial site in East Los Angeles was officially named Raúl Morín Memorial Square.

Meier and Rivera, *Dictionary of Mexican American History,* p. 239.

1964 • Horacio Rivero became the first Hispanic four-star admiral in the U.S. Navy. Born in Ponce, Puerto Rico, on May 16, 1910, Rivero graduated from the United States Naval Academy in 1931 and began serving on a variety of cruisers and battleships. During World War II, he saw considerable action in the Pacific and participated in the Iwo Jima and Okinawa campaigns and the first carrier raids on Tokyo. He was awarded the Legion of Merit for saving his ship and preventing loss of life during a fierce typhoon in 1945. In 1955, he was promoted to rear admiral and to vice admiral in 1962. In 1964, he was promoted to admiral and became vice chief of Naval Operations. In 1968, he commanded NATO forces as commander in chief of Allied Forces, Southern Europe. He retired in 1972 and was later named ambassador to Spain.

ADMIRAL HORACIO RIVERO.

Secretary of Defense, *Hispanics in America's Defense,* p. 89.

1973 • Lieutenant Everett Alvarez Jr. became the longest-held POW in U.S. history. He was also the first U.S. serviceman shot down over North Vietnam. The Salinas, California, native was captured after his plane was shot down over the Gulf of Tonkin, North Vietnam, and remained imprisoned for eight and a half years. He was repatriated by the North Vietnamese in February 1973.

Kanellos, *The Hispanic American Almanac,* p. 275; Secretary of Defense, *Hispanics in America's Defense,* p. 38.

1974 • The U.S. Navy named a ship for a Hispanic Vietnam hero, who was also awarded the Navy Cross. The forty-two-hundred-ton antisubmarine escort ship USS *Valdez,* named for the New Mexico native, Phil Valdez, who was killed while saving two marines on January 29, 1967.

Meier and Rivera, *Dictionary of Mexican American History,* p. 361.

1976 • Richard E. Cavazos became the first Hispanic general in the U.S. Army. Born in Kingsville, Texas, on January 31, 1929, he received a bachelor of science degree in geology at Texas Tech University and was commissioned a Second Lieutenant in 1951. During his thirty years of military service, he attended various military training schools and commanded forces in Vietnam as well as served in the Pentagon. In 1976, he became commanding general of the Ninth Infantry Division and post commander of Fort Lewis, Washington. From 1982 to 1984, General Cavazos was commander of the United States Armed Forces Command, Fort McPherson, Georgia. He retired in June, 1984.

Secretary of Defense, *Hispanics in America's Defense,* p. 91.

1979 • Edward Hidalgo became the first Hispanic to serve as secretary of the U.S. Navy. His two-year stint followed a career in which he had served as special assistant to the secretary of the navy, special assistant for economic affairs to the director of the U.S. Information Agency (USIA) and general counsel and congressional liaison for the Agency. From 1977 to 1979, he served as assistant secretary of the U.S. Navy. Hidalgo was born in Mexico City and immigrated to the United States as a child.

Meier and Rivera, *Dictionary of Mexican American History,* p. 161; Secretary of Defense, *Hispanics in America's Defense,* p. 217.

RICHARD E. CAVAZOS.

1980 · The U.S. government commemorated the Hispanic contribution to the American War of Independence by issuing a stamp recognizing General Bernardo de Gálvez's 1780 victory at the Battle of Mobile.

Secretary of Defense, *Hispanics in America's Defense*, p. 8.

1981 · President Ronald Reagan appointed war hero Everett Alvarez Jr. the first Hispanic deputy director of the Veterans Administration. The previous year, the president had appointed him deputy director of the Peace Corps.

See also The Military, 1973.

Kanellos, *The Hispanic American Almanac*, p. 275.

1996 · The first U.S. Navy ship to be named after a Hispanic Marine was the guided missile destroyer baptized *Sergeant Alfredo González,* after a Medal of Honor winner who was killed in Vietnam.

Hispanic Link Weekly Report, 7 October 1996, p. 1.

THE PERFORMING ARTS

DANCE

1831 • The first record of a professional dance troupe in performance in the United States is that of the theatrical company Compañía Española de Teatro, which performed in New Orleans at the Orleans Theater. Like many dramatic companies throughout the Spanish-speaking world, it presented dances, monologues, and more minor entertainments during acts as well as before and after the acts of the main play, which often numbered as many as five. *La abeja* (The Bee) newspaper stated that the company was performing national dances (of Spain), such as boleros and fandangos, as well as a fandango-style minuet, performed by "two well known and celebrated dancers," Tiburcio López and Mrs. Martínez. Throughout the nineteenth century and the early twentieth century, Hispanic theatrical companies included dances in their offerings, most of which represented the regional dances of Spain; in the twentieth century, the regional dances of Mexico, Cuba, and Puerto Rico gradually became more popular.

La abeja, 5 April 1831.

1932 • Dancer José Limón participated in the first appearance of modern dance on Broadway with the Humphrey-Weidman Company in the play *Americana.*

See also The Performing Arts: Dance, 1945.

Tardiff and Mabunda, *Dictionary of Hispanic Biography,* p. 486.

1934 • José Limón began teaching at the first summer school for modern dance, at Bennington College in Vermont.

See also The Performing Arts: Dance, 1945.

Tardiff and Mabunda, *Dictionary of Hispanic Biography,* p. 486.

1945 • José Limón (1908–1972), a Mexican immigrant raised in Los Angeles, began touring his own modern dance company and thus became the first Mexican American professional modern dancer to make a living and achieve renown with this art form. After serving in the U.S. Army during World War II, Limón reestablished his company and went on to outstanding international acclaim, but he was financially hard-pressed and therefore had to rely on

OPPOSITE PAGE:
JOSÉ LIMÓN.

teaching at various institutions. In 1950, he turned down an invitation from the Mexican government for a permanent post as a choreographer.

Limón often toured the world under the auspices of the U.S. State Department. He viewed dance as the highest expression of humanity. His most famous master works include *Lament for Ignacio Sánchez Mejía, La Malinche, The Moor's Pavane,* and *Danza de la muerte* (Dance of Death).

Meier and Rivera, *Dictionary of Mexican American History,* pp. 194–95; Tardiff and Mabunda, *Dictionary of Hispanic Biography,* pp. 485–87.

1950 • José Limón received an award from *Dance* magazine for outstanding achievement in modern dance choreography. He became the first Hispanic to receive such recognition.

See also The Performing Arts: Dance, 1945.

Tardiff and Mabunda, *Dictionary of Hispanic Biography,* p. 487.

1953 • Ballerina Lupe Serrano became the first Hispanic to serve as principal dancer for the American Ballet Theatre. During the nearly two decades that Serrano performed with the American Ballet Theatre, she appeared in more than fifty different roles.

Born in 1930 in Santiago, Chile, to a Spanish-Argentine musician father and a Mexican mother while they were on a performance tour, Serrano grew up in a performing arts environment. Her formal ballet training began in Mexico City at age thirteen, and by age eighteen she went on tour with the famed Cuban ballerina Alicia Alonso. She later performed with the famed Ballet Folklórico de México. At age twenty, Serrano was accepted into the Ballet Russe de Monte Carlo in New York City, where she was featured in her first solo performance. After becoming a principal dancer for the American Ballet Theatre, Serrano became one of its main attractions both in New York and around the world. She retired in 1971 to devote herself to teaching dance.

Tardiff and Mabunda, *Dictionary of Hispanic Biography,* p. 844; Telgen and Kamp, *Latinas! Women of Achievement,* pp. 355–59.

1995 • A song composed and recorded by a little-known Spanish flamenco duo, Los del Río, became the music for a line dance similar to the "Hokey Pokey," which took the United States by storm. "La Macarena" became so popular that it has become standard fare in all ballroom and school dances and even is performed in "human wave" fashion by spectators during football and baseball games. In the summer of 1996, a remix by the Bayside Boys made "La Macarena" the number one song on *Billboard's* pop chart.

Houston Chronicle, 8 September 1996, p. A27.

MUSIC

1598 • With the colonizing expedition into New Mexico led by Juan de Oñate, both European and mestizo ecclesiastic and secular music were introduced to the Southwest, and they have continued as part of religious and folk tradition to this day. In particular, the folk music, as represented by ballads and other songs, is the oldest folk music in the United States, except for that of the American Indians. Because the missionaries discovered that music was especially effective in evangelizing the Indians, it was taught more extensively to the natives than any other subject at the missions.

Campa, *Hispanic Culture in the Southwest,* pp. 234–42; Rosaldo et al., *Chicano,* p. 143.

CA. 1605 • The first European music teacher to arrive in the Spanish provinces that would become the Southwest of the United States was Percival de Quinanes, who even carried an organ with him to New Mexico.

Rosaldo et al.,*Chicano,* p. 143.

1700 • By the turn of the century, operas were not only being performed but also composed in Mexico City and Peru. Thus, the first opera and European classical music was introduced to North America by the Spaniards, and it has had an unbroken tradition to date.

Kanellos, *Chronology of Hispanic American History,* p. 53.

1750 • The first symphony orchestra in the Americas was organized in Caracas, Venezuela.

Kanellos, *Chronology of Hispanic American History,* p. 55.

1824 • The first conservatory of music in the Americas was founded by José Mariano Elízara in Mexico City.

Kanellos, *Chronology of Hispanic American History,* p. 81.

1912 • The first Hispanic operatic diva in the United States was Lucrezia Bori, who made her debut at the Metropolitan Opera in New York City in 1912. Born in Valencia, Spain, on December 24, 1888, Bori studied opera in Milan, Italy, and began her career there. However, she spent the better part of her career with the Met in New York from 1921 to 1936. During this time, she also appeared frequently in Hispanic theatrical productions in New York. When the Met's existence was threatened because of economic problems during the Depression, she became chairperson of Save the Metropolitan Opera, and thanks to her leadership the opera survives to this day. After Bori went into retirement in 1936, she became the first woman opera singer to be elected a member of the board of directors of the Metropolitan Opera. She served on the board until her death in 1960.

Hispanics in U.S. History, p. 26.

1927 · With Luisa Espinel's debut recital at New York's famed Edith Totten Theater, the singing and dramatic career of the first U.S.-born and bred Hispanic musical star in both Hispanic and Anglo mainstream venues was launched. During the 1930s, Espinel—the Tucson, Arizona, native changed her name from Ronstadt—toured Southwest theaters, opera houses, and college campuses singing the folk music of Spain in a bel canto voice. Espinel had received formal training in San Francisco, Paris, and Madrid and had personally researched the folk songs and dances of Spain by traveling the Spanish countryside and living among the folk.

Sheridan, *Los Tucsonenses,* pp. 190–91.

1930 · By the early 1930s modern Mexican American *conjunto* music had been born. When Narciso Martínez began his commercial recording career, the first steps had been taken toward cementing the core of the modern conjunto—the accordion and *bajo sexto* combination. These two instruments would later become inseparable. Meanwhile, Martínez, who is considered the father of modern conjunto, devised a new technique for the accordion, one that differed radically from the old Germanic style. He stopped using the left-hand base-chord buttons, leaving the accompaniment to the bajo sexto. The resulting sound was dramatically novel—a clean, spare treble and a staccato effect that contrasted sharply with the Germanic sound of earlier northern Mexican accordionists. The Martínez style quickly took hold and became the standard that younger accordionists emulated, particularly those who established themselves after World War II.

Kanellos, *The Hispanic American Almanac,* p. 604.

1930 · Cuban popular musician Arsenio Rodríguez became the father of modern salsa music. In the early 1930s, the basic *son* of Afro-Cuban music was upgraded when Rodríguez added a second trumpet, conga drums, and, most important, a piano, giving the ensemble a more urban and sophisticated sound. Rodríguez also anticipated some of the greatest modern *salseros* (salsa musicians) by moving away from romantic themes of earlier *sones* and incorporating texts that addressed nationalist and social issues.

Kanellos, *The Hispanic American Almanac,* p. 615.

1933 · Xavier Cugat and his band became the first Hispanic music group to have its own radio program, *Dinner at the Waldorf.* This was followed by *Let's Dance* in 1934 and 1935, the *RCA Magic Key* program in 1936, and *Xavier Cugat's Rumba Review* in 1941 and 1942.

Tardiff and Mabunda, *Dictionary of Hispanic Biography,* p. 263.

1936 · Spanish-born opera star Lucrezia Bori became the first female opera singer to be elected to the board of directors of the Metropolitan Opera of New York. She served until her death in 1960.

See also The Performing Arts: Music, 1912.

Hispanics in U.S. History, p. 26.

1940 · The first Hispanic music to cross over into American popular music was the songs and compositions composed by Ernesto Lecuona (1896–1963). They became standards beginning in the 1940s.

Lecuona, the beloved Cuban composer of popular and semiclassical music, was born in Guanabacoa, near Havana, into a family of musical performers. Having been afforded piano lessons from early childhood, Lecuona was composing by the age of eleven and teaching music in the city schools by the age of sixteen. At seventeen, he graduated from the Conservatorio Nacional de Cuba and later studied with Joaquín Nin. His musical training and virtuosity as a pianist took him to the founding of what became a very successful and historically important band, Lecuona's Cuban Boys, which cut numerous records.

Much of the Latin music recording business emanated from New York during the 1940s, and Lecuona spent quite a bit of time there. Some of his popular compositions became standards of not only Latin music but also American popular music; most noteworthy of these are "Siboney" (the name of a pre-Columbian Indian tribe of Cuba) and "Malagueña" (Girl from Málaga, Spain). Lecuona also composed serious music, such as his *Rapsodia negra* (Black Rhapsody) for piano and orchestra, as well as numerous *zarzuelas* (Hispanic operettas) and radio scores. After the triumph of the Cuban Revolution, Lecuona went into exile in Santa Cruz de Tenerife, Canary Islands, where he died on November 19, 1963.

Kanellos, *Chronology of Hispanic American History,* p. 130.

1956 · "Pancho López," a satiric version of the hit song "Davey Crockett" became one of the first cross over hit recordings nationally for composer and performer Lalo Guerrero (1917–), a native of Tucson, Arizona. Guerrero has performed and recorded his songs for more than four decades, expressing the humor and the popular sentiments of the working classes in his songs. Another burlesque of a mainstream standard is his "Tacos for Two."

Sheridan, *Los Tucsonenses,* pp. 246–47.

1957 · At age twenty-two, Jorge Mester (1935–) became the youngest teacher-conductor at the Juilliard School of Music and for six years was conductor at the Juilliard Opera Theatre. Born in Mexico City to Hungarian immigrant parents, he immigrated to the United States and received his higher education in southern California. In 1967, he became the conductor of the Louisville Orchestra and in 1970 became the director of the annual Aspen Festival.

Meier and Rivera, *Dictionary of Mexican American History,* p. 219.

1957 · Columbia University hosted the world premiere of the opera *The Visitors* by Mexican composer Carlos Chávez. Mexico's leading composer of classical music, Carlos Chávez y Ramírez, was born on June 13, 1899, in a suburb of Mexico City. He was one of six children raised by a widowed mother.

CARLOS CHÁVEZ.

Chávez's first music lessons came from his older brother, who was studying piano with the famed composer Manuel M. Ponce; he later studied with Ponce himself, from 1909 to 1914. As a composer, for the most part he was self-taught. He began writing piano pieces and writing arrangements for popular songs when he was sixteen and completed a symphony by the age of nineteen. In 1921, he began presenting his own works and won a government commission for a ballet, *El fuego nuevo* (The New Fire), which was based on an Aztec story. From 1926 to 1928, Chávez lived in New York City, where he composed a great deal of abstract music and worked with Edgard Varese. In 1928, he returned to Mexico City to direct the newly founded Orquesta Sinfónica de México and to direct the Conservatorio Nacional de Música. In 1931, he debuted his ballet *H.P.* (Horsepower), which he had written during his New York years. Over the years he wrote significant pieces of chamber and symphonic music.

During the 1930s, infused with revolutionary spirit and class consciousness, Chávez began offering concerts for workers, producing such works as *Sinfonía India* (Indian Symphony); *Obertura Republicana* (Republican Overture); *Cantos de Méjico* (Mexican Cantos), the latter based on folk songs and instruments; *Llamadas* (Calls), a "proletarian symphony"; and *Xochipilli Macuilxochitl,* in which he attempted to re-create ancient Aztec music.

During the 1940s, his most productive decade as a composer, Chávez wrote the ballet *La Hija de Cólquide* (The Daughter of Colchis) for Martha Graham (who produced it as *Dark Meadow*), a great deal of choral music, concertos, and chamber music. From 1947 to 1952, Chávez served as the director of the Instituto Nacional de Bellas Artes (National Fine Arts Institute). After leaving the institute, he composed five more symphonies and his only opera, *The Visitors,* which was premiered at Columbia University in New York in 1957. Chávez is considered to have been the most important unifying force in Mexican serious music. He died in 1978.

Kanellos, *Chronology of Hispanic American History,* pp. 141, 144.

1957 • The Casals Music Festival was founded in San Juan, Puerto Rico, in honor of the greatest cellist that ever lived, Pablo Casals. The yearly classical music festival, which takes place every June for sixteen days, was the first classical music festival to honor a Hispanic virtuoso. Pablo Casals moved to Puerto Rico from his native Spain as a refugee from the Spanish Civil War.

1958 • Ritchie Valens (Ricardo Valenzuela) became the first Mexican American rock star with his hit recording of "Come On, Let's Go." In October of the same year, he became the first Mexican American rocker to be featured on the national television show *American Bandstand* in Philadelphia. His second recording in 1958 was his most important, with both sides, "La Bamba" and "Donna," becoming hits. Both climbed to the top ten by December. Just as his career was taking off, Valens died in a plane crash with other rock stars. In 1987, Luis Valdez wrote and directed a hit movie biography of Valens entitled *La Bamba*.

Tardiff and Mabunda, *Dictionary of Hispanic Biography,* p. 914.

1960 • Spanish classical guitarist, Celedonio Romero (1908–1996) formed the first classical guitar quartet to tour and perform with major symphony orchestras in the United States. The quartet went on to become the most important classical guitar dynasty in American music. Romero formed the quartet with his three sons, Angel, Pepe, and Celín, and in addition to performing at symphonies also performed at the White House and at the Vatican. Romero composed and recorded hundreds of works for guitar, including ten concerts for guitar and orchestra. After dictator Francisco Franco's death, Spain embraced Romero, and King Juan Carlos presented him with the Order of Isabel, the monarch's highest civilian honor. The Vatican made Romero a Knight of the Holy Sepulchre in 1991. Romero died in San Diego, California, in 1996.

Houston Chronicle, 11 May 1996, p. D5.

1962 • Mexican American singer Joan Baez became the first U.S. Hispanic entertainer to appear on the cover of *Time* magazine, after she sang to a crowd of 350,000 gathered at the Lincoln Memorial for Martin Luther King Jr.'s "I Have a Dream" speech. Along with Bob Dylan, Baez was one of the moving forces behind the pop and folk music support for the 1960s generation's youth activism and protest against the Vietnam War. During this time, Baez's recording albums were very successful; her first such album, entitled *Joan Baez,* reached number three on the charts.

Baez, *A Voice to Sing With;* Tardiff and Mabunda, *Dictionary of Hispanic Biography,* pp. 81–82.

1964 • Rafael Méndez (1906–) became the first Hispanic trumpet player to play a solo performance at Carnegie Hall. Born in Mexico to a musical family, Méndez immigrated with is family to the United States in 1920. He played for years with the Russ Morgan band.

Meier and Rivera, *Dictionary of Mexican American History,* p. 219.

1964 • Lead guitarist Jerry García founded the Grateful Dead, one of the greatest rock bands of all times. The son of a musician who emigrated from Coruña, Spain, García was ranked among the top ten moneymaking Latino performers at the time of his death in 1995. So popular was García's band that it became the subject of a cult followed by thousands of "Deadheads."

Hispanic Link Weekly Report, 14 August 1995, p. 1.

1966 • Spanish-born flamenco guitarist José Montoya composed the first flamenco music concerto, *Suite Flamenco,* for solo guitar and orchestra, which was debuted in January, 1966, by the Saint Louis Symphony Orchestra.

Tardiff and Mabunda, *Dictionary of Hispanic Biography,* p. 569.

1967 • Vikki Carr (1940–) became the first U.S. Hispanic singer or entertainer to be invited to a command performance for Queen Elizabeth II in London. The following year, she set a precedent for sold-out concerts in Germany, Spain, France, England, Australia, Japan, and Holland. In the United States, she became a favorite of the White House, performing repeatedly for each of the last four presidents. To date, Carr has recorded forty-nine best-selling records, including fifteen gold albums. In 1985, she won a Grammy for her Spanish-language album *Simplemente Mujer* (Simply a Woman). For her Spanish-language records, she has won gold, platinum, and diamond records. Her 1989 album, *Esos Hombres,* won gold records in Mexico, Chile, Puerto Rico, and the United States. Among her other awards are the *Los Angeles Times* 1970 "Woman of the Year," the 1972 American Guild of Variety Artists's "Entertainer of the Year," the 1984 "Hispanic Woman of the Year," and the 1991 Girl Scouts of America Award.

Kanellos, *Chronology of Hispanic American History,* pp. 215, 257, 272.

1968 • Cuba-born Tania J. León (1943–) became the first musical director of the Dance Theater of Harlem. She is one of a very small handful of women conductors in the United States. Since 1968, she has maintained a busy schedule as a composer, recording artist, and guest conductor at most of the important symphonies throughout the United States and Puerto Rico, as well as in Paris, London, Spoleto, Berlin, and Munich. From 1977 to 1988, she was the director of the Family Concert Series for the Brooklyn Philharmonic Community. In 1985, León joined the faculty of Brooklyn College as an associate professor teaching both composition and conducting. She has also served as music director for Broadway musicals, such as *The Wiz.* Her honors include the Dean Dixon Achievement Award in 1985, the ASCAP Composer's Award from 1987 to 1989, the National Council of Women Achievement Award in 1980, the 1991 Academy-Institute Award in Music from the American Academy and Institute of Arts and Letters, and many others.

Kanellos, *Chronology of Hispanic American History,* pp. 219, 252.

1968 • Pop singer José Feliciano became the first Puerto Rican artist to win a Grammy Award. Actually, he won two: one for Best New Artist, and the other for Best Contemporary Pop Vocal Male Performer. The Grammys were awarded for his rendition of "Light My Fire."

Hispanics in American History: 1865 to the Present, p. 49.

1969 • Mexican American pop singer Linda Ronstadt became one of the first singers to fuse country and rock styles in such albums as *Hand Sown . . . Home Grown* (1960) and *Silk Purse* (1970).

Tardiff and Mabunda, *Dictionary of Hispanic Biography,* p. 774.

1969 • Mexican American rock musician Carlos Santana and his group were the first pop group to experiment with the fusion of rock and salsa styles and to perform at Woodstock, which led to the group's being the first

Hispanic salsa-rock group to appear on television's *Ed Sullivan Show*. In his career, Santana has recorded more than thirty albums, with nine of them achieving platinum status and sixteen gold status.

Tardiff and Mabunda, *Dictionary of Hispanic Biography*, p. 818.

1970 • Mexican-born opera singer Gilda Cruz-Romo was named a lead soprano for New York's Metropolitan Opera, becoming the first U.S. Hispan-

TANIA J. LEÓN.

ic to attain this position, which she garnered by winning the Met's national auditions. She had previously starred in the Dallas Civic Opera and the New York City Opera.

Kanellos, *The Hispanic American Almanac,* p. 724.

1971 • Princeton University professor and composer Mario Davidovsky won the Pulitzer Prize for his "Synchronism No. 6." Davidovsky was born in Buenos Aires, Argentina, in 1934.

Kanellos, *The Hispanic American Almanac,* 1996.

1972 • Mexican American singer Vikki Carr was the first Hispanic performer to be named Entertainer of the Year by the American Guild of Variety Artists.

See also The Performing Arts: Music, 1967.

Tardiff and Mabunda, *Dictionary of Hispanic Biography,* p. 182.

1974 • Mexican Eduardo Mata (1942–1995) became the first Hispanic conductor of a major American symphony, the Phoenix Symphony. From 1977 until the 1993–94 season, Mata led the Dallas Symphony as music director, while also touring extensively and even continued to serve as the principal conductor and musical advisor of the Phoenix Symphony until 1978. He also served as principal guest conductor of the Pittsburgh Symphony beginning in 1989. Mata was named conductor emeritus of the Dallas Symphony beginning with the 1994 season.

Eduardo Mata was born in Mexico City and became one of Mexico's most outstanding symphonic directors. Educated at the National Conservatory of Music from 1954 to 1963, and through private instruction, he began his conducting career in 1964 with the Guadalajara Symphony Orchestra. From 1966 to 1975, he was music director and conductor of the Orquesta Filarmónica of the National University in Mexico City. In 1975, he became director of the National Symphony in Mexico City and also directed a number of international music festivals, including the 1976 Casals Festival in Mexico.

Kanellos, *The Hispanic American Almanac,* pp.729–31.

1975 • The country's oldest salsa music festival was founded in New York City. The festival is staged annually at Madison Square Garden.

Hispanic, August 1995, p. 76.

1975 • Singer Freddy Fender (Baldemar Garza Huerta) became the first Mexican American country and western star to have a national hit song, "Before the Next Teardrop Falls," cross over to pop and become a gold record. He also released his first album that year, which also became gold. In 1976, he became the first Hispanic to receive a Country Music Association Award for Single of the Year and a Grammy for Best Male Country Vocal Performance.

Tardiff and Mabunda, *Dictionary of Hispanic Biography,* p, 327.

1978 • Cuban American composer-conductor Tania J. León became the first Hispanic to serve as the music director and conductor for a Broadway hit musical: *The Wiz,* as well as for the *Dance in America* series for public television. León has served as guest conductor for symphonies throughout the United States and has had her compositions recorded.

See also The Performing Arts: Music, 1968.

Kanellos, *The Hispanic American Almanac,* p. 729; Tardiff and Mabunda, *Dictionary of Hispanic Biography,* p. 479.

1982 • The Guadalupe Cultural Arts Center in San Antonio, Texas, founded the annual Tejano Conjunto Festival to celebrate Tejano music, the Texas brand of northern Mexican music, which has become one of the most popular Hispanic varieties of dance music. Today, the festival draws bands from throughout the United States, Mexico, and as far away as Japan. Prizes and honorable mentions are awarded annually in four related categories. In addition, each year the Conjunto Hall of Fame honors the giants in the field of Tejano music at the festival; a total of thirty-one musicians have been thus honored to date.

Hispanic, July 1995, *p. 9.*

1984 • The recording "Conga" by Cuban American singer Gloria Estefan and her Miami Sound Machine was the first record in history to make it onto *Billboard*'s pop, dance, black, and Latin charts simultaneously. The single was part of the Miami Sound Machine's first English-language album, *Eyes of Innocence.*

Tardiff and Mabunda, *Dictionary of Hispanic Biography,* p. 316.

1986 • Salsa singer Celia Cruz became the first Hispanic musical performing artist to be given the Ellis Island Medal of Honor, also known as the Mayor's Liberty Award, by the National Ethnic Coalition of Organizations.

See also The Performing Arts: Music, 1995.

Tardiff and Mabunda, *Dictionary of Hispanic Biography,* p. 257.

1991 • Mariah Carey (1970–) became the first Hispanic pop singer to win Grammys for Best Female Pop Vocalist and Best New Artist with her very first album *Mariah Carey.* Carey was only the third artist in history to be nominated in the same year for Best Album, Best Song, and Best New Artist. The eleven songs on the album were co-written by Carey, and she produced "Vanishing," a piano and vocal track. The track "Visions of Love" was number one on *Billboard*'s pop, black, and adult contemporary charts. In the first year of the album's release, *Mariah Carey* remained number one for twenty-two weeks and sold some six million copies.

Tardiff and Mabunda, *Dictionary of Hispanic Biography,* p. 175; Telgen and Kamp, *Latinas! Women of Achievement,* pp. 51–55.

1992 • Salsa musician and composer Tito Puente became the first Hispanic recording artist to record one hundred albums. He is also the holder of four Grammy Awards and has published more than 400 compositions. He has also been honored with a star on the Hollywood Walk of Fame.

Tardiff and Mabunda, *Dictionary of Hispanic Biography*, p. 706–707.

1994 • *Lydia Mendoza: A Family Autobiography,* edited by Chris Strachwitz and James Nicopolus, became the first Hispanic book to receive the Association for Sound Collections Award for Excellence in the field of ethnic music. The book was an edited transcription of the dictated memoirs of Lydia Mendoza and her family of singers and vaudevillians. Mendoza was the first great Mexican American recording star, the first to sing in the vernacular, rather than the cultivated operatic style, and to appeal to a broad section of working-class Mexican Americans. Beginning in the early 1930s, her career as a recording star and performer lasted well into the 1960s, and her fame extended throughout the Southwest, Mexico, Central America and northern South America.

Strachwitz and Nicopolus, *Lydia Mendoza.*

1994 • Tania J. León became the first U.S. Hispanic composer to win the BMW Prize for best composition at the Munich Biennale for New Music Theater for her opera *Scourge of Hyacinths.* She may be the only U.S. Hispanic composer of serious music to be internationally recognized.

See also The Performing Arts: Music, 1968.

Tardiff and Mabunda, *Dictionary of Hispanic Biography*, p, 479.

1994 • Plácido Domingo and José Carreras, together with Luciano Pavarotti—the three most prominent living operatic tenors—began a series of concerts entitled "The Three Tenors" for the largest opera audiences in history and staging their events in stadiums and broadcasting them live internationally, as well as marketing videos and CDs of the concerts. The first of these megaopera events was held in San Francisco Giants Stadium on the eve of the World Cup finals before an audience of fifty-eight thousand people.

Both Spanish tenors have performed often in the United States, with Domingo regarded by American aficionados as one of the greatest operatic tenors. So beloved is his voice that Domingo has recorded popular Latin American songs for the U.S. Hispanic audience as well as songs in English for American mainstream listeners. Born in Madrid in 1941, Domingo grew up in Mexico and made his debut there in 1961. He made his debut with the New York City Opera in 1965 and with the Metropolitan Opera in 1968. In 1996, Domingo became the director of the Washington (D.C.) Opera, becoming the first Hispanic to direct a major company in the United States.

Profiles, March 1996, pp. 34–36.

1995 • Salsa singer Celia Cruz became the first Hispanic pop singer to be awarded the National Medal for the Arts, presented by President Bill Clinton. Cruz is the acknowledged "queen of salsa" and the female artist who

CELIA CRUZ.

has recorded the most salsa records in history. She immigrated to the United States as a refugee from Communist Cuba and has sung with many of the leading salsa bands, including the Willie Colón band.

Tardiff and Mabunda, *Dictionary of Hispanic Biography*, pp. 255–58.

1995 • Cuban composer-bandleader Israel "Cachao" López was the first Hispanic recipient of the National Heritage Fellowship award in a White House ceremony. The fellowships celebrate the lifelong achievements of masters of folk and traditional arts in the United States. Cachao is credited with starting or influencing many of the traditions that have made up salsa music, including contributing to the development of the mambo and the *descargas,* or freestyle improvisational jam sessions. Cachao was born in 1918 into an extended family with some fifty musicians as members. As a string bassist, he made his debut at age twelve with the Havana Philharmonic and later, along with his brothers, played with the historically important *charanga* orchestra of Antonio Arcaño. Cachao, who immigrated to the United States as a refugee, has won several Grammys.

Hispanic Arts News, October 1995, p. 12.

1995 • Mexican American pop singer Selena (1978–1995) set the record for attendance at the largest venue for country and western concerts, the Houston Livestock Show and Rodeo. She drew a crowd of sixty thousand at her performance during the same year that her life ended tragically.

Tardiff and Mabunda, *Dictionary of Hispanic Biography*, p. 837.

1995 • Pop singer Selena's album *Dreaming of You,* issued posthumously, entered the Billboard 200 at number one—the second highest chart debut after Michael Jackson's *HIStory*.

Tardiff and Mabunda, *Dictionary of Hispanic Biography*, p. 838.

1995 • Santiago Rodríguez, the first Cuban American classical musician of note, made his first recording to outstanding critical acclaim, *Rachmaninoff Edition, Volumes 1, 2, and 3.* Rodríguez is a professor of piano at the University of Mayland.

USA Today, 12 December 1995.

1996 • Salsa bandleader-composer Tito Puente was the first Hispanic popular musician to be honored by the Smithsonian Institution's National Museum of American History for his sixty years in the music industry. He donated a pair of timbales to the museum on the occasion.

Hispanic Link Weekly Report, 14 October 1996, p. 1.

1996 • The Houston Grand Opera staged the world premiere of a specially commissioned opera by Mexican composer Daniel Catán, *Florencia en Amazonas,* based on a short story by Nobel Prize-winning writer Gabriel García Márquez. The libretto was written by Marcela Fuentes-Berain, a Mexican scriptwriter who has coauthored films with García Márquez. *Florencia en Amazonas* is the story of a famous opera singer traveling down the Amazon River searching for lost love. It is the first Spanish-language opera commissioned by an American opera company. Up to that point, no operas in the standard opera repertoire had Spanish-language texts.

"Myth, Magic, and Spirit, *Houston Chronicle Zest Magazine,* 20 October 1996, pp. 8–9, 15.

1997 • Eduardo "Lalo" Guerrero became the first Chicano musician to receive the government's highest honor for an artist, the 1996 National Medal for the Arts, presented by President Bill Clinton in a White House ceremony. Born in Tucson, Arizona, in 1917, Guerrero has led a life devoted to composing and performing popular music. He scored his first hit, "La Canción Mexicana," when he was still in his teens, and wrote and recorded hits throughout the 1940s and 1950s. He currently resides in southern California, where he still performs on occasion.

Hispanic Link Weekly Report, 13 January 1997, p. 1.

RELIGION

1509 • Pope Julius II authorized the Catholic Kings of Spain to administer the Catholic church in the Americas in exchange for underwriting the costs of evangelization in the New World. In 1511, he issued a bull, the Pontifex Romana, which established various dioceses in the New World. This was the official introduction of Christianity to the New World.

Kanellos, *Chronology of Hispanic American History*, p. 26.

1511 • The Diocese of San Juan Bautista (Puerto Rico) was established by Pope Julius II. The first bishop for Puerto Rico, Alonso Manso, was named that year; in effect, he became the first bishop to be named in the Americas, and the first bishop in lands that are now part of the United States. He said his first Mass in Puerto Rico in 1513. He also became the first inquisitor in the Americas, and functioned as such until he was replaced by Rodrigo Bastidas in 1539.

Kanellos, *Chronology of Hispanic American History*, p. 27.

1512 • The first cathedral, Santo Domingo, and the first hospital, that belonged to the Dominicans and also named Santo Domingo, were built by the Spaniards on the island of Española (now Hispaniola). The first school was also located here.

Kanellos, *Chronology of Hispanic American History*, p. 27.

1521 • The first Catholic priests to set foot in what would later become the United States were the missionaries in Juan Ponce de León's abortive mission to colonize Florida. Subsequent expeditions to colonize Florida during the sixteenth century also had missionaries with them; for the most part, they were Dominicans and Franciscans. In 1567, Jesuit missionaries arrived to reinforce the efforts to Christianize the Indians.

Fontana, *Entrada*, p. 47.

1531 • The first appearance of the Virgin Mary in the New World reportedly took place in Mexico. According to the Catholic faithful, on December 12 the Virgin Mary, Our Lady of Guadalupe, a version of the Virgin of Spanish origin, appeared to the Indian Juan Diego on the hill of Tepeyac, just out-

OPPOSITE PAGE:
VIRGIN OF GUADALUPE.

side Mexico City. She appeared to Juan Diego with Indian features on the site of a temple devoted to the Aztec goddess Malintzin and miraculously caused her image to be emblazoned on his poncho. This image is the one guarded at today's Shrine of the Virgin of Guadalupe, built on the original site, and duplicated in the thousands of churches bearing the Virgin's name, wherever Mexicans live.

The Virgin of Guadalupe was named the patron saint of Mexico and the Americas and has become a symbol of the Catholic church in those countries, a church for Indians, mestizos, and Creoles. The miraculous appearance led to the rapid and massive conversion of many of the Amerindian peoples in Mexico and the other Indian lands being conquered and incorporated by the Spaniards. By the time of Father Miguel Hidalgo's shout for independence from Spain in 1810, the cult of the Virgin of Guadalupe had become so strong among Indians, mestizos, and Creoles that he invoked her name as a rallying cry. From then on, she became a symbol of Mexican nationalism.

Kanellos, Chronology of Hispanic American History, *p. 34.*

1565 • The first sustained religious conversion and ministering to the Indians in what would become the United States began with Pedro Menéndez de Avilés's colonization of La Florida. In 1566, the Nombre de Dios Mission was established at what is today the northern edge of Saint Augustine, Florida. It was the longest-surviving mission in La Florida, the only one existing beyond 1706 in its original location. In all, there were more missions established in Florida (some one hundred) than in California (forty), the latter built much later. The Florida missions stretched from the coast of what became South Carolina across north Florida to the vicinity of Marianna. Jesuits made the initial inroads among the Calusa and Tequesta Indians of south Florida and the Guale and Escamacu Indians of Georgia and South Carolina. The Franciscans began working these areas in 1753, especially among the Timicua Indians.

Fontana, *Entrada,* pp. 47, 71; Henderson and Mormino, *Spanish Pathways in Florida,* pp. 140–42.

1565 • Some historians claim that the first Thanksgiving held in what would become the United States was that celebrated by priests and Timicuan Indians sharing a feast after Mass was said by the priests in Pedro Meléndez de Avilés's colonizing mission. Today a stainless steel cross and a chapel mark the site of these events, which led to the establishment of the first Catholic parish, Nuestra Señora de la Leche (Our Lady of Milk), in what would become part of the continental United States.

See also Religion, 1565 (previous entry).

Florida Department of State, *Florida Cuban Heritage Trail,* p. 56.

1566 • Father Pedro Martínez became the first Jesuit missionary to be martyred by the Indians; he was clubbed to death near present-day Cumberland Island.

Fontana, *Entrada,* p.48.

1573 • The Franciscan order arrived in Florida to establish the first missions in lands that would later become the United States. A century later their missions would extend along the east coast of North America from Saint Augustine, Florida, to North Carolina. The Franciscans also established a string of missions from Saint Augustine westward to present-day Tallahassee. In the seventeenth century, the Franciscans established more missions and acculturated more Indians in northern New Spain—what would become the Southwest of the United States—than any other order.

Kanellos, *Chronology of Hispanic American History,* p. 46.

1602 • The first Christian parish in the United States was founded in Saint Augustine. The Cathedral of Saint Augustine today houses a replica of the chapel of the church first founded on that site in 1602.

Fontana, *Entrada,* p. 49.

1690 • On May 24, 1690, the first permanent Spanish settlement in Texas, San Francisco de los Tejas, was founded near the Neches River by two Spanish priests, Father Massanet and Father Fontcubierta.

Kanellos, *Chronology of Hispanic American History,* p. 52.

1691 • Father Eusebio Kino (1645–1711), an untiring Jesuit missionary, made the first inroads into Arizona. By 1700, Kino had established a mission at San Xavier del Bac, near present-day Tucson; he later established other missions in Arizona, including Nuestra Señora de los Dolores, Santa Gertrudis de Saric, San José de Imuris, Nuestra Señora de los Remedios, and San Cayetano de Tumacácori.

Kanellos, *Chronology of Hispanic American History,* p. 52.

1699 • The first religious book in the Spanish language published in the United States was Cotton Mather's *La fe del Christiano: en veinticuatro artículos de la institutción de Christo embiada a los españoles, para que abran sus ojos, para que se conviertan de las Tinieblas a la luz, y de la potestad de Satanás a Dios: para que reciban por la fe que es en Jesús Christo. remisión de pecado, y suerte entre los santificados* (The Faith of the Christian: In Twenty-four Articles on the Christian Institution Sent to the Spanish So That They Might Open Their Eyes in Order for Them to Convert from Darkness to Light, and from the Power of Satan to God: So That They Receive Through Faith in Jesus Christ the Remission of Their Sins and the Fortune of the Sanctified). It was issued in Boston by B. Green and J. Allen; the Harvard University Library has a reproduction of the original. This was the first publication in what would become a large industry in the United States: the publication of religious books in Spanish, especially by Protestant denominations wishing to convert Hispanics.

Online Computer Library Center.

CONCELEBRATION OF MASS NEAR SITE OF MISSION SAN FRANCISCO DE LOS TEJOS.

1769 • On July 3, 1769, Fray Junípero Serra established the first mission in Alta California at the site of present-day San Diego. Serra eventually found-

ed ten missions, traveled more than ten thousand miles on foot, and converted close to sixty-eight hundred Indians.

Kanellos, *Chronology of Hispanic American History,* p. 58.

CA. 1790 ⋆ The Brotherhood of Penitentes, a mystic lay order, was first introduced to New Mexico from New Spain (Mexico). In a province far from the metropolitan centers and the reach of the established Church, the Penitentes took on many of the responsibilities of priests and of government, enforcing law, order, and religiosity on the frontier. Although some of their practices, such as flagellation, harkened back to medieval Christianity, the Penitentes were responsible for the survival of the faith and the conservation of many religious and cultural practices on the frontier.

Rosaldo et al., *Chicano,* pp. 137–45.

1812 ⋆ The first book by a Hispanic promoting freedom of religion was written anonymously and published in Philadelphia. It was entitled *A todos los que habitan las islas y el vasto continente de la América española: obrita curiosa, interesante, y agradable seguida de un discurso sobre la intolerancia religiosa* (To All Who Inhabit the Islands and the Vast Continent of Spanish America: A Curious, Interesting and Agreeable Little Work, Followed by a Discourse on Religious Intolerance.) The book was signed by "Amigo de los Hombres" (Friend of Men) and was probably an effort to communicate the liberal ideas fostered during the American Revolution to the people of the Spanish colonies who were beginning their revolutionary movements.

Online Computer Library Center.

1840 ⋆ Francisco García Diego y Moreno (1785–1846) became the first Catholic bishop of California. The seat of the first bishopric was San Diego, and the diocese included both California and Baja California. García Diego y Moreno ordained the first priests in California in June 1842 at Mission Santa Barbara.

Meier and Rivera, *Dictionary of Mexican American History,* p. 143.

1844 ⋆ The first Catholic seminary was founded in California near Mission Santa Inés. Bishop Francisco García Diego y Moreno founded the seminary to prepare priests for service in California and Baja California.

Meier and Rivera, *Dictionary of Mexican American History,* p. 143.

1848 ⋆ José Sadoc Alemany (1814–1888) became the first bishop in California under U.S. rule, in the diocese of Monterey. Alemany was from Cataluña, Spain. He had immigrated to the United States in 1840 as a member of the Dominican Order. In 1853, he became the first archbishop of the new diocese of San Francisco, which included the whole state of California.

Kanellos, *Chronology of Hispanic American History,* p. 96.

FATHER ANTONIO
JOSÉ MARTÍNEZ.

1857 • Father Antonio José Martínez (1793–1867) became the first priest to be excommunicated by the Catholic church in the United States. After repeated battles with the new bishop of New Mexico, John Baptiste Lamy, who Martínez believed was prejudiced against New Mexicans, Bishop Lamy excommunicated the priest for insubordination. Martínez formed his own schismatic church, which he led until his death on July 28, 1867.

Meier and Rivera, *Dictionary of Mexican American History,* p. 10; Sánchez, *Memories of Antonio José Martínez.*

1865 • Bishop José Sadoc Alemany appointed the first pastor in the United States to specifically serve a Hispanic community. He named Father Gabriel Serrano *pastor hispanorium.* Serrano was appointed to work with the Spanish-speaking community in San Francisco.

Dolan and Hinojosa, *Mexican Americans and the Catholic Church, 1900–1965,* p. 134.

1875 • Bishop José Sadoc Alemany established Our Lady of Guadalupe parish as the first national Hispanic parish to tend specifically to the Spanish-speaking residents of San Francisco and to unite the Spanish- speaking community.

Dolan and Hinojosa, *Mexican Americans and the Catholic Church, 1900–1965,* p. 134.

1884 • Father Jean Baptiste Ralliere became the first person to collect the Spanish religious songs of New Mexico and publish them for use by local churches in New Mexico. Entitled *Cánticos espirituales recogidos por el Padre Juan B. Ralliere* (Spiritual Canticles Collected by Father Juan B. Ralliere), the successful hymnal was used well into the twentieth century.

Dolan and Hinojosa, *Mexican Americans and the Catholic Church, 1900–1965,* p. 29.

1897 • A group Los Angeles Catholic churchwomen established the first Hispanic settlement house in the United States, El Hogar Feliz (The Happy Home), to serve the Mexican community. The house included a clinic and a school. After operating at various sites, the school finally settled next to the Plaza Church in the heart of the Mexican community.

Dolan and Hinojosa, *Mexican Americans and the Catholic Church, 1900–1965,* p. 156.

CA. 1900 • The first Catholic hymnal for the Hispanic community in the United States, *Cánticos espirituales* (Spiritual Canticles), was published by *Revista Católica.* Consisting of music mostly from Spain, it included many folk hymns that became the staples especially for Hispanic Catholic communities in New Mexico.

Online Computer Library Center.

1917 • Brother Angélico Chávez became the first native New Mexican to become a Franciscan friar. From the time of his ordination in 1917, at the age of twenty-seven, until age sixty-two, he served as pastor in several towns and Indian pueblos in New Mexico. Chávez is also known as the greatest religious poet of U.S. Hispanic origin.

See also Literature, 1939.

Dictionary of Literary Biography, Vol. 82: *Chicano Writers,* pp. 86–90.

1927 • The first major Hispanic religious procession was started in East Los Angeles in honor of our Lady of Guadalupe. Held annually, the procession attracts as many as five thousand marchers and thirty thousand spectators.

Dolan and Hinojosa, *Mexican Americans and the Catholic Church, 1900–1965*, pp. 181–82.

1933 • The first group of nuns whose mission was to work exclusively with Hispanics in the United States was founded. The Missionary Catechists of Divine Providence worked among the poor Mexicans and Mexican Americans in south Texas. In 1946 the group was approved as an official branch of the Sisters of Divine Providence for Mexican Americans.

Dolan and Deck, *Hispanic Catholic Culture in the United States*, p. 188; Dolan and Hinojosa, *Mexican Americans and the Catholic Church, 1900–1965*, pp. 66–67.

1936 • Mariano S. Garriga (1886–1965) was appointed bishop of the diocese of Corpus Christi, thus becoming the first Hispanic and first Mexican American to be named a Catholic bishop in modern times. No other Hispanic Catholic bishop was named until Patricio Flores of the diocese of San Antonio in 1970. Before the decade of the 1970s was over, eight other Hispanics had been named to bishoprics, thus serving the needs of the burgeoning Hispanic population in the church.

Meier and Rivera, *Dictionary of Mexican American History*, pp. 86, 144.

1944 • The first seminar on the Spanish-speaking within the Catholic church in the United States was held in San Antonio, Texas, under the sponsorship of Archbishop Robert E. Lucey. Fifty delegates from western and southwestern states met for three days to discuss the condition of Hispanics within the church. This and following meetings led to the formation of Catholic councils for the Spanish-speaking in 1945.

Dolan and Deck, *Hispanic Catholic Culture in the United States*, pp. 133–34.

1945 • The Bishop's Committee for the Spanish-Speaking was founded by the Catholic church to care for the spiritual and social welfare of Hispanic Catholics, at first in the four episcopal provinces of Los Angeles, Santa Fe, Denver, and San Antonio. In 1964, the committee became national, extending everywhere in the United States where there were considerable concentrations of Hispanics. The Bishop's Committee was extended through diocesan-level councils in these Hispanic population centers. Most of the leaders of these councils were Hispanic laypersons. The first projects undertaken included the construction of clinics, settlement houses, and community and catechetical centers. Later phases extended programs to migrant workers and provided education and recreation for the young. By the early 1960s, representatives of some seventy dioceses worked with the committee. Today, 60 percent of the 176 dioceses in the United States support a Hispanic apostolate office. The Bishop's Committee has come to define Hispanic ministry.

Dolan and Deck, *Hispanic Catholic Culture in the United States,* pp. 134–35, 234–36; Dolan and Hinojosa, *Mexican Americans and the Catholic Church, 1900–1965,* pp. 113–16.

1953 • Pope Pius XII decorated lawyer Reynaldo G. Garza with the Medal Pro Ecclesia et Pontifice for his work with the Knights of Columbus. The pope recognized him again in 1954 as a Knight of the Order of Saint Gregory the Great. Garza went on to become an outstanding federal judge in Texas.

See also Government: Politics, 1979 and 1987.

Kanellos, *The Hispanic American Almanac,* p. 252.

1953 • Spanish American Catholic Action was founded in New York City under Francis Cardinal Spellman, mostly to deal with Puerto Ricans and their culture within the Catholic church. Under its auspices, the famed priest Ivan Illich set up his Institute for Intercultural Communication in Ponce, Puerto Rico.

Dolan and Deck, *Hispanic Catholic Culture in the United States,* p. 137.

1957 • Two Spanish air cadets in Waco, Texas, conducted the first *cursillo,* or short courses, on Christianity given by Hispanic laymen in order to reenergize Hispanic Catholics. The cursillo grew into a dynamic movement within Hispanic Catholic communities in the United States, building community solidarity and lay leadership. The cursillo movement even became one of the bases on which the United Farm Workers began its union in 1965, as César Chávez recruited many of his first members from among his fellow *cursillistas.*

Dolan and Deck, *Hispanic Catholic Culture in the United States,* pp. 216–20; Dolan and Hinojosa, *Mexican Americans and the Catholic Church, 1900–1965,* pp. 116–19, 222–24.

1958 • The Caballeros de San Juan (Knights of Saint John), an organization under the auspices of the Catholic church, became the largest society of Spanish-speaking people in the Midwest as the number of Puerto Ricans migrating there exploded.

Dolan and Hinojosa, *Mexican Americans and the Catholic Church, 1900–1965,* p. 291.

1959 • The Catholic church in Miami established the first center to assist Cuban refugees, the Centro Hispano Católico. The center offered such services as housing and job referrals, English classes, a day nursery, educational programs for children, an outpatient clinic, small loans, and used clothing, among other items.

García, *Havana USA,* p. 19.

1963 • Saint Vincent de Paul Seminary in Boynton Beach, Florida, became the nation's first bilingual, multiculutral seminary in order to deal with the explosion of the Hispanic population that resulted from the number of Cubans coming into exile in the United States.

Dolan and Deck, *Hispanic Catholic Culture in the United States,* p. 193.

1965 ⬩ The Migrant Ministry of the National Council of Churches, a Protestant organization, became the first religious group in the history of labor organizing to support the formation of a union among farmworkers and to offer long-term support for their efforts. From the beginning of the United Farm Workers Union, led by César Chávez, members of the Migrant Ministry walked alongside the workers on the picket lines. This support came from a Protestant organization, whereas Catholic parish priests refused to support the predominantly Catholic farm workers at first.

See also Labor, 1965.

Dolan and Deck, *Hispanic Catholic Culture in the United States,* p. 147.

1967 ⬩ Antonio Tinajero was the first Hispanic named national director of the Bishop's Committee for the Spanish-Speaking. Subsequent directors have been Hispanic, as have many of the leaders at the diocesan level.

Dolan and Deck, *Hispanic Catholic Culture in the United States,* p. 136.

1969 ⬩ Padres Asociados para Derechos Religiosos, Educativos y Sociales (Priests United for Religious, Economic and Social Rights; PADRES) was the first organization of Mexican American priests to press for services to the Spanish-speaking within the Catholic church. Some fifty Mexican American priests met October 7–9, 1969, in San Antonio, Texas, to found the organization and draft twenty-seven resolutions, one of which called for the naming of native Hispanic bishops. From its inception, the organization participated in civil rights and labor movement struggles of Mexican Americans in the Southwest and pushed for reforms in the church. By the time of its 1975 national convention, PADRES counted four Hispanic bishops in its membership.

Dolan and Deck, *Hispanic Catholic Culture in the United States,* p 154.

1970 ⬩ Patricio Flores became the first Hispanic native-born bishop of the Catholic church in the United States when Archbishop Francis J. Furey named him auxiliary bishop. During his first few years after elevation to bishop, Flores functioned as the unofficial shepherd of Hispanics in the United States, lending his support to the important causes of Hispanics, including the farmworkers's union and the National Chicano Moratorium on the Vietnam War. He also served for a number of years as chair of the Texas Advisory Committee to the U.S. Commission on Civil Rights. Flores later rose to archbishop. Between 1970 and 1992, twenty-two other Hispanic bishops were named.

See also Labor, 1965; Government: The Civil Rights Struggle, 1970.

Dolan and Deck, *Hispanic Catholic Culture in the United States,* pp. 149–50.

PATRICK F. FLORES.

1971 • Las Hermanas, an organization of fifty Hispanic Catholic nuns, was formed to promote "effective and active service to the Hispanic people" in the fields of education, health, pastoral work, and sociology. As one of its first issues, Las Hermanas addressed the cause of more than one thousand Mexican nuns working in seminaries, retreat houses, and convents in the United States doing domestic work, rather than ministering to the needs of the Hispanic lay community in the United States. Las Hermanas also lobbied for the naming of Hispanic bishops and for direct services to Hispanic communities.

Dolan and Deck, *Hispanic Catholic Culture in the United States,* pp. 152–53, 261–66.

1971 • The Catholic church established the first institute for training Hispanics for the ministry, the Mexican American Cultural Center in San Antonio, Texas. Serving as an entry point for Latin American liberation theology, the center administered courses to some nine thousand laypersons and clergy, half of whom were Anglos. The courses dealt with everything from culture and pastoral service to research and leadership development.

Dolan and Deck, *Hispanic Catholic Culture in the United States,* p. 156.

1972 • The First National Hispanic Pastoral Encounter (Encuentro) took place in Washington, D.C. It was designed to assess the relationship of the Catholic church with Hispanics in the United States. Demands were made for representation of Hispanics in the church and appropriation of resources. The second pastoral encounter met in 1977, and subsequent meetings have been held every few years.

Dolan and Deck, *Hispanic Catholic Culture in the U.S.,* pp. 111, 142–44.

1972 • The Mexican American Cultural Center was founded in San Antonio, Texas, by the Catholic church as the first national seminary dedicated exclusively to the preparation of Mexican American priests. Father Virgilio Elizondo, the leading Mexican American theologian, became its first director.

Dolan and Deck, *Hispanic Catholic Culture in the United States,* pp. 230–31.

1973 • New Mexico-born teacher and clergyman Robert Sánchez (1934–) became the first Mexican American archbishop of the Catholic church chosen by the pope to be the Archbishop of Santa Fe.

Meier and Rivera, *Dictionary of Mexican American History,* p. 318.

1973 • The first wholesale institutional support by the Catholic church for the union effort of farmworkers came with the vote of the Catholic bishops to support the national grape and lettuce boycotts. The bishops requested the legislature and the governor of California to authorize secret, free elections for the farm workers to choose the union that would represent them. The bishops supported the establishment of the Agricultural Labor Relations Board to mediate disputes between the union and the growers.

See also Labor, 1965.

Dolan and Deck, *Hispanic Catholic Culture in the United States,* p. 148.

1973 • San Antonian Carlos Rosas became the first person to compose Mexican American songs to be sung at Catholic Mass. Among his most popular compositions for Mass, many of which are still sung, are "Virgencita, Bendice Estos Dones" (Little Virgin, Bless These Gifts), "Misa de San Juan" (Saint John's Mass), and "Rosas de Tepeyac" (Roses of Tepeyac).

Dolan and Deck, *Hispanic Catholic Culture in the United States,* p. 385.

1974 • Under the leadership of Pablo Sedillo, the National Conference of Catholic Bishops' (NCCB) Committee for the Spanish-speaking for the first time rises to the top of the church hierarchy in the United States, becoming the secretariat for the Spanish-speaking.

Dolan and Deck, *Hispanic Catholic Culture in the United States,,* p. 139.

1974 • Allan Figueroa Deck, S.J., became the first U.S. Hispanic to earn a doctorate in theology. He obtained his degree from Fordham University in New York City. Today Father Figueroa Deck is an associate professor of theology at Loyola Marymount University in Los Angeles. He is also the editor of *Frontiers of Hispanic Theology in the United States.*

Dolan and Deck, *Hispanic Catholic Culture in the United States,* p. 192.

PABLO SEDILLO.

1977 • The first national meeting of Hispanic catechists took place in Corona, California, in December 1977. Its purpose was to identify catechetical needs of the Hispanic community. The meeting was made possible with a grant from the American Board of Catholic Missions.

Dolan and Deck, *Hispanic Catholic Culture in the United States,* p. 190.

1977 • The Catholic church established the first National Hispanic Youth Task Force in response to initiatives by Hispanic youth in the Northeast, who had earlier established Concilio Pastoral Juvenil (Youth Pastoral Council).

Dolan and Deck, *Hispanic Catholic Culture in the United States,* p. 295.

1979 • Patrick F. Flores became the first Mexican American to be named an archbishop of the Catholic church. Born Patricio Fernández Flores in Ganado, Texas, the seventh of nine children, Flores attended Saint Mary's Seminary in La Porte, Texas, and Saint Mary's Seminary in Houston. He was ordained a Catholic priest on May 26, 1956, and served in a variety of functions in the diocese of Galveston-Houston. He became the director of the Bishop's Committee for the Spanish-Speaking, serving until March 18, 1970, when Pope Paul VI appointed him to serve as auxiliary to the archbishop of San Antonio. On May 5, 1970, he was consecrated a bishop. Bishop Flores was the first Mexican American elevated to the hierarchy of the Catholic church in the United States since 1936.

On May 29, 1978, Bishop Flores was installed as the bishop of the diocese of El Paso, where he served until he was installed as the archbishop of San Antonio on October 13, 1979. Flores has pioneered programs in the church and in government on behalf of the civil rights of Hispanics and immigrants. In 1983, he was one of four bishops elected to represent the hierarchy of the United States at the Synod of Bishops in Rome; he was the first U.S. Hispanic ever selected. In 1986, he was awarded the Medal of Freedom (Ellis Island Medal of Honor) in honor of the Statue of Liberty's 100th birthday.

Kanellos, *Chronology of Hispanic American History,* pp. 195, 256.

1979 • The Instituto de Liturgia Hispana (Hispanic Liturgy Institute) was founded as the first Catholic liturgy center to specifically serve the liturgical needs of the Hispanic Catholic community.

Dolan and Deck, *Hispanic Catholic Culture in the United States,* pp. 372–73.

1980 • Cuban Catholic priest Father Felipe J. Estevez became the first Hispanic rector of a seminary in the contemporary United States, serving at Saint Vincent de Paul Seminary in Boynton Beach, Florida.

Dolan and Deck, *Hispanic Catholic Culture in the United States,* p. 193.

1981 • The first seminar for renewal of ministry targeted specifically for Hispanics by the Catholic church, the Committee of Religious in Hispanic Ministry (CORHIM), was held. CORHIM has offered three-week seminars of renewal for members of religious orders to assist participants in improving their ministry to Hispanics.

Dolan and Deck, *Hispanic Catholic Culture in the United States,* pp. 156–57.

1983 • The National Council of Catholic Bishops published its first pastoral letter dealing with Hispanic Catholics. Whereas previously, Hispanics in the United States were seen by the Catholic church as a problem, the letter signaled a turning point in the view of the Catholic hierarchy toward the church's Hispanic constituency. Entitled, "The Hispanic Presence: Challenge and Commitment," the letter stated that "we recognize the Hispanic community among us as a blessing from God." The letter recognized the particular history and culture of Hispanics within the church, and pledged that the church would accommodate and learn from them: "This Hispanic presence challenges us all to be more *catholic,* more open to diversity of religious expression."

Dolan and Deck, *Hispanic Catholic Culture in the United States,* pp. 152–53.

1983 • The First National Hispanic Liturgical Conference was held in New York City.

Dolan and Deck, *Hispanic Catholic Culture in the United States,* pp. 373–74.

1988 • The first school to train Hispanic theologians in the United States was founded by Jesuit Father Allan Figueroa Deck at Berkeley: The Academy of Hispanic Theology. Academy membership was limited to Hispanic clergy with a doctoral degree. The major objective of the academy was the development of an indigenous Hispanic theology in the United States.

Dolan and Deck, *Hispanic Catholic Culture in the United States,* p. 158.

1988 • The Most Reverend Robert O. González became the youngest Catholic bishop in the United States upon being named auxiliary bishop of the archdiocese of Boston. He was also the first Hispanic bishop of Boston. In 1995, it was announced that González would succeed as the next bishop of Corpus Christi, Texas.

Houston Chronicle, 17 May 1995.

1989 • The National Organization of Catechists for Hispanics, *Voz catequética,* began publishing the first Spanish-language catechetical journal for the continuing education of Hispanics catechists in the United States.

Dolan and Deck, *Hispanic Catholic Culture in the United States,* p. 191.

1990 • Hispanic ministry within the Catholic church came of age when the first consortium of movements, institutes, regional offices for Hispanic ministry and religious congregations was organized as the National Catholic Council for Hispanic Ministry (NCCHM). According to founder Father Allan Figueroa Deck, NCCHM was formed to promote the articulation of theological, pastoral and social issues and concerns of special interest to Hispanics, through forums, workshops, research and publications, and to facilitate communication between grassroots communities and church, civic, and professional organizations. It held its first meeting at Mary Center in Burlingame, California, and its first major activity was the Hispanic Congress '92: Roots and Wings.

Today, the council counts some fifty organizations as members, including regional offices of Hispanic ministry; professional association of ministers, such as priests, deacons, and catechists; pastoral institutes and centers; church congregations; apostolic movements; and media and publishing organizations. Its first congress drew 750 participants in 1992.

Dolan and Deck, *Hispanic Catholic Culture in the United States*, p. 159; Rosazza, "Distinctive contributions of Hispanic Catholics," *Texas Catholic Herald*, pp, 20–21.

1992 ◆ Sister Anita de Luna became the first Mexican American woman religious to be elected president of the Leadership Conference of Women Religious.

Dolan and Deck, *Hispanic Catholic Culture in the United States*, p. 188.

1992 ◆ María Cantón became the first layperson (also the first woman and the first Hispanic) to be given the Pope Paul VI Award for Leadership in Evangelization by the National Council for Catholic Evangelization. Cantón, a Cuban exile, started a storefront Catholic evangelization center in Miami soon after her escape from Cuba in the Mariel Boatlift.

Dolan and Deck, *Hispanic Catholic Culture in the United States*, p. 189.

1992 ◆ The Conference of Catholic Bishops established in Washington, D.C., the first national Secretariat for Hispanic Affairs, with Pablo Sedillo as its first director.

Dolan and Deck, *Hispanic Catholic Culture in the United States*, p. 234.

1995 ◆ Father Leopoldo Alard was the first Hispanic elected a bishop of the Episcopal church. On September 9, 1995, Alard was consecrated suffragen bishop of the Episcopal Diocese of Texas, a diocese of forty-nine thousand square miles. The suffragen bishop acts as an assistant to the bishop. Previously, Alard had served fifteen years as a parish priest and Episcopal school headmaster in Homestead, Florida. In 1986, he became the executive director of the Center for Hispanic ministries in Austin, Texas. After that he served as vicar of Santa Cruz, the diocese's fastest-growing parish, located near the Port of Houston. Alard was born in Matanzas, Cuba, and immigrated to the United States at age twenty after becoming disillusioned with Fidel Castro's revolution. Alard received his divinity degree from the Episcopal Seminary of the Caribbean in 1967.

Hispanic, December 1995, p. 12; *Houston Chronicle,* 13 May 1995, p. 29A.

SCIENCE AND TECHNOLOGY

AGRICULTURE

1493 • Sugar cane was introduced to the New World by Christopher Columbus during his second voyage. Originally from India, the plant was taken first to Hispaniola and then to the rest of the Americas for its cultivation. The first sugar mill was built in 1508 or 1509 on Hispaniola. From Santo Domingo; from there New World sugar was shipped to Spain beginning in 1516. All the technology, plants, and technicians involved in sugar production were brought to the New World by the Spaniards. By 1523, there were twenty-four mills operating on the island.

Kanellos, *Chronology of Hispanic American History,* pp. 24, 31; Sidney W. Mintz, "Pleasure, Profit, and Satiation," in Viola and Margolis, *Seeds of Change,* p. 117.

1508 • The first agricultural product introduced to the Americas by the Spaniards was sugar. Originally from India, the plant was taken first to Hispaniola and then to the rest of the Americas for its cultivation. The first sugar mill was built in 1508 or 1509 on Hispaniola. The first samples of sugar were sent to Spain about 1515. By 1523, there were twenty-four mills operating on the island.

Kanellos, *Chronology of Hispanic American History,* p. 24.

1521 • The Spaniards Hernán Cortés and Gregorio Villalobos introduced ranching to Mexico when they imported cattle from Cuba for breeding purposes. This was the beginning of the ranching industry and culture on the mainland; it would travel north and eventually become one of the principal industries of the American Southwest. Not only were cattle introduced but also all of the components of ranch ecology, including cattle, sheep, goats, hogs, and the plant species these animals consume.

Deb Bennett and Robert S. Hoffmann, "Ranching in the New World," in Viola and Margolis, *Seeds of Change,* pp. 90–95.

1521 • Spanish explorers took horses and cattle to Florida on Juan Ponce de León's second trip. Hernando de Soto was next to import livestock to Florida, including more than three hundred horses and some cattle in 1539. It was in Florida that the Spanish established the first stock raising in what is now the

United States. Missions spearheaded settlement and stock raising. By 1565, some stock raising was established around Saint Augustine and Tallahassee. The first ranchers raised cattle for local consumption but also smuggled stock to Cuba. Ranching was difficult in the swamps and tropics; it did not flourish as it later did in California and Texas. By 1800, the Spanish tax rolls showed only thirty-four ranches with some fifteen thousand to twenty thousand cattle.

Slatta, *Cowboys of the Americas,* p. 10.

CHRISTOPHER
COLUMBUS.

1535 · Although horses were introduced by the Spaniards into areas that became present-day Florida as early as 1521, Antonio de Mendoza was the first to bring horses to the mainland of the Americas for breeding purposes, introducing them into Mexico in 1535. By 1650, there were countless herds of mustangs in northwest Mexico, and they later made their way into the Great Plains of North America. The first breeding herds of horses were brought to Florida by Pedro Meléndez de Avilés in 1565. Juan de Oñate's colonization of New Mexico brought more horses north in 1598. During the next three centuries, Santa Fe, New Mexico, served as the center for distribution of horses.

Deb Bennett and Robert S. Hoffmann, "Ranching in the New World," in Viola and Margolis, *Seeds of Change,* pp. 107–108.

1539 · Hernando de Soto drove a herd of pigs from Florida to Arkansas, with numerous pigs escaping along his path; these became the foundation for the feral populations of North America. Later populations of pigs were introduced by the Franciscan missionaries in Texas and elsewhere. The razorback, prized by hunters throughout the South, arose from these populations.

Deb Bennett and Robert S. Hoffmann, "Ranching in the New World," in Viola and Margolis, *Seeds of Change,* p. 103.

1564 · Spanish Mexican missionaries introduced grapes to California, the future site of the most important wine industry in the United States. The European vine, *V. vinifera,* was introduced from Mexico and by 1600 was producing grapes principally for sacramental wine in and around San Diego

HERNANDO DE SOTO, PORTRAYED BY AN UNKNOWN EIGHTEENTH-CENTURY ARTIST.

and Los Angeles. In 1767, the Franciscan brothers introduced what was later called the mission grape. By the early 1800s, surplus wine was sold to consumers.

Henry Hobhouse, "New World, Vineyard to the Old," in Viola and Margolis, *Seeds of Change,* p. 61.

1598 • Cattle and ranching were first introduced north of the Rio Grande by Spanish Mexican colonists headed by Juan de Oñate when they crossed the river with seven thousand head of cattle somewhere near present- day El Paso into what became New Mexico. Besides cattle, Oñate brought in more than four thousand head of shaggy sheep, which became the foundation of the churro breed of the Navajos. The first ranches along the Rio Grande in Texas were founded from 1659 to 1682. During the next century, cattle ranching flourished all along the north of the river, and by the 1830s cattle had been driven from California to northern Oregon.

Deb Bennett and Robert S. Hoffman, "Ranching in the New World," in Viola and Margolis, *Seeds of Change,* pp. 98–100.

1600 • The Spanish settlers along the Rio Grande Valley introduced the plow and beasts of burden to the Pueblo Indians, ushering in an agricultural technology that would endure for centuries in what would become the American Southwest. They also introduced irrigation and new craft techniques, such as those involved in carpentry and blacksmithing, and a new profit-driven economy.

Fontana, *Entrada,* pp. 80–81.

1600 • A more efficient and rapid sugar mill was invented in Mexico or Peru and later disseminated throughout areas of the Americas engaged in sugar production. This was the vertical three-roller mill, which allowed for a quicker and more thorough extraction of the sugar juice.

Sidney W. Mintz, "Pleasure, Profit, and Satiation," in Viola and Margolis, *Seeds of Change,* p. 120.

1760 • The Spanish governor of Texas proposed that the heavy traffic in cattle from Texas to French Louisiana be licensed and regulated. This proposal underscored the realization that Hispanic cowboys had been driving cattle to Louisiana for decades and that it was a lucrative trade. The first cattle drives to take place in what would become the United States had already begun. After the United States acquired the Louisiana Territory in 1803, the cattle drives continued—as smuggling.

Slatta, *Cowboys of the Americas,* p. 19.

1830 • The first Longhorn cattle appeared, a result of the crossbreeding of the Spanish Retinto and animals brought to Texas by Anglo settlers. Immune to tick fever and accustomed to the tough brush country of south Texas, the Longhorn became the basis for the western livestock industry.

Slatta, *Cowboys of the Americas,* p. 19.

ENGINEERING

1610 · The first irrigation canals and irrigation systems north of the Rio Grande were built in Santa Fe, New Mexico, by Spanish, Indian, and mestizo colonizers. They dug two *acequias madres* (main ditches) on each side of the small river that passed through the center of the town they were establishing. The Spanish had strict codes and plans for the construction of irrigation systems for the towns they were founding in the arid present-day Southwest; such systems were often constructed in advance of the building of the forts, houses, and churches. The undertaking was quite often massive, calling for digging, dredging, and transporting materials, and the feeding of humans and animals. This was the case in the founding of Albuquerque in 1706, of San Antonio in 1731, and of Los Angeles in 1781. The canals of San Antonio were so well planned, lined with stone and masonry as they were, that many of them are still functioning today.

Meyer, *Water in the Hispanic Southwest,* pp. 37–41; Simmons, "Spanish Irrigation Practices in New Mexico," pp. 138–39.

CA. 1790 · The idea for a transcontinental road first occurred to the Spanish governor of California, Pedro Fages, who wrote his viceroy for permission to contact George Washington about constructing a continental trail from Virginia to California, with the roads meeting at the Spanish fort at Saint Louis. The idea did not take hold until 1869 when the transcontinental railroad finally linked East and West.

Joseph P. Sánchez, "Hispanic American Heritage," in Viola and Margolis, *Seeds of Change,* p. 182.

1790 · The first schools of mining in the New World were founded in Mexico City and Guatemala City.

Kanellos, *Chronology of Hispanic American History,* p. 62.

1837 · The first railroad in Spanish America was built in Cuba, between Havana and Guines.

Kanellos, *Chronology of Hispanic American History,* p. 89.

1885 · Spanish immigrant Rafael Guastavino (1842–1908) obtained the first of his twenty-five patents, this one for new mortars he developed for tiled floor and ceiling vaults, partitions and stairs. Over the years this architect and contractor developed fireproofing innovations and perfected traditional cohesive masonry for modern use; he was responsible for building the tiled vaults for such New York City monuments as Grand Central Station, Carnegie Hall, the old Penn Station, the Metropolitan Museum of Art, the Plaza and Biltmore hotels, the Cathedral of Saint John the Divine, and many others. Born in Valencia, Spain, Guastavino studied architecture in Barcelona, where he built factories, houses, and theaters, incorporating many of the traditional technologies of Mediterranean architecture.

Guastavino immigrated to the United States in 1881 in search of broader markets and better mortars and went on to become one of the most recognized designers and builders of vaults, domes, and tiled surfaces, promoting their acoustics, elegance, and economy. By 1891, Guastavino's company had offices in New York, Boston, Providence, Chicago, and Milwaukee. In 1892, Guastavino documented his successful system of construction in his book *Essay on the Theory and History of Cohesive Construction.* After his death, Guastavino's business was continued by his son Rafael II, who expanded the company and was responsible for numerous patents of his own. In all, the Guastavinos were responsible for domes built at state capitals, major universities, museums, and railroad stations throughout the United States, as well as the Supreme Court building and the Natural History Museum in Washington, D.C.

"Master Builders," *Humanities* 16/3 (May/June 1995), pp. 29–30.

1989 • Environmental engineer Margarita Colmenares became the first woman elected to the presidency of the Society of Hispanic Professional Engineers. Colmenares is an air-quality specialist at the Chevron refinery in El Segundo, California.

Tardiff and Mabunda, *Dictionary of Hispanic Biography,* pp. 237–38.

1990 • Mexican American Ellen Ochoa became the first Hispanic female astronaut. Ochoa earned both a master's degree and doctorate in electrical engineering from Stanford University.

Tardiff and Mabunda, *Dictionary of Hispanic Biography,* p. 617.

ELLEN OCHOA.

1991 • Margarita Colmenares, a Mexican American born and raised in Sacramento, California, was the first Hispanic engineer to be selected for a White House fellowship since the program was established in 1964.

Tardiff and Mabunda, *Dictionary of Hispanic Biography,* p. 237.

1992 • Teresa Mendoza was the first Hispanic to become chief of the U.S. Army Corps of Engineers's Earthquake Preparedness Center of Expertise. Mendoza was a founder of this center in 1991 and its first chief. The center guides, trains, and prepares the Corps of Engineers for this inevitable catastrophic disaster. In 1979, Mendoza received her degree in civil engineering from San Jose State University and from 1980 on worked her way up the ranks of the U.S. Army Corps of Engineers. As chief of the Earthquake Preparedness Center, she has been involved in dealing with most of the major earthquakes suffered in the United States since 1980. She has won numerous awards for her work on the Loma Prieta and the Northridge earthquakes. In 1993, she was named Hispanic Engineer of the Year.

Biography of Teresa Mendoza supplied by U.S. Army Corps of Engineers.

1995 • Senior Research Physicist F. J. Duarte of Eastman Kodak Company became the first Hispanic to win the Engineering Excellence Award presented by the Optical Society of America. He was recognized for his work in developing systems to assess the density of photographic film, for which he and Kodak earned a patent in 1993.

"About People," *Hispanic Business,* April 1996, p. 68.

GEOGRAPHY

1509 • Juan Ponce de León (1460–1520) colonized the first New World area to later become part of the United States—the island of San Juan Bautista (Puerto Rico). He was then appointed governor as a reward for his labors. Ponce de León was noted for putting down Indian uprisings in Puerto Rico. He was removed as governor of the island in 1511, and he returned to Spain in 1512.

Kanellos, *Chronology of Hispanic American History,* pp. 24, 26.

1513 • On February 4, 1513, the Gulf Stream was discovered by pilot Antonio de Alaminos during Juan Ponce de León's voyage to Florida. Antonio de Alaminos had served as the pilot on Christopher Columbus's fourth voyage (1502–04). This discovery resulted in Havana's becoming a major port of assembly and Florida's becoming a strategic stopping place for voyages. The current runs from the Straits of Florida into the Bahama channel, past the coast of the Carolinas into the open ocean, where it forks northward to Norway and east to the Azores. Spanish ships, therefore, headed for the Azores, refitted, and returned to Spain.

Kanellos, *Chronology of Hispanic American History,* p. 30.

1513 • Juan Ponce de León became the first European to explore the mainland of what would become the United States. In negotiations with the Spanish Crown, it was decided that Ponce de León would lead expeditions to settle Bimini (Florida). He had to cover expenses himself but would receive 10 percent of all royal revenues derived from the exploitation of Bimini. Ponce de León's expedition left Spain on March 4, 1513, and arrived at the coast of Florida on April 3. After exploring the coast, he returned to Spain to make a report to the Council of the Indies and to make new proposals to the Crown. He was granted new concessions and appointed captain general of an armada against the Carib Indians. In 1520, Ponce de León set out on his last journey to take possession of Florida for the Crown. His expedition was subsequently destroyed by the Indians of the peninsula, and Ponce de León returned to Cuba with an arrow wound that took his life.

Kanellos, *Chronology of Hispanic American History,* p. 13.

1519 • Alonso Alvarez de Pineda discovered the coast of the Gulf of Mexico and claimed Texas for Spain. The first map to chart the entire Gulf of Mexico was created from information from this exploration. Alvarez de Pineda's map is the first document of Southwest history.

Chipman, *Spanish Texas, 1519–1821,* p. 243; Fontana, *Entrada,* p. 17; Kanellos, *Chronology of Hispanic American History,* p. 33.

1520 • Explorer Alonso Alvarez de Pineda settled the question of Florida's geography, proving that it is not an island, but part of a vast continent. He, in effect, proved the existence of North America.

Kanellos, *Chronology of Hispanic American History,* p. 33.

1524 • Esteban Gómez was the first Hispanic to explore the northeastern coast of North America in search of a passage to the Orient. After leaving from La Coruña, Spain, and crossing the Atlantic, he explored from the coast of Nova Scotia down to Florida. Gómez went on to explore Hudson Bay and the Delaware and Connecticut Rivers some eighty years before Henry Hudson. His exploration contributed to many of the maps of the coast that were created during the sixteenth century.

Fontana, *Entrada,* pp. 18–19; Kanellos, *Chronology of Hispanic American History,* p. 34.

1526 • San Miguel de Guadalupe, the first settlement in what is now the United States, was founded by the Spaniards on the coast of present-day Georgia near the Savannah River. Founded by Lucas Vásquez de Ayllón in what was then called La Florida, the colony was abandoned in early 1592, after more than four hundred people had died of disease and hunger.

Kanellos, *Hispanics in U.S. History,* p. 20.

1540 · Francisco Vásquez de Coronado and the members of his expedition became the first Europeans to explore the Grand Canyon. In 1540, Coronado set out from Mexico leading several hundred Spaniards and Indian allies on an expedition financed by his wife to search for Cíbola (or Quivira), where the seven cities of gold were rumored to be located. Along the way north into the present-day Southwest, Coronado conquered various Indian tribes, including Zuñis, living in what were thought to be the cities of gold. On August 25, 1540, the expedition encountered the Grand Canyon; they later encountered the Rio Grande, which they named Nuestra Señora (Our Lady).

All along the way, the Europeans had their first encounters, some peaceful, others violent, with many native groups; included in these were the massacres of the Tiguex and Cicuye Indians. Coronado never found the supposed cities of gold but reached as far north as today's state of Nebraska. Coronado wrote to the king that he had found lands poor in metals but rich in livestock and very suitable for farming; however, Coronado had traveled and explored more land in the shortest period of time than any other explorer to that date. In so doing, he prepared the way for future settlement of what has become the American Southwest. He returned to Nueva Galicia in 1541. He died in Mexico City in 1554.

Kanellos, *Chronology of Hispanic American History,* p. 40.

1541 · From 1539 to 1542, Hernando de Soto (1500–1542) explored the present states of Florida, Alabama, Mississippi, Tennessee, North Carolina, Arkansas, and Louisiana. In May 1541, he arrived at the Mississippi River, the largest river he had ever seen. He named it Río Grande de la Florida

ARTIST FREDERIC REMINGTON'S DEPICTION OF CORONADO'S TREK ACROSS THE SOUTHWEST.

(Great River of Florida). De Soto and his men were the first Europeans to see the Mississippi River. During the course of his journeys, De Soto lost one thousand men and then also took ill and died at the age of forty-two.

Fontana, *Entrada*, pp. 22–25; Kanellos, *Chronology of Hispanic American History*, p. 40.

1542 • On September 28, 1542, Juan Rodríguez de Cabrillo, a Portuguese sailor commissioned by the Spanish viceroy, sailed north of Mexico's west coast in search of treasures. He entered and explored what he described as an excellent port—present-day San Diego, California.

Kanellos, *Chronology of Hispanic American History*, p. 40.

1560 • The Spanish founded Santa Elena in what is today the state of South Carolina; it was the first European settlement in what became the continental United States. Both Santa Elena and Saint Augustine predate Jamestown, which was founded in 1607 by the British, and the arrival of the *Mayflower* in 1620.

Kanellos, *Chronology of Hispanic American History*, p. 45.

1562 • Diego Gutiérrez (1485–?), a pilot and a chart and instrument maker in Seville, created the largest, most complete print map of the Americas, relying on the data collected by Spain during its explorations. The map included information on the people and settlements and the fauna and flora from Tierra del Fuego all the way up to Labrador on the east coast of the hemisphere and to California on the west coast. His was the largest printed map of the hemisphere known up to that time.

James Lockhart, "The Central Areas during and after the Conquest," in Herbert, *1492*, p. 146.

1565 • The first permanent European settlement in what is now the United States was Saint Augustine, Florida, founded by Pedro Menéndez de Avilés on the order of King Philip II of Spain. Menéndez de Avilés established seven settlements in all on the coast of La Florida. The Spaniards were welcomed by the Timicua Indians, who gave the soldiers and settlers shelter in their huts. The site of the original village of Saint Augustine was moved a year later, in 1566, to a more strategic site. Saint Augustine became the most successful strategic post for the Spaniards in defending the Florida coast. It was the only one that endured storms, fires, famine, and raids by the French and English. In 1586, the English privateer Francis Drake looted and burned Saint Augustine, forcing the villagers to flee to the forest. Once the privateer was gone, they returned to rebuild.

During the seventeenth century, the city and other areas of Florida received a considerable number of emigrants from Spain and the Spanish Caribbean. The population of Saint Augustine grew to two thousand by the turn of the eighteenth century. The city was afforded more security by the building of the San Marcos Fort, begun in 1672 and finished in 1756.

In 1763, the region of the Florida peninsula, called Eastern Florida—as opposed to Western Florida, which ranged from the Georgia coast to the

Mississippi River—came under British control as a result of the Treaty of Paris. This area included Saint Augustine. In 1783, under the Treaty of Versailles, Eastern Florida was returned to Spain. It remained a possession of Spain until 1821, when it was surrendered to the United States. Louisiana, which had been discovered by the Spanish but settled by the French from Canada, remained a French colony until 1763, when it, too, passed into Spanish possession as a result of the Treaty of Paris. Louisiana was ceded to France in 1801 but was sold to the United States by Napoleon in 1803.

Kanellos, *Chronology of Hispanic American History*, p. 45.

1590 • Juan de Fuca navigated his ships to the northern coast of present-day Washington State. Spanish maps from the period show the Strait of Juan de Fuca as a possible Northwest Passage.

Kanellos, *Chronology of Hispanic American History*, p. 47.

1602 • With three ships, Sebastián Vizcaíno explored and charted the coast of California. He identified Monterey as an ideal place for major Spanish settlement.

Fontana, *Entrada*, p. 69.

1693 • The great Spanish Mexican scientist and mathematician Carlos de Sigüenza y Góngora (1645–1700) accompanied Admiral Andrés de Pez on a scientific expedition into what is today the southeastern United States. Sigüenza y Góngora studied the topography, fauna, and flora and later published his findings in Mexico City, becoming the first scientist and university professor to study the region. He published his findings in his book *Descripción de la bahía de Santa María de Galve (antes Penzacola), de la Movila o Mississippi, en la costa septentrional del seno mejicano* (Description of the Bay of Santa María de Galve [previously Penzacola], of Mobile or Mississippi, on the eastern coast of the Gulf of Mexico).

Sigüenza y Góngora authored numerous books in all the fields of his broad interests and also has the distinction of publishing the first newspaper in Mexico, *El Mercurio Volante* (Winged Mercury). He was also one of the first to write scholarly accounts of territories that would become part of the United States. In addition to his book about the lands around the northeastern Gulf of Mexico, he also published *Historia de la provincia de Tejas* (History of the Province of Texas). Finally, his encyclopedic knowledge and study extended to include what might be considered anthropology today. He researched and wrote about the Aztecs and the Chichimecas in his books *Genealogía de los reyes mejicanos* (Genealogy of the Mexican Kings) and *Historia del imperio de los chichimecas* (History of the Chichimeca Empire). Sigüenza y Góngora died in 1700 in Mexico City. Unfortunately, a devastating fire in Mexico City in 1792 consumed many of his manuscripts.

Fontana, *Entrada*, p.77; Kanellos, *Chronology of Hispanic American History*, pp. 44, 49.

1774 • Led by a Spanish Franciscan missionary by the name of Pedro de Garcés, government official Juan Bautista de Anza (1735–1788) pioneered a route across the Sonora and Mohave Deserts to southern California. Because of his success, he was next requested by the viceroy of Mexico to find a route to Alta California and lead soldiers and settlers there to found a colony on San Francisco Bay.

Meier and Rivera, *Dictionary of Mexican American History,* p. 17.

1775 • Captain Bruno de Hezeta explored and mapped the mouth of the Columbia River and its interior for twenty miles—some thirty years before American explorers Lewis and Clark arrived there. A companion ship commanded by Peruvian Juan Francisco de la Bodega y Cuadra got as far north as 58° 30' north latitude in Alaska.

Fontana, *Entrada,* p. 181–82; Joseph P. Sánchez, "Hispanic American Heritage," in Viola and Margolis, *Seeds of Change,* p. 182.

1775 • Retired soldier Carlos Butrón (or Buitrón) and his Indian wife received the first land grant in California, consisting of a few acres near the San Carlos Barromeo Mission close to Monterey. This land grant policy was developed in Spain to encourage settlement in its faraway lands and ensure agricultural productivity. During the Mexican regime, the number of land grants accelerated greatly, so that by the time of Anglo- American migration, most of the best land was already in the possession of Hispanic Californians.

Fontana, *Entrada,* p. 171.

1776 • The first pioneers to make their way overland to California were led by Juan Bautista de Anza from San Miguel de Horcasitas in Sonora, Mexico, to the California coast, where they would establish the port and city of San Francisco, California. The pioneers founded the San Francisco Presidio on September 17, 1776, and the Dolores Mission in October. Father Pedro Font was the first to give the name San Francisco to the bay. The train of wagons included some 240 persons (more colonists were picked up along the way), among them were soldiers and their families, cowboys, muleteers, and servants. They took along with them 302 head of beef cattle, 140 pack mules, and 340 saddle animals.

Fontana, *Entrada,* pp. 160–64, 172; Meier and Rivera, *Dictionary of Mexican American History,* p. 17.

1777 • The governor of Alta California, Felipe de Neve, established his capital in Monterey and also founded the village of San José with some of the settlers brought earlier by José Moraga.

Kanellos, *Chronology of Hispanic American History,* p. 58.

1779 • Ignacio de Arteaga sailed to the mouth of Prince William Sound in Alaska, named the port Santiago de Apóstol, and claimed it for Spain; this was the northernmost point ever taken possession of by Spanish subjects.

Fontana, *Entrada,* p. 183.

1781 • California Governor Felipe de Neve went south from Monterey with other settlers and established Nuestra Señora la Reina de los Angeles de Porciúncula (Los Angeles).

Kanellos, *Chronology of Hispanic American History,* p. 58.

1784 • The first land grants for ranches in California were given by the Spanish crown. These gave the recipients title to huge tracts of land suitable for raising livestock.

Fontana, *Entrada,* p. 171.

1790 • Alejandro Malaspina became the first man to explore and map the Pacific coast of North America. On a scientific expedition that included naturalists, astronomers, and artists in search of a northern route from the Pacific to the Atlantic Oceans, Malaspina was finally deterred when an impassable glacier in Alaska blocked his path. That glacier is now known as Malaspina Glacier. Because of the Malaspina expedition, Spain was able to claim possessions as far north as Alaska and found settlements such as those in Valdez and Córdoba. At Yakutat Bay, artists Tomás de Suría and José Cardero made drawings of the Tlingit people who inhabited the region. These are believed to be the first drawings by Europeans (or their Hispanic descendants in the New World) of Alaskan natives.

Fontana, *Entrada,* p. 186; *Hispanics in U.S. History,* p. 44.

1792 • Naturalist José Mariano Moziño Suárez Losada, on an expedition led by Juan Bodega y Cuadra, was the first to study and describe the Nootka region of Alaska, leaving for posterity detailed written accounts of the native inhabitants. His companion, Atanasio Echeverría y Godoy, became the first artist to depict the plants, animals, people, and scenes in the Nootka region.

Fontana, *Entrada,* p. 186.

1800 • The first map published by a Hispanic in the United States was Miguel González's *Carta esférica del Océano Atlántico* (Spherical Map of the Atlantic Ocean), issued by C.& I. Honig.

Online Computer Learning Center.

1806 • When Zebulon Montgomery Pike crossed the Missouri River in his exploration of the West, he was actually following a trail blazed by Captain Facundo Melgares of Santa Fe, who had been trading among the Pawnees and working out peace treaties with them.

Joseph P. Sánchez, "Hispanic American Heritage," in Viola and Margolis, *Seeds of Change,* p. 182.

MINING

1842 • The first man to discover and mine gold in California was a Mexican herder by the name of Francisco López. He made his find on March 19, 1842, in Feliciano Canyon near Los Angeles. Mexicans worked diggings from Los Angeles up to Santa Cruz from this time on, years prior to James Marshall's discovery at Sutter's Mill on January 24, 1848, which led to the California gold rush.

Meier and Rivera, *Dictionary of Mexican American History,* pp. 200–201.

1845 • Andrés Castillero, a Mexican army captain, discovered mercury in red cinnabar rocks close to San José, California, and founded the New Almadén mine and mining town with local Indian and Mexican workers. But the outbreak of the Mexican-American War and his need for finances ended his and his workers business. By 1850, the British company of Barron and Forbes had bought the mine, and it was later taken over by the New York Quicksilver Mining Corporation. The mine became the second-largest producer of quicksilver in the world during the reminder of the nineteenth century.

Meier and Rivera, *Dictionary of Mexican American History,* pp. 253–55.

PHYSICAL AND SOCIAL SCIENCES

1512 • The first hospital in the Western Hemisphere was founded at the cathedral of Santo Domingo in the city of that name on the island of Hispaniola. It was built by the Spaniards. The first school was also located there.

Kanellos, *Chronology of Hispanic American History,* p. 27.

1536 • The first social science and biological document of the indigenous peoples and the flora and fauna of the South and Southwest, particularly Texas and the Mariam, Avavar, Karankawa, and other Indians of the region, was a report written in 1536 in Mexico City by three shipwrecked Europeans and an Afro-European, one of whom was Alvar Núñez Cabeza de Vaca. No other region in the present-day United States was described so early with so much detail.

Chipman, *Spanish Texas, 1519–1821,* pp. 243–46.

1541 • Rodrigo Rangel and a soldier known only as the Gentleman of Elvas were the first to describe the culture of the Caddo Indians, which they observed on the expedition of Hernando de Soto to southern Arkansas and east Texas.

Chipman, *Spanish Texas, 1519–1821,* p. 244.

1542 • Alvar Núñez Cabeza de Vaca (1490–1557) can be considered the first anthropologist and ethnographer of the New World because of his accounts of the Indians of the South and Southwest of the present-day United States. He documented his observations and experiences in his book *The Account,* which was published in Spain in 1542 after his return from the New World. In the winter of 1528, Cabeza de Vaca was only one of fifteen survivors of a shipwreck off the coast of Florida. The Indians, who were suffering from illness, forced the survivors to become "healers," and Cabeza de Vaca began his career as a renowned physician among the Indians.

During the six years that he remained among the Indians along the Gulf Coast, as far west as Texas, Cabeza de Vaca also became a merchant and a translator. He recorded in great detail for the first time many observations about the Indians of the South and Southwest. In 1534, he and three other marooned survivors set out on a march west in search of New Spain. They marched on foot completely across Texas and into New Mexico, going from one tribe to the next as healers and traders. They finally encountered Spaniards in what is today northwestern Mexico in 1536. Cabeza de Vaca's nine-year journey from Florida to New Mexico ended when he set sail in April 1537, for Spain. His memoir *La relación* (The Account) may be considered the first ethnographic study of the Americas, as well as a literary masterpiece, possibly the first book of "American literature" written in a European language.

Chipman, *Spanish Texas, 1519–1821,* pp. 243–44; Kanellos, *Chronology of Hispanic American History,* pp. 13, 26, 38.

ALVAR NÚÑEZ
CABEZA DE VACA.

1595 · The first European to study and translate the languages of Indians residing in what is today the United States was Father Francisco Pareja, who, from 1595 until his death sometime after 1626, became an expert in the Timicuan language and published four works on the language. These studies are the basic texts used by modern linguists to understand the now extinct language. Father Pareja was a missionary to the Timicuan Indians at the San Juan del Puerto Mission, founded in 1587, in what is now Georgia.

Fontana, *Entrada,* p. 49.

1805 · The first hospital in the Southwest was founded in San Antonio, Texas, under Spanish rule. It was located in the Alamo. By 1806, the Alamo hospital was caring for eighteen patients, with a waiting list of twenty others. It closed by 1814.

Chipman, *Spanish Texas, 1519–1821,* p. 258.

1807 · The first medical publication by a Hispanic in the United States was Valentín de Foronda's *Cartas presentadas a la Sociedad Filosófica de Philadelphia* (Letters Presented to the Philadelphia Philosophic Society), published by Duane in Philadelphia. In 1810, a Sephardic Jew, Jacob de la Motta, published another medical treatise, *An Investigation of the Properties and Effects of the Spiraea Trifoliata of Linnaeus, or Indian Physic.* In 1820, de la Motta gave an address to the Georgia Medical Society entitled "On the Causes of the Mortality among Strangers, during the Late Summer and Fall," which was later published.

Simonhoff, *Jewish Notables in America, 1776–1865,* pp. 189–92.

1823 · The first book of prescriptions (pharmaceuticals) written and published in the Spanish language in what would become a state of the Union was published in Sonoma, California, by the Imprenta del Gobierno (Government Printing House) under the title *Botica general de los remedios esperimentados; que a beneficio del público se reimprime por su original en Cádiz* (General Collection of Proven Remedies; Reprinted from the Original of Cádiz for the Benefit of the Public).

Online Computer Learning Center.

1827 · The first handbook of medical treatments written by a Hispanic scholar was published in Philadelphia. *Compendio de la medicina: o medicina práctica . . .* (Compendium of Medicine: or Practical Medicine . . .), by Juan Manuel Venegas, claimed to have drawn its remedies from observations of medicine in New Spain, presumably influenced by the medicine practiced by the Native Americans.

Online Computer Learning Center.

1827 · The first book on Cuban horticulture to be published in the United States, Ramón de la Sagra's *Memorias para servir de introducción a la horti-*

cultura cubana (Memories to Serve as Introduction to Cuban Horticulture), was issued in New York.

Online Computer Learning Center.

CA. 1836 • Sephardic Jew Jacob de la Motta of Charleston, South Carolina, became the first Hispanic pharmacist on record when he bought and operated Apothecaries Hall, reputed to be the first pharmacy in the Americas, supposedly started in 1780. The equipment, the brass scales, and the interior woodwork of this old pharmacy are housed today in the Charleston Museum.

See also Science and Technology: Physical and Social Sciences, 1807.

Simonhoff, *Jewish Notables in America, 1776–1865,* p. 191.

1836 • The first Hispanic known to have graduated from an Ivy League school (University of Pennsylvania) in medicine was David Camden DeLeón, who came from a multitalented Sephardic Jewish family of Charleston, South Carolina. After graduation in 1836, DeLeón enlisted in the army and was sent to the Florida tropics to treat the sick and wounded soldiers of the Seminole Wars. He later became a hero at the Battle of Chapultepec in the Mexican War and later a hero of the Confederacy in the U.S. Civil War. DeLeón became the first surgeon general of the Confederacy. After the defeat of the Confederacy, DeLeón moved to Mexico. At the request of President Ulysses S. Grant, DeLeón eventually returned to the United States and settled in New Mexico, where he practiced medicine and wrote for medical journals.

Simonhoff, *Jewish Notables in America, 1776–1865,* pp. 297–300.

1881 • Carlos Juan Finlay, a Cuban doctor educated in Philadelphia, proposed that yellow fever was spread by the *Aedes aegypti* mosquito and was met with skepticism from the medical community. It was not until the American occupation of Cuba in 1900, when American soldiers were dying of the disease and army doctor Major Walter Reed visited with Finlay and observed his experiments, that the medical community took his work seriously enough to implement a program of eradication of the dreaded mosquito. Under the direction of engineer William Gorgas, the U.S. Army destroyed the swamps where the mosquito lived.

Hispanics in U.S. History, p. 8.

1900 • The famous Mexican faith healer, Teresa Urrea (1873–1906), known as La Santa de Cabora (The Saint from Cabora), was hired by an American medical company to make her talents available to the masses. By 1904, she had become disillusioned with the commercialism of the company and withdrew from her contract to continue working as a free agent in Clifton, Arizona.

Frank B. Putnam, "Teresa Urrea, 'The Saint of Cabora,'" *Southern California Quarterly,* 45 (September 1963); pp. 245–64.

NOBEL PRIZE-WINNING
PHYSICIST LUIS
WALTER ALVAREZ.

1943 • Hispanic physicist Luis Walter Alvarez (1911–1988) left his post at the Massachusetts Institute of Technology to join the Manhattan Project to develop the first atomic bomb. He was responsible for the development of the triggering device of the first plutonium bomb, and he flew in a B-29 following the *Enola Gay* to observe the bomb's detonation over Hiroshima.

See also Science and Technology: Physical and Social Sciences, 1968.

Tardiff and Mabunda, *Dictionary of Hispanic Biography,* p. 39.

1959 • Biochemist and professor at New York University, Severo Ochoa (1905–1993) became the first Hispanic to win a Nobel Prize in physiology (medicine). He shared the prize with his former student Arthur Kornberg for their work in discovering the enzymes that help produce nucleic acids. In effect, these two scientists had discovered how to synthesize both RNA and DNA. Ochoa was born in Spain but became a naturalized American citizen in 1956. He taught at universities in Spain, Germany, England, and the United States.

Hispanics in U.S. History, p. 83; Tardiff and Mabunda, *Dictionary of Hispanic Biography,* p. 621.

1965 • California-born zoologist Evelyn Margaret Rivera (1929–) received the UNESCO Award from the International Cell Research Organization for her research on cancer and the biology of tumors.

Kanellos, *The Hispanic American Almanac,* p. 692.

1966 • California-born David Pimentel (1925–) became the first U.S. Hispanic to be named to the President's Science Advisory Committee. The Cornell educated entomologist has also served UNESCO, the National Academies of Science, the Department of Energy, and the Environmental Protection Agency.

Kanellos *The Hispanic American Almanac,* p. 691.

1968 • Luis Walter Alvarez (1910–1988) became the first U.S.-born Hispanic to win the Nobel Prize for physics. Born on June 13, 1910, in San Francisco, California, Luis Alvarez was one of the United States's most distinguished and respected physicists. With B.S. (1932) and Ph.D. (1936) degrees from the University of Chicago, Alvarez also received a number of honorary degrees from universities in the United States and abroad. He developed most of his work at the University of California-Berkeley from 1936 until his death. From 1954 to 1959 and from 1976 to 1978, he served as associate director of the prestigious Lawrence Berkeley Lab. In 1986, Alvarez was awarded the Nobel Prize in physics in recognition of his work in the development of bulle chambers for the detection and identification of subatomic particles. He had also received the Collier Trophy (1946), the Scott Medal (1953), the Einstein Medal (1961), the National Medal of Science (1964), in addition to many other awards. He was the first U.S. Hispanic to win most of these awards. Alvarez was a pioneer in particle physics, astrophysics, ophthalmic and television optics, geophysics, and air navigation. Alvarez died in 1988.

Kanellos, *Chronology of Hispanic American History,* pp. 165, 272; Tardiff and Mabunda, *Dictionary of Hispanic Biography,* pp. 38–40.

1969 • Cuba-born chemist Fausto Ramírez (1923–) became the first U.S. Hispanic to be awarded the Silver Medal by the city of Paris. His research concerns organic synthesis and molecular biology.

Kanellos, *The Hispanic American Almanac*, p. 692.

1969 • Colombia-born theoretical physicist Albert William Saenz (1923–) became the first Hispanic to receive the Pure Research Award from the Naval Research Lab of the United States. His research interests include relativity, quantum mechanics, and quantum scattering theory.

Kanellos, *The Hispanic American Almanac*, pp. 692–93.

1970 • Celso Ramón García (1921–) became the first U.S.-born Hispanic to hold an endowed chair in medicine at an Ivy League medical school: the William Shippen Jr. Chair in Human Reproduction at the University of Pennsylvania Medical School. Born in New York City in 1921, García has held teaching positions at various universities, from Harvard to the University of Puerto Rico.

Kanellos, *The Hispanic American Almanac*, p. 687.

1972 • After his appointment as an assistant professor in the Wayne State School of Medicine in 1972, Puerto Rican anatomist José Alcalá conducted the research that would make him the foremost expert on the cell makeup of the human eye lens. In his research, Alcalá developed laboratory methods to study the histology of ocular tissue, which ultimately helped to explain the development of cataracts, among other maladies of the eye.

Tardiff and Mabunda, *Dictionary of Hispanic Biography*, p. 8.

1975 • San Antonio-born physicist John Taboada (1943–) received the U.S. Air Force's Outstanding Science Achievement Award for his work on lasers and optics. Born in Tampico, Mexico, Taboada received his M.S. and Ph.D. degrees in physics from Texas A&M University in 1968 and 1973, respectively. He has worked as a scientist for the air force since 1966.

Kanellos, *The Hispanic American Almanac*, pp. 693–94.

1975 • Neurobiologist Rodolfo Llinas became the first Hispanic scientist to serve as editor of the *Neuroscience Journal*. Born in Bogotá, Colombia, Llinas is chairman of the Department of Physiology and Biophysiology of New York University, where he conducts structural and functional studies of neuronal systems and also studies the evolution and development of the central nervous system.

Kanellos, *The Hispanic American Almanac*, p. 689.

1975 • José R. Coronado became the first Hispanic to direct a major U.S. hospital, the Audie L. Murphy Veterans Hospital, a 704-bed tertiary facility and a 120-bed nursing home affiliated with the University of Texas Health Sciences Center in San Antonio. Coronado was born on April 3, 1932, in Benavides, Texas, and obtained an M.S. degree in educational administration from Texas A&I in Kingsville in 1959 and an M.S. in hospital administration from Baylor University in Waco in 1973.

Kanellos, *The Hispanic American Almanac,* pp. 723–24.

GEORGE CASTRO.

1978 • George Castro (1939–) discovered the mechanism of the intrinsic charge carrier of organic photoconductors. Years later, such materials in the form of organic polymeric films became the basis for flexible photoconductors that are used in photocopying machines and high- speed printers.

Born in Los Angeles, California, Castro received his B.S. in chemistry from the University of California-Los Angeles in 1960 and his Ph.D. in physical chemistry from the University of California-Riverside in 1965. He has worked as a researcher for IBM since 1968. Since 1986, he has been the manager of Synchrotron Studies for IBM at the Almaden Research Center. In 1978, he received the Outstanding Innovation Award from IBM and, in 1990, he was elected a fellow of the American Physical Society. Castro assumed the leadership of the Physical Sciences division of the IBM San Jose Research Lab in 1975, three years after its formation. He has built the organization into one that is world famous for its scientific discoveries. These include the discovery of the first superconducting polymer, novel organic metals and superconductors, high-resolution laser techniques, and new methods of investigating magnetic materials.

Kanellos, *Chronology of Hispanic American History,* pp. 211, 276.

1978 • Dr. Mario E. Ramírez (1926–) became the first Hispanic to be named by *Good Housekeeping* magazine as the Family Doctor of the Year. The family practitioner was born in Roma, Texas, and received his medical degree from the University of Tennessee College of Medicine in Knoxville in 1948.

Kanellos, *The Hispanic American Almanac,* pp. 734–35.

1980 • Physicist Luis Alvarez became the first scientist to develop the theory that the extinction of the dinosaurs was due to the crash of a giant meteor into the earth; the meteor raised so much dust into the atmosphere that it blocked out the sun and caused the vegetation consumed by dinosaurs to die.

Tardiff and Mabunda, *Dictionary of Hispanic Biography,* p. 40.

1983 • Cuba-born chemist Richard Isaac Martínez (1944–) became the first Hispanic scientist to be awarded the Bronze Medal from the Department of Commerce for his work as a research chemist at the National Bureau of Standards. In 1983, he also received the Independent Research 100 Award. He has worked on the development and application of tandem mass spectrometry to the study of the kinetics of complex organic reaction systems relevant to oxidation and atmospheric chemistry.

Kanellos, *The Hispanic American Almanac*, p. 690.

1986 ⋆ Franklin Chang-Díaz became the first Hispanic in space; the astronaut spoke to television viewers from the space shuttle *Columbia* in Spanish. Chang-Díaz was born and raised in Costa Rica, the grandchild on his paternal side of a Chinese immigrant to Costa Rica. Chang-Díaz immigrated to the United States in 1969 and studied mechanical engineering at the University of Connecticut. He received a Ph.D. in physics from the Massachusetts Institute of Technology in 1977 and three years later was chosen by National Aeronautics and Space Administration (NASA) for the space program.

Hispanics in U.S. History, p. 80.

FRANKLIN CHANG-DÍAZ.

1986 ⋆ Antonia Novello (1944–) became the first Hispanic to serve as deputy director of one of the National Institutes of Health, the National Institute of Child Health and Development, where she nurtured a special interest in children with AIDS. At the time, she was also a clinical professor of pediatrics at Georgetown University Hospital. Novello became surgeon general in the Bush administrations.

See also Science and Technology: Physical and Social Sciences, 1989.

Kanellos, *The Hispanic American Almanac*, p. 731; Telgen and Kamp, *Latinas! Women of Achievement*, pp. 273–78.

1989 ⋆ Dr. Mario J. Molina became the first Hispanic scientist to receive the NASA Medal for Exceptional Scientific Achievement. That same year he was also the first Hispanic to receive the United Nations Environmental Programme Global 500 Award. Molina's research on fluorocarbon depletion of the earth's ozone shield has resulted in nations around the world taking steps to curb the use of materials that emit fluorocarbons.

Kanellos, *The Hispanic American Almanac*, 1986, pp. 447–48.

1989 ⋆ Venezuela-born biologist Francisco Dallmeier (1953–) became the director of the Smithsonian Institution's famous Man and the Biospehere Biological Diversity Program, which coordinates field biodiversity research and training in the United States and various Latin American countries.

Kanellos, *The Hispanic American Almanac*, p. 684.

1989 ⋆ Antonia Novello became the nation's first Hispanic surgeon general. Born and educated through medical school in Puerto Rico, Novello received a Ph.D. in medicine from the Johns Hopkins University School of Medicine in 1982. Prior to her being named the nation's top doctor, Novello had become an international leader and respected researcher in children's health and nephrology.

Kanellos, *The Hispanic American Almanac,* p. 731; Telgen and Kamp, *Latinas! Women of Achievement,* pp. 273–78.

1990 • Ellen Ochoa became the first Hispanic woman to serve as an astronaut. Born in Los Angeles on May 10, 1958, Ochoa graduated as valedictorian from both high school and San Diego State University, where she majored in physics. Ochoa went on to Stanford University, where she earned both a master's degree and a Ph.D. in electrical engineering. Ochoa is also an accomplished researcher who has three patents in optical processing to her name.

Telgen and Kamp, *Latinas! Women of Achievement,* pp. 279–85.

1990 • Emyré Barrios (1926–), founder of Barrios Technology, became the first Hispanic to serve as chair of the Texas Space Commission, which has duties related to the National Aeronautics and Space Administration (NASA), in Clear Lake, Texas. Barrios is a businesswoman who has been recognized repeatedly for her leadership.

Kanellos, *The Hispanic American Almanac,* p. 363.

1990 • Adriana Ocampo, a science coordinator for the Jet Propulsion Laboratory in Pasadena, California, developed the concept for "Space Conference for the Americas: Prospects in Cooperation," in conjunction with the United Nations. The purpose of the conference, which was held in Costa Rica and has since been repeated in Chile, was to further cooperation among the Panamerican countries in the areas of science and technology for

ADRIANA OCAMPO.

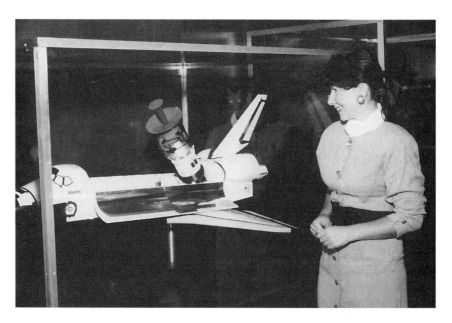

peaceful uses of space. This conference followed in the wake of other conferences she helped to develop in Costa Rica, Colombia, Nigeria, Egypt, and Mexico to involve third world nations in the space program.

Vita of Adriana Ocampo supplied by Jet Propulsion Laboratory.

1990 • Dr. Richard Tapia, a mathematics professor at Rice University in Houston, Texas, became the first Hispanic mathematician to be named a fellow of the American Physical Society. Tapia, who has also been a leader in bringing minorities into the study of math and sciences, received the Martin Luther King Jr. Award in 1987.

Hispanic, September 1996, p. 40.

1991 • Argentine American mathematician Alberto P. Calderón became the first Hispanic to receive the National Medal of Science, conferred by President George Bush. In large part the distinction recognized his groundbreaking work on singular integral operators and their application to important problems in partial differential equations. Calderón had presented his first revolutionary paper on the topic as early as 1985 at the American Mathematical Society. Calderón's theory of singular operators has contributed to linking several branches of mathematics and has had practical applications in physics and aerodynamic engineering.

Tardiff and Mabunda, *Dictionary of Hispanic Biography,* pp. 152–53.

1991 • Alberto Vinicio Baez (1915–) advanced the study of x-ray imaging optics. The S.P.I.E. conferred the Dennis Gabor Award on Baez, a Mexico-born, U.S.-trained physicist, and co-researcher Paul Kirkpatrick "in recognition of their important role in the development of x-ray imaging optics. Their early discoveries that grazing incidence optical systems could be used to focus x-rays gave birth to the field of x-ray imaging optics. . . . Their pioneering contributions to this field include the Kirkpatrick-Baez x-ray double reflecting imaging system. The Kirkpatrick-Baez Lamar x-ray telescope has been approved for flight on the Freedom Space Station." In his research, Baez specialized in x-ray radiation, optics and microscopy, as well as science and environmental education.

Kanellos, *Chronology of Hispanic American History,* pp. 173, 277.

PLANT CHEMIST ELOY RODRÍGUEZ. PHOTO BY FRANK DIMEO.

1992 • One of the world's leading plant chemists, Eloy Rodríguez, reported to the American Association for the Advancement of Science that he and his colleague Richard Wrangham had identified a process for finding plants with medicinal properties by observing animal behavior and interaction with plants. Rodríguez and Wrangham coined the term "zoopharmacognosy" to describe this process, and since then many animal behaviorists have been reporting on animal usage of curative plants, thus leading to a revolution in finding new medicines. In addition to identifying new medicinal plants, Rodríguez has also found plant chemicals that kill fleas and mites by observing how monkeys rub leaves with these chemicals on their fur. Rodríguez also

studies native peoples in the tropics to uncover their traditional uses of curative plants. Rodríguez is one of the very few Hispanics with an endowed chair in science at an American university; the Texas native is the James A. Perkins Professor of Environmental Studies at Cornell University.

Metta Winter, "Animals Point to Nature's Medicines," *Cornell Focus,* 5/1 (1996); pp. 5–7.

1993 • Dr. David Cardús of Houston, Texas, became the first Hispanic to serve as president of the International Society for Gravitational Physiology.

Tardiff and Mabunda, *Dictionary of Hispanic Biography,* p. 173.

1993 • Dr. Ralph R. Ocampo became the first Hispanic to be elected president of the California Medical Association.

Hispanic Link Weekly Report, 22 March 1993, p. 1.

1994 • Dr. Richard A. Tapia became the first recipient of the National Nico Haberman Award for promoting the representation of minorities and women in the computational sciences, given by the Computer Research Association, Washington, D.C. A Los Angeles native, Tapia received his B.S., M.S, and Ph.D. degrees in mathematics from the University of California at Los Angeles and has developed his career at Rice University in Houston.

Biography of Richard A. Tapia supplied by Rice University.

1994 • Francisco Ayala, professor of ecology and evolutionary biology at the University of California-Irvine, became the first Hispanic to serve as president of the American Association for the Advancement of Science, Washington, D.C.

Hispanic Business, October 1994, p. 70.

1995 • Mario Molina, a researcher and professor at the Massachusetts Institute of Technology (MIT), shared the Nobel Prize in chemistry with two others for work that led to an international ban on chemicals believed to be depleting the ozone protective layer of the earth. A native of Mexico with a B.S. in chemical engineering from the National Autonomous University of Mexico (1965) and a Ph.D. in physical chemistry from the University of California-Berkeley (1972), he has taught and conducted research at various universities in the United States. From 1982 until 1989, Molina was a senior research scientist at the Caltech Jet Propulsion Laboratory. In 1989, he was appointed professor in the Department of Earth, Atmospheric and Planetary Sciences at MIT. In 1992, he became the Lee and Geraldine Martin Professor of Environmental Sciences at MIT.

Molina has been a world leader in developing scientific understanding of the chemistry of the stratospheric ozone layer and its susceptibility to man-made perturbations. He has explained through his laboratory experiments new reaction sequences that enable the catalytic processes that account for most of the observed ozone destruction in the Antarctic stratosphere. His other awards include the NASA Medal for Exceptional Scientific Achievement (1989), the United Nations Environmental Programme Global

500 Award (1989), the appointment as Pew Scholar on Conservation and the Environment from 1990 to 1992, and the Hispanic Engineer National Achievement Award (1992).

Houston Chronicle, November 4, 1995, p. A29.

1995 • Lydia Aguilar-Bryan and her husband, Joseph Bryan, endocrinologists at Houston's Baylor College of Medicine, were the first researchers to

NOBEL PRIZE-WINNING CHEMIST MARIO MOLINA. PHOTO BY DONNA COVENEY.

solve the problem of hyperinsulinism. After a decade of research, they were able to discover how the body regulates the secretion of insulin and prepare the way for a cure or better treatment of diabetes. Thanks to their work, there may soon be a prenatal test for hyperinsulinism and, down the road, a genetic remedy. As a researcher and doctor, Aguilar-Bryan is particularly interested in diabetes because it strikes people of Mexican descent in unusually high numbers. She is a native of Mexico City who watched her grandmother and her uncles die of the disease. As a graduate student at the University of Texas, she studied diabetes in Mexican American populations in Starr County, Texas, and has continued to work on the problem since joining the Baylor College of Medicine in 1985.

Helen Thorpe, "Lydia Aguilar-Bryan and Joseph Bryan," *Texas Monthly,* September 1995, pp. 116–17, 148–49.

1995 • In an undertaking reminiscent of that in the science fiction film *Jurassic Park,* Hispanic scientist Raúl Cano of the California Polytechnic State University was the first Hispanic biologist to revive several hundred specimens of bacteria from ancient bees, gnats, and beetles trapped in amber as much as 135 million years ago. Cano exerts this effort in his search for new enzymes and antibiotics that can be used in pharmaceuticals. Cano is the leading biologist in reviving ancient spores.

Houston Chronicle, 19 May 1995, p. A6.

1995 • Engineer José Hernández of the Lawrence Livermore National Laboratory in California was instrumental in developing a computerized digital mammography system that may improve early detection of breast cancer. In 1995, he received the Hispanic Engineer National Achievement Award for Outstanding Technical Contribution.

Hispanic Link Weekly Report, 16 October 1995, p. 1.

1995 • U.S. Surgeon General Antonia Novello became the first Hispanic to win the Ronald McDonald Children's Charities Award for Medical Excellence of $100,000 for her work in fighting preventable diseases. Her work led to an overhaul of the nation's immunization programs.

Hispanic Link Weekly Report, 16 October 1995, p. 1.

1996 • A team of researchers led by Hanna and Antonio Damasio at the University of Iowa College of Medicine became the first to disprove the idea that the human brain has a central "dictionary" for language. Rather, they have shown that words originate in widely dispersed parts of the brain and are probably linked to experience. Even meaning, construction, and pronunciation areas are widely scattered in the brain. The findings have widespread implications not only for neuropsychology but or general learning as well.

"The Brain Has a Way with Words," *Houston Chronicle,* 13 April 1996.

1996 • Florida International University engineering professor Milton Torres developed a liquid polymer called PantherSkin that strengthens old metal, resists fire, and even contains explosions. The polymer is applied in a foam, and it is believed it can be used in safeguarding airplanes from explosions. He specifically set out to develop PantherSkin in 1988 in response to an airplane explosion that caused the death of a flight attendant.

"New Technologies Could Ensure Safer Flights," *Houston Chronicle,* 3 September 1996.

1996 • There were finally enough Hispanic representatives in the sciences in the United States to be featured in a six-part documentary series for television, *The Changing Face of Science,* focusing on minorities in American science. Mathematician Richard A. Tapia, a professor at Houston's Rice University, and engineer-entrepreneur Israel Galván, also of Houston, were among the twenty minority scientists and technologists featured. Tapia, a Los Angeles native, joined the faculty at Rice University in 1970 and has helped to make his department the number one department in the United States for graduating women and minority Ph.D. degrees. He was also the first native-born Hispanic to be elected into the National Academy of Engineering.

Biography of Richard A. Tapia supplied by Rice University.

1996 • Alexander H. Reyes, a Ph.D. student in electrical engineering at Texas A&M University, became the first Hispanic to win the Outstanding Young Author Award from the Institute of Electrical Engineering and Electronics Engineers for a paper on wireless volume control for hearing aids. The award is usually given to assistant professors; it was the first time that it was given to a second-year doctoral student.

Hispanic Business, September 1996, p. 70.

1996 • The National Society for Hispanic Physicists (NSHP), boasting more than one hundred members, was founded by David Ernst and Carlos Ordóñez. The NSHP operates an electronic bulletin board and mentoring and outreach programs to recruit Latino students into the physical sciences and help them attain post-graduate degrees.

Hispanic Link Weekly Report, 9 September 1996, p. 4.

1996 • President Bill Clinton named Joaquín Bustoz, a mathematics professor at Arizona State University (ASU), as one of ten teachers in the nation to receive the first Presidential Awards for Excellence in Science, Mathematics, and Engineering Mentoring. The award comes with a grant for $10,000. Professor Bustoz founded ASU's science honors program in 1986, which in ten years of existence brought more than one thousand minority students to campus for intensive summer instruction and mentoring.

Hispanic Business, December 1996, p. 58.

1996 • President Bill Clinton appointed the first Hispanic member of the Nuclear Regulatory Commission, scientist Nils J. Díaz. Díaz is a professor and the director of the Innovative Nuclear Space Power and Propulsion Institute of the University of Florida, Gainesville. He is also president and principal engineer of Florida Nuclear Associates.

"One Hundred Influentials," *Hispanic Business,* October 1996, p. 58.

SPORTS

BASEBALL

1871 • Esteban Bellán became the first Spanish American ballplayer to play professional baseball in the United States. Bellán was a black Cuban recruited from Fordham College to play for the Troy Haymakers the same year as the founding of the National Baseball Association. He played three years in the majors. By the turn of the century, no blacks were allowed in the majors. Up until Jackie Robinson broke the color barrier, Hispanic blacks became regular players in the Negro leagues of the United States. White-looking Hispanics, however, were allowed to play throughout the history of professional baseball in the United States. At times, teams went to extremes to prove the racial purity of their Hispanic players, as did the Cincinnati Reds in 1911 in preparing affidavits to prove that their new Cuban players, Armando Marsans and Rafael Almeida, had the purest Castilian blood running through their veins.

Kanellos, *The Hispanic American Almanac,* p. 699.

1878 • The Liga de Béisbol Profesional Cubana, the Cuban professional baseball league, was founded just seven years after the National Baseball League was founded in the United States. Professional baseball in Spanish America is almost as old as it is in the United States. The Cuban leagues became important contributors of players to the Negro and white professional leagues in the United States and also offered major league players a place to play during the off-season.

Kanellos, *Chronology of Hispanic American History,* p. 114.

1909 • Cuban José Méndez (1886–?) was the first Hispanic pitcher to achieve the outstanding record of forty-four wins with only two losses for his first two seasons of play. He accomplished this incredible feat while playing for the Cuban Stars of the Negro leagues. Because of his African ancestry and dark skin, Méndez was never allowed to play in the majors. Instead, he played in the Negro National League and in Cuba, and thus many of his statistics are missing. Such witnesses as Hall of Famer John Henry Lloyd said that he never saw a pitcher superior to Méndez, and Giants Manager John

McGraw said that Méndez would have been worth $50,000 in the majors, an unusually high figure in those days. During the winters he played in Cuba, where he compiled a record of 62–17 by 1914. From 1912 to 1916, Méndez played for the All-Nations of Kansas City, a racially mixed barnstorming club. From 1920 to 1926, he served as a player- manager for the Kansas City Monarchs and led them to three straight Negro National League pennants from 1923 to 1925. During his long career, he also played for the Los Angeles White Sox, the Chicago American Giants, and the Detroit Stars.

Kanellos, *Chronology of Hispanic American History,* p. 121.

1921 • The best batter in Cuban baseball, and probably one of the best to ever play the game, was Alejandro Oms, who played with the Cuban Stars and the New York Cubans in the Negro Leagues from 1921 to 1935. In the winter season, Ohms managed to put in outstanding seasons in Cuba.

Alejandro Oms was born into a poor family in Santa Clara, Cuba, in 1895. As a child he had to work in an iron foundry. He started playing organized baseball in 1910 as a center fielder. On the most famous Cuban team of all time, Santa Clara, Oms batted .436 in the 1922–23 season. In Cuba, Oms achieved a lifetime batting average of .352; his average in the United States is unknown. He was batting champion on the island three times: in 1924–25 with .393; in 1928–29 with .432; and in 1929–30 with .380. In 1928, he established a Cuban record for most consecutive games with hits—30. In his last years, he was penniless and his vision had failed; he died at the age of fifty-one in 1946.

Kanellos, *The Hispanic American Almanac,* pp. 128, 189.

1923 • Adolfo Luque became the first Hispanic American to play in the World Series, as a member of the Cincinnati Reds. Luque, who was a dark-skinned Cuban, broke into the majors in 1914 with the Boston Braves, where he was incessantly jeered at and subjected to racial epithets. Despite his emotionally rocky career because of the racism he faced, he had one of the longest careers of any Hispanic baseball player, serving until 1935 for the Boston, Cincinnati, Brooklyn, and New York teams. Luque pitched in two World Series, being credited with the decisive win in one of them. In 1923, Luque became the first Hispanic to win the pitching championship in professional baseball in the United States, with 27 wins, an earned run average of 1.93, and six shutouts.

Kanellos, *The Hispanic American Almanac,* p. 700.

1930 • One of the greatest baseball pitchers of all time, Vernon "Lefty" Gómez (1907–1989), began his major league career. Born in Rodeo, California, Gómez ranks third in regular-season wins in the history of baseball, with 189 for the New York Yankees. He also holds the record for World Series wins without a loss (6–0) and three wins against one loss in all-star play. Gómez was active from 1930 to 1943, pitching 2,503 innings, winning 189 games to 102 losses, with an earned-run average of 3.34. He scored twenty wins or more in 1931, 1932, 1934, and 1937. Gómez is number thirteen on the all-time winning percentage list. Gómez made all-star teams every year from 1933 to 1939, and he is a member of the Hall of Fame. During winter seasons, he played in Cuba, where he also served as manager of the Cienfuegos team, and once he taught a class on pitching at the University of Havana. Gómez died on February 2, 1989, in San Rafael, California.

Kanellos, *The Hispanic American Almanac,* p. 160.

1938 • Puerto Rico began winter-league baseball, under the name La Liga de Béisbol Profesional de Puerto Rico, by hosting off-season major league baseball players and preparing many future star athletes in Class AAA play. Today, the Puerto Rican Winter League is the oldest such league in operation in the world.

Van Hyning, *Puerto Rico's Winter League,* p. 4.

1942 • Hiram Bithorn joined the Chicago Cubs, becoming the first Puerto Rican baseball player in the major leagues.

1951 • Cuban Orestes (Minnie) Miñoso (1922–) became the first Hispanic American ballplayer in professional baseball in the United States to steal the most bases (thirty-one) in a season. Miñoso had made his debut with the New York Cubans of the Negro leagues in 1948, but made it to the Cleveland Indians in 1946 when the color barrier was broken. Miñoso had a long career playing for various teams. In 1976, when he served as a designated hitter for the Chicago White Sox, he became one of only six players to have been active during four decades.

Kanellos, *The Hispanic American Almanac,* p. 710.

1951 • The first Hispanic American ballplayer to be selected for the all-star game was Venezuelan shortstop Alfonso (Chico) Carrasquel. Carrasquel served as the opening player in that position in 1951.

Kanellos, *Chronology of Hispanic American History,* p. 231.

1954 • Mexican second baseman Roberto (Beto) Avila became the first Hispanic American to win the batting championship in professional baseball in the United States. Playing for Cleveland in 1954, he batted .341, drove in 67 runs, and scored 112, fifteen of them home runs.

Kanellos, *Chronology of Hispanic American History,* p. 235–36.

1956 • Venezuelan shortstop Luis Aparicio (1934–)became the first Hispanic American in U.S. professional baseball to be named Rookie of the Year. Playing for Baltimore in 1956, Aparicio drove in fifty-six runs, scored sixty-nine runs, and led the leagues in stolen bases. He was inducted into the Baseball Hall of Fame in 1984.

Kanellos, *The Hispanic American Almanac,* p. 702.

1960 • Cuban Orestes (Minnie) Miñoso became the first Hispanic American ballplayer in U.S. professional baseball to lead both leagues in hits, with 184 for the Chicago White Sox.

Kanellos, *Chronology of Hispanic American History,* p. 242.

1962 • Pedro "Tony" Oliva (1940–), a native Cuban, became the only baseball player in history to win batting championships during his first two major league seasons. While playing for the Minnesota Twins, he won Rookie of the Year in 1964 and the league batting title in 1964, 1965, and 1971. Oliva also won the Golden Glove in 1966 as the league's best defensive right fielder.

Kanellos, *The Hispanic American Almanac,* pp. 710–11.

1963 • Dominican pitcher Juan Marichal (1937–) became the first Hispanic American to throw a no-hitter in professional baseball in the United States. Pitching for the San Francisco Giants, he beat Houston 1–0 on July 15, 1963.

Kanellos, *The Hispanic American Almanac,* p. 709.

1964 • Minnesota Twins baseball player Tony Oliva set the American League record—which still stands today—for most hits by a rookie, 217.

Reichler, *The Great All-Time Baseball Record Book,* p. 305.

1967 • Kansas City's Bert Campaneris became the first Hispanic baseball player to hit three triples in a game, thus joining an elite club of most triples hitters in one game in the major leagues.

Reichler, *The Great All-Time Baseball Record Book,* p. 98.

1968 • San Francisco Giants pitcher Juan Marichal became the first Hispanic to tie the record for the most consecutive wins, ten. He repeated the feat in 1969. In 1988, Juan Agosto of the Houston Astros became the second Hispanic to join the exclusive club.

Reichler, *The Great All-Time Baseball Record Book,* p. 241.

1970 • Venezuelan shortstop Luis Aparicio won more Gold Gloves as the best American League shortstop in the history of baseball. He won every year from 1958 to 1962 and then again in 1964, 1966, 1968, and 1970. He led the American League shortstops in fielding for eight consecutive seasons and broke a major league record by leading the American League in assists for six straight years.

Tardiff and Mabunda, *Dictionary of Hispanic Biography,* p. 45.

1971 • While playing for the Minnesota Twins, baseball player Pedro "Tony" Oliva led the league in hits five times in his career and made all-star teams from 1964 to 1971, tying Joe Dimaggio's record of having been named an all-star in each of his six first seasons.

Kanellos, *The Hispanic American Almanac*, pp. 710–11.

ROBERTO CLEMENTE,
HALL-OF-FAME
BASEBALL PLAYER.

1973 • Roberto Clemente (1934–1972) became the first Puerto Rican baseball player to be named to the Hall of Fame and was the first player in history for whom the Hall of Fame waived its five-year waiting period.

Born in Carolina, Puerto Rico, Clemente rose from an impoverished background to become a star outfielder for the Pittsburgh Pirates from 1955 to 1972. He assisted the Pirates in winning two World Series in 1960 and 1971. Among Clemente's achievements as a player, he was four times the National League batting champion—in 1961, 1964, 1965, and 1967—and he was voted the league's most valuable player in 1966. He was awarded twelve Golden Gloves and set a major league record in leading the National League in assists five times. He served on fourteen all-star teams, and he was one of only sixteen players to have three thousand or more hits during their career. Clemente was promising a great deal more before his untimely death in a plane crash while bringing relief to victims of an earthquake in Nicaragua. Clemente had accumulated 240 home runs and a lifetime batting average of .317.

See also Sports: Baseball, 1984.

Kanellos, *Chronology of Hispanic American History*, pp. 251, 257; Tardiff and Mabunda, *Dictionary of Hispanic Biography*, pp. 233–35.

1973 • Orlando Cepeda became the first Hispanic baseball player to tie the record for most doubles in a game, four, while playing for the Boston Red Sox. In 1986, two more Hispanic players, Dámaso García and Rafael Ramírez, joined that elite group.

Reichler, *Great All-Time Baseball Record Book*, pp. 96–97.

1976 • José Morales of the Montreal Expos set the record for the most pinch hits, twenty-five, in a season of major league play. That record still stands.

Reichler, *Great All-Time Baseball Record Book*, p. 163.

1977 • Panama-born baseball player Rod Carew received more than four million all-star votes, more than any other player in history. Spending most of his career as an outfielder for the Minnesota Twins, Carew played in eighteen consecutive all-star games and batted over .300 for fifteen consecutive seasons.

Kanellos, *The Hispanic American Almanac*, pp. 702–703.

1977 • When baseball player Al López (1908–)was elected to the Hall of Fame, he was considered the seventh-best catcher and the seventh-best manager of all time. For many years, he held the record for the highest number of games caught in the major leagues (1918) and for the most years (twelve) spent in the National League, catching in one hundred games or more. He tied the record for the most games caught in the National League without a passed ball (114) in 1941. As a manager for the Indians and the White Sox, he compiled a record of .581, the ninth all-time highest.

Kanellos, *The Hispanic American Almanac,* p. 708.

1981 • Baseball pitcher Fernando Valenzuela (1960–) became the first rookie ever to win the Cy Young Award. The Los Angeles Dodger led the league in strikeouts, and, in the shortened season that year, he tied the rookie record for the most shutouts—eight. He also won the Rookie of the Year and the *Sporting News* Player of the Year awards.

Kanellos, *The Hispanic American Almanac,* p. 716.

1983 • Juan Marichal (1937–) became the first Dominican baseball player to be inducted into the Hall of Fame. Marichal started his career as a pitcher with the San Francisco Giants in 1962, and from 1962 to 1971 he averaged twenty wins per year. He led the National League in wins in 1963 with a record of 25–8 and in 1968 with 26–9 and in shutouts in 1965 with ten. He also had the highest earned run average (ERA)—2.10—in 1969. He pitched in eight all-star games with a record of 2–0 and a 0.50 ERA for eighteen innings. Marichal's total innings pitched were 3,509, for a record of 243–142 and an ERA of 2.89. He was an all-star from 1962 to 1969 and again in 1972.

Kanellos, *Chronology of Hispanic American History,* pp. 209, 247, 269.

1984 • Venezuelan Luis Aparicio was inducted into the Baseball Hall of Fame as one of the greatest shortstops of all time in professional baseball in the United States. He still holds the records for games played, assists, and double plays, and the American League record for put-outs. His record of 506 stolen bases still ranks among the highest. Playing most of his career for the Chicago White Sox, Aparicio began his career in 1956 as Rookie of the Year and continued to play inspired baseball until his retirement in 1973. Aparicio played on all-star teams from 1958 to 1964 and again from 1970 to 1972. He won the Golden Glove eleven times.

Kanellos, *The Hispanic American Almanac,* pp. 529–30.

1984 • While playing Class AAA baseball, José Canseco became the first ballplayer in history to hit the ball out of Cheney Stadium in Tacoma, Washington.

Tardiff and Mabunda, *Dictionary of Hispanic Biography,* p. 162.

1984 • Roberto Clemente became the first Hispanic baseball player to be featured on a U.S. postage stamp; he was only the second baseball player to be so honored.

I Have a Dream, pp. 50–51; *Total Baseball,* pp. 324, 1026.

1986 • Baseball pitcher Fernando Valenzuela tied Carl Hubbell's record of five straight strikeouts in an all-star game. Valenzuela was selected for the all-star team five times.

Kanellos, *The Hispanic American Almanac,* p. 716.

1988 • José Canseco became the only baseball player in history to hit forty home runs (actually forty-two) and steal forty bases in the same season. He accomplished his feat while playing for the Oakland A's; he also batted .307 and scored 120 runs that season.

Reichler, *The Great All-Time Baseball Record Book,* p. 85; Tardiff and Mabunda, *Dictionary of Hispanic Biography,* p. 162.

1989 • Cuban American baseball player José Canseco signed the highest-paying contract up to that point in baseball history—for $23.5 million over five years—with the Oakland A's.

Tardiff and Mabunda, *Dictionary of Hispanic Biography,* p.162.

1991 • Baseball player Rod Carew was inducted into the Baseball Hall of Fame in the first year of his eligibility; he was only the twenty-third player in history to be inducted in his first year.

Tardiff and Mabunda, *Dictionary of Hispanic Biography,* p. 173.

1992 • Bobby Bonilla became the highest-paid baseball player in the major leagues, signing a contract with the New York Mets for $29 million over five years. He proved his worth in 1993—he was the sole Mets representative in the all-star game.

Tardiff and Mabunda, *Dictionary of Hispanic Biography,* p. 129.

1993 • Linda Alvarado (1951–), the president of a construction company, became the first Hispanic owner of a major league baseball team in the United States. The president of Alvarado Construction became a partner in the Colorado Rockies franchise from its inception.

See also Business and Commerce, 1993.

Tardiff and Mabunda, *Dictionary of Hispanic Biography,* p. 32; Telgen and Kamp, *Latinas! Women of Achievement,* pp. 15–17.

1995 • Montreal Expos manager Felipe Alou became the first Hispanic to win baseball's Manager of the Year award.

Hispanic Link Weekly Report, 29 August 1995, p. 1.

1996 • Alex Rodríguez of the Seattle Mariners became the first shortstop to hit more than thirty home runs in a season. The twenty-one-year-old also maintained a batting average of .360.

1996 • Texas Rangers baseball player Iván Rodríguez doubled in the eighth inning against the Minnesota Twins to set the new record for doubles by a catcher in one season, forty-three.

Houston Chronicle, 3 September 1996, p. B5.

BASKETBALL

1991 · Houston Rockets basketball forward Carl Herrera became the first Venezuelan to be signed by the National Basketball Association. That year he became only the fifth rookie in the team's history to shoot .500 or better. Herrera had previously played for the University of Houston Cougars, becoming their top offensive rebounder and winning Southwest Conference Newcomer of the Year and All-Southwest Conference first team choice in 1989–90.

"One Hundred Most Influential Hispanics," *Hispanic Business,* October 1993.

1995 · Rebecca Lobo became the first Hispanic woman basketball player to be named All-American center. Lobo led her team, the University of Connecticut, to a national championship with a record of 35–0. The six-feet-four Southwick, Massachusetts, native scored record points (thirty-five) and record rebounds (seventeen). She was the only Big East basketball player in history to win both Big East Player of the Year and Scholarship Athlete of the Year, and she accomplished this feat twice.

Hispanic, August 1995, p. 28.

1996 · The first Hispanic woman to win an Olympic gold medal in basketball was Rebecca Lobo, who competed on the undefeated championship team of the United States. Lobo had helped her college team, the University of Connecticut, win the 1995 National Collegiate Athletic Association championship, where she was named final four Most Valuable Player.

Hispanic Business, May 1996, p. 28.

BODYBUILDING

1980 · Mexican American bodybuilder Rachel Elizondo McLish became the first winner of the U.S. Women's Bodybuilding Championship. She went on to become Ms. Olympia in 1980 and 1983, and world champion in 1982. She has become the most famous female bodybuilder of all time.

Born in 1958 in Harlingen, Texas, to Rafael and Rachel Elizondo, Rachel Elizondo McLish found her way to athletics through the study of ballet and her father's interest in weightlifting. McLish intensified her weight training while in college at Pan American University in Edinburgh, Texas, and during that time began working as a trainer at a spa. In 1978, McLish graduated with a degree in health and physical education from Pan American and became a partner in the Sport Palace Spa, the first and largest health club in south Texas. She began competing in bodybuilding tournaments and soon became known as the World's First Female Bodybuilding Champion. During the 1990s, McLish began a successful film acting career. She has also written books and designed sportswear.

Hispanic, September 1993, pp. 50–54; Kanellos, *The Hispanic American Almanac,* p. 709.

RACHEL ELIZONDO
MCLISH.

BOWLING

1870 • Real estate mogul Leopoldo Carrillo opened the first bowling alley in Tucson, Arizona. It might have been the first bowling alley in the Southwest.
Sheridan, *Los Tucsonenses,* p. 50.

1989 • Venezuelan Amleto Andrés Monacelli (1961–) became the first Hispanic to win the U.S. Professional Bowlers Association Player of the Year Award. Monacelli is a college graduate who began the Professional Bowling Association tour in 1982. By 1991, he was winning $81,000 in prizes annually, and in 1989 even achieved a record $213,815.

The list of tournaments he has won includes the Japan Cup (1987), the Showboat Invitational (1988), the Miller Challenge (1989), the Wichita Open (1989 and 1990), the Budweiser Touring Players Championship (1989), the Cambridge Mixed Doubles (1989 and 1990), the Columbus Professional Bowling Classic (1990), the Quaker State Open (1991), and the True Value Open (1991). Among his many awards are the Professional Bowlers Association Player of the Year (1989 and 1990) and the Harry Smith Point Leader Award in 1989. In 1990, he won the Budweiser Kingpin Competition for the highest average of the year. And in 1990, sportswriters named him Bowler of the Year; this was the first time that a foreigner has ever been named Bowler of the Year in the United States. In his professional career, Monacelli has rolled sixteen perfect games, seven of them during the 1989 season, which established a new record for perfect games in a year. Three of these were accomplished during one week, tying the record.
Kanellos, *The Hispanic American Almanac,* p. 710.

BOXING

1931 • Cuba's "Kid Chocolate" became the first Hispanic boxer to win a world title, in the junior lightweight class. He was born Eligio Sardiñas in Havana on October 28, 1910, and his career became an example of the fate of boxers who battle their way out of poverty into fame and temporary riches. After winning eighty-six amateur fights and twenty-one professional fights in Cuba, he made his New York debut in 1928 and fought more than one hundred bouts in the United States over the next ten years. He became a true champion, supported his community, and was memorialized on stage and screen. However, he was severely exploited by his managers and owners and ultimately was done in by poverty and alcoholism.
Kanellos, *Chronology of Hispanic American History,* pp. 163, 199.

1936 • Sixto Escobar became the first Puerto Rican boxer to win a world championship when he knocked out Tony Marino. Fighting as a bantamweight boxer, Escobar is one of only a very few boxers to have regained his crown—twice.
Kanellos, *Chronology of Hispanic American History,* p. 209.

BOXING CHAMPION
"KID CHOCOLATE".

1942 • Manuel Ortiz of El Centro, California, became the first Hispanic to win the bantamweight boxing championship on August 7, 1942, when he beat Lou Salica. Ortiz totaled forty-one knockouts in his career and never suffered one himself in 117 bouts. Ortiz tied Henry Armstrong in defending his title twenty times (only two fighters had defended more often).

Kanellos, *The Hispanic American Almanac,* pp. 711–12.

1956 • José Luis "Chegüi" Torres (1936–)became the first U.S. Latino to win a silver medal in the light middleweight boxing division of the Olympics.

JOSÉ "CHEGÜI" TORRES.

He was also the first Puerto Rican athlete on the American team and the first to win a medal. Torres went on to become a professional boxer, winning the middleweight championship in 1965 with a technical knockout of Willie Pastrano in Madison Square Garden. After finding no more rivals in the middleweight division, Torres rose to middle heavyweight and won the crown, which he defended successfully until 1966.

Torres was born and raised in Ponce, Puerto Rico. He dropped out of high school and joined the U.S. Army, where he became a champion boxer. After the army, Torres moved to New York and pursued his amateur and then professional boxing careers, but he also pursued a career as a singer and musician. The multitalented Torres later became a respected columnist for the *New York Daily News*.

Kanellos, *Chronology of Hispanic American History*, p. 239; Kanellos, *The Hispanic American Almanac*, pp. 714–15.

1969 • Boxer Armando Ramos (1948–) became the first Mexican American to win the world lightweight championship with his victory over Carlos Cruz in Los Angeles. In 1972, he went on to win the World Boxing Congress lightweight championship over Pedro Carrasco.

Kanellos, *The Hispanic American Almanac*, p. 712.

1974 • Mexican American boxer Carlos Palomino became the first Hispanic to win the world welterweight championship. Born in Sonora, Mexico, Palomino immigrated to the United States with his family when he was a child. While serving in the U.S. Army, he became world military champion, and after compiling a record of thirty wins and one loss as a professional, he captured the world welterweight championship.

Meier and Rivera, *Dictionary of Mexican American History*, p. 270.

1984 • The Los Angeles Olympics registered the most U.S. Hispanics to ever have competed on the U.S. Olympic team. Local hero Paul Gonzales of East Los Angeles won a gold medal in boxing. He became the first Mexican American to win an individual gold medal for the United States.

Kanellos, *Chronology of Hispanic American History*, p. 271.

1985 • Boxer Héctor Camacho became the first Puerto Rican to win the World Boxing Council and World Boxing Organization championships in the lightweight division.

Tardiff and Mabunda, *Dictionary of Hispanic Biography*, p. 156.

1989 • Panamanian boxer Roberto Durán (1951–)became the first Hispanic boxer in history to have held championship titles in four different weight divisions: lightweight, welterweight, junior middleweight, and middleweight. In 1989 at the age of thirty-seven, Durán won his last title, in the World Boxing Council middleweight division.

Tardiff and Mabunda, *Dictionary of Hispanic Biography*, pp. 299–300.

1992 • Oscar de la Hoya became the only boxer to win a gold medal for the United States in the Summer Olympics held in Barcelona.

Hispanic, October 1995, pp. 28–32.

1995 • Oscar de la Hoya became the first Mexican American boxer to win the International Boxing Federation Lightweight Championship. He defeated Rafael Ruelas in the second round to remain undefeated. Born in Los Angeles in 1973, De la Hoya was the only boxing gold medal winner for the United States in the 1992 Olympics. In May 1996, he went on to beat Mexico's great champion Julio César Chávez in the junior welterweight class, becoming the world champion at that weight.

Hispanic, October 1995, pp. 28–32.

1995 • Rose Quiñones Trentman became the first woman to serve as a New York State Boxing Commissioner. Of Puerto Rican origin, Trentman is also a bilingual teacher in the New York City schools.

Hispanic, April 1995, pp. 8–9.

CYCLING

1995 • Mariano Friedrick became the first Hispanic cyclist to win a bronze medal in the world championships. His grandfather was a three-time national cycling champion in Argentina.

Hispanic Business, May 1996, p. 28.

1995 • David Juárez became the first U.S. Hispanic to win a gold medal in cycling at the Pan American Games. In 1989, the Californian turned pro in mountain bike racing.

Hispanic Business, May 1996, p. 28.

FENCING

1900 • Ramón Fonst of Cuba was the first person in the world to win a gold medal in épée, or fencing. He won the medal in the second Olympic games of the modern era, which were held in Paris.

Kanellos, *Chronology of Hispanic American History,* p. 145.

1904 • The Cuban Olympic team made a clean sweep of all the medals in fencing at the Olympiad in Saint Louis, Missouri. The team was composed of second-time gold medal winner Ramón Fonst, Manuel de Díaz, Charles Tatham, and Albertson Von Zo Post. They won four gold medals, two silver, and three bronze. The only medal not taken was a bronze in the saber.

Kanellos, *Chronology of Hispanic American History,* p. 153.

1932 • The first Hispanic athletes to make the U.S. Olympic team were fencer Miguel A. Capriles and triple jumper Roland Lee Romero. Capriles also became the first U.S. Hispanic to win a medal, the bronze, in these games.

Kanellos, *Chronology of Hispanic American History,*. p. 201.

1951 • Fencer Miguel A. de Capriles became the first U.S. Hispanic to represent the United States in the Pan American Games. Capriles also made the U.S. Olympic team three times.

Kanellos, *Chronology of Hispanic American History,* p. 201.

1962 • Argentina-born fencer Hugo M. Castelló (1914–) became the coach of the first U.S. Olympic fencing training camp. In 1935 and 1936, he had been National Intercollegiate Foil Champion. In 1936, he competed with the U.S. Olympic team. From 1946 to 1975, he served as fencing coach at New York University, where he became one of a select number of coaches to have won at least ten national collegiate team fencing championships. Only five other NCAA coaches in all sports have won ten national team titles. Castelló is a member of the Helms Sports Hall of Fame.

Kanellos, *The Hispanic American Almanac,* p. 703.

1972 • Fencer Alfonso Morales became the first U.S. Hispanic athlete to compete four times in the Olympics.

Kanellos, *Chronology of Hispanic American History,* p. 258.

1989 • Natalia Sainz Lederer-Peterson became the first Hispanic female fencer to win the U.S. national championship in epee. The Cuba-born Lederer- Peterson had studied fencing and had belonged to the Cuban Professional Club before she immigrated to the United States. Over the years, Lederer-Peterson participated on numerous U.S. national teams in international championships and Olympic games. In 1972, she won the Pacific Coast Women's Foil Championship, the Grand International Women's Foil Championship, and the Espada de Honor Trophy. In 1989, she won the gold medal in women's epee at the U.S. national championship.

Kanellos, *The Hispanic American Almanac,* 1996, p. 736.

FLYING

1956 • Korean War ace Manuel J. Fernández set a new world record for air speed, flying at 666.661 miles-per-hour in his F-100C Super Sabre at the Bendix Trophy Race in September 1956.

See also The Military, 1952.

Secretary of Defense, *Hispanics in America's Defense,* p. 35.

FOOTBALL

1970 • Stanford University football quarterback Jim Plunkett, became the first Hispanic Heisman Trophy-winner. Of German-Irish and Mexican ancestry, Plunkett was born and raised in San Jose, California, and after college went on to become a record-breaking quarterback for the Boston (now New England) Patriots and the San Francisco 49ers.

Meier and Rivera, *Dictionary of Mexican American History*, p. 279.

1971 • Jim Plunkett became the first Hispanic to start as quarterback in the National Football League, and in his debut year he became Rookie of the Year while playing for the Boston (now New England) Patriots and passing for 2,158 yards and nineteen touchdowns.

Kanellos, *The Hispanic American Almanac*, p. 712.

1973 • Manuel José "Manny" Fernández received the highest distinction of any Hispanic in football—he was named to the All-Time Greatest Super Bowl All-Star Team. Fernández played on one of professional football's winningest teams, the Miami Dolphins, from 1968 to 1977. Fernández was voted the Dolphins's Most Valuable Defensive Lineman six consecutive years, from 1968 to 1973. He helped the Dolphins win two Super Bowls, in 1972 and 1973, and become the only undefeated team in National Football League history in 1973. Fernández may also be the only Hispanic football player to have started in three Super Bowls.

Kanellos, *The Hispanic American Almanac*, p. 706; Tardiff and Mabunda, *Dictionary of Hispanic Biography*, p. 332.

1978 • Thomas Flores became the first Hispanic American to be named coach of a professional football team in the United States. He succeeded John Madden to the post for the Oakland Raiders in 1978 and was officially named in 1979. Flores, born on March 21, 1937, in Fresno, California, into a family of Mexican American farmworkers, went on to become one of the most successful coaches in the history of the National Football League. He led the Raiders to two Super Bowl championships.

Kanellos, *The Hispanic American Almanac*, pp. 706–707.

1989 • Outstanding coach of professional football Thomas Flores (1937–), became president and general manager of the Seattle Seahawks, the highest rank ever attained by a Hispanic in professional sports in the United States.

Kanellos, *The Hispanic American Almanac*, pp. 706–707.

1991 ✦ Professional football player Anthony Muñoz became the first Hispanic player to be named Offensive Lineman of the Year by the American Football Conference. Also, for several years he held the unofficial title of the NFL's Strongest Man.

Tardiff and Mabunda, *Dictionary of Hispanic Biography,* p. 591.

THOMAS FLORES.

GOLF

1963 ⁖ Juan "Chi Chi" Rodríguez became the first Puerto Rican and first Hispanic golfer to win the Denver Open. He went on to become one of golfing's all-time greats, also being the first Hispanic to win in more than a decade of open golfing competitions.

   Born in Río Piedras, Puerto Rico, in 1935, Rodríguez came from an extremely impoverished family and found his way into golf as a caddy on the

"CHI CHI" RODRÍGUEZ, GOLF GREAT.

links that served Puerto Rico's booming tourism. His is one of the most famous Hispanic "rags to riches through sports" tales—his career earnings have passed the $3 million mark. He has contributed financially to numerous charities and to the Chi Chi Rodríguez Youth Foundation in Clearwater, Florida. Included among the important tournaments that he has won are the Denver Open (1963), the Lucky Strike International Open (1964), the Western Open (1964), the Dorado Pro-Am (1965), the Texas Open (1967), and the Tallahassee Open (1979). As a member of the Senior Professional Golf Association (PGA) Tour, he has won numerous tournaments, including the Silver Pages Classic (1987), the GTE Northwest Classic (1987), and the Sunwest Senior Classic (1990).

Kanellos, *Chronology of Hispanic American History*, p. 207.

1968 • Lee Treviño (1939–) became the first Mexican American to win a major professional golf championship at the U.S. Open, and he became the first player in history to shoot all four rounds of the event under par. Born in Dallas, Texas, to a cleaning lady and raised by her and her father, a gravedigger, Treviño got involved in golf because their four-room farmhouse was located at the back of the Glen Lakes Country Club fairways. As a boy, Treviño studied the form of golfers on the course from his own backyard. He dropped out of school in the seventh grade and made his way into what was then an exclusively Anglo rich man's sport by working as a caddy and greenskeeper.

In 1966, Treviño became a professional golfer, and achieved his first major victory in 1968 at the U.S. Open. In 1970, he was the leading money winner on the Professional Golf Association (PGA) tour. In 1971, Treviño won the U.S. Open for a second time, won five tournaments between April and July, and also won the British Open in that year and again in 1972. In 1971, Treviño became the first Hispanic ever named PGA Player of the Year, Associated Press Athlete of the Year and *Sports Illustrated* Sportsman of the Year. After that, he won the 1974 PGA again, among many other tournaments. He was also awarded the Vardon Trophy for the fewest strokes per round (69.73 for eighty-two rounds), the lowest since Sam Snead in 1958. Treviño retired from the PGA tour in 1985, with his thirty victories and a total career earnings of more than $3 million (third highest). Treviño has been elected to the Texas Sports, American Golf, and World Golf Halls of Fame.

Kanellos, *Chronology of Hispanic American History*, pp. 211, 257.

1978 • Nancy López became the first Hispanic to win the Ladies Professional Golf Association Tournament. One of the greatest women's golf champions of all time, López was born in 1957 to Mexican American parents in Torrance, California. She was raised in Roswell, New Mexico, and rose to become one of the youngest women golfers to experience professional success. She learned golf from her father and by the age of eleven, she was already beating him. López won the New Mexico Women's Open when she was only twelve. In high school, she was the only female member of the golf team, and as an eighteen-year-old senior, she placed second in the U.S. Women's Open. In 1978, during López's first full season as a pro, she won nine tournaments, including the Ladies Professional Golf Association (PGA). She was named Rookie of the Year, Player of the Year and Female Athlete of the Year; she also won the Vare Trophy. Also in 1978, she set a new record for earnings by a rookie, $189,813.

LEE TREVIÑO.

In 1983, López took a break from her career when she became the mother of Ashley Marie, the child of her marriage to baseball star Ray Knight. Two months after having Ashley, López began touring again, and by 1987 she had won thirty-five tournaments and qualified to become the eleventh member of the Ladies Professional Golf Association Hall of Fame; in all, López had nearly fifty tournament victories. López's most outstanding year was 1985, when she won five tournaments and finished in the top ten at twenty-five others; that year she also won the LPGA title again. Through 1987, she had earned more than $2 million.

Kanellos, *The Hispanic American Almanac,* p. 708; Telgen and Kamp, *Latinas! Women of Achievement,* pp. 209–12.

HANDBALL

1985 • Los Angeles native Sandra Lynn de la Riva-Baza, the daughter of Mexican immigrant parents, became the first Hispanic U.S. national champion in team handball. Since the late 1970s, de la Riva-Baza has played team handball, making the U.S. national team for nine years, including participation in the 1984 and 1988 Olympics. De la Baza was U.S. national champion in 1985 and 1986 and served as team captain in the 1986 world championships. She is the winner of gold medals at the 1987 U.S. Cup and the Pan American Games. At the 1988 U.S. national championships, she was selected Most Valuable Player. Since 1994, de la Riva-Baza has served as vice president of the United States Team Handball Foundation. She is the first Hispanic to accomplish all of these firsts in handball.

Kanellos, *The Hispanic American Almanac,* 1996, p. 731.

HORSE RACING

1974 • Puerto Rican jockey Angel Cordero (1942–) won the Kentucky Derby to became the first U.S. Hispanic to win one of the races of the Triple Crown. Cordero went on to win the Derby again in 1976 and 1985. He also won the Preakness Stakes in 1980 and 1984 and the Belmont Stakes in 1976. In 1982, he was named Jockey of the Year.

Kanellos, *The Hispanic American Almanac,* p. 705.

1988 • Puerto Rican jockey Angel Cordero became the first Puerto Rican to be inducted into the Thoroughbred Racing Hall of Fame. In his thirty-one-year career, Cordero won more than seven thousand races, including three Kentucky Derbies.

Tardiff and Mabunda, *Dictionary of Hispanic Biography,* p. 240.

JUDO

1988 • René Capo became the first Hispanic to compete on the Olympic men's judo team. Capo was born in Pinal del Río, Cuba, in 1965 and has studied judo since the age of six. Capo was ranked number one in the United States in his weight class of 95 kilos (210 pounds). He is a business management graduate of the University of Minnesota.

Hispanic Business, May 1996, p. 27.

1996 • Celita Schultz became the first Hispanic woman to make the U.S. Women's Olympic Judo Team and the first to be elected captain of the team. Born in Houston, Texas, in 1968, Schultz has been competing in judo since the age of seven. She is a graduate in art from Yale University.

Hispanic Business, May 1996, p. 28.

RODEO

1883 • One of the first champion riders, Mexican *vaquero* Antonio Esquivel, performed in Buffalo Bill Cody's "Wild West Show" intermittently from 1883 to 1905.

Slatta, *Cowboys of the Americas,* p. 146.

1900 • The first cowboy to win the World Championship of Trick and Fancy Roping was Vicente Oropeza, a famous Mexican roper who had made his debut in competition in the United States in 1891 and became a star of Buffalo Bill Cody's touring "Wild West Show" for sixteen years. He is credited with having introduced trick and fancy roping into the United States and was the most influential Hispanic rodeo performer of all time. Oropeza was inducted into the National Rodeo Hall of Fame.

Mary Lou LeCompte, "The Hispanic Influence on the History of Rodeo," *Journal of Sports History,* 12 (spring 1985); pp. 21–38.

1939 • José Romero became the first rodeo performer to rope a full grown eagle in flight at a rodeo in Tucson, Arizona on May 31, 1939.

Rosaldo et al., *Chicano,* p. 10.

1965 • Ramón Ahumado, known as *el Charro Plateado* (The Silver-Plated Cowboy), was the first known Mexican rodeo champion in the United States. He was elected posthumously to the National Cowboy Hall of Fame. A real cowboy who punched cattle on the Mexican ranches of Arizona in the 1880s and participated in rodeo-type events, Ahumado was a dazzling horseman.

Sheridan, *Los Tucsonenses,* p. 98.

SKATING

1956 • Catherine Machado became the first U.S. Hispanic athlete to ever compete on the U.S. Winter Olympic Team. She was the senior women's figure skating champion. She finished eighth in overall competition in women's singles.

Kanellos, *Chronology of Hispanic American History,* pp. 238–39.

1958 • Catherine Machado became the first U.S. Hispanic to win the World Professional Figure Skating Championship, held in England. After competing in the Olympics, Machado developed a career with the Ice Capades but also continued to compete professionally.

Kanellos, *Chronology of Hispanic American History,* pp. 238–39.

1987 • Rudy Galindo became the first Hispanic to win the world junior championship in men's figure skating. In 1996, he went on to win the U.S. national championship.

"Edge of a Dream," *Time,* 18 March 1996.

1989 • Rudy Galindo became the first Hispanic to win a national championship in pairs figure skating as the partner of Kristi Yamaguchi. The duo won the championship again in 1990.

"Edge of a Dream," *Time,* 18 March 1996.

1996 • Rudy Galindo became the first Hispanic National Figure Skating champion of the United States. Two weeks after winning the U.S. title in his hometown of San Jose, California, Galindo became the first Hispanic to win a bronze medal in the World Figure Skating Championships. Born to Mexican American parents in San Jose, and educated in the San Jose public schools, Galindo began skating at the age of eight. When he and his sister became outstanding skaters, their truck-driving father, Jess Galindo, worked overtime for many years to finance the lessons and the travel that his children needed to compete regionally and nationally. Beginning in 1987, when Rudy Galindo won the world junior championships and the Central Pacific senior championships, he became a leading figure in national and world competitions. His first national championship, however, was as a partner in pairs figure skating with Kristi Yamaguchi in 1989, which was repeated in 1990. Galindo was singles champion in the Pacific Coast Senior competition in 1992, 1993, 1994, and 1995. In March 1996, Galindo won first place in singles figure skating at the National Senior Figure Skating championship. Galindo's international titles include, first place in the Vienna Cup in 1994 as well as second place in the Prague Skate in 1993. In 1996, he placed third in the World Skating championship.

"Edge of a Dream," *Time,* 18 March 1996.

SOFTBALL

1979 • Silvia Ortiz became the first U.S. Hispanic woman to compete on the U.S. team at the Pan American Games, in softball.

1996 • The star pitcher for the first gold medal—winning women's softball team in the Summer Olympics was Lisa Fernández. Like her teammates, Fernández won her gold medal the same year that softball was admitted as an official Olympic sport.

Born in Lakewood, California, in 1972, Fernández is the daughter of Cuban immigrant parents who played baseball and softball. She is considered among the greatest women softball players ever. In high school she threw sixty-nine shutouts and in college was a four-time All-American for the University of California, Los Angeles. As a pitcher, she helped UCLA win two National Collegiate Athletic Association Women's College World Series. Fernández is also an outstanding batter, leading the nation with a .510 average in 1993 and batting .382 during her college career. She holds the records for singles (225), runs scored (142), walks (65), hits (287), pitching wins (93), career percentage (.93), and no-hitters (11).

Hispanic Business, May 1996, p. 8.

SWIMMING AND DIVING

1964 • At the Tokyo Olympics, Donna De Varona became the first U.S. Hispanic to win a gold medal in swimming; she actually won two gold medals, in the 400-meter individual medley and in the 4 × 100 freestyle. That same year, De Varona was named Most Outstanding Female Athlete in the World by both the Associated Press and United Press International. Donna De Varona has been inducted into the International Swimming Hall of Fame and the San Francisco Bay Area Hall of Fame.

Kanellos, *The Hispanic American Almanac, 1996, p. 731.*

1965 • Olympic gold medal swimmer Donna De Varona became the youngest person (eighteen years old) and the first woman to be a sportscaster on network television. She has continued in that career, often appearing as host and cohost for Olympic coverage. In addition, De Varona is one of the founders of the Women's Sports Foundation.

Kanellos, *The Hispanic American Almanac,* 1996, p. 731.

1985 • Wendy Lucero-Schayes became the first Hispanic diver to win the National Collegiate Athletic Association one-meter diving championship;

she also won the national title in the Phillips 66 Outdoor Championships in 1984 and 1985. For these years, she was also named Academic All-American for her performance in the classroom. Lucero-Schayes was born on June 26, 1963, the daughter of Don Lucero, the son of a Spanish immigrant, and Shirley Lucero, of Irish descent.

Telgen and Kamp, *Latinas! Women of Achievement,* pp. 219–26.

1987 • Diver Wendy Lucero-Schayes became the first Hispanic diver to win the America Cup II championship in three-meter diving; that year she also came in first in the U.S. Olympic Festival. She went on to compete in the 1988 Olympics in Seoul, South Korea.

Telgen and Kamp, *Latinas! Women of Achievement,* p. 223.

1987 • U.S. Hispanics competing at the Pan American Games on the U.S. team won the most medals ever, thirteen. Tracy Ruiz-Conforto won two, and became the first U.S. Hispanic woman to win the gold in the Pan American Games.

1991 • Olympic diver Wendy Lucero-Schayes became the first U.S. Hispanic to win a silver medal in the World Championships. The Denver, Colorado, native had previously made the U.S. Diving National Team and had competed in the Olympics in 1988. Lucero-Schayes was also voted the U.S. Female Diving Athlete of the Year in 1990 and 1991.

Tardiff and Mabunda, *Dictionary of Hispanic Biography,* pp. 497–99; Telgen and Kamp, *Latinas! Women of Achievement,* pp. 219–26.

1991 • Olympic swimmer Donna De Varona, 1964 gold medal winner, was the first woman to receive the International Swimming Hall of Fame Gold Medallion as an inspiration for all swimmers. In recognition of her pioneering work for girls and women in all sports, she also received the American Woman Award in 1992 from the Women's Research and Education Institute.

Kanellos, *The Hispanic American Almanac,* 1996, p. 731.

1993 • Francisco Ferreras Rodríguez set the new world record in deep free diving in Freeport, Bahamas. by diving without air to 410 feet beneath the sea. Rodríguez was clocked at two minutes and nine seconds, thus setting new depth and new time records. Born in Matanzas, Cuba, but now a resident of Florida, Rodríguez competed on the Cuban Olympic team in 1980.

Hispanic, September 1994, p. 9.

TENNIS

1948 • Richard Alonso "Pancho" González (1928–), one of the greatest tennis professionals ever, became the first Hispanic to win the U.S. singles championship at Forest Hills. He repeated this feat again in 1949. After having won the U.S. grass, clay, and indoor championships, González turned pro. From 1954 to 1962, he was world professional singles champion. In 1968, he was named to the International Tennis Hall of Fame.

Kanellos, *The Hispanic American Almanac,* p. 707.

1966 ⁘ Rosemary Casals (1948–) teamed with Ian Crookenden to win the U.S. hard-court mixed doubles tennis championship. The daughter of Salvadoran immigrants thus became the first Hispanic to win the mixed doubles championship.

Telgen and Kamp, *Latinas! Women of Achievement,* p. 59.

1967 ⁘ Rosemary Casals, the daughter of Salvadoran immigrants to the United States, joined Billie Jean King to win the doubles tennis championship at Wimbledon. They went on to win it again another four times. King and Casals also won the U.S. Ladies Association doubles championship twice at Forest Hills. In the years that followed, Casals and King won fifty-six titles in total to become one of the most successful doubles teams in history. Nine times Casals was rated as number one in doubles by the United States Lawn Tennis Association. She was the first U.S.-born Hispanic female athlete to become a top-rated tennis professional.

Kanellos, *The Hispanic American Almanac,* p. 703; Telgen and Kamp, *Latinas! Women of Achievement,* pp. 57–62.

1968 ⁘ Richard Alonso "Pancho" González became the first Hispanic tennis player to coach the U.S. Davis Cup team. That year, 1968, he also became the first U.S. Hispanic to be named to the International Tennis Hall of Fame.

Kanellos, *The Hispanic American Almanac,* pp. 707–708.

ROSEMARY CASALS.

1970 · In response to unfair and unequal prize money for women's professional tennis, Rosemary Casals and other women players established the annual Virginia Slims Invitational Women's Tennis Tournament in Houston, Texas—despite the disapproval of the U.S. Ladies Tennis Association. Casals became the first winner of the tournament, taking home the top prize of $1,600. The success of the Virginia Slims Invitational led to Casals becoming a member of the Virginia Slims eight-tournament women's professional circuit and to an end to any financial problems she had experienced. She went on to become one of the top money winners.

Telgen and Kamp, *Latinas! Women of Achievement,* p. 61.

1973 · Tennis player Rosemary Casals collected the largest prize ever awarded in women's tennis to that time, defeating Nancy Richey Gunter in the finals of the Family Circle Tournament and winning $30,000.

Telgen and Kamp, *Latinas! Women of Achievement,* p. 61.

1990 · Dominican American tennis player Mary Joe Fernández became the highest ranked U.S. Hispanic women's single tennis player in history. She also ranked fourth in the world from late 1990 to early 1991.

Tardiff and Mabunda, *Dictionary of Hispanic Biography,* p. 334.

1990 · Tennis player Rosemary Casals became the first Hispanic to win the U.S. Open senior women's championship in doubles, teaming up with Billie Jean King.

Telgen and Kamp, *Latinas! Women of Achievement,* p. 62.

1991 · Dominican American tennis player Mary Joe Fernández became the winningest Hispanic women's tennis player in history when she became the thirty-third woman to earn more than $1 million in prize money.

Tardiff and Mabunda, *Dictionary of Hispanic Biography,* p. 334.

1991 · Gigi Fernández became the first Puerto Rican professional women's tennis player to rank in the top twenty of the world's best players; she is also the first Puerto Rican tennis player to be ranked number one in doubles in the world. Just six years after her professional debut, Fernández ranked seventeenth in the world.

Gigi Fernández was born in San Juan, Puerto Rico, and has been playing tennis since she was eight years old, when her parents enrolled her in tennis lessons. She has played consistently since then and went to Clemson University on a tennis scholarship. During her freshman year, she made the National Collegiate Athletic Association finals. She turned pro in 1985 and by 1991, was ranked seventeenth in the world—her highest ranking to date.

Fernández is the winner of six Grand Slam women's doubles titles, including the U.S. Open in 1988, 1990, and 1992, the French Open in 1991 and 1992, and Wimbledon in 1992. In 1991, she and her partner, Mary Joe Fernández (no relation), were ranked number one in doubles tennis. In the 1992 Barcelona Olympics, the two Fernándezes won the gold medal, making Gigi the first Puerto Rican to win Olympic gold.

Tardiff and Mabunda, *Dictionary of Hispanic Biography,* p. 329; Telgen and Kamp, *Latinas! Women of Achievement,* pp. 129–31.

1991 • Puerto Rican tennis star Gigi Fernández and Dominican American tennis star Mary Joe Fernández were ranked number one in the world in women's double tennis.

Tardiff and Mabunda, *Dictionary of Hispanic Biography,* p. 329; Telgen and Kamp, *Latinas! Women of Achievement,* pp. 137–40.

1992 • The doubles tennis team of Gigi Fernández and Mary Joe Fernández became the first U.S. Hispanic doubles team to win a gold medal in the Olympics.

Tardiff and Mabunda, *Dictionary of Hispanic Biography,* p. 329.

TRACK AND FIELD

1932 • The first Hispanic athletes to make the U.S. Olympic team were triple jumper Roland Lee Romero and fencer Miguel Capriles. Capriles became the first Hispanic of the United States to win a medal, the bronze.

Kanellos, *Chronology of Hispanic American History,*. p. 201.

1979 • Cuba-born marathoner Alberto Bauduy Salazar (1958–) set the U.S. road record of 22:13 for five miles. In 1980, he made the U.S. Olympic team, but that was the year that the United States boycotted the games in Moscow. However, that same year, he went on to win the New York Marathon, becoming the first U.S. Hispanic to do so. In winning the marathon, he set the record for the fastest first marathon in history, as well as the second-fastest time ever run by an American.

Kanellos, *The Hispanic American Almanac,* pp. 713–14.

1980 • Alberto Bauduy Salazar set a new world record in the New York Marathon of 2:08:13. That year, he was also selected as the top U.S. road racer. In 1982, Salazar won the Boston and New York Marathons. In addition to his world record, Salazar has set six U.S. records, the most since Steve Prefontaine.

Kanellos, *The Hispanic American Almanac,* pp. 713–14.

1987 • U.S. Hispanics competing at the Pan American Games on the U.S. team won the most medals ever, thirteen. Mike González won one in the decathlon.

1994 • Long-distance runner Alberto Bauduy Salazar came back in 1994 after a long slump and a series of illnesses, and stunned the sports world by winning the fifty-three-mile supermarathon in South Africa. He was the first Hispanic runner to do so.

Kanellos, *The Hispanic American Almanac,* pp. 713–14.

VOLLEYBALL

1992 • Carlos Briceño became the first U.S. Hispanic to win an Olympic medal in volleyball. In international play, Briceño has consistently ranked among the top three and in 1995 shared the number one men's team ranking. At the 1992 Barcelona Olympics, Briceño won a bronze medal for the United States, and in 1993 he won a silver medal at the NORCEA championships.

Hispanic Business, May 1996, p. 28.

WEIGHTLIFTING

1987 • U.S. Hispanics competing at the Pan American Games on the U.S. team won the most medals ever, thirteen. Weightlifter Mario Martínez won three gold medals.

WRESTLING

1971 • Sergio González became the first U.S. Hispanic to win a gold medal in the Pan American Games. The wrestler won the gold in the light-weight class.

THEATER

~~~~~~

1598 • Juan de Oñate's colonizing mission to New Mexico marked the introduction of European theater into lands north of the Rio Grande. The soldiers in the company, led by a certain Captain Farfán de los Godos performed the folk play *Moros y Cristianos,* a pageant reenactment of the victory of Spanish Christian forces over Moors in medieval Spain, which accompanied Spanish soldiers all over the world as they saw themselves battling paganism. The troupe also improvised plays based on their historic journey. As missionaries began evangelizing the Native Americans in the Southwest, they also introduced religious plays, such as *Los Pastores* (The Shepherds), that eventually would become a staple part of the folktheater of the U.S. Southwest and survive well into the twentieth century.

Kanellos, *The Hispanic American Almanac,* p. 505.

1789 • In what became the Southwest of the United States, the first plays for subscription (i.e., professional or semiprofessional) were performed as early as 1789. The manuscript copy of a three-act cloak-and-dagger play, Fernando de Reygados's *Astucias por heredar un sobrino a su tío* (The Clever Acts of a Nephew in Order to Inherit His Uncle's Health), bears that date and shows evidence of having been toured through California settlements. By the 1840s there was a steady stream of itinerant theatrical companies performing Spanish melodramas at the ranches and settlements in Alta California.

Kanellos, *A History of Hispanic Theater,* pp. 1–3.

1825 • The first Spanish-language play was published in the United States. Félix Megía's two-act play *Lafayette en Mount Vernon,* dramatizing the ideas of American democracy, was also published that same year in English translation, *Lafayette in Mount Vernon,* making it the first English-language translation of a Hispanic play in the United States. Both were issued in Philadelphia.

Online Computer Library Center.

1831 • The first Spanish-language professional theatrical company of record in the South was the Compañía Española de Teatro, which performed for a season in New Orleans at the Orleans Theater. Included in its repertory were five-act melodramas, such as *Bolero,* and three-act plays by the Spanish master Lope de Vega, which were performed along with music, dance, and shorter comic pieces, such as *Madre e hija* (Mother and Daughter). The leading actor of the company was Bernardo Arsilla, who had made his reputation on the stages of Spain. According to the *La abeja* (The Bee) newspaper, all of the actors in the small company—which had to be reinforced with local amateurs—were Spanish and had performed in Europe and the Americas.

La abeja, 5 April 1831.

1846 • The first Mexican circus-theaters (*maromas*) were documented as performing in the Monterey, California, area. Tent-covered performing companies offered a mixture of circus acts and melodrama, Spanish operetta (*zarzuela*), and song and dance. For the next one hundred years, numerous Hispanic circuses and tent theaters would crisscross what would become the U.S. Southwest. By the 1870s, Mexican circuses were the most frequent professional performing companies in the Southwest, and by the 1870s San Antonio had become a home base for the circuses and tent shows.

Kanellos, *A History of Hispanic Theater in the United States,* pp. 96–103.

1848 • The first Spanish-language theater house in the Southwest was Antonio F. Coronel's in Los Angeles. It was built as an addition to his house and seated three hundred; it included a covered stage with a proscenium, a drop curtain, and a good supply of scenery. Before then, professional performances were housed in halls or billiard parlors or held in the open air. Various other theaters were opened during the decades to follow in Los Angeles, but the real flowering of the stage, especially in Los Angeles and San Antonio, took place during the 1920s when numerous houses, bearing such names as Teatro California, Teatro México, Teatro Hidalgo, Teatro Nacional, and Teatro Zendejas, were opened.

Kanellos, *A History of Hispanic Theater in the United States,* pp. 2–3.

1860 • By the 1860s, resident Spanish-language theatrical companies were established in the Southwest as such formerly itinerant groups as the Compañía Española de la Familia Estrella settled down in San Francisco. The company was led by leading actor Gerardo López del Castillo, who is known in the history of the Mexican stage as the first impresario to take theater on tour to the provinces.

Kanellos, *A History of Hispanic Theater in the United States,* pp. 3–6.

1890 • Following the construction of railroads along the U.S.-Mexican border, Mexican theatrical companies began performing along a circuit that started at Laredo and extended west to California. During the early twentieth century, the Southwest would see a flowering of the Spanish- language professional stage in the major cities of the Southwest and West, such as Laredo, San Antonio, El Paso, Tucson, Los Angeles, and San Francisco.

Kanellos, *A History of Hispanic Theater in the United States,* pp. 17–20.

1891 • A portion of the Cuban cigar industry was transferred to Florida when Ybor City was founded in the swamps just outside of Tampa in 1886. The factory owners and workers soon constructed mutual aid societies to serve the transplanted cigar-making community. The societies were the first Hispanic mutual aid societies to house theaters in their buildings and to run full-range theatrical programs by and for the workers as well as to house professional companies on tour from Cuba, Spain, and later New York and other parts of the United States.

The first of these societies to open was the Centro Español in 1891. The Centro Español's original building included a theater hall, which was used for dramatic and musical comedy productions as well as for dances and other community events. A new building proudly erected in 1912 included a first-rate theater with a stage twenty-eight by thirty-five feet with a proscenium arch twenty-four feet high, an orchestra pit, box seats, 231 seats in the balcony and 465 in the orchestra.

Over the years, Ybor City became a Hispanic theatrical center that launched the careers of many professional theater people as well as entire companies. During the Depression, it was the only community to support a

A TOURING THEATRICAL COMPANY IN ARIZONA IN THE 1890S.

Hispanic Federal Theater Project company as part of the Works Progress Administration.

Kanellos, *A History of Hispanic Theater in the United States,* pp. 146–75.

1911 • The first Spanish-language play supporting women's rights and exhorting women to liberate themselves, *Julia y Carlota,* was written; excerpts from the play were published anonymously in Tampa's Centro Obrero (Workers's Center) newspaper *La Federación* on November 2, 1911. The excerpt that appeared in the newspaper exhorted Carlota to break the bonds of family and religion that are meant to keep women in their place, oppressed, and divorced from politics so that they do not reform civil laws.

Kanellos, *A History of Hispanic Theater in the United States,* p. 169.

1914 • The Centro Asturiano mutual aid society in Ybor City included in its newly constructed center a first-rate twelve-hundred-seat theater with a stage twenty-seven by eighty feet for productions by its own company and by professional theater companies on tour to the Tampa area. It is the only theater constructed by Hispanics still in use today as a theater. In addition, it was the only theater to house a Hispanic Federal Theater Project during the Depression.

Kanellos, *A History of Hispanic Theater in the United States,* p. 152.

1915 • The first Hispanic woman to become a theater impresario was Carmen Soto Vásquez, who constructed and operated the most important theater house for Tucson, Arizona's Mexican community. Teatro Carmen was Tucson's largest theater to that date, seating fourteen hundred spectators. During its heyday, from 1915 to 1922, the theater hosted both professional Spanish-language touring companies and local amateurs performing melodramas, comedies, *zarzuelas,* operettas, and musical concerts. According to Thomas E. Sheridan, "To the Mexican elite of Tucson, Teatro Carmen was a powerful symbol of self-identity, living proof of the depth, power, and beauty of their culture. . . . The dramas of Spain's Golden Age or contemporary works of Mexico's finest playwrights and composers gave lie to the derogatory stereotypes of Mexicans so prevalent in the Southwest."

Kanellos, *A History of Hispanic Theater in the United States,* pp. 185–86; Sheridan, *Los Tucsonenses,* pp. 200–201.

1917 • The first published labor theater piece in the history of Hispanic drama in the United States was *¡Vivan las cadenas!* (Long Live the Chains), published in Tampa's Centro Obrero newspaper *El Internacional* on August 24, 1917. *¡Vivan las cadenas!* is set in a cigar factory and deals with upcoming union elections at the Centro Obrero. Like many indoctrination and agitation works, the one-act play attempted to inspire workers to assume the responsibilities of leadership in their union. But here the argument is presented humorously as a group of tobacco workers is depicted playing cards, ogling the girls, and wasting time rather than helping the union.

Kanellos, *A History of Hispanic Theater in the United States,* p. 169.

~~~~~~

1919 • The first Spanish-language theater house was founded in New York. El Teatro Español, which was the former Park Theatre, was leased by Spanish director and leading man Manuel Noriega in partnership with other businessmen. Prior to this date, Spanish-language theatrical companies leased theaters only for the run of plays or to house companies on tour. Noriega formed a stock company, Gran Compañía de Opera y Zarzuela, to occupy the house when touring companies were not performing there.

Kanellos, *A History of Hispanic Theater in the United States,* pp. 109–11.

1921 • The Teatro Principal in Los Angeles became the first Hispanic theatrical entity in the United States to establish a playwriting contest. Following this lead, playwriting contests sponsored by the many Spanish- language theaters in Los Angeles gave rise to a boom in original works written for the stages of the Southwest. Many of the plays were based on local themes, and some even elaborated plots based on Hispanic culture of the Southwest dating back to missionary and colonial times. Locally written plays became so popular in Los Angeles that the largest crowds were registered at the theaters every time that new plays by local writers were featured. The Teatro Principal invited local playwrights to submit works in any theatrical genre in prose or verse. The winning works were chosen for production by director Romualdo Tirado, and their authors were paid royalties based on the box office sales. At the end of the run, the newly produced plays competed in an additional contest in which the plays were judged by a panel and audience acclamation. The first- and second-place winners were awarded prizes of $100 and $50, respectively.

Kanellos, *A History of Hispanic Theater in the United States,* pp. 44–45.

1922 • The first Puerto Rican play to be published in New York was Gonzalo O'Neill's *La india borinqueña* (The Puerto Rican Indian). O'Neill was a prosperous businessman who was also a poet and playwright and an investor in the most important theater houses of the 1930s, the Teatro Hispanic. He wrote nationalistic plays that supported Puerto Rican independence and identity, such as his *Bajo una sola bandera* (Under One Flag), which was produced on stage and published in 1928.

Kanellos, *A History of Hispanic Theater in the United States,* pp. 140–43.

1924 • The first playwright contracted to write works to be produced on a Hispanic stage in the United States was Guz Aguila (Antonio Guzmán Aguilera). Impresario and theater-owner Meyer Trallis hired the renowned Mexican author of musical-comedy revues for $1,000 per month to write original *Revistas* (revues) for production at the Teatro Hidalgo in Los Angeles. The Teatro Hidalgo also committed a company of thirty performers to be directed by Guz Aguila, as well as new scenery and costumes.

The production of original material based on the lives and culture of Mexicans in Los Angeles had become so important in the intensely competitive theatrical environment of Los Angeles that such publicity and production strategies had become common. The contracting of playwrights led to the greatest boom in Spanish-language playwriting ever experienced in the United States.

During the next decades, numerous other theaters were leased or purchased and rebaptized as Hispanic houses, such as the Teatro Campoamor, the Teatro Cervantes, the Teatro Hispano, the Teatro San José, and the Teatro Variedades.

Kanellos, *A History of Hispanic Theater in the United States,* pp. 64–65.

1930 • Beatriz Escalona (1903–1980), known onstage as La Chata Noloesca, split from the Hermanos Areu vaudeville company to form her own touring company, made up mainly of Mexican American young women from San Antonio, Texas. She was the first U.S.-born Hispanic to not only become an outstanding theatrical performer but also rise to the status of the greatest vaudeville actress. Born on August 20, 1903, in San Antonio, Texas, Escalona was discovered while working as an usherette and box office cashier at the Teatro Nacional. She became associated with the Spanish-Cuban troupe of Hermanos Areu (Areu Brothers)—she married José Areu—and played everything from melodrama to vaudeville with them, beginning in 1920, when she made her stage debut in El Paso. Over the course of the 1920s, Escalona developed and perfected her comic persona of the streetwise maid, a *peladita,* or underdog character, who maintained a spicy and satirical banter.

By 1930, La Chata Noloesca had split from the Areus and formed her own company, Atracciones Noloesca, and continued to tour the Southwest and northern Mexico. In 1936, she re-formed her company in her native San Antonio and set out to weather the Depression by performing in Tampa, Chicago, and New York—as well as Puerto Rico and Cuba—as the Compañía Mexicana. La Chata's novel idea was to bring to the Cubans, Puerto Ricans and others Mexican vaudeville, music, folklore, and her own brand of humor. In 1941, the company set down roots in New York for a stretch of nine years, during which time it was a mainstay on the Hispanic vaudeville circuit made up of the Teatro Hispano, the Teatro Puerto Rico, the Teatro Triboro, and the 53rd Street Theater. Back in San Antonio, she periodically performed for special community events until her death in 1980.

Kanellos, *Chronology of Hispanic American History,* pp. 149, 108.

1936 • The Tampa Hispanic unit of the Federal Theater Project (FTP) was the only Hispanic company involved in the effort by the historically important Works Progress Administration's (WPA) effort to save the American stage by employing theatrical artists. The company was directed by professional leading actor and director Manuel Aparicio, who had risen from the Ybor City stages to perform in New York, Cuba, and Spain. Manuel Aparicio became the only Hispanic director in all of the FTP.

The company, headquartered at the Centro Asturiano, performed mostly standard *zarzuelas* along with some other works required by the FTP. Ultimately, because of language differences and misunderstandings about citizenship, the Hispanic unit lost twenty-five of its members in 1937 when

LA CHATA NOLOESCA (LEFT).

Congress passed the ERA Act of 1937, which effectively removed foreigners from the WPA. This led to the demise of the unit.

Kanellos, *A History of Hispanic Theater in the United States,* pp. 156–60.

1937 • The first play published by a Puerto Rican woman playwright of New York was *Los Hipócritas* (The Hypocrites) by Franca de Armiño. It was also the first play of record by a Hispanic woman produced on the stages of

MANUEL APARICIO
(LEFT) IN A FEDERAL
THEATER PROJECT PLAY.

New York. *Los Hipócritas,* which debuted in three performances at the Park Palace Theatre in New York on April 15 and 16, 1933, by the Compañía Manuel Santigosa, is a social drama in four acts and eight scenes. The author dedicated the play to the oppressed of the world and to those who work for social renovation. Franca de Armiño was a labor organizer and a columnist for *Gráfico* (Graphic) newspaper.

Kanellos, *A History of Hispanic Theater in the United States,* pp. 139–40.

1937 • The first Hispanic theater to conscientiously support the solidarity of a pan-Hispanic identity was New York's Teatro Hispano, which opened in August 1937. Under the leadership of Mexican impresario Señor del Pozo, the Teatro Hispano developed a formula for featuring the national culture of the diverse Hispanic ethnic groups of the New York community. The theater would offer a week of Puerto Rican theater and variety acts, then one of Cuban, followed by Spanish or Mexican or Argentine in an effort to bring all of the diverse ethnic groups together and, of course, benefit financially from this cooperation and solidarity.

Kanellos, *A History of Hispanic Theater in the United States,* pp. 131–34.

1952 • Puerto Rican dancer Chita Rivera became the first Hispanic star dancer on Broadway in 1952 when she accepted a role as a principal dancer in *Guys and Dolls.* She went on to star in numerous Broadway hit musicals during the golden age of musicals, including *Can-Can, Mr. Wonderful,* and *West Side Story.* She also became the first Hispanic show dancer to be featured on all of the top television variety shows, including *The Garry Moore Show, The Ed Sullivan Show, The Arthur Godfrey Show, The Sid Caesar Show,* and others.

Telgen and Kamp, *Latinas! Women of Achievement,* pp. 313–19.

1957 • Panamanian American director José Quintero became the first Hispanic director to be nominated for a Tony Award for a Broadway production, *Long Day's Journey into Night.* Quintero is one of the few Hispanic directors to have made a career on Broadway and in major American theaters, directing the works of such international masters as Federico García Lorca, Jean Genet, Thornton Wilder, and Tennessee Williams.

Tardiff and Mabunda, *Dictionary of Hispanic Biography,* p. 718.

1957 • Broadway musical *West Side Story* was the first mainstream production to have a Hispanic theme and to showcase the talents of Hispanic actors and dancers, some of whom, such as Chita Rivera and Rita Moreno, went on to make important contributions to stage and film. The musical ran for 732 performances on Broadway and garnered a Tony nomination for Chita Rivera, the first such nomination for a Hispanic performer.

Telgen and Kamp, *Latinas! Women of Achievement,* p. 316.

1963 • The first play that can be called "Chicano" was Luis Valdez's *The Shrunken Head of Pancho Villa,* which he wrote while he was a student at San Jose State University. The drama department produced the play in 1963, making it the first produced Chicano play. Luis Valdez went on to be called by many critics "the father of Chicano theater" for his founding El Teatro Campesino in 1965 and defining, introducing, and promoting a form and style of people's theater called *teatro chicano.*

Kanellos, *The Hispanic American Almanac,/i>, pp. 539–40.*

CHITA RIVERA.

1965 • Luis Valdez (1940–) founded El Teatro Campesino, the first farm-worker theater, in Delano, California. His efforts inspired young Chicano activists across the country to use theater as a means of organizing students, communities, and labor unions.

Valdez was born into a family of migrant farm workers in Delano, California. Although his education was constantly interrupted, he finished high school and went on to San Jose State College, where he majored in English and pursued his interest in theater. In 1965, Valdez enlisted in César Chávez's mission to organize farm workers in Delano into a union. It was there that Valdez brought together farm workers and students in El Teatro Campesino to dramatize the plight of the farm workers. The publicity and success gained by the troupe led to the spontaneous appearance of a national Chicano theater movement.

In 1967 Valdez and El Teatro Campesino left the unionizing effort to expand their theater beyond agitprop and farm-worker concerns. Since then, Valdez and the theater have explored most of the theatrical genres that have been important to Mexicans in the United States. During the late 1960s and the 1970s El Teatro Campesino produced many of Valdez's plays, including *Los vendidos* (The Sell-Outs; 1967), *The Shrunken Head of Pancho Villa* (1968), *Bernabé* (1970), *Dark Root of a Scream* (1971), *La Carpa de los Rascuachis* (1974), and *El Fin del Mundo* (The End of the World; 1976). Valdez later broke into mainstream theater and film.

González Broyles, *El Teatro Campesino;* Kanellos, *Chronology of Hispanic American History,* pp. 248, 274

1965 • Cuban American playwright María Irene Fornés (1930–) became the first Hispanic playwright to win an Obie for distinguished playwriting for *The Successful Life of Three.* She went on to win five other Obies, the most of any Hispanic playwright, for her plays *The Danube, Mud, Sarita, The Conduct of Life,* and *Abingdon Square.*

Tardiff and Mabunda, *Dictionary of Hispanic Biography,* pp. 345–347; Telgen and Kamp, *Latinas! Women of Achievement,* pp. 141–48.

1967 • Broadway and Hollywood actress Miriam Colón founded the first mobile Puerto Rican theater in the United States, the Puerto Rican Traveling Theater (PRTT), to take full-scale productions, often including salsa bands, into neighborhoods and parks of New York City. Unlike the community-based Chicano theater, which performed short improvisational *actos,* the PRTT produced full-length conventional plays by Latin American and Latino playwrights in Spanish and English.

Kanellos, *The Hispanic American Almanac,* pp. 525–28.

1968 • Luis Valdez's El Teatro Campesino became the first Mexican American company (and he the first Mexican American playwright) to win an Obie. Valdez would win two more Obies, in 1972 and 1978.

Tardiff and Mabunda, *Dictionary of Hispanic Biography*, p. 911.

1968 • Luis Valdez and El Teatro Campesino left the struggle to establish a farm-worker union in order to dedicate themselves to establishing a national theater for Chicanos. They founded Teatro Nacional de Aztlán (TENAZ), at first with the idea that the best members of companies from around the country would join TENAZ to form a national performing company; but in fact it was El Teatro Campesino that became the national company for Chicanos. In the mid-1970s, Valdez and El Teatro Campesino left TENAZ, which had become an association of Chicano theaters, organizing festivals, seminars, and conferences. Valdez had been severely criticized for not abandoning religious mysticism and for not becoming as radical as many of the other groups had become.

Kanellos, *The Hispanic American Almanac*, p. 521–23.

1969 • The only Hispanic repertory company specializing in both production of the classics of the Spanish Golden Age as well as contemporary drama, the Teatro Repertorio Español was founded in New York City and continues to be the most active Hispanic company in the United States. It is also one of the few companies in the United States to stage nineteenth-century *zarzuelas*. Operating today out of the Gramercy Arts Theater, which has a tradition of Spanish-language theater that goes back to the 1920s, the Teatro Repertorio Español caters both to educational and community-based audiences, with productions in both Spanish and English.

Kanellos, *The Hispanic American Almanac*, p. 526.

1971 • Cuban American playwright Iván Acosta's play *Abdala-José Martí* was the first Spanish-language play produced at the Lincoln Center Theater Festival.

Sánchez-Grey Alba, "El Tema del Desarraigo en el Teatro de Iván Acosta," *Círculo: Revista de Cultura* 24 (1995): p. 119.

1973 • José Quintero became the first Hispanic to win a Tony Award for Best Director for his work on the Broadway production of *A Moon for the Misbegotten* by Eugene O'Neill.

Tardiff and Mabunda, *Dictionary of Hispanic Biography*, p. 718.

1973 • Mexican American comedian Cheech Marín and his partner Tommy Chong, of the team of the Cheech and Chong, was the first Hispanic and Asian American comedians to win a Grammy for Best Comedy Recording for their album *Los Cochinos* (The Pigs). During the 1970s, Cheech and Chong were among the first entertainers to introduce a new brand of comedy spoofing hippies and marijuana smokers. After signing with Warner

Bros., Cheech and Chong made a series of comedy albums that were all smash hits. Marín later went on to star in comedy films of his own.

Tardiff and Mabunda, *Dictionary of Hispanic Biography,* p. 518.

1973 • Actress Carmen Zapata launched the Bilingual Foundation of the Arts, the first Hispanic theater to serve as a showcase of Hispanic acting and playwriting for Hollywood.

Tardiff and Mabunda, *Dictionary of Hispanic Biography,* p. 966.

1973 • Luis Valdez and El Teatro Campesino were the first Hispanic theatrical director and troupe to win a special Emmy for the PBS broadcast of the television version of their play *Los vendidos* (The Sellouts).

Tardiff and Mabunda, *Dictionary of Hispanic Biography,,* p. 518.

1974 • The first Broadway hit play by a Hispanic was *Short Eyes* by Miguel Piñero (1946–1988). It was also the first Hispanic-authored play to win major drama awards on Broadway, including the New York Drama Critics Circle Award for Best American Play, an Obie, and the Drama Desk Award. After the success of *Short Eyes,* Piñero went on to write other successful plays and scripts for such television dramas as *Barreta, Kojak,* and *Miami Vice.* In all, Piñero wrote eleven plays that were produced, most of which are included in his two collections, *The Sun Always Shines for the Cool, A Midnight Moon at the Greasy Spoon, Eulogy for a Small-Time Thief* (1983), and *Outrageous One-Act Plays* (1986). Piñero also authored of a book of poems, *La Bodega Sold Dreams* (1986).

Kanellos, *Chronology of Hispanic American History,* pp. 224, 260.

1974 • The Puerto Rican Traveling Theater became the first Hispanic theater to open a theater house in the Off-Broadway section of New York City and to be accepted and reviewed as an Off-Broadway house. Founded by Miriam Colón in 1967, the theater had previously performed in the open air in various Hispanic neighborhoods of New York City.

Kanellos, *The Hispanic American Almanac,* pp. 525–28.

1975 • Rita Moreno became the first Hispanic actress to win a Tony Award for Best Supporting Actress in the Broadway production of *The Ritz,* which ran for more than four hundred performances.

Telgen and Kamp, *Latinas! Women of Achievement,* p. 266.

1975 • The Hispanic Organization of Latin Actors (HOLA) was founded in New York City to provide support services to Hispanic artists in theater, film, television, radio, dance, video and music. HOLA publishes the oldest newsletter for Hispanic actors and performers.

Furtaw, *The Hispanic Americans Information Directory,* p. 15.

1976 • Playwright Estela Portillo Trambley became the first Mexican American to have a musical comedy produced. *Sun Images,* which she had written and staged in El Paso at the Chamizal National Monument, was published in 1979 in the historic anthology *Nuevos Pasos: Chicano and Puerto Rican Drama,* edited by Nicolás Kanellos and Jorge Huerta.

Kanellos, "Introduction," *Nuevos Pasos,* pp. v- ix.

1978 • Luis Valdez became the first Mexican American playwright to break into mainstream theater, with Los Angeles's Mark Taper Forum's production of his *Zoot Suit* and the 1979 Broadway production of the same play. In 1986, his play *I Don't Have to Show You No Stinking Badges* had a successful run at the Los Angeles Theater Center.

Kanellos, *The Hispanic American Almanac,* pp. 521–23.

1978 • Edward James Olmos became the first Mexican American actor to win the Los Angeles Drama Critics Circle Award for his role as the pachuco in Luis Valdez's play *Zoot Suit.*

Tardiff and Mabunda, *Dictionary of Hispanic Biography,* p. 626.

1980 • Playwright Luis Valdez became the first Hispanic to receive a Broadway production with his musical drama *Zoot Suit.* Unfortunately, the play did not experience the success that it did in Los Angeles, where it ran for more than a year; it closed shortly after opening when New York critics lambasted the effort.

Kanellos, *The Hispanic American Almanac,* pp.521–23.

1981 • Puerto Rican actor-director-producer José Ferrer became the first U.S. Hispanic actor inducted for acting into the Theater Hall of Fame.

See also Film, 1950.

Kanellos, *Chronology of Hispanic American History,* p. 167.

1981 • Cuban American playwright Dolores Prida became the first U.S. Hispanic to receive a Special Award from the Third World Theatre Competition in Caracas, Venezuela, for her play *La era latina* (The Latin Era). Written and first produced in 1980, this bilingual musical comedy toured to more than thirty Hispanic neighborhoods in New York City for open-air staging by the Puerto Rican Traveling Theatre.

This foray into bilingual theater next led her to write her most important and far-reaching work, *Coser y cantar* (Sewing and Singing; 1981), an experimental, psychological play about bilingualism-biculturalism and the conflicting roles that Hispanics, especially women, must play in U.S. soci-

SCENE FROM LUIS
VALDEZ'S PLAY <u>ZOOT
SUIT,</u> WITH EDWARD
JAMES OLMOS.

ety. By dividing the Americanized part of a woman's psyche from her "old country" consciousness, creating a character around each, and engaging the characters in bilingual dialog, Prida was able to illustrate the tensions and contradictions that need to be resolved by Hispanics everywhere in the United States.

Kanellos, *The Hispanic Literary Companion,* pp. 264–66.

1982 ⋅ Actress, director, and producer Miriam Colón became the first Hispanic artist to be awarded the New York City Mayor's Award of Honor for the Arts and Culture for her work as founder and director of the Puerto Rican Traveling Theater. Born in Ponce, Puerto Rico, to working-class parents, Colón won a scholarship to the world-renowned Erwin Piscator Dramatic Workshop in New York City, made her Broadway debut in 1953, and later appeared in such important Hollywood films as *One-Eyed Jacks* and *The Appaloosa,* opposite Marlon Brando. In 1967, she founded the Puerto Rican Traveling Theater to take Spanish-language and Hispanic theater into the neighborhoods of New York City in open-air productions. Later, she created a theater house from an old firehouse in the Off-Broadway section to house more conventional productions of Latino and Latin American plays.

Kanellos, *The Hispanic American Almanac,* pp. 525–26; Telgen and Kamp, *Latinas! Women of Achievement,* pp. 93–96.

1982 ⋅ Cuban American playwright María Irene Fornés became the first Hispanic to win an Obie for sustained achievement in theater. This was in addition to numerous other Obies that she had won during her career for individual plays.

Telgen and Kamp, *Latinas! Women of Achievement,* p. 147.

1983 ⋅ Playwright, director, and screen writer Luis Valdez became the first Hispanic to be awarded the National Medal for the Arts.
Tardiff and Mabunda, *Dictionary of Hispanic Biography,* p. 518.

1984 ⋅ Mexican American actor A. Martínez was the first Hispanic actor to break into daytime drama (soap operas) with a leading role; he played police officer Cruz Castillo in *Santa Barbara.* Martínez performed in the soap opera throughout its run, until 1992.

Tardiff and Mabunda, *Dictionary of Hispanic Biography,* pp. 525–26.

1985 ⋅ Miriam Colón, actress, director, and founder of the Puerto Rican Traveling Theatre, became the first Hispanic woman to receive the Athena Award from the New York Commission on the Status of Women.

Telgen and Kamp, *Latinas! Women of Achievement,* p. 96.

1985 ⋅ The Hispanic Playwrights Project was founded in Costa Mesa, California, to take plays by Hispanics through readings and workshops and produce the best of them in an annual national festival, which showcases them for theaters around the United States. Since its founding, more than half of the plays produced by the festival have gone on to productions by larger companies.

Hispanic, August 1995, p. 8.

MIRIAM COLÓN.

1985 • Cuban American writer María Irene Fornés became the first Hispanic playwright to win the prestigious American Academy and Institute of Arts and Letters Award in Literature, bestowed in recognition of sustained achievement.

Telgen and Kamp, *Latinas! Women of Achievement,* p. 147.

1987 • Luis Valdez became the first Mexican American screenwriter- director to break into Hollywood commercial films with his writing and directing of *La Bamba* (the name of a dance from Veracruz), the screen biography of Chicano rock-and-roll star, Ritchie Valens. Valdez's screenwriting career began with early film and television versions of Corky González's poem "I Am Joaquín" (1969) and the play *Los vendidos* (The Sellouts) and gathered momentum with a film version of "Zoot Suit" (1982).

Valdez's plays, essays, and poems have been widely anthologized. He has published two collections of plays, *Luis Valdez—The Early Works* (1990) and *Zoot Suit and Other Plays* (1992). Valdez's awards include an Obie (1968), Los Angeles Drama Critics Awards (1969, 1972, and 1978), and a special Emmy Award (1973) for Best Musical from the San Francisco Bay Critics Circle (1983)

Kanellos, *Chronology of Hispanic American History,* p. 274.

1987 • Director José Quintero became the first Hispanic to win the Unique Contributions to the Theatre Award from the Drama League. The Panamanian-born Quintero has made a career of directing the works by the great American playwrights Tennessee Williams and Eugene O'Neill.

Tardiff and Mabunda, *Dictionary of Hispanic Biography,* p. 718.

1989 • Arte Público Press received a grant for $133,000 from the Ford Foundation to publish collections of Hispanic plays—the first ever concerted effort to issue the works of Hispanic playwrights of the United States. In the following three years, the press published anthologies of Chicano, Cuban American, and Puerto Rican plays, respectively, as well as individual collections of plays by such playwrights as Iván Acosta, Carlos Morton, Miguel Piñero, Dolores Prida, and Luis Valdez. The press also issued anthologies of Hispanic women's plays and plays for children.

Kanellos, *The Hispanic American Almanac,* p. 523.

1989 • Josefina López, as a seventeen-year-old Mexican immigrant, became the youngest Hispanic playwright to have a play, *Simplemente María, or The American Dream,* air nationally on the Public Broadcasting System. López has since then gone on to become a scriptwriter for television and film.

Hispanic, August 1995, p. 28.

1990 • In 1990, Carmen Zapata of the Bilingual Foundation for the Arts was the first Hispanic director to receive the prestigious Civil Order of Merit from His Majesty Juan Carlos I, king of Spain, in recognition of her commitment to Hispanics in theater and film and for her community service. In

1991, she, along with eight other artists and organizations, was conferred the California Governor's Award for the Arts.

Kanellos, *The Hispanic American Almanac,* p. 540.

1991 • The first history of Hispanic theater, *A History of Hispanic Theater in the United States: Origins to 1940,* was written by University of Houston professor Nicolás Kanellos. The book won the 1991 Texas Institute of Letters

JOSEFINA LÓPEZ.

Award for the Book Making the Most Significant Contribution to Knowledge. It also went on to book awards from the Southwest Conference on Latin American Studies and the San Antonio Conservation Society.

Kanellos, *A History of Hispanic Theater in the United States.*

1995 · Lionel G. García became the first Hispanic writer to win first place in the Texas Playwright Festival for his play *An Acorn on the Moon,* produced by Stages Repertory Theater of Houston, Texas, in 1995.

Kanellos, *The Hispanic Literary Companion,* pp. 99–109.

1996 · New York's Teatro Repertorio Español became the first Hispanic theatrical company to win an honorary Drama Desk Award for its excellence in presenting plays in Spanish and English.

Hispanic Link Weekly Report, 13 May 1996, p. 8.

BIBLIOGRAPHY

A

Almaguer, Tomás. *Racial Fault Lines: The Historical Origins of White Supremacy in California*. Berkeley: University of California Press, 1994.

Avila, Alex. "Freedom Fighter: Dr. Héctor P. García, Founder of the American G.I. Forum," *Hispanic,* January/February 1996, pp. 18–22.

B

Baez, Joan. *A Voice to Sing With*. New York: Summit Books, 1987.

Balderrama, Francisco, and Raymond Rodríguez. *Decade of Betrayal: Mexican Repatriation in the 1930s*. Albuquerque: University of New Mexico Press, 1995.

Broyles-González, Yolanda. *El Teatro Campesino: Theatre in the Chicano Movement*. Austin: University of Texas Press, 1994.

C

Campa, Arthur L. *Hispanic Culture in the Southwest*. Norman: University of Oklahoma Press, 1979.

Carter, Thomas P., and Roberto Segura. *Mexican Americans in the Public Schools: A History of Neglect*. Princeton, New Jersey: College Entrance Examination Board, 1979.

Castañeda, Carlos. *Our Catholic Heritage in Texas, 1519–1936*. New York: Arno Press, 1976.

Chipman, Donald E. *Spanish Texas, 1519–1821*. Austin: University of Texas Press, 1992.

Córdova, Alfredo C., and Charles B. Judah. *Octaviano Larrazolo: A Political Portrait*. Albuquerque: Department of Government, Division of Research, 1952.

Cotera, Martha. *Profile of the Mexican American Woman*. Austin: National Education Laboratory Publishers, 1976.

Crawford, James. *Bilingual Education: History, Policy, Theory and Practice*. Trenton, New Jersey: Crane Publishing, 1989.

Crocchiola, Stanley F. L., *The Civil War In New Mexico*. Denver: World Press, 1960.

Cruz, Gilbert C. *Let There Be Towns: Spanish Municipal Origins in the American Southwest, 1610–1810*. College Station: Texas A&M University Press, 1988.

D

Dobkins, Betty Eakle. *The Spanish Element in Texas Water Law*. Austin: University of Texas Press, 1959.

Dolan, Jay P., and Allan Figueroa Deck. *Hispanic Catholic Culture in the United States: Issues and Concerns*. Notre Dame, Indiana: University of Notre Dame, 1994.

Dolan, Jay P., and Gilberto M. Hinojosa. *Mexican Americans and the Catholic Church, 1900–1965*. Notre Dame, Indiana: University of Notre Dame Press, 1994.

E

Enciso, Carmen E., and the Hispanic Division, Library of Congress. *The History of the*

Congressional Hispanic Caucus. Washington, D.C.: U.S. Government Printing Office, 1981.

F

Fabre, Genvieve, ed. *European Perspectives on Hispanic Literature of the United States.* Houston: Arte Público Press, 1989.

Fernández, Roberta. *Twenty-five Years of Hispanic Literature in the United States.* Houston: University of Houston, M. D. Anderson Library, 1993.

Florida Department of State. *Florida Cuban Heritage Trail.* Tallahassee: Florida Department of State, Division of Historical Resources, 1995.

Fontana, Bernard L. *Entrada: The Legacy of Spain and Mexico in the United States.* Albuquerque: University of New Mexico Press, 1994.

Furtaw, Julia C., ed. *Hispanic Americans Information Directory: 1992–93.* Detroit: Gale, 1992.

G

Galarza, Ernesto. *Farm Workers and Agribusiness in California, 1947–1960.* Notre Dame, Indiana: University of Notre Dame Press, 1977.

Gallegos, Bernardo P. *Literacy, Education, and Society in New Mexico 1693–1821.* Albuquerque: University of New Mexico Press, 1992.

García, María Cristina. *Havana USA: Cuban Exiles and Cuban Americans in South Florida, 1959–1994.* Berkeley: University of California Press, 1996.

García, Mario T. *Memories of Chicano History. The Life and Narrative of Bert Corona.* Berkeley: University of California Press, 1994.

Gleiter, Jan, and Kathleen Thompson. *David Farragut.* Milwuakee, Wisconsin: Raintree Publications, 1989.

Gómez-Quiñones, Juan. *Roots of Chicano Politics, 1600–1940.* Albuquerque: University of New Mexico Press, 1994.

Gonzales, Juan L., Jr. *Mexican and Mexican American Farm Workers: The California Agricultural Industry.* New York: Praeger, 1985.

Griswold del Castillo, Richard, and Richard A. García. *César Chávez. A Triumph of Spirit.* Norman: University of Oklahoma Press, 1995.

Griswold del Castillo, Richard, Teresa McKenna, and Yvonne Yarbro-Bejarano, eds. *Chicano Art: Resistance and Affirmation, 1965–1985.* Los Angeles: Wight Art Gallery, University of California, Los Angeles, 1991.

Gutiérrez, Félix F., and Jorge R. Schement. *Spanish-Language Radio in the Southwestern United States.* Austin: Center for Mexican American Studies, University of Texas, 1979.

H

Henderson, Ann L., and Gary R. Mormino, eds. *Spanish Pathways in Florida.* Sarasota: Pineapple Press, 1991.

Herbert, John R., ed. *1492: An Ongoing Voyage.* Washington, D.C.: Library of Congress, 1992.

Hernández, Irene Beltrán. *Heartbeat Drumbeat.* Houston: Arte Público Press, 1993.

Hispanics in U.S. History: 1865 to the Present, two volumes. Englewood Cliffs, New Jersey: Globe Book Company, 1989.

J

Jamieson, Stuart. *Labor Unionism in American Agriculture.* New York: Arno Press, 1976.

Jenkins, John H. *Basic Texas Books: An Annotated Bibliography of Selected Works for a Research Library.* Austin: Texas State Historical Association, 1983.

Juárez, Tina. *Call No Man Master.* Houston: Arte Público Press, 1995.

K

Kanellos, Nicolás. *Chronology of Hispanic American History: From Pre-Columbian Times to the Present.* Detroit, Gale, 1995.

Kanellos, Nicolás. *Hispanic American Literature.* New York, HarperCollins, 1995.

Kanellos, Nicolás. *The Hispanic American Almanac,* Detroit, Gale, 1993; second edition, 1996.

Kanellos, Nicolás. *A History of Hispanic Theater in the United States: Origins to 1940.* Austin: University of Texas Press, 1989.

Kanellos, Nicolás. "Introduction," *Nuevos Pasos.* Houston: Arte Público Press, 1989; pp. v–ix.

Kanellos, Nicolás, and Claudio Esteva-Fabregat, *Handbook of Hispanic Cultures in the United States,* four volumes. Houston: Arte Público Press, 1994–95.

Keller, Gary D. *Hispanics and United States Film: An Overview and Handbook.* Tempe, Arizona: Bilingual Press, 1994.

Kloss, Heinz. *The American Bilingual Tradition.* Rowley, Massachusetts: Newbury House, 1977.

Knippling, Alpana Sharma, ed. *New Immigrant Literatures in the United States: A Sourcebook to Our Multicultural Heritage.* Westport, Connecticut: Greenwood Press, 1996.

Kushner, Sam. *Long Road to Delano: A Century of Farmworkers' Struggle.* New York: International Publishers, 1975.

L

Lanman, Charles. *Dictionary of the United States Congress.* Philadelphia: J. B. Lippincott, 1859.

LeCompte, Mary Lou. "The Hispanic Influence on the History of Rodeo," *Journal of Sports History,* 12 (spring 1985); pp. 21–38.

Lomelí, Francisco, and Carl R. Shirley, eds. *Dictionary of Literary Biography, Chicano Writers,* Detroit: Gale, Vol. 82, 1989; Vol. 122, 1992.

M

Mathews, Jay. *Escalante: The Best Teacher in America.* New York: Henry Holt, 1988.

McKnight, Joseph. "Law without Lawyers on the Hispano Mexican Frontier," *The West Texas Historical Association Year Book,* 64 (1990); pp. 51–65.

McKnight, Joseph. *The Spanish Elements in Modern Texas Law.* [Dallas], 1979.

McWilliams, Carey. *North from Mexico: The Spanish-Speaking People of the United States.* Philadelphia: Lippincott, 1949.

Meier, Matt S., and Feliciano Rivera. *Dictionary of Mexican American History,* Westport, Connecticut: Greenwood Press, 1981.

Meyer, Michael C. *Water in the Hispanic Southwest: A Social and Legal History 1550–1850.* Tucson: University of Arizona Press, 1984.

Montes Huidobro, Matías, ed. *El laúd del desterrado.* Houston: Arte Público Press, 1995.

Mora, Pat. *The Desert Is My Mother/El desierto es mi madre.* Houston: Arte Público Press, 1995.

Moritz, Charles, ed. *Current Biography Yearbook, 1963.* New York: H. W. Wilson, 1963.

Muñoz Marín, Luis. *Memorias: Autobiografía pública, 1940–1952* (Memories: Public Autobiography). San Germán, Puerto Rico: Universidad Interamericana, 1992.

Museum of Fine Arts, Houston. *Hispanic Art in the United States: Thirty Contemporary Painters and Sculptors.* New York: Abbeville Press, 1987.

N

"New Members, New Districts," *Congressional Quarterly,* 50/14 (November 7, 1992); p. 52.

P

Paredes, Américo. *With His Pistol in His Hand: A Border Ballad and Its Hero.* Austin: University of Texas Press, 1958.

Pendas, Miguel, and Harry Ring. *Toward Chicano Power: Building La Raza Unida Party.* New York: Pathfinder Press, 1974.

Pérez-Firmat, Gustavo. *Life on the Hyphen.* Austin: University of Texas Press, 1993.

Putnam, Frank B. "Teresa Urrea, 'The Saint of Cabora,'" *Southern California Quarterly,* 45 (September 1963); pp. 245–64.

Q

Quirarte, Jacinto. *Mexican American Artists.* Austin: University of Texas Press, 1973.

R

Reddy, Marlita A., ed. *Statistical Record of Hispanic Americans.* Detroit: Gale, 1995.

Reichler, Joseph L. *The Great All-Time Baseball Record Book.* New York: Macmillan, 1993.

Reyes, Luis. "Hollywood's Hispanic Heritage," *DGA News,* (August/September 1994); pp 16–20.

Rodríguez, Eugene. *Henry B. González: A Political Profile.* New York: Arno Press, 1976.

Rodríguez, Lori. "New Mission, New Leaders for Hispanics," *Houston Chronicle,* January 7, 1996; pp. A23–24.

Rosaldo, Renato, Robert A. Calvert, and Gustav L. Seligmann. *Chicano: The Evolution of a People.* Minneapolis: Winston Press, 1973.

Rosales, Arturo. *Chicano! History of the Mexican American Civil Rights Movement.* Houston: Arte Público Press, 1996.

Rosazza, Marisa. "Distinctive Contributions of Hispanic Catholics," *Texas Catholic Herald.* August 23, 1996; pp. 20–21.

Ruiz de Burton, María Amparo. *The Squatter and the Don,* edited by Rosaura Sánchez and Beatriz Pita. Houston: Arte Público Press, 1993.

Ruiz de Burton, María Amparo. *Who Would Have Thought It?,* edited by Rosaura Sánchez and Beatriz Pita. Houston: Arte Público Press, 1995.

Ryan, Bryan, ed. *Hispanic Writers: A Selection of Sketches from Contemporary Authors.* Detroit: Gale, 1991.

S

San Miguel, Guadalupe, Jr. *Desegregation of Black and Hispanic Students from 1968 to 1980.* Washington, D.C.: Joint Center for Political Studies, 1981.

Sánchez, Pedro. *Memories of Antonio José Martínez.* Santa Fe: Rydal Press, 1978.

Schement, Jorge R., and Ricardo Flores. "The Origins of Spanish-Language Radio: The Case of San Antonio, Texas," *Journalism History,* 4 (February 1977); pp. 56–58.

Secretary of Defense, *Hispanics in America's Defense.* Washington, D.C.: U.S. Government Printing Office, 1990.

Sheridan, Thomas E. *Los Tucsonenses: The Mexican Community in Tucson.* Tucson: University of Arizona Press, 1986.

Simmons, Helen, and Cathryn A. Hoyt, eds. *Hispanic Texas: A Historical Guide.* Austin: University of Texas Press, 1992.

Simmons, Marc. "Spanish Irrigation Practices in New Mexico," *New Mexico Historical Review,* 47 (April 1972); pp. 138–39.

Simonhoff, Harry. *Jewish Notables in America, 1776–1865.* New York: Greenberg, 1956.

Slatta, Richard W. *Cowboys of the Americas.* New Haven: Yale University Press, 1990.

Sorell, Victor. "Barrio Murals in Chicago: Painting the Hispanic-American Experience on 'Our Community' Walls," *Revista Chicano-Riqueña,* 4/1 (1976); pp. 51–72.

Strachwitz, Chris, and James Nicopolus. *Lydia Mendoza: A Family Autobiography.* Houston: Arte Público Press, 1994.

T

Tabor, Mary B. W. "Loyalty and Labor: Nydia Margarita Velázquez," *New York Times,* September 16, 1992; p. B6.

Tardiff, Joseph C. and L. Mpho Mabunda, eds. *Dictionary of Hispanic Biography.* Detroit: Gale, 1996.

Telgen, Diane, and Jim Kamp, eds. *Latinas! Women of Achievement.* Detroit: Visible Ink Press, 1996.

Texas Hispanic, November 1994, p. 43.

U

Unterburger, Amy L., ed. *Who's Who among Hispanic Americans: 1992–93,* second edition. Detroit: Gale, 1992.

V

Vando, Gloria. *Promesas: A Geography of the Impossible.* Houston: 1994.

Van Hyning, Thomas E. *Puerto Rico's Winter League: A History of Major League Baseball's Launching Pad.* Jefferson, North Carolina: McFarland & Company, 1995.

Varela, Félix. *Jicoténcal,* edited by Luis Leal and Rodolfo Cortina. Houston: Arte Público Press, 1995.

Vigil, Maurilio E. *Chicano Politics.* Washington, D.C.: University Press of America, 1978.

Vigil, Maurilio E. *Los Patrones: Profiles of Hispanic Political Leaders in New Mexico History.* Washington, D.C.: University Press of America, 1980.

Viola, Herman J., and Carolyn Margolis, eds. *Seeds of Change: A Quincentennial Commemoration.* Washington, D.C.: Smithsonian Institution Press, 1991.

W

Winter, Metta. "Animals Point to Nature's Medicines," *Cornell Focus,* 5/1 (1996); pp. 5–7.

Wroth, William. *Furniture from the Hispanic Southwest.* Santa Fe: Ancient City Press, 1984.

Y

Young, Jan. *The Migrant Workers and César Chávez.* New York: Julian Messner/Simon and Schuster, 1972.

Z

Zavala, Iris M., and Rafael Rodríguez. *The Intellectual Roots of Independence: An Anthology of Puerto Rican Political Essays.* New York: Monthly Review Press, 1980.

INDEX BY YEAR

first Puerto Rican baseball player named to the Hall of Fame and first player for whom the five-year waiting period was waived, 278

first U.S. Hispanic woman in modern times to have her literary works published by the major commercial publishing houses, 165

first U.S. museum devoted completely to Mexican art, 12

first wholesale institutional support by the Catholic church for the union effort of farmworkers, 242

longest-held POW in U.S. history, 213

1974

first Broadway hit play by a Hispanic, 315

first Hispanic conductor of a major American symphony orchestra, 226

first Hispanic governor of New Mexico in fifty years, 96

first Hispanic special assistant to the president, 96

first Hispanic theater to open an Off-Broadway theater house, 315

first Hispanic to win the world welterweight championship, 286

first large Hispanic voter registration organization, 129

first major exhibitions of Chicano art, 12

first pro–Cuban Revolution magazine in the United States, 167

first prounion legislative act in California, 148

first U.S. Hispanic to earn a doctorate in theology, 243

first U.S. Hispanic to win one of the races of the Triple Crown, 294

first woman to win the national award for Chicano literature, 167

first women's muralist group, 13

1975

first anthology of Nuyorican literature, 167

first Chicano novelist to have a book published in Spanish in Mexico, 167

first Hispanic actress to win a Tony Award for Best Supporting Actress, 315

first Hispanic director of a major U.S. hospital, 265

first Hispanic governor of Arizona, 96

first Hispanic scientist to serve as editor of the *Neuroscience Journal,* 265

first Hispanic writer to win the Academy of American Poets Prize, 167

first Mexican American country and western star to have a national hit song cross over to pop and become a gold record, 226

first salsa music festival in the United States, 226

first woman president of a California bank, 33

1976

first baseball player with twenty-five pinch-hits in a season of major league play, 278

first Hispanic appointed to the Colorado Supreme Court, 97

first Hispanic general in the U.S. Army, 214

first literary magazine founded by Cuban exile writers outside of Miami, 168

first major broadcasting company to distribute programming directly to its affiliates via domestic satellites, 197

first major daily to publish a Spanish-language insert in its issues, 189

first Mexican American to have a musical comedy produced, 316

first Spanish-language news service, 193

first U.S. Hispanic writer and first American to win the Premio Casa de las Américas from Cuba, 168

first U.S. Hispanic writer to win the United States Award of the International Poetry Forum, 168

1977

first baseball player to receive more than four million all-star votes, 278

first Hispanic director of the Community Services Administration, 97

first Hispanic director of the U.S. Immigration and Naturalization Service, 97

first Hispanic woman ambassador, 97

first Hispanic writer to win the National Literary Contest of the Coordinating Council of Literary Magazines, 168

first national meeting of Hispanic catechists, 244

GENERAL INDEX

A

Abreu, Juan, 172
Academia de San Alejandro, 14
academic journals, 51
academies of fine arts, 3
Academy Award, 60, 62, 64, 66, 67
Academy for Young Ladies, 45
Academy of American Poets, 167
Academy of Hispanic Theology, 245
Academy of Our Lady of Light, 43
Academy of San Fernando, 4, 5
acequias, 77
Acosta, Iván, 67, 314, 320
Acosta-Belén, Edna, 190
actors, 57, 58, 60-62, 64, 65, 67, 70, 304, 311, 315, 316, 318
actresses, 58, 59, 67, 220, 308, 309, 313, 315, 318
Acuña, Rodolfo, 48, 49
adoption, 73, 74
AdulTV/Latin America, 203
advertising, 36, 110, 192
affirmative action, 105
AFL-CIO, 139, 146
Afro-Cuban music, 196
Afro-Hispanics, 81
Agosto, Juan, 277
agribusiness, 26
Agricultural Labor Relations Board, 243
agricultural workers, 141
agriculture, 21, 247
Aguayo, Marquis of, 23
Aguila, Guz (Antonio Guzmán Aguilera), 307
Aguilar-Bryan, Lydia, 271, 272
Ahumado, Ramón, 295
AIDS, 193, 267
airlines, 34
Alaminos, Antonio de, 253
Alarcón, Alonso de, 79
Alarcón, Raúl, 193
Alard, Leopoldo, 246
Alcalá, José, 265
alcaldes, 79

alcaldes ordinarios, 77
alcoholism, 177
Aleandro, Norma, 67
Alegría, Ricardo, 9
Alemany, José Sadoc, 238
alférez real, 77
Algarín, Miguel, 167
alguaciles, 77
Alinaza Federal de Mercedes, 126
Alianza Hispano Americana, 115, 120
Alinzky, Saul, 121
Allende, Isabel, 184
Alliance for Progress, 93
All-Star players, 276, 278, 279
Almaraz, Carlos, 13
Almeida, Rafael, 274
Almendros, Nestor, 66
Alou, Felipe, 280
Alurista, 163-165
Alvarado, Linda, 37, 38
Alvarado, Tony, 109
Alvarez, Everett Jr., 101, 213
Alvarez, Julia, 174, 177
Alvarez, Luis, 264, 266
Alvarez, María Elena, 38
Alvarez de Pineda, Alonso, 254
Amalgamated Clothing Workers of America, 149
ambassadors, 37, 53, 93, 94, 97, 100, 159, 213
Ambert, Alba, 183
American Association of Hispanic CPAs, 33
American Ballet Theatre, 218
American Book Award, 171
American Federation of Labor (AFL), 133-135
American Federation of Teachers, 52
American Folkore Society, 54
American G.I. Forum, 130, 213
American Golf Hall of Fame, 292
American Guild of Variety Artists, 226
American Institute, 129
American Institute of Architects, 17, 20
American literature, 261

H

Herrera, Juan José, 115, 133
Herron, Willie, 12
Hezeta, Bruno de, 258
Hidalgo, Edward, 100, 214
Hidalgo y Costilla, Miguel, 207, 234
hides, 21, 26, 28
highways, 30
Hijuelos, Oscar, 174, 176
Hinojosa, María, 193-195, 199
Hinojosa, Rolando, 163, 164, 168, 169
Hispanic American Police Command Officers
    Association, 96
Hispanic battallion, 209
Hispanic Business, 190
Hispanic Designers Association, 15
Hispanic Institute, 159
Hispanic National Bar Association, 100, 107
Hispanic Organization of Latin Actors, 315
Hispanic Playwrights Project, 319
Hispanic Radio Network, 195
Hispanic Women in Higher Education, 51
Hispano U.S.A., 194
historians, 100, 158
historical documentaries, 254
Hogar Feliz, El, 238
hogs, 247
Home Box Office (HBO), 199
Homenaje a Frida Kahlo, by Irene
    Cervántez, 18
Homestead Act, 31, 72
homesteading, 22
horse racing, 294
horses, 21, 24, 25, 28, 247, 249
        mustangs, 249
        tarding, 24
horticulture, 262
Hospital, Carolina, 175
hospitality industry, 33
hospitals, 232, 260, 262
House of Balmain, 17
House Un-American Activities Committee, 144
housing, 93
Houston Grand Opera, 231
Houston, Sam, 28
Hoya, Oscar de la, 287
Hoyos, Angela de, 161
Hubbell, Carl, 280
Hudson, Henry, 254
Huerta, Dolores, 122, 147
Huerta, Jorge, 316
Humanitas International, 129
humanities, 176
hymns, 238
hyperinsulinism, 272

I

Ibáñez, Dora, 120
IBM, 266

Idar, Jovita, 188
Idar, Nicasio, 116
identity, 307
    Aztec, 163
    pan-Hispanic, 311
Iglesias Pantín, Santiago, 133
Illich, Ivan, 240
illustrators, 11, 166
immigrants, 25, 28, 35, 47, 95, 102, 120, 130,
    131, 137, 141, 145, 186, 192, 193, 214, 216,
    221, 223, 244, 246, 267, 294, 299
immigration, 131, 158, 177, 194
Immigration and Nationalization Service
    (INS), 145
immigration literature, 175
Immigration Reform and Control Act, 93, 131
Imperialism, 156
impressarios, 306
Impressionism, 3, 5
independence
    Mexico, 234
    Northern Mexico, 207
    Texas, 155
independence movements
    British Colonies, 204
    Cuba, 24, 32, 113, 154
    Mexico, 82, 207
    Puerto Rico, 113, 122, 123, 128, 307
    Spanish America, 237
    Venezuela, 204
independent sector, 132
Indian pueblos, 78
Indians, 22, 26, 29, 30, 40, 73, 78, 79, 81, 154,
    164, 204, 206, 211, 219, 221, 232, 234, 235,
    237, 238, 250, 251, 253, 255, 258-262, 303
    Avavar, 260
    Aztec, 41, 222, 234, 257
    Caddo, 260
    Carib, 254
    Chichimeca, 257
    Cicuye, 255
    Creek, 23
    Escamacu, 234
    Florida, 185
    Guale, 234
    Karankawa, 260
    Mariam, 260
    Mestizo, 40, 73, 234
    Navajo, 22
    Otomí, 41
    Pima, 23
    Pueblo, 250
    Siboney, 221
    Tiguex, 255
    Timicua, 234, 256, 262
    Yamassee, 204, 255
    Zuñi, 255
Indians for Justice, 110
Industrial Areas Foundation, 130
Inquisition, The, 151, 232

Hispanic firsts :
973 KANELLOS   32928003204306

Kanellos, Nicol~as.
GLOUCESTER CO LIBRARY SYSTEM